Faithfully Yours

Charles Dickens

LIFE OF

CHARLES DICKENS.

BY

R. SHELTON MACKENZIE, LL.D.
LITERARY EDITOR OF THE "PHILADELPHIA PRESS."

WITH

PERSONAL RECOLLECTIONS AND ANECDOTES;—LETTERS BY 'BOZ,'
NEVER BEFORE PUBLISHED;—AND UNCOLLECTED
PAPERS IN PROSE AND VERSE.

WITH PORTRAIT AND AUTOGRAPH.

PHILADELPHIA:
T. B. PETERSON & BROTHERS;
No. 306 CHESTNUT STREET.

DEDICATION.

TO HON. JOHN W. FORNEY.

My Dear Forney,

I beg leave to dedicate to you, wishing that it were worthier of your acceptance, this biographical sketch of Charles Dickens, knowing, during all the years of my relations with you, how warmly you have admired the genius of the great and good man whose loss the world mourns. In the fulness of his fame, Dickens has departed. Of late years, there have been several of these public misfortunes. Macaulay and Thackeray soon followed Hood and Jerrold; John Leech left us in his prime, and still later, two more of Dickens's friends—Maclise, the great painter, and Mark Lemon, Editor of *Punch*—were smitten by the inevitable shaft. These men died not much beyond middle age; but nearly all of them were suddenly stricken. Charles Dickens, in his fifty-ninth year, has followed, and the shock is great; for of him, it might be said, as of the great Hebrew in the olden time, that when he died, "his eyes were not dim, nor his natural force abated."

In the most aristocratic country in the world, Charles Dickens stood, not merely among but above all his contemporaries as a Man of the People. Scott, Bulwer, Macaulay, Thackeray, and others who taught great truths through the press, either were of high family descent or had received the best education that Universities could bestow. Their writings are crowded with references to the classic authors of their youth. Dickens, son of an obscure Government clerk, whose pedigree no one has cared to trace, received only such an education as, free of cost, every State in our Union bestows upon its children. It has been argued by great scholars, that Shakespeare was familiar not only with classical but modern European literature; but Dickens was master of *one* language—that which is spoken, not alone in his island-home, but in Asia, in Australia, and most of all, in our United States. He knew, and was proud in the knowledge, that for every one reader he had at home, there were fifty *here*.

In the following pages, I have attempted to give a sketch of his literary and personal history—stating plain facts, introducing some of his correspondence never before printed, adding such anecdotes and traits of character as illustrate his double position of Man of Letters and Man of the People, and stating such particulars as have reached me concerning the originals, from whom he is known, or supposed, to have drawn many of the characters in his tales.

In the body of this volume, I have expressed my admiration of the ability of the necessarily rapid tributes to the genius and worth of Mr. Dickens, which appeared in the American newspapers. I had intended to publish the best of these, kindly selected for me by Mr. W. W. Nevin, of Philadelphia, but they were so numerous that I had to abandon the idea. For assistance rendered, or offered, while I was writing this life, (with the temperature ranging at from 90° to 96° in the shade,) I am very grateful, and would particularly offer my thanks to the Hon. Ellis Lewis and Mr. John E. McDonough, of Philadelphia; Mr. Philp and Mr. Solomon, of Washington; and Mr. Henry May Keim, of Reading. An old friend of Mr. Dickens, now resident in New York, has placed me under great obligations by giving me many of his personal reminiscences.

R. Shelton Mackenzie

August 1st, 1870.

CONTENTS.

CHAPTER I.

CHAPTER II.

CHAPTER III.

CHAPTER IV.

CHAPTER V.

CHAPTER VI.

CHAPTER VII.

CHAPTER VIII.

CHAPTER IX.

CHAPTER X.

CHAPTER XI.

CHAPTER XII.

CHAPTER XIII.

CHAPTER XIV.

CHAPTER XV.

CHAPTER XVI.

CHAPTER XVII.

CHAPTER XVIII.

CHAPTER XIX.

CHAPTER XX.

CHAPTER XXI.

CHAPTER XXII.

CHAPTER XXIII.

UNCOLLECTED PIECES.

BY CHARLES DICKENS.

WILL OF CHARLES DICKENS.

LIFE OF CHARLES DICKENS.

CHAPTER I.

LESSON OF HIS LIFE AND WRITINGS.—CHARACTER OF HIS GENIUS.—ANCESTRY.—JOHN DICKENS, THE GOVERNMENT CLERK.—HIS FAMILY.—REMOVAL TO LONDON.—NEWSPAPER REPORTER.—MICAWBER AND MRS. NICKLEBY.—CHARLES DICKENS'S EDUCATION.—TRUTH IN FICTION.—ROCHESTER VISITED BY THE PICKWICKIANS.—WATTS'S HOSPITAL.—CLOISTERHAM.—GAD'S HILL.

THE greatest writer of his age is gone, and the sudden blow has smitten the great heart of humanity. There is no part of the civilized world where the name of Charles Dickens is unknown, where his genial and elevating writings are not valued. They have been translated into many languages, and the characters which he created and the adventures in which he placed them have passed into the current literature of the world. Every reader mourns for him—the lowliest as well as the highest participate in one common sorrow. Life has been better and brighter for what he has done. He was the champion of the oppressed, he was the censor of the selfish rich. In a single one of his tales was matter far more serious and convincing than could be found in a pyramid of lengthy homilies, in which Christian charity was distinguished by its absence. Even when he amused, he taught. No vile thoughts, no prurient suggestions, no foul words are to be found in the writings of Charles Dickens. Even when he treated of crime and poverty his language was not base or low. The practical spirit he endeavored to inculcate was that of comprehensive Christianity. His personal character was in accordance with his teaching. Charitable, kind-hearted, affectionate, temperate in living, ever doing his work as if he felt it a pleasure rather than a labor, there was a daily beauty in his life, in its earnestness, in its simplicity, in its purity, which was an exemplar in itself.

To him, even more appropriately than to the brilliant but erratic genius to whom they were addressed, might be applied the stanzas which spoke of one

"Whose mind was an essence, compounded with art,
From the finest and best of all other men's powers;
Who ruled, like a wizard, the world of the heart,
And could call up its sunshine, or bring down its showers;—

"Whose humor, as gay as the firefly's light,
Play'd round every subject, and shone as it played;—
Whose wit, in the combat, as gentle as bright
Ne'er carried a heart stain away on its blade;—

"Whose eloquence,—brightening whatever it tried,
Whether reason or fancy, the gay or the grave,—
Was as rapid, as deep, and as brilliant a tide,
As ever bore freedom aloft on its wave!"

In ordinary cases, a biography begins with some geneological narrative, intended to show that the person presented to the notice of the reader had particular ancestors. In England, it is considered something to boast of that the first-known of a man's family "came in with the Conqueror." In Scotland, it suffices for this founder of the line to have belonged, in his time, to some Celtic marauder or early Border raider. In Ireland, it is the fashion to go back to some period—before the island lost her nationality, "when Malachi wore the collar of gold which he won from the proud invader." In our own Northern States the New Englanders count back some two hundred and fifty years, dating from the Landing of the Pilgrim Fathers, while the chief boast of the South is that their lineage, more remote, dates from the colonization in the time of Elizabeth. As with families, so with individuals. Walter Scott was prouder of his distant cousinship with the ducal house of Buccleugh than of his own great genius which cast a flood of living glory upon his native land. Byron never forgot, and would have all the world remember, that, long before Henry the Eighth forcibly wrested Newstead Abbey from the monks, and bestowed it upon Sir John Byron—he with the long beard,—sundry members of the family had fought in the Holy Land, during the Crusades. Even Washington Irving, who was nothing if not an American and a republican, could not resist the temptation, when writing the life of George Washington, of showing that one of his English progenitors was "Washingatune," during the reign of Saxon Edgar, in the tenth century, a time when few could spell, and fewer write. It has been, in fact, an ordinary weakness, this ambition of showing that a distinguished personage was not wholly what, in our ordinary parlance, is called "self-made." The majority of biographers exhibit it; though Thomas Moore, who devoted some space, in his Life of Byron, to the glorification of the family-tree, had the good sense to reject it for himself. On one occasion, when he was the favored guest of the then Prince of Wales, afterwards George the Fourth, and was brightening the horizon of the board with wit and song, his Royal host observed, "By the way, Moore, your surname is the same as that of the Marquis of Drogheda? I shall ask him here, one of these days, to meet you. Of course, you belong to his family?" There was a moment's pause, and then the Poet answered, "Our common descent is the same, I believe—from Adam. But I desire to inform your Royal Highness, that I am not akin to the Peerage. *My* father was son of a County Kerry farmer, and to this day keeps a grocer's shop in Dublin, where I was born and bred." The manliness and independence of this response certainly did not injure Moore—who usually was somewhat of a tuft-hunter,—in the opinion of those who heard it. Lord Thurlow was less independent, because less accurate, in his reply to the gentleman from the Herald's College, who waited upon him, in June, 1778, when he was created a peer, for particulars of his descent, out of which to construct a family pedigree, and said, "I suppose I may safely set you down as of the same blood with another Norfolk celebrity, John Thurloe, who was Secretary of State to the Commonwealth, under Oliver and Richard Cromwell?" Thurlow, who was impetuous and rough, immediately blustered out, "You are wrong altogether, John Thurloe was an Essex man, and I am from Suffolk. *He* came of an old stock. There was one Thurlow, in my part of the county, who was a common carrier, and I think as he was an honest man, that you had better derive my lineage from *him*."

Charles Dickens, like many other illustrious personages, whose names are not written in the Herald's books at Doctor's Commons, had no ancestry to boast of, went through life extremely well, without crest or scutcheon, and was content to draw his nobility direct from the Creator. His father, plain John Dickens, who died some time ago, full of years, after having seen his son's universal popularity, and profited by his continuous bounty, was a Government clerk, stationed at Portsmouth Dockyard, in Hampshire, when his eldest son was born. He was in the Paymaster's office, and, in that capacity, had to travel from place to place, to pay charges and salaries, during the great war which closed at Waterloo. Sometimes he went as far to the southwest of the English coast as Falmouth and Plymouth—oftener to Gosport, Dover, Sheerness, Chatham and Gravesend. He was a trusted and trustworthy person, to whom much money was confided, the "wooden walls" being costly in those days, and men-of-war's-men apt to get angry if, on landing at a port, after a long cruise, their arrears of wages were not immediately paid up. How foolishly, how recklessly they lavished this money, can be judged from the naval romances " of the period " as written by Marryat, Chamier, Edward Howard, Johnson Neale, and others.

Mr. John Dickens was married in the early part of the present century, and his wife, Mrs. Elizabeth Dickens, has been described to me as having much resembled Mrs. Nickleby, of happy memory, in the charming inaccuracy of her memory and the curious insecutiveness of her conversation. In later years she was tall and thin, with a wasp's waist, of which she was very vain, and was what is called "dressy." She was a good wife, very fond of her husband, devoted to her children, and extremely proud of her son Charles, who was kind and liberal to her from the time it was in his power to be so. Her family further consisted of the following children :

1. Fanny Dickens, who was a music-teacher for some time before her marriage with Mr. Bennett, a lawyer. She is dead.

2. Charles Dickens, "the world's heir of fame," born at Landport, a suburb of Portsmouth, on the 7th of February, 1812 ; died at Gad's Hill, near the old Cathedral, city of Rochester, in Kent, on Thursday, the 9th of June, 1870, and interred in Westminster Abbey, on Tuesday, the 14th of June, 1870.

3. Letitia Dickens, married to Mr. Austen, engineer and architect in London. She is the only surviving member of this household.

4. Frederic William Dickens, who, through the influence of Lord John Russel, an old and warm friend of Charles Dickens, obtained a clerkship in the Foreign Office, London, but after some years, received a hint that from certain irregularities, his resignation would be accepted. On the 23d of October, 1868, he died of abscess on the lungs, at Darlington, where he had been stationed during the preceding twelve months. He had suffered greatly during the last three weeks of his illness. The newspaper obituary

which mentions this, adds: "The geniality—it was something more to those who could see below the surface—of Mr. Frederic Dickens's nature, and his ready fund of humor and anecdote, will not readily be forgotten by those who knew him best, and liked him best." Mr. Frederic Dickens may best be characterized, perhaps, as belonging to that numerous and careless class who enjoy life, on small means, without much regard for health. "Nobody's enemy but his own," is the general conversational epitaph on a man of this sort.

5. Alfred Dickens, was an architect or engineer, perhaps a little of both, upon the Malton Railroad, and is dead.

6. Augustus Dickens, was brought up in the counting-house of John Chapman & Co., No. 2 Leadenhall street, London, and came to this country, some ten or twelve years ago. He became a clerk in the Illinois Railroad Company, and died in Chicago, five years ago. His second wife (Miss Bertha Phillips, daughter of the late Charles Phillips, the celebrated Irish orator,) whom he brought here and married, died on Christmas eve, 1868, at Chicago, leaving three beautiful children. She was alive when Charles Dickens last was in America, but, as none of the family had recognized her, and he thought it not impossible that she might be intruded upon him, as believed to be his sister-in-law, he did not visit Chicago. It is stated that, on hearing of her distressed circumstances, he sent her a handsome pecuniary present. Augustus was the original "Boses."

Charles Dickens may be considered less a townsman than a towns-baby of Landport, near Portsmouth. When he was only twelve months old, his father removed from Portsmouth Dockyard to Somerset House, London, where he was intrusted with some very important duties, that do not appear to have suited his taste any better than they did his peculiar abilities, for Mr. John Dickens was undeniably a man of talent and energy, gifted with a lively and convivial spirit that made him, wherever he went, "a hail fellow well met," and a man so generally liked that his company was much sought after, which his personal friends hint led him to "launch out," like many other kindred spirits, a little more than his means would permit, and as a natural consequence, he was not altogether free from those peculiar anxieties and troubles that follow such indulgences. Somerset House, then, was not a congenial place for Mr. Dickens, and that worthy gentleman, with his wife and young Charles, one fine morning embarked in one of the hoys then plying between London and Chatham, taking his household effects with him, and after a day or so settled down as an official in Chatham Dockyard, selecting as his place of abode a plain-looking house, with a whitewashed plaster front, and a small garden, front and behind, in St. Mary's place, or the Brook, which belonged to a Mr. Smart, and was next to an original and humble-looking building, also of plastered exterior, long known as the Providence Chapel, belonging to a sect of Baptists, where Charles's schoolmaster, the Rev. Mr. Giles, officiated as pastor. Charles, like most children who have the good fortune to be first-born sons, was his mother's pet. Mr. Dickens, sen., here again was not permitted to settle down quietly, but was destined to follow a roving kind of commission between the dockyards of Chatham, Sheerness, and other Government places; and in course of time young Charles grew up to be a boy old enough to wear a broad white collar, blue jacket, buckled shoes, and a large peaked cap.

Mr. John Dickens, the father, was superannuated in 1816, while yet in the prime of life, and allowed a pension,—according to the liberal practice in England. There was a general reduction of the naval and military establishments, at the close of the war, and therefore Mr. Dickens was dismissed. He wrote an unusually good hand, round and clear, (as I perceive by a note of his now before me, dated thirty years after this period,) and, removing his household goods to London, succeeded in obtaining an engagement as reporter upon the *Morning Chronicle.* Active in mind and body, with a great deal of energy, and a remarkable aptitude for work, John Dickens was a useful journalist. He continued on the *Chronicle,* I have heard, until the *Daily News* was established, in January, 1846, when Charles Dickens placed him and Mr. George Hogarth on the staff of that paper, and I believe he remained on it to the last. It was a constant joke, among newspaper-men, that Charles Dickens had drawn upon his father's actual character, when he was writing *David Copperfield,* and put him into that story as Micawber; but though there was a great deal of "waiting until something should turn up," in much that John Dickens did, (and did not,) a man who had kept himself in London, during a period of over forty years, upon the newspaper press, with only a single change, and that for the better, was considerably *above* the Micawber scale. Some traits of the *living* may have been transmitted, with the novelist's natural exaggeration, to the *fictitious* character. A journalist, with wife and six young children, must always find it difficult to keep his head above water in London, where, (the price of bread regulating all other prices of provisions,) the four pounds loaf then cost twenty-five cents. It is possible that a man may have found it rather difficult to "raise" a brood of six children, "my dam and all her little ones," upon four or five guineas a week, to say nothing of their schooling. Now and then, perhaps, the reporter may have had some "outside" chances, but it may be presumed that an avuncular relation, sporting the three golden balls of Lombardy over his place of business, may have been resorted to when money was scarce. Perhaps, too, on an emergency, money had to be raised by "a little bill." The Micawber mode of financiering, as developed in *David Copperfield,* a tale which avowedly gives many of its author's own experiences, may have been drawn less from imagination than memory, and it may be noticed that while Micawber does and says many unwise things, he never goes into anything which he considered dishonest or dishonorable. For my own part, I see no reason why John Dickens should *not* have been the original of Wilkins Micawber. He considered himself rather complimented in thus being converted into literary "capital" by his son.

How and where the Dickens children were educated, on the father's small salary, is to me unknown. We have to look after the eldest son only. Charles's education was plain enough. He received it, for the most part, in a school at Chatham. It included some little study of the Eton Latin Grammar, but no Greek. Perhaps, the experiences of poor David Copperfield may have been those of young Charles Dickens. It is known that, at an early age, the heroes of Fielding's and Smollett's novels, of Goldsmith's Dr. Primrose, of Le Sage's French-Spanish Gil Blas, of Cervantes's immortal Knight of La Mancha, and De Foe's life-like Robinson Crusoe, were familiar friends of the lad—for he has told us that he fell into a habit of impersonating each of them, in turn, for periods of from a week to a month, and thus lived in the ideal world of romance. Then there were the Arabian Nights and the Tales of the Genii, throwing a chastened Oriental glamour over all, while a balance of realism, one halfpenny worth of bread to a vast quantity of sack, was supplied by sundry volumes of voyages and travels.

The miserable experiences at Salem House, with the cruel practices in which Mr. Creakle, its brute of a master, used delightedly to indulge, most probably were those of Dickens himself;—he could scarcely have invented them. The boy, notwithstanding, picked up a plain education, with as much Latin grammar as enabled him, by and by, to write English with propriety, and prepared him, after he had attained manhood and celebrity, to master the French language, so as to translate it with ease, and finally to speak it with fluency and a good accent. In his European tour, and by subsequent study, he picked up some knowledge of Italian.

Charles Dickens was intimately acquainted, from his boyish days, with that part of Kent, containing the ancient episcopal city of Rochester, situated on the river Medway, which surrounds the naval yard and harbor of Chatham. In the preface to *Nicholas Nickleby*, this sentence is to be found: "I cannot call to mind, now, how I came to hear of Yorkshire schools, when I was not a very robust child, sitting in by-places, near Rochester Castle, with a head full of Partridge, Strap, Tom Pipes, and Sancho Panza."

This neighborhood, early and late, had a great influence on Dickens. In 1836, when he began *The Pickwick Papers*, (the date of the story being 1827, a pre-railroad period,) he makes the hero start from the Golden Cross, Charing Cross, then a great coaching centre, with the resolution of making Rochester his first halting-place. When the party, accompanied by Jingle, reach Rochester Bridge, (erected in the time of King John, six hundred and fifty years ago,) the magnificent ruin of Rochester Castle, built by Bishop Gundulph, and the splendid Cathedral, still well preserved, and erected by Bishop Odo, brother of William the Conqueror, are signally praised. Moreover the party are made to pull up at the Bull Inn, in the High street, next door to Wright's, which Jingle describes as "dear—very dear—half a crown in the bill if you look at the waiter,—charge you more if you dine at a friend's than they would if you dined in the coffee-room—rum fellows—very." None but one very well acquainted with the locality could have grouped together the four towns, Stroud, Rochester, Chatham, and Brompton, which are thus described:

The principal productions of these towns, (says Mr. Pickwick,) appear to be soldiers, sailors, Jews, chalk, shrimps, officers, and dock-yard men. The commodities chiefly exposed for sale in the public streets, are marine stores, hard-bake, apples, flat-fish and oysters. The streets present a lively and animated appearance, occasioned chiefly by the conviviality of the military. It is truly delightful to a philanthropic mind, to see these gallant men, staggering along under the influence of an overflow, both of animal and ardent spirits; more especially when we remember that the following them about, and jesting with them, affords a cheap and innocent amusement for the boy population. Nothing (adds Mr. Pickwick) can exceed their good humor. It was but the day before my arrival, that one of them had been most grossly insulted in the house of a publican. The bar-maid had positively refused to draw him any more liquor; in return for which, he had (merely in playfulness) drawn his bayonet, and wounded the girl in the shoulder. And yet this fine fellow was the very first to go down to the house next morning, and express his readiness to overlook the matter, and forget what had occurred! The consumption of tobacco in these towns (continued Mr. Pickwick) must be very great: and the smell which pervades the streets must be exceedingly delicious to those who are extremely fond of smoking. A superficial traveller might object to the dirt which is their leading characteristic; but to those who view it as an indication of traffic and commercial prosperity, it is truly gratifying.

No one, except he were to the manor born, could have described that place so sententiously. It was upon the Lines of Rochester that the grand military review took place, at which Pickwick, Winkle and Snodgrass "came to grief," but finally fell into good luck by becoming acquainted with Mr. Wardle, an improbable gentleman farmer of the Weald of Kent.

Dickens did not often describe scenery, but here, opening the fifth chapter of *Pickwick*, is a charming sketch of this favorite locality:

Bright and pleasant was the sky, balmy the air, and beautiful the appearance of every object around, as Mr. Pickwick leaned over the balustrades of Rochester Bridge, contemplating nature, and waiting for breakfast. The scene was indeed one, which might well have charmed a far less reflective mind, than that to which it was presented.

On the left of the spectator lay the ruined wall, broken in

many places, and in some, overhanging the narrow beach below in rude and heavy masses. Huge knots of sea-weed hung upon the jagged and pointed stones, trembling in every breath of wind; and the green ivy clung mournfully round the dark and ruined battlements. Behind it rose the ancient castle, its towers roofless, and its massive walls crumbling away, but telling us proudly of its old might and strength, as when, seven hundred years ago, it rang with the clash of arms, or resounded with the noise of feasting and revelry. On either side, the banks of the Medway, covered with corn-fields and pastures, with here and there a windmill, or a distant church stretched away as far as the eye could see, presenting a rich and varied landscape, rendered more beautiful by the changing shadows which passed swiftly across it, as the thin and half-formed clouds skimmed away in the light of the morning sun. The river, reflecting the clear blue of the sky, glistened and sparkled as it flowed noiselessly on; and the oars of the fishermen dipped into the water with a clear and liquid sound, as the heavy but picturesque boats glided slowly down the stream.

This is, literally, a beautiful picture in words—a pen and ink view.

Many years after *Pickwick* was written, its author again went back to Rochester, remembering that, ever since the year 1579, Watts's Hospital, for the nightly entertainment of Six Poor Travellers, had been a noted institution, and telling how the effigy of worthy Master Richard Watts was to be seen in the Cathedral, and how he had restricted his charity (lodging and entertainment gratis for one night, with fourpence each) for the Six, as aforesaid; they "not being Rogues, or Proctors." He says:

I found it to be a clean white house, of a staid and venerable air, with the quaint old door already three times mentioned (an arched door), choice little long low lattice-windows, and a roof of three gables. The silent High Street of Rochester is full of gables, with old beams and timbers carved into strange faces. It is oddly garnished with a queer old clock that projects over the pavement out of a grave red-brick building, as if Time carried on business there, and hung out his sign. Sooth to say, he did an active stroke of work in

Rochester, in the old days of the Romans, and the Saxons, and the Normans; and down to the times of King John, when the rugged castle—I will not undertake to say how many hundreds of years old then—was abandoned to the centuries of weather which have so defaced the dark apertures in its walls, that the ruin looks as if the rooks and daws had picked its eyes out.

What was done and said at Watts's, is it not to be read in that Christmas story by Dickens entitled "The Seven Poor Travellers," and doth it not show, if evidence were needed, what a place Rochester had in his memory? *The Uncommercial Traveller* mentions it again and again.

Yet more. In *The Mystery of Edwin Drood*—that story begun in so much hope and after a great deal of thought, which must remain a fragment, reminding us of

> "him who left untold
> The story of Cambuscan bold,"

—Rochester was again brought up. Its resemblance to Cloisterham Cathedral, is obvious from the first. In its antiquity, even the likeness prevails, for, next to Canterbury, the see of Rochester is the oldest in England;—and the Cathedral was built in the year of grace 604. Thus in early manhood, in his prime, and in the sere and yellow leaf, Dickens wrote about the old place, which had been familiar to him in his boyhood. When he was able to purchase a homestead, the old house at Gadshill, near Rochester and Chatham, became his. In one of his *Uncommercial* sketches, he "noticed by the wayside a very queer small boy." Here is what follows:

"Halloa!" said I, to the very queer small boy, "where do you live?"

"At Chatham," says he.

"What do you do there?" says I.

"I go to school," says he.

I took him up in a moment, and we went on. Presently the very queer small boy said, "This is Gadshill we are coming to, where Falstaff went out to rob those travelers, and ran away."

"You know something about Falstaff, eh?" said I.

"All about him," said the very queer small boy. "I am old (I am nine), and I read all sorts of books. But *do* let us stop at the top of the hill, and look at the house there, if you please!"

"You admire that house?" said I.

"Bless you, sir," said the very queer small boy, "when I was not more than half as old as nine, it used to be a treat for me to be brought to look at it. And now, I am nine, I come by myself to look at it. *And ever since I can recollect, my father seeing me so fond of it, has often said to me, 'If you were to be very persevering and were to work hard, you might some day come to live in it.'* Though that's impossible!" said the very queer small boy, drawing a low breath, and now staring at the house out of the window with all his might.

I was rather amazed to be told this by the very queer small boy; for that house happens to be my house, and I have reason to believe that what he said was true.

It was even so. In the very queer small boy, nine years old, who read all sorts of books, admired Gadshill, knew its Shakespearian association, and was paternally told that if he worked hard, he might live in such a house, we find realized the famous Wordsworthian aphorism, "The Child is father of the Man," the idea of which, by the way, is to be found in two lines,

> "The childhood shows the man
> As morning shews the day,"

which were written in *Paradise Regained*, by an almost inspired blind old man, named John Milton, who is more talked about than read, in *our* days.

He repeatedly declared his desire to be buried without pomp, in the burial ground of St. Nicholas Parish near the Cathedral—marked 3 on the diagram on next page. Thirty years ago, when, in company with a friend, to whom I am indebted for much personal information about him, he was looking down, from the top of Rochester Castle, upon the quiet burial-ground, he said "There, my boy, I mean to go into dust and ashes."

Here, from memory, is a sketch of that part of Rochester. He desired to rest beneath the grand old castle, which stands "a noble wreck in ruinous perfection," with the Medway flowing between grassy banks, within a hundred feet of its base. There is scarcely any spot in England more beautifully picturesque, and the last thirteen years of Charles Dickens's life was passed within four miles of this familiar and beautiful old city :—

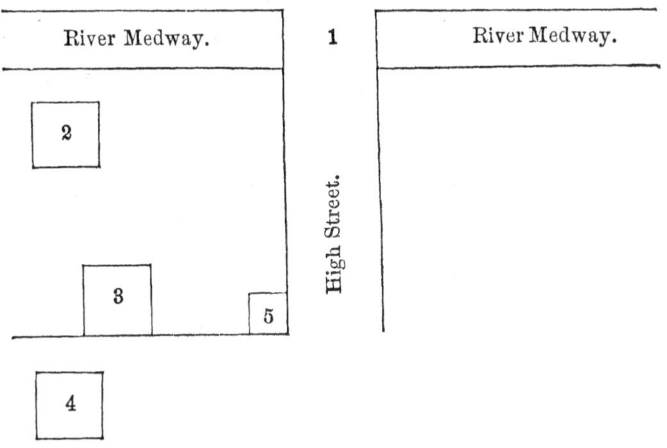

1. Rochester Bridge.
2. The Castle.
3. St. Nicholas Church Yard.
4. The Cathedral.
5. Wright's Hotel.

Wright's Hotel, of which Mr. Jingle spoke in such disparaging terms, and where the Pickwickians did not stop, was the scene of the Ball in which the rencontre between Jingle and Dr. Slammer of the 97th took place, though the consequent duel did not.

CHAPTER II.

ENGLISH LAWYERS.—ARTICLED CLERKS.—SHORT-HAND WRITING.—DICKENS AS A REPORTER.—MIRROR OF PARLIAMENT.—TRUE SUN.—MORNING CHRONICLE.—FIRST AUTHORSHIP.—WRITING THE "SKETCHES."—JOHN BLACK, OUR OLD-TIME EDITOR.—RECOLLECTIONS BY N. P. WILLIS.—PUBLISHER.

IT has been stated that "Charles Dickens began life as a lawyer, got tired of the dull routine, and turned to literature." This is erroneous, for he never had even a chance of becoming a lawyer,—either in the higher grade of outer barrister, or "counsel learned in the law," or in the lower, but often more lucrative, class of attorney. In England, before a young man can enter his name as "student," at one of the Inns of Court, to enable him to be "called" to the bar, after a lapse of three years, it is necessary for him to deposit about one hundred pounds, with the treasurer of the Inn of Court, as a sort of guarantee for his respectability, which sum is returnable when "called," though it has to be paid out again for the stamp-duty upon the certificate of his admission to the bar. In the case of an attorney, a properly qualified person could be admitted to practice, after a prescribed examination, as to his knowledge of the principle and practice of the law, provided he had been an apprentice, or "articled clerk," to some practising attorney for five years. But, upon the "articles" or indenture of apprenticeship, be the premium high or low, it was necessary to pay a stamp-duty of one hundred and twenty pounds. There could be no "articles" unless the documents were stamped, at the beginning of the five years, at the said cost of £120. It is writ, in literary history, that Mr. Disraeli commenced as an attorney, like Dickens and Ainsworth. The latter really was admitted as an attorney, after having been a five years' articled clerk, but did not practice. Mr. Disraeli was a not articled clerk, but was in an attorney's office, for a few months and then took to literature.

Thriftless John Dickens, with a small salary, and a large family, had not the means of placing his eldest son, Charles, as an "articled clerk" in an attorney's office. The boy was taken from school, at the age of sixteen and put, as writing clerk, into the office of an attorney, in Southampton Buildings, Bedford Row, London,—like one of the young gentlemen who "chaffed" Mr. Pickwick on the memorable occasion when he paid a visit, without being sent for, to Messrs. Dodson & Fogg. The articled clerk looks to being in business, on his own account, as soon as he has served his five years, but the writing clerk can have no such hope. He has to do all the rough work in the office, as well as out of doors, is perpetually copying documents when not running about, in the courts and out of them, and, commencing upon a salary of about five dollars a week, may consider himself fortunate if he has thrice that amount, at the close of twenty or thirty years' service. Very frequently, in this poverty and the recklessness which it has a facile tendency to engender, the clerk declines into a careless ne'er-do-well, like Dick Swiveller, or an out-at-elbows hack, like Weevle, in *Bleak House*. Here the distinction lies. The "young man of the name of Guppy," clerk in the office of Kenge and Carboy, attorneys for Mr. Jarndyce, comes out of his articles, (to use his own words,) at the end of five years, passes his examination, gets his certificate, is admitted on the roll of attorneys, and opens his office in Walcot Square, Lambeth; but his friend, and senior, Weevle, *alias* Jopling, who has not been articled, remains a mere clerk—*his* clerk, in fact, and never can rise above that dead level. The English system differs so much from our own that, for the benefit of possible legal readers, I have thus explained it.

After a sufficiently long trial of this sort of life, in the course of which he probably had occasion to visit police-offices, courts of law, judges' chambers, and the taxing-master's room; to serve subpœnas and copies of writs; to look after bail and execution; to hunt out witnesses's facts; to copy folio after folio of the lengthy documents facetiously called *briefs*, Charles Dickens picked up, not a knowledge of the law, for he has made some legal mistakes in his stories, but a familiar acquaintance with the routine practice in an attorney's office, and after a sufficiently long trial, bade farewell to that hopeless ever-go-round, and resolved to set up for himself. His reliance was on the newspaper press, and, like his own David Copperfield, he had labored hard and successfully to obtain facility as a short-hand writer. He was nearly twenty when he got employment upon a publication called *The Mirror of Parliament*, conducted by Mr. Barrow, a barrister, and established as a rival to *Hansard's Parliamentary Debates.* In England there is no official reporting of the proceedings in Parliament, but each London morning paper has a full staff of private reporters. Their reports are made, submitted for correction to the gentlemen who have taken part in the proceedings, and then reprinted in a separate publication, in convenient book-form. At present and for many years past, Hansard's has been the only work of this character, and is generally referred to as authority. On Barrow's rival publication, throughout the great Reform debates of 1832, Charles Dickens not only attended the debates, but also acted as a sort of sub-editor of the work. It was a great object to get it before the public in advance of its rival, and by means of the good system the new hand established, this was usually done.

The connection thus established made him well known at many editorial rooms, and soon procured him an engagement as reporter upon the *True Sun*, a London evening paper, then lately established. There had been a misunderstanding between Mr. Grant, chief proprietor, and Mr. Murdo Young, sole editor of *The Sun*, which ended in the latter gentleman obtaining legal possession of the paper, which he had forced into great notoriety, at vast expense, by making it the vehicle for special and late parliamentary reports. This was before Railwayism had spread all over the country, before the electric telegraph had annihilated time and space. The mails for all parts of England then left the General Post Office about half-past seven o'clock each evening and received no newspapers after six. Except by rare efforts, the second editions of the evening papers gave no news after 5 P. M. In 1826, when Mr. Canning explained how he had sent an army and fleet to Lisbon, to prevent the invasion of Portugal; in 1829, when Catholic Emancipation was debated and conceded; in 1831–32, during the debates on the Reform Bill, and on other important occasions, *The Sun*, sending relays of its own stenographers into the Lords and Commons, gave long reports of these discussions, sometimes not ending until morning—and expressed large numbers of these late editions to all parts of the country, by means of post-chaises and four, at enormous cost, but with commensurate increase of prestige and circulation, because the morning papers were thus anticipated. *The True Sun*, established in rivalry, had also to make great exertions. Mr. Dickens was soon found to be one of the most rapid, ready, and reliable of its reporters. As the great pressure on these gentlemen was far from frequent—say, twice or thrice in each session, their actual labor averaged only a few hours each evening. There was abundance of leisure, if not very magnificent remuneration, for these afternoon reporters. Among those who made profitable use of it was Charles Dickens, who then wrote several of his *Sketches*, and visited the nooks and corners of London, taking observations.

In the parliamentary session of 1835, Mr. Dickens was engaged as a reporter for the *Morning Chronicle*, in the House of Commons, and immediately took rank in the van, for the accuracy and neatness of his reports, and the rapidity with which he transcribed his notes. At one of the dinners of the Press Fund, in London, where he occupied the chair, he told his audience that the habits of his early life as a reporter so clung to him, that he seldom listened to a clever speech without his fingers mechanically and unconsciously going through the process of reporting it.

All that is now remembered of him in "the Gallery," is that he was reserved, but not shy, and that he took unusual pains with his work. Some time before this, he rented what are called "chambers," in Furnival's Inn, Holborn Bars,—one of the two Inns of Chancery attached to Lincoln's Inn, and mentioned not only in *Pickwick*, but also in the fourth part of *Edwin Drood.*

Mr. James Grant, author of "Random Recollections of the Houses of Lords and Commons," and of numerous other matter-of-fact works which were very sharply ridiculed by Thackeray in *Fraser's Magazine*, has given the following detailed account of Mr. Dickens's entrance into authorship:

It was about the year 1833–34, before Mr. Dickens's connection with the *Morning Chronicle*, and before Mr. Black, the editor of that journal, had ever met with him, that he commenced his literary career as an amateur writer. He made his *debût* in the latter end of 1834 or beginning of 1835, in the *Old Monthly Magazine*, then conducted by Captain Holland, a friend of mine. He sent, in the first instance, his contributions to that periodical anonymously. These consisted of sketches, chiefly of a humorous character, and were simply signed "Boz." For a long time they did not attract any special attention, but were generally spoken of in newspaper notices of the magazine as "clever," "graphic," etc. Early in 1836 the editorship of the *Monthly Magazine*—the adjective "Old" having been by this time dropped—came into my hands; and in making the necessary arrangements for its transfer from Captain Holland—then, I should have mentioned, proprietor as well as editor—I expressed my great admiration of the series of "Sketches by Boz," which had appeared in the *Monthly*, and said I should like to make an arrangement with the writer for the continuance of them under my editorship. With that view I asked him the name of the author. It will sound strange in most ears, when I state that a name which has for so many years filled the whole civilized world with its fame, was not remembered by Captain Holland. But, he added, after expressing his regret that he could not at the moment recollect the real name of "Boz," that he had received a letter from him a few days previously, and that if I would meet him, at the same time and place next day, he would bring me that letter, because it related to the "Sketches" of the writer, in the *Monthly Magazine*. As Captain Holland knew I was at the time a Parliamentary reporter on the *Morning Chronicle*, then a journal of high literary reputation, and of great political influence—he supplemented his remarks by saying that "Boz" was a Parliamentary reporter; on which I observed that I must, in that case, know him, at least by sight, as I was acquainted in that respect, more or less, with all the reporters in the gallery of the House of Commons. Captain Holland and I met, according to appointment, on the following day, when he brought the letter to which he had referred. I then found that the name of the author of "Sketches by Boz," was Charles Dickens. The letter was written in the most modest terms. It was simply to the effect that as he (Mr. Dickens) had hitherto given all his contributions—those signed "Boz"—gratuitously, he would be glad if Captain Holland thought his "Sketches" worthy of any small remuneration, as otherwise he would be obliged to discontinue them, because he was going very soon to get married, and therefore would be subjected to more expenses than he was while living alone, which he was during the time, in Furnival's Inn.

A writer in the *Liverpool Albion* (England) says for himself, "it may not be an inadmissible souvenir of the all-mourned idol to state here, that the first lines ever Mr. Dickens composed were submitted unconditionally to the writer of these remarks, submitted as the merest matter of professional literary business, hap-hazard, without any introduction or intervention of any kind, and without critic or author having the faintest idea of each other's individuality. It is, perhaps, not a too extravagant hypothesis to surmise that, had the judgment been adverse, there might never have been another appeal elsewhere by the hand which has held the whole reading world in captive admiration to its multitudinous spells ever since—a period of some thirty-five years."

He confirms Mr. Grant's statement, with additions, thus:

At that time the *Old Monthly*, as it was called, to distinguish it from the *New*, about which latter, Colburn, with Campbell for editor, kept blowing such trumpets, was still a puissance, though it had lately parted with its principal contributor, Rev. Dr. Croly, whose *Salathiel* was yet in the flow of its original success; and his "Notes of the Month" were always a piquant feature, even in an age of trenchant and polished penmanship. Under Croly the magazine was ardently tory; but it had become the property of Captain Holland, formerly one of Bolivar's aides-de-camp—a high bred man of a type now passed away, most variedly accomplished, and the centre of a congenial circle as gifted as himself, including many who afterwards made the fame of *Fraser*. Holland's Hispañolan liberalism, stimulated by the hot and turbid English reform agitation, still seething, and the Campbell and Colburn competition, led him to look for fresh blood to revive the drooping circulation. Hence one reason why Dickens, then buoyantly radical, was drawn thitherwards, although there was nothing whatever political in the slight initial paper, of less than half a dozen pages, he ventured upon. Nor was there in the three or four similar ones he afterwards furnished, and which attracted only the most cursory notice from his fellow-contributors. These articles sufficed, however, to induce Dr. Black, an old friend of his father's, to recommend the acceptance of others like them, but of a mere "social" character, in the after manner of the master, for *Bell's Life*—the proprietor of which was lavishing large means, in every form of publicity, upon his three journals, morning, evening, and weekly. Then the success of "her Majesty's Van" (Peel's newly-devised hearse-like vehicle for conveying prisoners to and from the police courts), and a few more of the like category, though printed in the smallest and densest newspaper type, some two-thirds of a column in length, obtained in all journals the extensive quotation which led to the Chapman and Hall alliance that resulted in "Pickwick," and in the unexampled celebrity thereupon supervening, and sustained *crescendo* to the last. Unique in all things, Dickens was pre-eminently singular in this, that, though "a gentleman of the press" to a degree undreamed of in the vocabulary of the right honorable personage who affectedly disavows any other escutcheon, he had no assailants, no traducers, no enemies. And for this reason, that, without being in the least mawkish, tuft hunting, or mealy-mouthed—on the contrary, being the most out-spoken extirpator of shams, imposture, and, in his own all-exhaustive phrase, of "Pecksniffism," he nevertheless traduced, maligned, satirized nobody. Not even his censors. For he had many such. It would be like descending into the catacombs of criticism, so to speak, to unearth proofs of how leading journals, now blatant in his posthumous praise, once ridiculed his pretensions to delineate anything beyond the Marionettes at a peep-show; what jubilant clapping of hands there was over Jupiter's pseudo-classic joke, *Procumbit humi Boz*, in reference to his first and last dramatic fiasco, "The Village Coquettes," under Braham's management, at the St. James, a quarter of a century back; and what a titter of sardonic approval was evoked by the Superfine Reviewer's pedantic scoff, that Mr. Dickens's readings appeared to be confined to a perusal of his own writings. His first steps were beset with Rigbys, whose "slashing articles" cried out, "This will never do!" pointing out how thorough a cockney he was, once his foot was off the flagways of the bills of mortality, and anticipating the late vixenish verdict of a certain screaming sister of the sensational school, that his works are stories of pothouse pleasantries. He won his way into universal favor in virtue of an ill-assimilative geniality against which no predetermination of resistance was proof, as in the case of Sydney Smith, who, with characteristic candor, avowed his intolerance of what he believed to be the cant of Dickens's popularity, and promptly ended in becoming an enthusiastic apostle of the propaganda himself.

When Dickens was engaged on the *Morning Chronicle*, Mr. John Black, biographer of Torquato Tasso, and translator of the lectures of William Augustus and Frederick Schlegel, was its editor. Of great learning and remarkable memory, with very liberal political opinions, this gentleman had been in charge of the *Chronicle* long before the death of Mr. James Perry, who, if he did not found, established that paper as the mouthpiece of the Whigs, after he became its proprietor and editor. It was Mr. Perry who initiated the employment of relays of reporters—the effect of which has been to make the closing part of a report, however extended, as full and vigorous as the commencement. Mr. Black was an editor, *sui generis.* A ten-line "leader" would have appalled him, by its brevity, for he resembled some of the Old World soldiers, in his predilection for charging in long "columns." He never could understand why Mr. Perry paid Thomas Moore very liberally for the satirical squibs which were finally collected under the title of "The Two-penny Post-bag," always contending that Poetry could say nothing which might not be much better expressed in Prose! His plan in writing a leading article, was to meditate upon it from morning until night, and then write two or three heavy sticksful, closing with a quotation, at least a column in length, from Bayle, Pascal, Thomas Aquinas, Dun Scotus, or some other light writer. It has always puzzled me to know why, not having the slightest sense of humor, he admitted Dickens's *Sketches* into the *Chronicle.* It is true, they were only published in a tri-weekly afternoon issue for the country.

Mr. Gruneison, long connected with the London press, confirms the statement that some of the *Sketches* appeared in *Bell's Life in London,* the great sporting paper, which had a large circulation, and paid contributors liberally. It was then conducted by a very able man, Mr. Vincent Dowling, known in the profession, from his great height, by the sobriquet of "The Long Scribe."

To this period (1835), when he may be said to have been "in a transition state," belongs a reminiscence of Charles Dickens, from the pen of N. P. Willis. Filtering out of it a certain assumption of superiority, on the part of the "Pencillings by the Way" author, it may give some idea of what a professed and professional man of society felt on meeting such a gem as Dickens and not seeing the sparkle.

Mr. Willis's letter, written from London to the *National Intelligencer* at Washington, reads thus:

I was following a favorite amusement of mine one day in the Strand, London—strolling toward the more crowded thoroughfares, with cloak and umbrella, and looking at people and shop windows. I heard my name called out by a passenger in a street cab. From out the smoke of the wet straw peered the head of my publisher, Mr. Macrone, (a most liberal and noble-hearted fellow, since dead). After a little catechism as to my damp destiny for that morning, he informed me that he was going to visit Newgate, and asked me to join him. I willingly agreed, never having seen this famous prison, and after I was seated in the cab he said he was to pick up on the way a young paragraphist for the *Morning Chronicle*, who wished to write a description of it. In the most crowded part of Holborn, within a door or two of the Bull and Mouth Inn (the great starting and stopping-place of the stage-coaches), we pulled up at the entrance of a large building used for lawyers' chambers. Not to leave me sitting in the rain, Macrone asked me to dismount with him. I followed by a long flight of stairs to an upper story, and was ushered into an uncarpeted and bleak-looking room, with a deal table, two or three chairs and a few books, a small boy and Mr. Dickens for the contents. I was only struck at first with one thing (and I made a memorandum of it that evening, as the strongest instance I had seen of English obsequiousness to employers), the degree to which the poor author was overpowered with the honor of his publisher's visit! I remember saying to myself, as I sat down on a ricketty chair, "My good fellow, if you were in America with that fine face and your ready quill, you would have no need to be condescended to by a publisher." Dickens was dressed very much as he has since described Dick Swiveller—*minus* the swell look. His hair was cropped close to his head, his clothes scant, though jauntily cut, and after changing a ragged office coat for a shabby blue, he stood by the door, collarless and buttoned up, the very personification, I thought, of a close sailor to the wind. We went down and crowded into the cab (one passenger more than the law allowed, and Dickens partly in my lap and partly in Macrone's), and drove on to Newgate. In his works, if you remember, there is a description of the prison, drawn from this day's observation. We were there an hour or two, and were shown some of the celebrated murderers confined for life, and one young soldier waiting for execution; and in one of the passages we chanced to meet Mrs. Fry on her usual errand of benevolence. Though interested in Dickens's face, I forgot him, naturally enough, after we entered the prison, and I do not think I heard him speak during the two hours. I parted from him at the door of the prison, and continued my stroll into the city. Not long after this, Macrone sent me the sheets of "Sketches by Boz," with a note saying that they were by the gentleman who went with us to Newgate. I read the book with amazement at the genius displayed in it, and in my note of reply assured Macrone that I thought his fortune was made as a publisher, if he could monopolize the author.

Two or three years afterwards I was in London, and was present at the complimentary dinner given to Macready. Samuel Lover, who sat next me, pointed out Dickens. I looked up and down the table, but was wholly unable to single him out without getting my friend to number the people who sat above him. He was no more like the same man I had seen than a tree in June is like the same tree in February. He sat leaning his head on his hand while Bulwer was speaking, and with his very long hair, his very flash waistcoat, his chains and rings, and with all a much paler face than of old, he was totally unrecognizable. The comparison was very interesting to me, and I looked at him a long time. He was then in his culmination of popularity, and seemed jaded to stupefaction. Remembering the glorious work he had written since I had seen him, I longed to pay him my homage, but had no opportunity, and I did not see him again till he came over to reap his harvest, and upset his hay-cart in America. When all the ephemera of his imprudences and improvidences shall have passed away —say twenty years hence—I should like to see him again, renowned as he will be for the most original and remarkable works of his time.

Remembering what manner of man Mr. N. P. Willis was, fashioning himself on the model of Count D'Osray, that mere tailor's block for the exhibition of unpaid-for garments, the above description is to be taken, like his own *notes of hand*, at a considerable discount. The idea of taking, or mistaking Charles Dickens then, with a good engagement, for "a young paragraphist for the *Morning Chronicle*," and of fancying that he resembled Dick Swiveller, "*minus* the swell look" in his appearance, is too heavy a draught upon human credulity. It is only surprising, when he mentioned the "hair cropped close to his head," that this self-appointed "arbiter elegantiarum" did not suggest that probably it had not grown since Dickens had last taken his month's exercise upon the treadmill at the House of Correction in Brixton! Yet the writer of such stuff would have been terribly offended if any one had told him it was impertinent and ungentlemanly, with a probable seasoning of spite and falsehood.

CHAPTER III.

THE ORIGIN OF THE NAME OF "BOZ."—VARIETY OF THE "SKETCHES."—EPIGRAM.—THE DEMOSTHENES OF THE TAP. —OLD BAILEY CHARACTERS.—FAGIN AND THE ARTFUL DODGER SHADOWED FORTH.—BUMBLE AND MRS. GAMP.—CRUIKSHANK'S ILLUSTRATIONS.—THE COUNTESS AND THE PUBLISHER.

WHEN Mr. Macrone published two volumes of *Sketches* by "Boz," with illustrations by George Cruikshank, it was known only to a few newspaper folks that a young man named Charles Dickens, was the author. As we have seen, he had put "Boz," as his *nom de plume*, to sundry magazine and newspaper stories and sketches. In one of his later prefaces to *Pickwick*, he explained the origin of this pseudonym, saying it "was the nickname of a pet child, a younger brother, whom I had dubbed Moses, in honor of the Vicar of Wakefield; which being facetiously pronounced through the nose, became Boses, and being shortened, became Boz. * * Boz was a very familiar household word to me, long before I was an author, and so I came to adopt it."

Not having received this derivation at first, the human

race fell into the interminable mistake of mispronouncing the *sobriquet.* Every one sounds it like the first syllable of the word *pos*-itive ; whereas, according to its author's own version, it ought to be pronounced *Boze.*—Having thus disposed of this important philological episode, I return to the narrative.

The *Sketches* contain the earliest productions of their author, "written," as he has stated, "from time to time to meet the exigencies of a newspaper or a magazine. They were originally published in two series: the first in two volumes, and the second one in one ;" this was in 1836. Fourteen years later, when he supervised a collective edition of his writings, Mr. Dickens prefaced them with the statement:

> The whole of these Sketches were written and published, one by one, when I was a very young man. They were collected and re-published while I was still a very young man ; and sent into the world with all their imperfections (a good many) on their heads. They comprise my first attempts at authorship—with the exception of certain tragedies achieved at the mature age of eight or ten, and represented with great applause to overflowing nurseries. I am conscious of their often being extremely crude and ill-considered, and bearing obvious marks of haste and inexperience; particularly in that section of the present volume which is comprised under the general head of Tales. But as this collection is not originated now, and was very leniently and favorably received when it was first made, I have not felt it right either to remodel or expunge, beyond a few words and phrases here and there.

The collection contains Sketches from our Parish, Scenes in London and its vicinity, Characters, and a dozen Tales. Most of these "Sketches of English Life and Character" had already attracted no small attention. Several provincial Journalists, of whom I was one, appreciating their spirit and fidelity, duly "conveyed" them to their own weekly journals—at that time there not being a daily paper in Great Britain, out of London, though there were several in

Dublin. I, for one, was very glad to reprint these lively sketches, the authorship of which was unknown, then and until the success of the *Pickwick Papers* revealed it. At first, it was believed, that "Dickens" was as fictitious a name as "Boz." An indifferent but much quoted epigram published about this time, in *the Carthusian*, ran thus:

> "Who the Dickens 'Boz' could be
> Puzzled many a learned elf;
> But time unveiled the mystery,
> And 'Boz' appeared as Dickens' self."

The *Sketches* had the great merit of being faithful as well as humorous and spirited, and were infinitely superior to Mr. Wight's "Morning in Bow street," from the *Morning Herald*, which had been collected into two volumes, a few years earlier—also with the great advantage of being illustrated by George Cruikshank. No doubt "Boz" and Cruikshank, with pen and pencil, were exaggerated as well as sprightly—but it was an exaggeration whose racy humor scarcely misrepresented the truth. It has been charged that the *Sketches*, however graphic and varied, chiefly depicted vice, vulgarity, and misery: the drunken clerk making a night of it; the degraded and desperate female convict; the abandoned drunkard hurrying on his own fearful end; the retired shopkeeper making a fool of himself by falling in love; the contemptible squabbles and intrigues of a city boarding house; the overtasked youth expiring in the arms of a widowed mother. But the writer was neither vicious nor vulgar. He had to show the shadows as well as the lights of society which had come under his observation, and after all, fun and frolic predominate. The author's own taste was apparent in several sketches of private theatricals. A description of a balloon-ascent from Vauxhall Gardens is full of life, and some of the character-sketches are wonderfully good. For example, the Parlor Orator—Demosthenes of the tap—who allows no one to speak but himself, and has obtained, and keeps, his position, by objecting to whatever other people say, by calling on them to *prove* the most as well as the least abstract propositions.

We stand, (he says,) in these times, upon a calm elevation of intellectual attainment, and not in the dark recess of mental deprivation. Proof is what I require—proof, and not assertions, in these stirring times. Every gen'lm'n that knows me, knows what was the nature and effect of my observations, when it was in the contemplation of the Old-street Suburban Representative Discovery Society, to recommend a candidate for that place in Cornwall there—I forget the name of it. "Mr. Snobee," said Mr. Wilson, "is a fit and proper person to represent the borough in Parliament." "Prove it," says I. "He is a friend to Reform," says Mr. Wilson. "Prove it," says I. "The abolitionist of the national debt, the unflinching opponent of pensions, the uncompromising advocate of the negro, the reducer of sinecures and the duration of Parliament; the extender of nothing but the suffrages of the people," says Mr. Wilson. "Prove it," says I. "His acts prove it," says he. "Prove *them*," says I. "And he could not prove them," said the red-faced man looking round triumphantly; "and the borough didn't have him; and if you carried this principle to the full extent, you have no debt, no pensions, no sinecures, no negroes, no nothing. And then, standing upon an elevation of intellectual attainment, and having reached the summit of popular prosperity, you might bid defiance to the nations of the earth, and erect yourselves in the proud confidence of wisdom and superiority. This is my argument—this always has been my argument—and if I was a Member of the House of Commons to-morrow I'd make 'em shake in their shoes with it." And the red-faced man having struck the table very hard with his clenched fist, by way of adding weight to the declaration, smoked away like a brewery.

He is opposed, this Mr. Rogers, by a common-sense green-grocer who holds to the optimist principle, and denies that he is a slave:

"What is man? (continued the red-faced specimen of the

species, jerking his hat indignantly, from its peg on the wall.) What is an Englishman? Is he to be trampled upon by every oppressor? Is he to be knocked down at everybody's bidding? What's freedom? Not a standing army. What's a standing army? Not freedom. What's general happiness? Not universal misery. Liberty ain't the window-tax, is it? The Lords ain't the Commons, are they." And the red-faced man, gradually bursting into a radiating sentence, in which such adjectives as "dastardly," "oppressive," "violent," and "sanguinary," formed the most conspicuous words, knocked his hat indignantly over his eyes, left the room, and slammed the door after him.

In a sketch of the Old Bailey, we have the germs of two well known characters, in Oliver Twist. The first will remind the reader of the trial of Fagin:

Turn your eyes to the dock; watch the prisoner attentively for a few moments, and the fact is before you, in all its painful reality. Mark how restlessly he has been engaged for the last ten minutes, in forming all sorts of fantastic figures with the herbs which are strewed upon the ledge before him; observe the ashy paleness of his face when a particular witness appears, and how he changes his position and wipes his clammy forehead, and feverish hands, when the case for the prosecution is closed, as if it were a relief to him to feel that the jury knew the worst.

The defence is concluded; the judge proceeds to sum up the evidence, and the prisoner watches the countenances of the jury, as a dying man, clinging to life to the very last, vainly looks in the face of his physician for one slight ray of hope. They turn round to consult; you can almost hear the man's heart beat, as he bites the stalk of rosemary, with a desperate effort to appear composed. They resume their places—a dead silence prevails as the foreman delivers in the verdict—"Guilty!" A shriek bursts from a female in the gallery; the prisoner casts one look at the quarter from whence the noise proceeded, and is immediately hurried from the dock by the jailer.

In the same sketch, is a young pickpocket, who in reply to the question, "Have you any witnesses to your character?" answers "Yes, my Lord; fifteen gen'lm'n is a vaten outside, and vos a vaten all day yesterday, vich they told me the night afore my trial vos a comin' on." When the witnesses fail to appear, because they never existed, and the jailer states that the urchin has been under his care twice before, he resolutely denies it, in some such terms as—"S'elp me 'God, gen'lm'n, I never vos in trouble afore—indeed, my Lord, I never vos. It's all a howen to my having a twin brother, vich has wrongfully taken to prigging, and vich is so exactly like me, that no vun ever knows the difference atween us."

If this youth was not own cousin to the Artful Dodger, there is no truth in family resemblances! Further, when the boy is sentenced to seven years' transportation, we are told that "finding it impossible to excite compassion, he gives vent to his feelings in an imprecation bearing reference to the eyes of 'old big vig!' and as he declines to take the trouble of walking from the dock, he is forthwith carried out by two men, congratulating himself on having succeeded in giving everybody as much trouble as possible." Surely, in speech and action the Artful here stands confessed? In *Oliver Twist,* he jocosely chaffs the police officers at Bow street; asks the jailer to communicate "the names of them two files as was on the bench;" turns on the magistrate with an air of abstraction, and "Did you redress yourself to me, my man?" vehemently declares that his attorney is a "breakfasting with the Wice-President of the House of Commons;" when committed, threatens the Bench with his vengeance; and, finally retires "grinning in the officer's face, with great glee and self-approval." The Parish Beadle, who appears in several of these sketches, was reproduced, ere long, as Mr. Bumble, and when an interesting event occurs in the house of Mr. Robinson, who married one of the four Misses Willis, and the street is "very much alarmed at hearing a hackneyed coach stop at Mrs. Robinson's door, at half-past two o'clock in the morning, out of which emerged a fat old woman, in a cloak and nightcap, with a bundle in one hand,

and a pair of pattens in the other, who looked as if she had been suddenly knocked up out of bed for some very special purpose," who can doubt, for a moment, that he stands, thus early, in the august presence of Mrs. Sarah Gamp, friend of *that* Mrs. Harris, and subsequently painted at full length in the remarkable adventures of the Chuzzlewit family. It is not unusual for authors to develop at length characters of which they had originally given glimpses. Scott, in this manner, drew, for some of his novels, upon anecdotes which he had previously related in the notes to his Scottish minstrelsy and other poems.

Cruikshank's admirable illustrations considerably aided the popularity of the *Sketches*. Before Dickens was born, Cruikshank had made himself familiar with the by-ways of London, and with the various classes to be found in them. Perhaps he even presented such "happy hunting grounds" in these large but not very respectable districts to the clever young writer, who also had a taste for examining various phases of society. Some of Cruikshank's happiest "bits" are among these illustrations. The rotund personage who, in "The Parish Engine," assails the street-door, is the very incarnation of Beadledom. The crowd of children, in another plate, who rush forth hatless and bonnetless, to call a hackney coach, is *chef d' œuvre* in its quiet effect, and the numerous interiors, with tenier-like wealth of detail, are wonderful little pictures. As for the two plates of "The Steam Excursion," they are the Before and After of pleasure anticipated and destroyed. Artist and author are seen in thorough unison throughout these remarkable *Sketches*. They worked together, as Captain Cuttle would say, "with a will." Following up the success of the two volumes of "Sketches," illustrated by Cruikshank, and published by Mr. J. Macrone, a third volume soon appeared. In a few weeks the demand for them was so great, that the supply fell short of the demand. It is a tradition in "the trade," that a lady of title called at Macrone's, in St. James's Square, for a copy of the work. He had sold the last, but promised that she should be supplied by noon, next day, fresh from the binder. Could he lend her his own two volumes? Unfortunately he had sold them. She said she would look in the shop for herself, and he handed her out of her carriage. She rummaged for a copy, but ineffectually, and at last, having lost time and temper, drove off in a pet, without having the civility even to bow to the handsome young publisher. As the book cost a guinea, it was almost unknown to the people. *Pickwick*, in shilling numbers, was within the reach of all, and hit the taste of all. The lady who figures in this tale of tales, was the Countess Cowper, subsequently married to Lord Palmerston.

CHAPTER IV.

FIRST LAURELS WON.—HOW THE "PICKWICK PAPERS" WERE BEGUN.—THE SHILLING NUMBER SYSTEM.—GREEN PAPER COVERS.—LEVER AND THACKERAY.—MR. SERGEANT TALFOURD.—COPYRIGHT.—PROPOSED NIMROD CLUB.—MR. PICKWICK FOUND AT RICHMOND.—RECEPTION OF PICKWICK.—INTRODUCTION OF SAM WELLER.—AUTHOR AND PUBLISHERS.—BULWER.—THE GREAT LITERARY REVIEWS.—MISS MITFORD'S CRITICISM.—SCOTT AND DICKENS.—WHAT PICKWICK HAS DONE.—IN A PICKWICKIAN SENSE.—LADY JERSEY'S SAM WELLER' BALL.

In 1836, then in his twenty-fifth year, Charles Dickens reached the culminating point in his career. Many a man who has had the consciousness of power has panted for the opportunity of exercising it. "Give me a fulcrum," Archimedes is reported to have said, "and I will move the earth." The one thing wanted in human life is opportunity. Without this, aspiration and even ability may be said, in the words of one who was himself a powerful man of genius, to resemble, "silent thunder." It was in no vain boasting mood that Manfred, as his baffled career was nearing its close, said,

> "Ay —— father! I have had those earthly visions,
> And noble aspirations in my youth,
> To make my mind the mind of other men,
> The enlightener of the nations."

So, more or less, genius has ever felt. Rarely does it realize its early ambition. Here, in 1836, Dickens had conquered one great difficulty. Youthful and unknown, without patrons or friends, he had succeeded in getting his *Sketches* placed before the world, in the substantive form of a book, and a publisher saw sufficient in them to warrant the expense of having them illustrated by George Cruikshank, then very famous for the spirit, truth, and humor of his designs. The *Sketches* had been favorably, kindly noticed in the public journals, and their author was laboring in preparing a third volume, when an incident occurred which is best told in his own words.

I was a young man of two or three-and twenty, when Messrs. Chapman & Hall, attracted by some pieces I was at that time writing in the *Morning Chronicle* newspaper, or had just written in the old *Monthly Magazine* (of which one series had been lately collected and published in two volumes, illustrated by Mr. George Cruikshank), waited upon me to propose a something that should be published in shilling numbers—then only known to me, or, I believe, to any body else, by a dim recollection of certain interminable novels in that form, which used to be carried about the country by peddlers, and over some of which I remember to have shed innumerable tears before I had served my apprenticeship to Life.

When I opened my door in Furnival's Inn to the partner who represented the firm, I recognized in him the person from whose hands I had bought, two or three years previously, and whom I had never seen before or since, a paper —in the "Sketches" called Mr. Minns and his Cousin—

dropped stealthily one evening at twilight, with fear and trembling into a dark letter-box, in a dark office, up a dark court in Fleet street—appeared in all the glory of print; on which occasion I walked down to Westminster Hall, and turned into it for half an hour, because my eyes were so dimmed with joy and pride that they could not bear the street, and were not fit to be seen there. I told my visitor of the coincidence, which we both hailed as a good omen; and so fell to business.

The idea propounded to me was, that the monthly something should be a vehicle for certain plates to be executed by Mr. Seymour; and there was a notion, either on the part of that admirable humorous artist, or of my visitor (I forget which), that a "Nimrod Club," the members of which were to go out shooting, fishing, and so forth, and getting themselves into difficulties through their want of dexterity, would be the best means of introducing these. I objected, on consideration, that although born and partly bred in the country, I was no great sportsman, except in regard of all kinds of locomotion; that the idea was not novel, and had been already much used; that it would be infinitely better for the plates to arise naturally out of the text; and that I should like to take my own way, with a freer range of English scenes and people, and was afraid I should ultimately do so in any case, whatever course I might prescribe to myself at starting. My views being deferred to, I thought of Mr. Pickwick, and wrote the first number; from the proof-sheets of which, Mr. Seymour made his drawing of the Club, and that happy portrait of its founder, by which he is always recognized, and which may be said to have made him a reality. I connected Mr. Pickwick with a club, because of the original suggestion, and I put in Mr. Winkle expressly for the use of Mr. Seymour. We started with a number of twenty-four pages instead of thirty-two, and four illustrations in lieu of a couple. Mr. Seymour's sudden and lamented death before the second number was published, brought about a quick decision upon a point already in agitation; the number became one of thirty-two pages with two illustrations, and remained so to the end. My friends told me it was a low, cheap form of publication, by which I should ruin all my rising hopes; and how right my friends turned out to be, everybody now knows.

He added, in a foot-note, "this book [Pickwick] would

have cost, at the then established price of novels, about four guineas and a half." It was sold, when completed, neatly half-bound, for one guinea, which, to use a sporting phrase, gave an advantage of nine to two in favor of the purchaser, without taking into account the addition of forty-three engravings from original designs. In a subsequent chapter, Dickens's artists will be separately treated of.

The issue in shilling numbers, which Dickens's friends objected to, as a low, cheap form of publication, was by no means a new idea. Two publishing houses, at the head of which were Mr. Henry Fisher and Mr. Kelly, respectively, were then doing an immense business throughout England, by the sale of various works in shilling numbers, distributed by peripatetic agents, and Chapman & Hall, the new firm with whose fortunes those of Charles Dickens were long to be associated, having considerable knowledge of "the trade," shrewdly believed that an attractive novel, published in monthly parts, at a low price, might safely venture to compete with the thrilling issues of the "History of the War," sent out by Mr. Kelly, or even such novelties as "The Pilgrim's Progress," "Pamela," "Clarissa Harlowe," and "Sir Charles Grandison," printed from worn-out stereotype plates.

The first number of the Pickwick Papers had a green paper cover, on which many emblematic designs were given, was published on the last day of March, 1836, and the final issue, containing title-page, index, dedication, and brief preface, and consisting of Parts 19 and 20, was in October, 1837. The covers of every other serial monthly by Dickens was of green paper, like the first, and he often referred to it. Some years later, when Charles Lever adopted the serial form of publication, "Harry Lorrequer" and its followers invariably had *red*, while Thackeray's "Vanity Fair" appeared in *yellow* covers. These differences of hue were severally retained to the end by all three authors. Dickens more than once mentioned his "green leaves."

The dedication to Mr. Sergeant Talfourd was at once a memorial of private friendship, and, the words ran, "as a slight and most inadequate acknowledgment of the inestimable services you are rendering to the literature of your country, and of the lasting benefits you will confer upon the authors of this and succeeding generations, by securing to them and their descendants a permanent interest in the copyright of their works." Talfourd, who then sat in the House of Commons, as member for Reading, his native town, had introduced a new copyright act, in the session of 1837, which, still bearing the title of "Talfourd's Act," was passed, with some modifications, in 1842, and extended the term of author's copyright from twenty-eight to forty-two years. This, the existing copyright law of Great Britain and Ireland, made Talfourd very popular among authors. In its operation, however, it has been less advantageous to authors than to publishers, who do not pay more for a forty-two than for a twenty-eight years' copyright. With some other enthusiasts, Dickens believed that this extension of copyright would greatly benefit "those who devote themselves to the most precarious of all pursuits," (literature,) and, still addressing his friend, said, "Many a fevered head and palsied hand will gather new vigor in the hour of sickness and distress, from your excellent exertions; many a widowed mother and orphan child, who would otherwise reap nothing from the fame of departed genius but its too frequent legacy of poverty and suffering, will bear, in their altered condition, higher testimony to the value of your labors than the most lavish encomiums from lip or pen could ever afford."

In the Preface, of 1837, Dickens said that his original purpose "was to place before the reader a constant succession of characters and incidents; to paint them in as vivid colors as he could command; and to render them, at the same time, life-like and amusing." He added that "deferring to the judgment of others in the outset of the undertaking, he adopted the machinery of the club, which was suggested as that best adapted to his purpose; but, finding that it tended rather to his embarrassment than otherwise, he gradually abandoned it, considering it a matter of very little importance to the work whether strictly epic justice were awarded to the club or not." He claimed, also, as well he might, that throughout the book no incident or expression occurs which could call a blush into the most delicate cheek, or wound the feelings of the most sensitive person, and his closing words are, "If any of his imperfect descriptions, while they afford amusement to the perusal, should induce only one reader to think better of his fellow-men, and to look upon the brighter and more kindly light of human nature, he would indeed be proud and happy to have led to such a result."

The title of the book was almost fortuitously created. *Nimrod*, as above stated, was first proposed, but, we are told, a better name was soon found. Mr. Dickens rushed into the publisher's office one day exclaiming with evident delight, "I've got it—Moses Pickwick, Bath, coach-master." He had just seen painted on the door of a stage coach that was passing along the street the name and address "Moses Pickwick & Co., Bath," that worthy firm being the proprietors of a line of stages running from the great metropolis to the well-known seat of fashion in the West of England. Moses was changed into Samuel, and so the hero got his name. After the trial, when Mr. Pickwick resolved to visit Bath, and proceeded to the White Horse Cellar, Piccadilly, a noted coaching and booking hotel in those days, Sam Weller drew his attention to the fact that PICKWICK was inscribed on the stage-coach, in gilt letters of goodly size, and adds "that ain't all: not content vith writin' up Pickwick, they puts 'Moses' afore it, vich I call addin' insult to injury, as the parrot said ven they not only took him from his native land, but made him talk the English langwidge arterwards." His indignation and sorrow when he found that "nobody is to be whopped for taking this here liberty," are duly recorded and cannot be forgotten. Mr. Chapman, one of the publishers, is said to have described an elderly gentleman, with spectacles and gaiters, whom he met looking over the Thames at Richmond, and Seymour is believed to have embodied this idea, in his full-length of Mr. Pickwick, which millions have smiled at.

The success of *Pickwick* was by no means so rapid and decided as has been generally supposed. The publishers did not advertise it extensively, and, though the mode of publication (monthly shilling numbers) certainly helped it on, the sale was comparatively small. Mr. James Grant says in the article already mentioned: "for the first five months of its existence, Mr. Dickens's first serial, the *Pickwick Papers*, was a signal failure, notwithstanding the fact, that Mr. Charles Tilt, at that time a publisher of considerable eminence, made extraordinary exertions, out of friendship for Messrs. Chapman & Hall, to insure its success. He sent out, on what is called sale or return, to all parts of the provinces, no fewer than fifteen hundred copies of each of the first five parts. This gave the *Pickwick Papers* a very extensive publicity, yet Mr. Tilt's only result was an average sale of fifty copies of each of the five parts. A certain number of copies sold, of course, through other channels, but commercially, the publication was a decided failure. The question was debated by the publishers whether they ought not to discontinue the publication of the serial. But just while the matter was under their consideration, Sam Weller, who had been introduced in the previous number, began to attract great attention and to call forth much admiration. The Press was all but unanimous in praising 'Samivel' as an entirely original character, whom none but a great genius could have created; and all of a sudden, in consequence of 'Samivel's' popularity, the *Pickwick Papers* rose to an unheard of popularity. The back numbers of the work were ordered to a large extent, and of course all idea of discontinuing it was abandoned. By the time the *Pickwick Papers* had reached their twelfth number—that being half of the numbers of which it was originally intended the work should consist—Messrs. Chapman & Hall were so gratified with the signal success to which it had now attained, that they sent Mr. Dickens a cheque for £500, as a practical expression of their satisfaction with the sale. The work continued to increase in circulation until its completion, when the sale had all but reached 40,000 copies. In the interval between the twelfth and concluding number, Messrs. Chapman & Hall sent Mr. Dickens several cheques, amounting in all to £3,000, in addition to the fifteen guineas per number which they had engaged at the beginning to give him. It was understood at the time, that Messrs. Chapman & Hall made a clear profit amounting to nearly £20,000 by the sale of the *Pickwick Papers*, after paying Mr. Dickens, in round numbers, £3,500."

It may be remembered that Samuel Weller was not introduced until after the four gentlemen of the Pickwick Club had visited the Wardle family at Manor Farm, Dingley Dell, and Jingle's elopement with the too sensitive middle-aged young lady, Miss Rachel Wardle. Mr. Jerdan, who had been over thirty years editor of the *Literary Gazette*, a great power in London when the *Athenæum* was not much read, takes credit, in his Autobiography, for having induced Dickens to make a great deal of Sam Weller. He says: "I was so charmed with the creation that I could not resist the impulse to write to the author, express my admiration, and counsel him to develop the novel character largely—to the utmost." Afterward, when "Pickwick" was finished, and a semi-business Pickwickian sort of dinner ensued, Jerdan was invited to be of the party, with this compliment: "I depend upon *you* above everybody; Faithfully yours, always, Charles Dickens." The author occupied the chair, with Mr. Serjeant Talfourd as Vice President, and Jerdan adds: "Then the pleasant and uncommon fact was stated, (all the individuals being present and toasted,) that *there never had been a line of written agreement, but that author, printer, artist and publisher had all proceeded on simply verbal assurances, and that there never had arisen a word to interrupt or prevent the complete satisfaction of every one.*"

This is at variance with Mr. Grant's statement that the terms upon which Mr. Dickens concluded an arrangement with Messrs. Chapman & Hall for the publication of the *Pickwick Papers*, were "fifteen guineas for each number, the number consisting of two sheets, or thirty-two pages. That was a rather smaller sum than he offered to me, just at the same time, to contribute to the *Monthly Magazine*, then under my editorship." In fact, the first number contained *twenty-four*, and each subsequent number *thirty-two* octavo pages.

Bulwer, writing in 1840, fifteen years after the beginning of his successful authorship, said, "Long after my name was not quite unknown in every other country where English literature is received, the great quarterly journals of my own disdained to recognize my existence." Dickens was far more fortunate. In October, 1837, when *Pickwick* was just completed, it was reviewed at length in the *Quarterly Review*, which frankly admitted "That a fresh vein of humor had been opened; that a new and decidedly original genius had sprung up; and the most cursory reference to preceding English writers of the comic order will show that, in his own peculiar walk, Mr. Dickens is not simply the most distinguished, but the first." Twelve months after this the *Edinburgh Review* had an article upon him, eulogizing his humanity and humor, his tenderness and truth.

There is no knowledge of the actual profits of *Pickwick* at this time. The impression, even while the story was in course of publication, was that they were immense. Miss Mitford, herself a deservedly popular author, writing to a friend in Ireland, in June, 1837, when *Pickwick* was in course of comple tion, said, "So you never heard of the *Pickwick Papers?* Well, they publish a number once a month, and print 25,000. The bookseller has made about £10,000 by the speculation. It is fun—London life—but without anything unpleasant; a lady might read it *aloud;* and this so graphic, so individual, and so true that you could courtesy to all the people as you see them in the streets. I did think there had not been a place where English is spoken to which 'Boz' had not penetrated. All the boys and girls talk his fun—the boys in the streets; and yet those who are of the highest taste like it the most. Sir Benjamin Brodie takes it to read in his carriage, between patient and patient; and Lord Denman studies *Pickwick* on the bench while the jury are deliberating. Do take some means to borrow the *Pickwick Papers.* It seems like not having heard of Hogarth, whom he resembles greatly, except that he takes a far more cheerful view, a Shakespearian view, of humanity. It is rather fragmentary, except the trial (No. 11 or 12), which is as complete and perfect as any bit of comic writing in the English language. You must read the *Pickwick Papers.*" In the same letter, criticizing Talfourd's Life of Charles Lamb, Miss Mitford says, "It consists almost wholly of his letters, which are entertaining, although not elegant enough to give one much pleasure. It is very odd that I should not mind the perfectly low-life of the *Pickwick Papers,* because the closest copies of things that are, and yet dislike the want of elegance in Charles Lamb's letters, which are merely his own fancies; but I think you will understand the feeling."

That Brodie, head of the medical profession in England, should have read *Pickwick* in his carriage, as he paid his usual round of visits, showed, no doubt, a great interest in the work. Another member of the same craft, nearly one hundred and fifty years earlier, had done more than *read,* for he actually *wrote* a popular poem in his chaise. This was Sir Samuel Garth, a famous London doctor, who, in

1699, published "The Dispensatory," a poem, which ran through seven editions in a few years, and was warmly com mended by Pope, a difficult critic as well as a great poet. As for Lord Denman, then Chief Justice of England, reading *Pickwick* on the bench, while a jury was deliberating on the verdict, literary history supplies a singular parallel, for Lockhart relates, in his "Life of Sir Walter Scott," that, one of the judges, in Edinburgh, felt so much interested in one of the Waverley Novels, just published, that he took it into court with him, and finding or fancying that the subject matter in one of its chapters somewhat bore upon a trial then proceeding, pulled out the volume, and read it, with infinite humor and gusto, as part of his charge to the jury!

Before "Pickwick" was completed, the sale rose to 40,000 a month, and the demand for back numbers to make up sets, was considerable. It has been said, without much consideration, that *Pickwick* rushed into more enormous popularity in a few months, than had ever been obtained by any first work of fiction except "Waverley." In 1814, when that romance appeared, Miss Edgeworth was the only living novelist who had any real hold on the public mind. In 1837, when *Pickwick* was being published, James, Ainsworth, Bulwer, Galt, Mrs. Gore, Mrs. Trollope, Disraeli, Grattan, Lover, Banim, Griffin, Warren, Theodore Hook, Miss Mitford, Miss Landon, Mrs. S. C. Hall, Horace Smith, Lister, Ward, Marryat, Lady Blessington, Croly, Hood, W. H. Maxwell, Lady Morgan, and many others, literally had the ear of the public. Therefore, the new and anonymous competitor for fame had to hold his own, like Ivanhoe at the tournament, against all comers. Scott had found an uncultivated waste, as it were, which soon bloomed in fragrance and beauty under his wand, truly that of an enchanter. Dickens, on the other hand, had an army of rivals to oppose, and only succeeded by proving himself equal, at least, to the greatest. Thackeray was then (1837) merely writing for bread, in *Fraser's Magazine.* Charles Lever had not then appeared.

Of all the rest, Bulwer best has kept his place, and it is a question whether, half a century hence, the Lord of Knebworth may occupy a place, on the roll of fame, as high as "Boz" himself; for if Dickens has sketched life in the middle and lower ranks of England, in the second quarter of the nineteenth century, Bulwer's Caxton novels have shown the political and fashionable phases of English society, with a spirit and fidelity which no one had exhibited before.

When "Waverley" was published (in July, 1814), it did not create any remarkable sensation. The first edition, of 1,000 copies, moved slowly off in five weeks. Then, on a report that none but Scott could have written the book, 3,000 copies more were sold before November. Author and publisher, on a fair division of the profits, each made £612 in these four months. Once established, however, and followed up, with all the abounding fertility of creative genius, by other novels and romances, in rapid succession, "Waverley" has held its own well, as "father of a line of kings," but without the early popularity of *Pickwick*.

No doubt, the admirers of the *Sketches by "Boz,"* which may be said to contain the germs of many of the characters which he subsequently elaborated, were glad to meet the author in a new work. They had found him shrewd and clever, truthful even when he ran into caricature, and unusually amusing. Attention was first drawn to Pickwick by the engravings. There was something very ludicrous in taking, as the hero of a novel, such an odd-looking little old gentleman as Mr. Samuel Pickwick, and, as he repeatedly came up in the whole twenty numbers, readers recognized him, as if he were a familiar acquaintance. Beginning merely to amuse, and in the secondary position of illustrating an artist's comic designs, it can readily be seen how soon and how completely this young author, then only twenty-four years old, rose above his original position. He would be an unusually acute reader who could clearly state what the plot of *Pickwick* really is. Had it been published, at first, as an entire book, without the illustrations, it would probably have been a failure. It contained as much letter-press as any three of the ordinary Waverley Novels, and might have been voted tedious. But, appearing in monthly parts, each (to use the words of Miss Edgeworth's postillion), closing with a sensational "gallop for the avenue," it did not too much or too long engage the attention, and there was left in the reader's mind a to-be-continued expectation of the next number.

Dickens, in his later preface, which explained how he was engaged to write the story, said:

> It has been observed of Mr. Pickwick, that there is a decided change in his character, as these pages proceed, and that he becomes more good and more sensible. I do not think this change will appear forced or unnatural to my readers, if they will reflect that in real life the peculiarities and oddities of a man who has anything whimsical about him, generally impress us first, and that it is not until we are better acquainted with him that we usually begin to look below these superficial traits, and to know the better part of him.

Glancing fourteen years back, Mr. Dickens said:

> I have found it curious and interesting, looking over the sheets of this reprint, to mark what important social improvements have taken place about us, almost imperceptibly, even since they were originally written. The license of Counsel, and the degree to which Juries are ingeniously bewildered, are yet susceptible of moderation; while an improvement in the mode of conducting Parliamentary Elections (especially for counties) is still within the bounds of possibility. But, legal reforms have pared the claws of Messrs. Dodson & Fogg; a spirit of self-respect, mutual forbearance, education, and co-operation, for such good ends, has diffused itself among their clerks; places far apart are brought together, to the present convenience and advantage of the Public, and to the certain destruction, in time, of a host of petty jealousies, blindnesses, and prejudices, by which the Public alone have always been the sufferers; the laws relating to imprisonment for debt are altered; and the Fleet Prison is pulled down!

He added, (this was twenty years ago, when little more than one-third of his literary career had been run):

With such a retrospect comprised within so short a period, who knows, but it may be discovered, within this Century, that there are even magistrates in town and country, who should be taught to shake hands every day with Common Sense and Justice; that even Poor Laws may have mercy on the weak, the aged, and unfortunate; that Schools, on the broad principles of Christianity, are the best adornment for the length and breadth of this civilized land; that Prison-doors should be barred on the outside, no less heavily and carefully than they are barred within; that the universal diffusion of common means of decency and health is as much the right of the poorest of the poor, as it is indispensable to the safety of the rich, and of the State; that a few petty boards and bodies—less than drops in the great ocean of humanity, which roars around them—are not to let loose Fever and Consumption on God's creatures at their will, or always to keep their little fiddles going, for a Dance of Death!

The object of the work, at first, was simply to amuse;—in the author's own words, "to place before the reader a constant succession of characters and incidents; to paint them in as vivid colors as he could command; and to render them, at the same time, life-like and amusing." The cumbrous machinery of the Pickwick Club, which opened the work, was soon dispensed with. All, except its tediousness, that now rests in the mind, is the quaint humor of Messrs. Pickwick and Blotton abusing each other, in the heartiest manner, like vestrymen at a parish meeting, and eventually ending the dispute by exchanging compliments, and declaring that they had respectively used harsh language "only in a Pickwickian sense." Just about that time a somewhat similar scene had taken place, in a great legislative body at Westminster, and the parties got out of it by mutually conceding that they had abused each other only "in a Parliamentary sense." This was the first hit in Pickwick that *told.* The idea was too good to be lightly parted with, so at Mr. Bob Sawyer's party, in his lodgings in the Borough, Lant-street,—the particular locality in which Mrs. Raddle was a house-keeper, has lately been swept away, I hear, to make room for the extension of a railroad station—it was worked up again. The great quarrel between Messrs. Noddy and Gunter, which had a "pistols for two and coffee for one" aspect, at one time, ends in both young gentlemen quietly eating their own words, and expressing their mutual admiration in the warmest terms.

Having to supply thirty-two octavo pages of letter-press each month, Mr. Dickens, starting with no settled purpose, except that of amusing his readers, now and then eked out his narrative by dipping into his portfolio for sketches and tales already written, and working these into his text. For the most part, he did this in a clumsy manner. Upon *Pickwick* were thus engrafted "the Stroller's Tale," related by the Dismal Man, at Rochester; "the Convict's Return," told by the Clergyman at Wardle's farm; "A Madman's Manuscript," purporting to have been written by the same; "the Bagman's Story," told in the Commercial room at Eatanswill; "the Story of the Queer Client," related by Jack Bamber of Gray's Inn; Wardle's "Story of the Goblins who stole a Sexton;" "the True Legend of Prince Bladud;" and "the Story of the Bagman's Uncle;" all of these had probably been written as portions of a new volume of "Sketches." They merely filled up space in *Pickwick* to save Dickens the trouble of composition, and very much clogged the story. Except in "Nicholas Nickleby," where, on the Yorkshire journey, a couple of gentlemen tell stories against each other, and in "Master Humphrey's Clock," where they legitimately came in as portions of the regular "works," Mr. Dickens never again tried to produce stories within a story.

The adventures of the Pickwickians in the country are fresh and lively, but the finding of the stone with the inscription and the subsequent proceedings thereon, are abundantly absurd. It was nothing new to burlesque the proceedings of an Antiquarian Society, and the idea of converting "Bil Stumps, his mark," into something which was taken or mistaken for an antique inscription, was evidently suggested by the A. D. L. L. which Jonathan Oldbuck, in "the Antiquary" fancied must signify *Agricola Dicavit Libens Lubens*, while Edie Ochiltree proved that it only indicated Archie Drum's Lang Ladle. It is no secret that Scott got his idea from an amusing incident recorded in the apocryphal Autobiography of Madame du Barry.

The adventures at Mr. Leo Hunter's, the quarrel with Mr. Peter Magnus about the Lady in Yellow Curl Papers, and a few such incidents, are feeble enough. But, the moment that Dickens brought us to Sam Weller, in the court-yard of the old Inn in the Borough, it was evident that he got upon *terra firma*. The way in which Sam, as "Boots" in that hostlerie, counts up the company there is inimitable:— "There's a wooden leg in number six; there's a pair of Hessians in thirteen; there's two pair of halves in the commercial; there's these here painted tops in the snuggery inside the bar; and five more tops in the coffee-room."

From that auspicious hour Sam Weller is master of the situation, and flavors the whole story. It has been stated, in a *Quarterly Review*, that while "The Pickwick Papers" were yet unfinished, a fashionable lady of high rank,—the Countess of Jersey, I think,—sent out invitations to a ball, the condition of acceptance pencilled upon each card being "Provided you will admit that Sam Weller is a gentleman."

Among the more striking incidents in *Pickwick*, are the duel which did *not* take place between Dr. Slammer of the 97th and Mr. Winkle; the sayings and doings of Mr. Alfred Jingle at Dingley Dell; the Election at Eatanswill; the Return Game between Sam Weller and Mr. Job Trotter; the Christmas in the country; the Bachelors' Party at Mr. Bob Sawyers; the Trial of Bardell *v.* Pickwick; the Footmen's Soirée at Bath; the scenes, alternately comic and touching, in the Fleet Prison; the final exit of Jingle and Trotter; the scenes where Mr. Soloman Pell figures as a legal gentleman of great powers; and the conclusion, in which Sam elects not to leave his master, and finally, like several others in the tale, settles down into matrimony.

The defect of the story, chiefly arising out of the aimless manner in which it had been begun, is the inconsistency of its principal characters. All its events take place within a single year, so that the mellowing of the leading personages cannot be the effect of age. Mr. Pickwick, when first encountered, is a mere butt, neither doing nor saying very wisely, and his immediate friends were made to match. These are Tupman, an obese *ci devant jeune homme*, ridiculous from his tendency to lose his head when he is in company with one of the softer sex; Mr. Winkle, a sporting character, who can neither ride, shoot, nor skate; and Mr. Snodgrass, "to this day reputed a great poet among his friends and acquaintances, although we do not find that he has ever written anything to encourage the belief." They start with all sorts of blunders and follies of speech and action, but as the story advances, severally exhibit common sense, instinctive good feeling, high principle, and a fine sense of propriety and honor. Mr. Pickwick in the Fleet, a voluntary prisoner, rather than satisfy the heavy exactions of some nefarious limbs of the law, but magnanimously paying Mrs. Bardell's law-costs, as well as his own, rather than that *she* should also be a prisoner in such a place, is not the ridiculous old gentleman who is presented in the opening chapter, standing upon a Windsor chair, in an extravagant position, making a speech to the assembled Pickwickians in the Club. It was a sagacious critic who wrote, "The fact is, that Phiz is consistent in *his* conception of Mr. Pickwick: throughout he is the same idiotic lump of bland blockheadism, unrelieved by thought or feeling, from beginning to end. In the hands of Boz, he commences a butt and ends as a hero."

CHAPTER V.

"THE WITS' MISCELLANY."—DICKENS EDITS BENTLEY'S.—DOUGLAS JERROLD.—ARTISTS AND AUTHORS.—DICKENS' CONTRIBUTIONS. — OLIVER TWIST. — PURPOSE AND MORAL.—AUTHOR'S LAW.—FAGIN'S CONVICTION.—JACOB'S ISLAND.—DRAMATIC VERSIONS.

THE Sketches by Boz, which so favorably drew the then new publishing firm of Chapman & Hall towards the then scarcely known young author, and the popularity which the *Pickwick Papers* had obtained among all classes of readers, also attracted the notice of Mr. Richard Bentley, of New Burlington-street, London, a publisher, educated at St. Paul's School, London, where two of his class-mates were Sir Frederick Pollock, Ex-Chief Baron of the Exchequer, and the Rev. Richard Harris Barham, to be remembered as author of "The Ingoldsby Legends." It had been Mr. Bentley's determination, for some time, to establish a periodical,—probably as a set-off to the *New Monthly Magazine*, long the property of his late partner, Mr. Henry Colburn. It had been announced under the title of *The Wits' Miscellany*, but an editor had not been found, though Theodore Hook had been spoken to, with a natural distrust, however, of his erratic and irregular habits. Just then, as if to give a spur to Bentley, *The Humorist* was advertised, which literally, before it was published, was incorporated with Colburn's *New Monthly*, of which Hook was made editor. At last, thinking that "Boz," who was then well-advanced with his *Pickwick Papers*, would be the right man in the right place, Mr. Bentley made him such an offer with a large editorial stipend, that he accepted it. On the first of January, 1837, appeared *Bentley's Miscellany*,

No. I., edited by "Boz." On the change of name, Douglas Jerrold, who was nothing if not satirical, said, "I can understand, Bentley, why you should give up the first title of the *Wits'* Miscellany, but am puzzled in thinking what could have induced you to run into the opposite extreme and call it '*Bentley's.*'" A strong and well-conducted periodical it was, during the two years Mr. Dickens was over it. He installed George Cruikshank as its artist in ordinary, R. W. Buss and H. K. Browne also contributing, as well as Samuel Lover, who etched the clever illustrations to his own "Handy Andy," the opening chapters of which appeared in *Bentley.* There also were portraits on steel of sundry celebrities—which had already done yeoman's service in others of Mr. Bentley's publications. The first number was opened with a Song of the Month, by Father Prout, and there were similar introductions in succeeding numbers, by Dr. Maginn, W. H. Ainsworth, Samuel Lover, and others.

Dickens gathered around him, as his staff, many celebrated writers of the time. Besides those already named, were Theodore Hook, T. L. Peacock, W. H. Maxwell, T. Haynes Bayly, J. Fenimore Cooper, Edward Howard, Charles Ollier, James Morier, J. Hamilton Reynolds, Charles Whitehead, Sir George Rose, William Jerdan, R. H. Barham, George Hogarth, Richard Johns, Captain Medwin, Prince Puckler Muskau, George Dance, and J. Sheridan Knowles. Here were the leading writers in Bentley's first volume, and Dickens, to use a term from the road, "had them well in hand." His own articles can soon be counted up:—"The Public Life of Mr. Tulrumble, Mayor of Mudfog," and "The Pantomime of Life," not included in Dickens' own collection of his writings, but republished in Petersons' editions of the *Sketches.* There also were two "Reports of the Proceedings of the Mudfog Association," burlesquing the proceedings of the then recently established "British Association for the Advancement of Science." These reports, which are characterized by humor rather broad than subtle, I republish in the present volume, with other inedited productions of "Boz."

The editorial address, dated November 30th, 1837, at the close of the first year, prefixed to the second volume of *Bentley's Miscellany*, was very brief, merely "hoping to make many changes for the better, and none for the worse; and to show that, while we have one grateful eye to past patronage, we have another wary one to future favors; in that, thus, like the heroine of the sweet poem, descriptive of the faithlessness and perjury of Mr. John Oakham, of the Royal Navy, we look two ways at once." This was not very brilliant, neither was the closing sentence—"These, and a hundred other great designs, preparations, and surprises are in contemplation, for the fulfilment of which we are already bound in two volumes cloth, and have no objection, if it be any additional security to the public, to stand bound in twenty more."

It may be stated here that a fac-simile reprint of *Bentley's Miscellany* was begun, with the illustrations, by William Lewer, publisher, New York. It commenced with the number for January, 1838,—so that Vol. III. of the English was Vol. I. of the American edition.

Perhaps this is the most suitable place for a poetical address to "Boz," which was published in *Bentley*, for January, 1838, and even was not reprinted in the author's own edition of the "Reliques of Father Prout." At this distance of time, it is a literary curiosity:

POETICAL EPISTLE FROM FATHER PROUT TO BOZ.

I.

A rhyme! a rhyme! from a distant clime,—from the gulph of the Genoese,
O'er the rugged scalps of the Julian Alps, dear Boz! I send you these,
To light the *Wick* your candlestick holds up, or, should you list,
To usher in the yarn you spin concerning Oliver Twist.

II.

Immense applause you've gained, oh, Boz! through continental Europe;
You'll make Pickwick œcumenick;* of fame you have a sure hope:
For here your books are found, gadzooks! in greater *luxe* than any
That have issued yet, hotpress'd or wet, from the types of GALIGNANI.

---

* ειδωλον της γης οικουμενης.

III.

But neither when you sport your pen, oh, potent mirth-compeller!
Winning our hearts "in monthly parts," can Pickwick or Sam Weller
Cause us to weep with pathos deep, or shake with laugh spasmodical
As when you drain your copious vein for Bentley's periodical.

IV.

Folks all enjoy your Parish Boy—so truly you depict him:
But I alack! while thus you track your stinted poor-law's victim,
Must think of some poor nearer home,—poor who, unheeded perish,
By squires despoiled, by "patriots" gulled,—I mean the starving Irish.

V.

Yet there's no dearth of Irish mirth, which, to a mind of feeling,
Seemeth to be the Helot's glee before the Spartan reeling;
Such gloomy thought o'ercometh not the glow of England's humor,
Thrice happy isle! long may the smile of genuine joy illume her!

VI.

Write on, young sage! still o'er the page pour forth the flood of fancy;
Wax still more droll, wave o'er the soul Wit's wand of necromancy.
Behold! e'en now around your brow th' immortal laurel thickens;
Yea, SWIFT or STERNE might gladly learn a thing or two from DICKENS.

VII.

A rhyme! a rhyme! from a distant clime,—a song from the sunny south!
A goodly theme, so Boz but deem the measure not uncouth.
Would, for thy sake, that "PROUT" could make his bow in fashion finer,
"*Partant*" (from thee) "pour la Syrie," for Greece and Asia Minor.

Genoa, 14th December, 1837.

The leading attraction of *Bentley's Miscellany* was a story called *Oliver Twist, or the Parish Boy's Progress*, written by Charles Dickens, and illustrated by George Cruikshank. It was begun in the second number, (February, 1837.)

Oliver Twist, evidently written with great care, is one of Dickens's most artistical productions, but the story is not in accordance with the sub-title: that is, the hero is only a parish boy for a very short time. In the chapter which treats of Dickens's relations with artists, this difference and its cause will be explained.

In his original preface to *Oliver Twist*, Mr. Dickens states that the greater part of that story was originally published in a magazine. Read as a whole, it bears little appearance of having been written from month to month, a great portion of it while *Pickwick* was also in hand, and published. The story, as a story, is well told, the characters are well grouped and strikingly contrasted; there is marked individuality in what they say and do, and poetical justice is awarded, at the close, by the punishment of Fagin, Sikes, and Monks —to say nothing of inferior personages. The parish boy gets into a den of thieves, from which he twice escapes, with the singular good fortune, each time, of falling into the hands of relations or friends. The comic humor of the author is largely exhibited in this tale. Mr. Bumble is amusing, from first to last, and his tea-table wooing of Mrs. Corney, matron of the workhouse, is one of the richest scenes in fiction. Master Charles Bates and the light-fingered but facetious "Artful Dodger," afford entertainment whenever they appear. There is a rough humor, too, in Mr. Noah Claypole, and his government of Charlotte, over whom he exercises a very rigid rule, is consistent throughout. Giles and "the Boy" Brittle are rather sketches than portraits. Mrs. Maylie, Rose and her lover, Mr. Losberne and Mr. Brownlow, to say nothing of Mr. Grimwig, whose talent chiefly consists in offering to eat his own head if such and such things did not occur, are rather commonplace characters, and, even thus early, Dickens showed and exhibited as much incapacity for writing love scenes as Cruikshank for sketching pretty women.

It is in the thieves' den that Dickens put forth his great power, exhibiting Rembrandt-like skill in the arrangement, by contrast of his lights and shadows. We are interested, despite of ourselves. We perceive that it is among a low and villainous gang that he has placed us: that, as he says himself, "Sikes is a thief, and Fagin a receiver of stolen goods, that the boy's a pickpocket, and the girl is a prostitute." He adds:

I confess I have yet to learn that a lesson of the purest good may not be drawn from the vilest evil. I have always believed this to be a recognized and established truth, laid down by the greatest men the world has ever seen, constantly acted upon by the best and wisest natures, and confirmed by the reason and experience of every thinking mind. I saw no reason, when I wrote this book, why the very dregs of life, so long as their speech did not offend the ear, should not serve the purpose of a moral, at least as well as its froth and cream. Nor did I doubt that there lay festering in Saint Giles's as good materials towards the Truth as any flaunting in Saint James's.

In this spirit, when I wished to show, in little Oliver, the principle of Good surviving through every adverse circumstance, and triumphing at last; and when I considered among what companions I could try him best, having regard to that kind of men into whose hands he would most naturally fall; I bethought myself of those who figure in these volumes. When I came to discuss the subject more maturely with myself I saw many strong reasons for pursuing the course to which I was inclined. I had read of thieves by scores—seductive fellows (amiable for the most part), faultless in dress, plump in pocket, choice in horseflesh, bold in bearing, fortunate in gallantry, great at a song, a bottle, pack of cards, or dice-box, and fit companions for the bravest. But I had never met (except in HOGARTH) with the miserable reality. It appeared to me that to draw a knot of such associates in crime as really do exist; to paint them in all their deformity, in all their wretchedness, in all the squalid poverty of their lives; to show them as they really are, for ever skulking uneasily through the dirtiest paths of life, with the great, black, ghastly gallows closing up their prospect, turn them where they may; it appeared to me that to do this, would be to attempt a something which was greatly needed, and which would be a service to society. And therefore I did it, as I best could.

There is great power, with some inconsistency, in the later development of Nancy Sykes :—she first appears as a drab, a loose liver, a drunkard, and a thief, but closes as a heroine. At the beginning, she talks the ordinary slang of London, but in her interview with Rose Maylie, near London Bridge, her language is pure, impressive, and dignified.

In *Oliver Twist*, as in *Pickwick*, *Nickleby*, and other

tales, Mr. Dickens brings his legal experience to account. But this is not so much knowledge of the law, as a recollection of the quirks of attorneys' clerks, and the practice of the courts. The trial-scene in *Pickwick*, which its author used to read with great dramatic effect, is one of his most successful productions, but it must have been a remarkable jury which could have given £750 damages in the case of Bardell *v.* Pickwick, on such slight evidence as was heard in court, and little Mr. Perker, defendant's attorney, must have been very careless, stupid, or ignorant, inasmuch as counsel, instructed by him, did not move the court, on the first day of next term, for a rule *nisi* to show cause why there should not be a new trial, on the ground that the verdict had been obtained on insufficient evidence. How Mr. Sergeant Talfourd, who read and revised most of Dickens's earlier novels, did not hit the legal "blot" in this case, must always be wondered at. So, in *Nicholas Nickleby*, we find Uncle Ralph, the Usurer, terribly frightened at the possible result of his dealings with Arthur Guide—such dealing consisting of the private execution of a bond, without witness or stamp, securing a sum of money to one rogue, on the celebration of marriage between another in the agreement, with a rich young lady. *That* was not illegal. So, finally, in *Oliver Twist*, Fagin is tried and convicted as an accessory before the fact in the murder of Nancy, whereas he had only made Noah Claypole, the spy, describe Nancy's private interview with Rose Maylie, at the bridge, which Sikes impatiently listened to and then burst out:

"Hell's fire!" cried Sikes, breaking fiercely from the Jew. "Let me go!" Flinging the old man from him, he rushed from the room, and darted wildly and furiously up the stairs.

"Bill, Bill!" cried the Jew, following him hastily. "A word—only a word."

The word would not have been exchanged, but that the housebreaker was unable to open the door, on which he was expending fruitless oaths and violence when the Jew came panting out.

"Let me out," said Sikes. "Don't speak to me—it's not safe. Let me out, I say!"

"Hear me speak a word," rejoined the Jew, laying his hand upon the lock. "You won't be——"

"Well," replied the other.

"You won't be—too—violent, Bill?" whined the Jew.

The day was breaking, and there was light enough for the men to see each other's faces. They exchanged one brief glance; there was a fire in the eyes of both which could not be mistaken.

"I mean," said Fagin, showing that he felt all disguise was now useless—"not too violent for safety. Be crafty, Bill, and not too bold."

Sikes made no reply, but pulling open the door of which the Jew had turned the lock, dashed into the silent streets.

Here Fagin, having taken means to work up Sikes into a passion, merely recommends him not to be too violent,—to be crafty, and not too bold. But Fagin is tried, as accessory—most powerful is that scene—and is really convicted only of having "exchanged one brief glance," there then being "a fire in the eyes of both which could not be mistaken." A Tombs' lawyer, with Fagin as his client, would have saved his life, I suspect, on the ground of want of *positive*, however strong might have been the *presumptive*, evidence against him. At the same time, every reader rejoices in the bad man's fate.

The anomaly in the book is that under such training as he had received from the "porochial authorities,"—Mrs. Mann and Mr. Bumble, the Beadle, Mr. Sowerberry the coffin-maker—and Fagin the fence, Oliver Twist should figure as a model of honesty, frankness, and refinement. Children who emerge from the meagre misery of work-house slavery, do not usually turn out so well as this.

Oliver Twist had the honor of being thrice introduced to the public. First, in the preface to the edition of 1839; next, in April, 1841, when the next edition was published; and finally in the edition of March, 1850. The third preface has not latterly been reprinted. It was a defence of the author against Sir Peter Laurie, a thickheaded alderman of London. In one of the closing chapters, which narrated, in a most effective manner, the well-merited fate of Sikes, that tragedy was located in a place called Jacob's Island, near that part of the Thames on which the church of Rotherhithe abuts, beyond Dockhead, in the Borough of Southwark, and Dickens described it as the filthiest, the strangest, the most extraordinary of the many localities that are trodden in London, wholly unknown by name to the great mass of its inhabitants. The view of this foul den, he thus presented:

To reach this place, the visitor has to penetrate through a maze of close, narrow, and muddy streets, thronged by the roughest and poorest of water-side people, and devoted to the traffic they may be supposed to occasion. The cheapest and least delicate provisions are heaped in the shops, the coarsest and commonest articles of wearing apparel dangle at the salesman's door, and stream from the house parapet and windows. Jostling with unemployed laborers of the lowest class, ballast-heavers, coal-whippers, brazen women, ragged children, and the very raff and refuse of the river, he makes his way with difficulty along, assailed by offensive sights and smells from the narrow alleys which branch off on the right and left, and deafened by the clash of ponderous wagons that bear great piles of merchandise from the stacks of warehouses that rise from every corner. Arriving at length in streets remoter and less frequented than those through which he had passed, he walks beneath tottering house-fronts projecting over the pavement, dismantled walls that seem to totter as he passes, chimneys, half crushed, half hesitating to fall, windows guarded by rusty iron bars, that time and dust have almost eaten away, and every imaginable sign of desolation and neglect.

In such a neighborhood, beyond Dockhead, in the Borough of Southwark, stands Jacob's Island, surrounded by a muddy ditch, six or eight feet deep, and fifteen or twenty wide, when the tide is in, once called Mill Pond, but known in these days as Folly Ditch. It is a creek or inlet from the Thames, and can always be filled up at high water by opening the sluices at the head mills, from which it took its old name. At such times, a stranger, looking from one of the wooden bridges thrown across it at Mill Lane, will see the inhabitants of the houses on either side lowering from their back doors and windows buckets, jars, domestic utensils of all kinds, in which to haul the water up; and when his eye is turned from these operations to the houses themselves, his utmost astonishment will be excited by the scene before him. Crazy wooden galleries, common to the backs of half-a-dozen houses, with holes from which to look upon the sluice beneath; windows broken and patched, with poles thrust out on which to dry linen that is never there; rooms so small, so filthy, so confined, that the air would seem too tainted even for the dirt and squallor which they shelter; wooden chambers thrusting themselves out above the mud, and threatening to fall into it—as some have done; dirt-besmeared walls and decaying foundations; every repulsive lineament of poverty, every loathsome indication of filth, rot, and garbage—all these ornament the banks of Folly Ditch.

In Jacob's Island the warehouses are roofless and empty, the walls are crumbling down, the windows are windows no more, the doors are falling into the street, the chimneys are blackened, but they yield no smoke. Thirty or forty years ago, before losses and chancery suits came upon it, it was a thriving place; but now it is a desolate island indeed. The houses have no owners; they are broken open and entered upon by those who have the courage, and there they live and there they die. They must have powerful motives for a secret residence, or be reduced to a destitute condition indeed, who seek a refuge in Jacob's Island.

This was written in the autumn of 1838. The late Bishop of London, (Dr. Charles James Blomfield,) who was active in promoting Social Reforms, presided, in February, 1850, at a public meeting in favor of Sanitary Reforms in London, and particularly stated that the houses in Jacob's Island could receive such sanitary improvements at a cost of about a penny three farthings per week per house. The Bishop mentioned that Mr. Dickens had described Jacob's Island, and Mr. Dickens, who also spoke, "confessed that soft impeachment." A few days after this meeting Sir

Peter Laurie addressed the Vestry of Marylebone, a parish some miles from Jacob's Island and in another county, ridiculed the idea of their being 1,300 houses on forty acres of ground, and added, "The Bishop of London, poor soul, in his simplicity thought there really was such a place, whereas it turned out that it existed *only* in a work of fiction, written by Mr. Charles Dickens ten years ago. The fact was admitted by Mr. Charles Dickens himself at the meeting, and he (Sir P. Laurie) had extracted his words from the same newspaper. Mr. Dickens had said, 'Now, the first of these classes proceeded generally on the supposition that the compulsory improvement of these dwellings, when exceedingly defective, would be very expensive. But that was a great mistake, for nothing was cheaper than good sanitary improvement, as they knew in this case of Jacob's Island, which he had described in a work of fiction some ten or eleven years ago.'" The comments which Mr. Dickens made on this blunder of the stolid Alderman, who believed that truth, when described in fiction, ceases to be truth, are too good to be any longer suppressed—as they were, after the death of the civic Knight, who had figured, in his life-time, as Alderman Cute, in the Christmas story of the *The Chimes*. Here is the reply—badinage charged with satire:

When I came to read this, I was so much struck by the honesty, by the truth, and by the wisdom of this logic, as well as by the fact of the sagacious vestry, including members of parliament, magistrates, officers, chemists, and I know not who else listening to it meekly (as became them), that I resolved to record the fact here, as a certain means of making it known to, and causing it to be reverenced by, many thousands of people. Reflecting upon this logic, and its universal application; remembering that when Fielding described Newgate, the prison immediately ceased to exist; that when Smollett took Roderick Randolph to Bath, that city instantly sank into the earth; that when Scott exercised his genius on Whitefriars, it incontinently glided into the Thames; that an ancient place called Windsor was entirely destroyed in the reign of Queen Elizabeth by two Merry Wives of that town, acting under the direction of a person of the name of Shakespeare; and that Mr. Pope, after having, at a great expense, completed his grotto at Twickenham, incautiously reduced it to ashes by writing a poem upon it;—I say, when I came to consider these things, I was inclined to make this preface the vehicle of my humble tribute of admiration to Sir Peter Laurie. But, I am restrained by very painful consideration—by no less a consideration than the impossibility of *his* existence. For Sir Peter Laurie having been himself described in a book (as I understand he was, one Christmas time, for his conduct on the seat of Justice), it is but too clear that there CAN be no such man!

The popularity of *Oliver Twist* was great from its first month, and the work has been repeatedly dramatized. Some of these adaptations still keep the stage, wherever the English language is spoken.

CHAPTER VI.

PUBLICATIONS UNAVOWED OR FORGOTTEN.—SUNDAY IN LONDON.—THE POOR MEN'S SUNDAY DINNER.—SKETCHES OF YOUNG LADIES AND OF YOUNG GENTLEMEN.—MEMOIRS OF GRIMALDI.—THE PIC-NIC PAPERS.— THOMAS MOORE'S PROSE AND VERSE.—DRAMATIC PERFORMANCES: THE STRANGE GENTLEMAN, VILLAGE COQUETTES, IS SHE HIS WIFE?—AMATEUR ACTING.—AUTHOR'S READINGS.

ONLY that I have a great objection to what are called "hard words," I might properly present what I have to place here, between the conclusion of Oliver Twist and the beginning of Nicholas Nickleby, as an intercalary chapter. It will treat of some of Dickens's productions, unacknowledged or almost forgotten.

In 1835, when the late Sir Andrew Agnew, M. P., a Scottish baronet, was making considerable stir in and out of Parliament, by vehement agitation in favor of rigid laws for the better observance of the Sabbath, and bringing no small ability, energy, and perseverence to this self-imposed duty, one class, among which Charles Dickens was to be found, objected to the course he was taking, on the ground that the execution of such laws would press lightly upon the rich and heavily upon the poor. He was unwilling to see a man of station—say Sir Andrew himself—riding to church in his own or a hired carriage, and afterwards partaking of a dinner, dressed by a French cook, while the omnibus within reach of the working man's limited means, was not to run on the Sabbath, and the public bakeries were to be closed on the same day, so as to prevent his children from having the accustomed baked joint and potatoes—perhaps their only regular dinner during the week.

There appeared, therefore, a *brochure* of some eighty pages, written by Dickens, about the time the first number of *Pickwick* was published. It was entitled

SUNDAY UNDER THREE HEADS:

AS IT IS: AS SABBATH BILLS WOULD MAKE IT:

AS IT MIGHT BE MADE.

BY

TIMOTHY SPARKS.

It was illustrated by Hablot K. Browne, whose pseudonyme was "Phiz." It was prefaced by a sarcastic dedication to the Right Reverend Father in God, Charles James, Lord Bishop of London. It was a strong plea for the poor. The description of a lot of children watching their father bringing the baked shoulder of mutton, with "taters" under it, from the public bakery, is capital. This book was a bold prophecy of *Pickwick* and subsequent works in which the side of the poor was taken. It has long been out of print, but a copy of it is preserved in the great library of the British Museum, London.

It was during the progress of "*Pickwick*," I think, that two small volumes, also illustrated by "Phiz," made their appearance. These, lively and graphic, were "Sketches of Young Gentlemen," and "Sketches of Young Ladies." They were so much in Dickens's style, that they were attributed to him for a time. They were republished in London a few years ago.

"Memoirs of Joseph Grimaldi," edited by "Boz," was a performance by Mr. Dickens when he was conducting *Bentley's Miscellany.* The introductory chapter is dated February, 1838. The subject of this biography was the most remarkable theatrical Clown that ever performed in any country. His father, Italian by descent and place of birth, arrived in London in 1758, during the reign of David Garrick at Drury Lane Theatre, and soon was appointed ballet-master and buffo-dancer. It was this ingenious gentleman, who, during the Riots of 1780, (afterwards so graphically described in "Barnaby Rudge,") when some of his terrified neighbors chalked "No Popery" upon their doors, to conciliate the furious anti-Catholic mob, wrote "No religion at all" upon *his*, in the expectation, which was realized, that all parties would leave him alone! In 1779, his son, Joseph Grimaldi, was born, and appeared in public, as a miniature Clown, before he was two years old. At the age of four he became a regular salaried member of the Sadler's Wells Company, and remained in that capacity, with the exception of one season, until he closed his professional career, forty-nine years afterwards. He took his farewell benefit in June, 1826. He devoted his leisure to the composition of his memoirs, and died on the last day of May, 1837,—five months after he had completed his last chapter. There was an immense quantity of manuscript, which was purchased by Mr. Bentley, who placed it in the hands of Mr. Dickens. In the introductory Chapter, after a characteristic dissertation on Pantomimes and Clowns, Mr. Dickens says of the memoirs:

His own share in them is stated in a few words. Being much struck by several incidents in the manuscript—such as the description of Grimaldi's infancy, the burglary, the brother's return from sea under the extraordinary circumstances detailed, the adventure of the man with the two fingers on his left hand, the account of Mackintosh and his friends, and many other passages—and thinking that they might be related in a more attractive manner (they were at that time told in the first person, as if by Grimaldi himself, although they had necessarily lost any original manner which his recital might have imparted to them), he accepted a proposal from the publisher to edit the book, and *has* edited it to the best of his ability, altering its form throughout, and making such other alterations as he conceived would improve the narration of the facts, without any departure from the facts themselves.

There was no book-making in the case. Grimaldi was allowed to tell his own story,—to relate the adventures of the most eminent Clown the stage ever possessed, and only where he had run into garrulity, was the pruning knife judiciously used. Mr. Dickens said "the account of Grimaldi's first courtship may appear lengthy in its present form: but it has undergone a double and most comprehensive process of abridgment. The old man was garrulous upon a subject on which the youth had felt so keenly; and as the feeling did him honor in both stages of life, the Editor has not had the heart to reduce it further."

The book, which is pleasant reading, like most theatrical biographies, had a portrait of Grimaldi, engraved on steel, for its frontispiece, and was further enriched with eight original illustrations by George Cruikshank.*

Mr. John Macrone, publisher of Dickens's *Sketches*, had endeavored to establish himself in business in London, with more experience in "the trade" than capital. He befriended Charles Dickens on his start into authorship, at a time

* The memoirs of Joseph Grimaldi are not included in any editions of Dickens, English or American, except those published by Messrs. T. B. Peterson & Brothers, Philadelphia.

when a young writer most requires encouragement, and, though the result proved the correctness of his judgment, risked what was a considerable sum, for a young publisher, in the production of the *Sketches*, with illustrations by Cruikshank. Mr. Macrone died when the success of "The Pickwick Papers" was an assured fact. For the benefit of his family, Mr. Dickens suggested and undertook to edit "The Pic-nic Papers," so called because the two volumes were made up from voluntary contributions. He opened with a lively sketch, called "The Lamplighter's Story." Thomas Moore presented a prose sketch, "The Student of Bagdad; from an unpublished Romance written in 1809-10:" Talfourd gave a sonnet; Geo. W. Lovell, author of "The Provost of Bruges," a poetic tale; Agnes Strickland, a couple of novelettes; Horace Smith, a mediæval Spanish story; Allan Cunningham, a Scotch sketch; W. H. Maxwell, an Irish adventure; W. H. Ainsworth, a fragment entitled, "The Old London Merchant;" Mr. John Forster, a clever paper on "John Dryden and Jacob Tonson." The acting editor of this collection, when his original materials ran short, helped himself out of "Charcoal Sketches," by the late Joseph C. Neal, of Philadelphia, to the extent of one hundred pages. The end was that Mr. Neal, whose name was not even mentioned in the English book, claimed his own, and, I believe, received some compensation. When "The Pic-nic Papers" were republished in America,* this portion was omitted. The work was illustrated by George Cruikshank and "Phiz," and realized a considerable sum for Mr. Macrone's family. As a literary curiosity, I quote a single sentence from Thomas Moore's little fragment:

> The sun had just set, and the modest Arabian jasmines, which had kept the secret of their fragrance to themselves all day, were now beginning to let the sweet mystery out, and make every passing breeze their confidant.

---

* By Messrs. T. B. Peterson & Brothers, of Philadelphia.

The author stated in a note, that this passage was thus versified afterwards in "Lalla Rookh:"

"From plants that wake when others sleep;
From timid jasmine buds that keep
Their fragrance to themselves all day,
But, when the sun-light dies away,
Let the delicious secret out
To every breeze that roams about."

Like the majority of newspaper men, Charles Dickens was fond of the stage. On Michaelmas day, 1836, just when he had introduced Sam Weller to the public, through the *Pickwick Papers*, commenced six months before, a farce, written by him, and entitled "The Strange Gentleman," was produced at the St. James's Theatre, on the opening of the season. Mr. John Pritt Harley, (now dead,) famous in what are called character-parts, was the hero of this piece, which was well received and had a fair run.

It could not have been a failure, as sometimes stated, for, at the same theatre, on the evening of Tuesday, December 6th, 1836, was produced "The Village Coquettes," an opera from his pen, the music of which was composed by Mr. John Hullah, also very young at the time, (he was born in 1812,) whose reputation may be said to have been established on this occasion. The *Era Almanac*, a London publication, which is authority upon dramatic and musical history, says: "The quaint humor, unaffected pathos, and graceful lyrics of this production found prompt recognition, and the piece enjoyed a prosperous run. 'The Village Coquettes' took its title from two village girls, Lucy and Rose, led away by vanity, coquetting with men above them in station, and discarding their humble though worthy lovers. Before, however, it is too late, they see their error, and the piece terminates happily. Miss Rainforth and Miss Julia Smith, were the heroines, and Mr. Bennett and Mr. Gardner were their betrothed lovers. Braham was the Lord of the Manor, who would have led astray the fair Lucy. There was a capital scene where he was detected by Lucy's father, played by

Strickland, urging an elopement. Harley had a trifling part in the piece, rendered highly amusing by his admirable acting."

Mr. Hullah, (who has made a great name as teacher of Music for the Million, and is now Professor of Vocal Music in King's College and Queen's College, London,) has repeatedly declared that the songs in "The Village Coquettes," had a good deal of Sheridan's sprightliness combined with the tenderness of Moore's lyrics.

On March 6th, 1837, a third piece by Dickens, called "Is She His Wife; or, Something Singular," was played, also at the St. James's Theatre. It was a farce, in which Harley played the principal character, Felix Tapkins, a flirting bachelor, and sang a song in the character of Pickwick, "Written expressly for him by Boz." The name of the author was not given in the playbill. This was Mr. Dickens's last dramatic production.

It has not been claimed for Charles Dickens that he was a very successful dramatist. His skill in construction, his facility in contriving startling situations—and, above all, his wondrous power of making his characters speak and act, like living creatures, and not according to the traditions of the stage, had scarcely been developed, certainly had not been matured, when he wrote two farces and an opera. Perhaps, had these been the production of any person but him, who was being recognized at the time, as a meteoric light on the horizon of letters, their success would have been more assured: for the dramatic element abounds in all his works, and no other writer has so thoroughly individualized the characters he created. They were not mere Marionettes, puppets moved by an unseen but not unsuspected hand behind the scene, but real people. Two or three of his novels were dramatized under his own inspection and with his own assistance, but nearly all of the other adaptations for the stage were got up in a hurry and in the most flimsy manner,—a collection of scenes, clipped out of the books, wholesale, for the sake of the dialogue. Some wit, unable to resist the temptation of putting a quotation from Virgil into an epigram, and not unwilling perhaps, to have a sly hit at his late colleague in "the gallery," wrote as follows:

Oh, Dickens, dear,
I sadly fear
That great will be our loss
When we shall say—
Alas, the day!—
"*Procumbit humi Boz.*"

Mr. Dickens, who was not a man to be content with a moderate success, especially at the very turn of the tide, when *Pickwick* was making him surprisingly popular, lost no reputation by his dramatic attempts,—which enterprising managers might now revive, with great prospect of success. For one person who knows anything about Sheridan's *School for Scandal*, five thousand are familiar with the *Pickwick Papers* and other works by Charles Dickens. His mission was to write humanizing tales rather than to waste his genius in writing funny plays for comedy-people to make reputation and fortune out of—for, at a theatre, we think not of the play-wright but the actors. If he were troubled, because his novels were more liked than his plays, being better, he might have consoled himself with the recollection that Thomas Moore, wit and poet, had also written for the stage, and had made a great failure, "M. P.; or, The Blue Stocking," a comic opera in three acts, which was produced at the Lyceum Theatre in October, 1811, just three months before Dickens was born. Moore devoted a long time to the composition of this opera, and assisted Horn, the composer, in arranging music for the songs. The cast included most of the best singers and dramatic performers, but nothing could save a piece, which was "comic" only in name. When published it did not sell, and was never included in Moore's collected works. It is preserved only in Galignani's very scarce edition, published in Paris in 1823. Compared with this, Dickens's "Village Coquettes" was triumphant indeed.

"The Village Coquettes" was published in 1836, and it would be difficult to obtain a copy now. Here, however, is the distribution of characters—technically the

DRAMATIS PERSONÆ.

Squire Norton, - - - - - - - - -	Mr. Braham.
The Hon. Spakins Flam (his friend,) - - -	Mr. Forrester.
Old Benson (a small farmer,) - -	Mr. Robert Strickland.
Mr. Martin Stokes (a very small farmer with a very large circle of particular friends,) - - - -	Mr. Harley.
George Edmunds (betrothed to Lucy,) - -	Mr. Bennett.
Young Benson, - - - - - - - - -	Mr. J. Parry.
John Maddox (attached to Rose,) - - -	Mr. Gardner.
Lucy Benson, - - - - - - - -	Miss Rainforth.
Rose (her cousin,) - - - - - - -	Miss J. Smith.

There was a notice, that the time occupied in representation was two hours and a half, that the period was the autumn of 1729, and that the scene was an English village. There was a Dedication, as follows:

TO J. P. HARLEY, ESQ.—MY DEAR SIR—My dramatic bantlings are no sooner born than you father them. You have my Strange Gentleman exclusively your own; you have adopted Martin Stokes with equal readiness; and you still profess your willingness to do the same kind office for all future scions of the same stock.

I dedicate, to you the first play I ever published; and you made for me the first play I ever produced:—the balance is in your favor, and I am afraid it will remain so.

That you may long contribute to the amusement of the public, and long be spared to shed a lustre, by the honor and integrity of your private life, on the profession which for many years you have done so much to uphold, is the sincere and earnest wish of, my dear sir, yours most faithfully,

December 15th, 1836. CHARLES DICKENS.

In addition, the author tendered his acknowledgment to the performers, in this semi-apologetic Preface:

Either the honorable gentleman is in the right, or he is not, is a phrase in very common use within the walls of Parliament. This drama may have a plot, or it may not: and the songs may be poetry, or they may not; and the whole affair from beginning to end may be great nonsense, or it may not, just as the honorable gentleman or lady who reads it may happen to think. So retaining his own private and particular opinion upon the subject (an opinion which he formed upwards of a year ago, when he wrote the piece), the author leaves every such gentleman or lady to form his or hers, as he or she may think proper, without saying one word to influence or conciliate them.

All he wishes to say is this—that he hopes Mr. Braham and all the performers who assisted in the representation of this opera will accept his warmest thanks for the interest they evinced in it, from its first rehearsal, and for their zealous efforts in his behalf—efforts which have crowned it with a degree of success far exceeding his most sanguine anticipations; and of which no form of words could speak his acknowledgment.

It is needless to add that the *libretto* of an opera must be, to a certain extent, a mere vehicle for the music; and that it is scarcely fair or reasonable to judge it by those strict rules of criticism which would be justly applicable to a five-act tragedy or a finished comedy.

Independent of other circumstances, including the dramatist's constant terror of not being done justice to, by actors and singers, there were several good reasons why Charles Dickens should no longer have written for the stage. First, the compensation, even for great success, would be comparatively small; and, next, his time was engrossingly occupied by his literary engagements, for he was midway in the *Pickwick Papers*, and had recently assumed the editorship of *Bentley's Miscellany*, in which he had commenced the story of *Oliver Twist.* To run a couple of serial novels, besides conducting a monthly magazine, was work enough,—even for Charles Dickens. Several years after this, when he was not so much pressed by hard work, his predilection for the drama brought him upon the stage, as the best amateur actor of the time, and, still later, led him to gratify the public, in both hemispheres, by giving effective dramatic Readings from his own works.

CHAPTER VII.

MARRIAGE.—GEORGE HOGARTH.—A COMPLIMENT FROM LOCKHART.—DICKENS A MAN OF METHOD.—THE MISSES HOGARTH. —FANNY HOGARTH'S SUDDEN DEATH.—PUBLICATION SUSPENDED.—MR. DICKENS INTERVIEWED.—"YOUNG BOZZES."

When he was still editor of *Bentley's Miscellany*, and enjoying fruitage of fame, with a liberal share of the substantial results which, in his case, so quickly fell into his lap, Charles Dickens was "Benedick the married man." The lady of his choice was a daughter of Mr. George Hogarth, a Scottish lawyer who had the rare good fortune of having been the friend and adviser of the two greatest writers of prose fiction his native and his adopted land had produced—Walter Scott and Charles Dickens. He was born in Scotland, in the far-off time, when the "Great Unknown" was a puny child; was a writer of the Signet, before the present century began; acted as Scott's confidential adviser, lawyer and friend, in the terrible year, 1826, when the compound failure of his Edinburgh and London publishers caused the ruin of the Lord of Abbotsford; afterwards became Charles Dickens's father-in-law; and died, at a very advanced age, only a few months ago. His sister was married to Mr. James Ballantyne, the printer, Scott's life-long friend, and on their death, feeling that the ties which connected him with Scotland were weakened, almost severed, he went to London, where, his practical and theoretical knowledge of music being great, he wrote several excellent works upon the subject. Lockhart, who never went out of his way to compliment any author, mentions Mr. Hogarth's History of Music as a work "of which all who understand that science speak highly." He had not been long in London before he became musical and dramatic critic upon the *Morning Chronicle*, upon which paper John Dickens and his gifted son were once employed together. When the *Daily News* was established, in the year 1846, Mr. Hogarth was placed on its staff as musical critic, and long retained that position, his labors ceasing only when he became far too old to attend concerts and operas.

Charles Dickens was quite a young man when he espoused Miss Catherina Hogarth, who, according to Shakespeare's sensible counsel, was still younger than her mate. Almost up to this time Mr. Dickens had continued to reside "in chambers," at Furnival's Inn. At the beginning of 1838, he had taken a step into Respectability, by becoming "a housekeeper," renting the house, 48 Doughty street, from which is dated *Nicholas Nickleby*, his next literary work. It was a good house, in a respectable and quiet old street, east of Russell Square, and near the Foundling Hospital, chiefly inhabited by professional men, in law and medicine. His residence there was not of long continuance, for he was residing in Devonshire Place, in July, 1840, when Mr. C. Lester Edwards saw him. A note to Mr. Serjeant Talfourd, written after *Nickleby* was completed and while *Master Humphrey's Clock* was in course of publication, (which note shall appear in a subsequent chapter, with other unpublished letters in my possession,) is dated "1 Devonshire Terrace, Tuesday, February sixteen, 1841." A later letter to myself, issued, with more geographical particularity, from "1 Devonshire Terrace, York Gate, Regent's Park, London; First September, 1842."

Charles Dickens was a thorough man of method, as well as a man of genius,—a notable illustration of the aphorism that Genius is only the perfection of Common Sense. Every document in his possession, from the commencement of his literary career, was duly docketed, dated, and deposited. "A place for every thing, and every thing in its place" was the ruling maxim of his life. I dare say that, among hundreds, even thousands of letters which he wrote, during his five-and-thirty years of literary correspondence, not so many as twenty letters were undated. I possess *one*, addressed to Talfourd, in which, though the day of the week and of the month are given in full, the *year* is not set down, but, as will be perceived, by and by, in the Chapter of his Correspondence, the text of this letter gave a clue to the year in which it was written.

Mrs. Charles Dickens had two sisters, younger than herself. These were Fanny and Georgina Hogarth, of whom only the latter, of whom all who know her speak well, alone survives. She is now over forty years old, and has literally dedicated her life to her brother-in-law's family—acting as friend, guide, and guardian ever since the unhappy disagreement, in 1858, which deprived them of the personal tenderness and care of a mother. A more exemplary woman than Miss Hogarth can rarely be found, and, believing this, I feel it my duty to say so, in this biographical sketch.

The original Preface to *the Pickwick Papers*, contained this paragraph: "The following pages have been written from time to time, almost as the periodical occasion arose. Having been written for the most part in the society of a very dear young friend who is now no more, they are connected in the author's mind at once with the happiest period of his life, and with its saddest and most severe affliction."

This refers to a melancholy event. Mr. Dickens was sitting after dinner, with his wife, her two sisters, Mr. John Forster, and Daniel Maclise, the artist. Miss Fanny Hogarth, who was older than her sister Georgina, was engaged to Maclise. The whole party were on the point of going to the theatre, to see Macready perform. Suddenly, Miss Fanny Hogarth fell back in her chair, and died, almost instantly, of heart disease. This heavy and unexpected blow had such an effect upon Dickens, that the publication of the serial which he was then writing was suspended for a month, public notice being given that this was caused by a severe domestic affliction, which had totally prostrated the author for a time.

Having already shown how even before he had appeared as author of a substantive work, Charles Dickens had been "interviewed" by Mr. N. P. Willis, it may not be out of place, here, to exhibit him, through another American medium, while yet the bloom of young success—its *purpurea juventus*—was his.

Mr. Charles Edwards Lester, subsequently U. S. Consul in Genoa, saw Mr. Dickens, in London, in July, 1840, and an account of his visit, in two volumes, of his experiences in England, was published, after his return home. Mr. Lester went to Devonshire Place, where Dickens then resided; pencilled a request, on his card, that he would see an American; was admitted into his library, and found him with a sheet of "Master Humphrey's Clock" before him. The great author, though disturbed by a curious stranger, was gentle and courteous, and expressed his gratitude for the favorable opinion of him entertained by American readers and critics. Mr. Lester then proceeds:

I inquired if, in portraying his characters, he had not, in every instance, his eye upon some particular person he had known, since I could not conceive it possible for an author to present such graphic and natural pictures except from real life. "Allow me to ask, sir," I said, "if the one-eyed Squeers, coarse but good John Browdie, the *beautiful* Sally Brass, clever Dick Swiveller, the demoniac and intriguing Quilp, the good Cheeryble Brothers, the avaricious Fagin, and dear little Nelly, are mere fancies?"

"No, sir, they are not," he replied; "they are copies. You will not understand me to say, of course, that they are true histories in all respects, but they are real likenesses; nor have I in any of my works attempted anything more than to arrange my story as well as I could, and give a true picture of scenes I have witnessed. My past history and pursuits have led me to a familiar acquaintance with numerous instances of extreme wretchedness and of deep-laid villany. In the haunts of squalid poverty I have found many a broken heart too good for this world. Many such persons, now in the most abject condition, have seen better days. Once they moved in circles of friendship and affluence, from which they have been hurled by misfortune to the lowest depth of want and sorrow. This class of persons is very large.

"Then there are thousands in our parish workhouses and in the lanes of London, born into the world without a friend except God and a dying mother. Many, too, who in circumstances of trial have yielded to impulses of passion, and by one fatal step fallen beyond recovery. London is crowded, and, indeed, so is all England, with the poor, the unfortunate, and the guilty. This description of persons has been generally overlooked by authors. They have had none to care for them, and have fled from the public gaze to some dark habitation of this great city, to curse the cold charities of a selfish world, and die. There are more broken hearts in London than in any other place in the world. The amount of crime, starvation, nakedness, and misery of every sort in the metropolis surpasses all calculation. I thought I could render some service to humanity by bringing these scenes before the minds of those who, from never having witnessed them, suppose they cannot exist. In this effort I have not been wholly unsuccessful; and there is nothing makes me happier than to think that, by some of my representations, I have increased the stock of human cheerfulness, and, by others, the stock of human sympathy. I think it makes the heart better to seek out the suffering and relieve them. I have spent many days and nights in the most wretched districts of the metropolis, studying the history of the human heart. There we must go to find it. In high circles we see everything but the heart, and learn everything but the real character. We must go to the hovels of the poor and the unfortunate, where trial brings out the character. I have in these rambles seen many exhibitions of generous affection and heroic endurance, which would do honor to any sphere. Often have I discovered minds that only wanted a little of the sunshine of prosperity to develop the choicest endowments of Heaven. I think I never returned to my home after these adventures without being made a sadder and a better man. In describing these characters I aim no higher than to feel in writing as they seem to feel themselves. I am persuaded that I have succeeded just in proportion as I have cultivated a familiarity with the trials and sorrows of the poor, and told their story as they would have related it themselves."

I spoke of the immense popularity of his works, and remarked that I believed he had ten readers in America where he had one in England.

"Why, sir, the popularity of my works has surprised me. For some reason or other, I believe they are somewhat extensively read; nor is it the least gratifying circumstance to me, that they have been so favorably received in your country. I am trying to enjoy my fame while it lasts, for I believe I am not so vain as to suppose that my books will be read by any but the men of my own times."

I remarked that he might consider himself alone in that opinion, and, it would probably be no easy matter to make the world coincide with him. He answered with a smile, "I shall probably not make any very serious efforts to do it!"

Looking through the library windows into a garden, Mr. L. saw "several rosy-cheeked children playing by a water fountain," and adds, "as the little creatures cast occasional glances up to us while we were watching their sports from the window, I thought I saw in their large, clear, blue eyes, golden hair, and bewitching smiles, the image of Charles Dickens. They were, in fact, young Bozzes." As it happened, they were *not*—seeing that in July, 1840, Dickens had not been four years married.

Mr. Lester wound up with the following rose-colored pen-portrait of his hero:

I think Dickens incomparably the finest-looking man I ever saw. The portrait of him in the Philadelphia edition of his works is a good one; but no picture can do justice to his expression when he is engaged in an interesting conversation. There is something about his eyes at such times which cannot be copied. In person he is perhaps a little above the standard height; but his bearing is noble, and he appears taller than he really is. His figure is very graceful, neither too slight nor too stout. The face is handsome. His complexion is delicate—rather pale generally; but when his feelings are kindled his countenance is overspread with a rich glow. I presume he is somewhat vain of his hair, and he can be pardoned for it too. It reminded me of words in Sidney's Arcadia: "His fair auburn hair, which he wore in great length, gave him at that time a most delightful show." His forehead, a phrenologist would say (especially if he knew his character beforehand), indicates a clear and beautiful intellect, in which the organs of perception, mirthfulness, ideality, and comparison, predominate. I should think his nose had once been almost determined to be Roman, but hesitated just long enough to settle into the classic Grecian outline.

But the charm of his person is in his full, soft, beaming eyes, which catch an expression from every passing object; and you can always see wit, half sleeping in ambush around them, when it is not shooting its wonted fires. Dickens has almost made us feel that

> "Wit is the pupil of the soul's clear eye,
> And in man's world, the only shining star."

And yet I think his conversation, except in perfect *abandon* among his friends, presents but few striking exhibitions of wit. Still there is a rich vein of humor and good feeling in all he says.

I passed two hours at his house, and when I left was more impressed than ever with the goodness of his heart. I should mention that during my visit I handed him Campbell's letter: it produced not the slightest change in his manner. I expressed, on leaving, the hope that little Nelly (in whose fate I confessed I felt a deeper interest than in that of most real characters) might, after all her wanderings, find a quiet and happy home. "The same hope," he replied, "has been expressed to me by others; and I hardly know what to do. But if you ever hear of her death in a future number of the Clock, you shall say that she died as she lived."

The portrait above referred to, was that engraved from the picture by Daniel Maclise, and will be remembered as the first authentic likeness of the young novelist then published. Mr. Lester, fairly excited, at last winds up with "Mr. Dickens is certainly one of the most *lovely* men I ever saw."—But that was thirty years ago, and was scarcely considered as saying too much, at the time, when little was known about the literary phenomenon, whose writings, popular as they were in his own country, were far more extensively read and prized in this Western empire. Mr. Lester's account of Dickens was very largely circulated, and prepared the American mind for the visit which he paid his transatlantic friends, a little later.

CHAPTER VIII.

RETIRES FROM BENTLEY'S MISCELLANY.—RETROSPECT.—YORKSHIRE SCHOOLS.—PICKS UP JOHN BROWDIE AND WACKFORD SQUEERS.—NICHOLAS NICKLEBY.—DOTHEBOYS HALL.—THE CRUMMLES PARTY.—CHEERYBLE BROTHERS.—CHANGE OF PLOT.—AUTHORSHIP AVOWED.—PORTRAIT BY MACLISE.—NICKLEBY ON THE PARISIAN STAGE.—MR. THACKERAY AND JULES JANIN.—CONTINUATION OF NICKLEBY.—TROOPS OF FRIENDS.

WE have now to go back a little. Fairly liberated from the great labor, however well paid, of editing, for he had retired from *Bentley's Miscellany*, at the close of 1838, with a genial valedictory about the old coachman introducing his successor, Mr. William Harrison Ainsworth, to its readers, Charles Dickens had leisure, at last, to devote his whole time and ability to the composition of a regularly constructed story. The *Sketches*, as their title implied, were odds and ends, forming a work of "shreds and patches." *Pickwick*, which had assailed imprisonment for debt as well as exposed the license of legal practitioners in English Courts of law, was begun without a plan, and had no plot; *Oliver Twist*, begun with the avowed object of exposing the mismanagement and inhumanity of the parish work-house system, soon abandoned that purpose, and took the boy to London, among the thieves. The new author had been exceedingly well received. Passages from his writings were upon men's lips, and Sam Weller had become a member of the great family of fiction. We knew everybody, in *Pickwick* and in *Oliver Twist*, as well as if we had constantly met them, in or out of society. It was almost universally admitted that a genius of uncommon brilliancy had arisen, and his next work was looked for with great expectation, particularly by a few who hinted that "the young man, a *farceur* at best, had written himself out." He was not a *farceur*, and so far from being exhausted, had over thirty years of great and successful work before him.

He took pains to prepare himself for another work, and the result was an onslaught upon the cheap Yorkshire schools, which were a crying shame and a detestable nuisance at that time. Mr. Wackford Squeers's advertisement of Dotheboys Hall, in the third chapter of *Nicholas Nickleby*, was scarcely a caricature thirty years ago. I have read scores of similar announcements in the Liverpool, Leeds, and Manchester papers, at Christmas and midsummer.

Mr. Dickens knew very little of Yorkshire schools, when he made up his mind to write about them. His own account is that, when himself a school-boy, he had "heard" of them. "My first impressions of them," he said, "were picked up at that time, and that they were, somehow or other, connected with a suppurated abscess that some boy had come home with, in consequence of his Yorkshire guide, philosopher, and friend, having ripped it open with an inky penknife. The impression made upon me, however made, never left me. I was always curious about them—fell, long afterwards, and at sundry times, into the way of hearing more about them—at last, having an audience, I resolved to write about them."

Whenever Lord Macaulay, writing history or criticism,

encountered a fact which he did not understand, or a date which he suspected, he would travel a hundred miles to verify or reject either. Scott had a good deal of the same tendency even in novel-writing. When he was writing *Quentin Durward*, with the scene in a part of France which he had never visited, he availed himself of the lively and accurate journal of a friend, who had lately traversed the district, and being as much artist as author, had executed a vast variety of clever drawings, representing landscapes and ancient buildings. But Scott wanted to describe the place where Louis XI. lived—and his letters to Constable, his publisher, are characteristic. "It is a vile place," he wrote, "this village of Plessis les Tours, that can baffle both you and me. It is a place famous in history; and moreover, as your Gazetteer assures us, is a village of a thousand inhabitants, yet I have not found it on any map, provincial or general, which I have consulted," and half in despair, he went on to suggest, that something about it must be found in Malte Brun's Geographical Works, or that Wraxall's History of France, or his Travels, might mention it. Finally he discovered that the place was on the banks of the Cher, a tributary of the Loire, and the readers of the romance, the first of the Waverley Novels which had its scene in France, may remember how well acquainted with the place, about which he despaired of learning anything, he has made *them*.

Mr. Dickens was as conscientious and as painstaking as Macaulay and Scott. He could have drawn upon his imagination for a description of the Yorkshire cheap school system, the cruelties of which, from vague reports, had long grieved and vexed him, but he preferred to write about what he *knew*. Therefore, at the beginning of 1839, he went down to Yorkshire, to judge for himself how much truth there was in the rumors which had reached him. In the extended preface, to the People's edition of his Works, he related what he had done; prefacing it with the remark that when the story was begun, there were a good many cheap Yorkshire schools in existence, and significantly adding "there are very few now." His object was to write about them, if he found that he ought to do so. He says:

With that intent, I went down into Yorkshire before I began this book, in very severe winter-time which is pretty faithfully described herein. As I wanted to see a schoolmaster or two, and was forewarned that those gentlemen might, in their modesty, be shy of receiving a visit from me, I consulted with a professional friend here, who had a Yorkshire connection, and with whom I concerted a pious fraud. He gave me some letters of introduction, in the name, I think, of my travelling companion; they bore reference to a suppositious little boy who had been left with a widowed mother who didn't know what to do with him; the poor lady had thought, as a means of thawing the tardy compassion of her relations in his behalf, of sending him to a Yorkshire school; I was the poor lady's friend, travelling that way; and if the recipient of the letter could inform me of a school in his neighborhood, the writer would be very much obliged.

I went to several places in that part of the country where I understood these schools to be plentifully sprinkled, and had no occasion to deliver a letter until I came to a certain town which shall be nameless. The person to whom it was addressed, was not at home; but, he came down at night, through the snow, to the inn where I was staying. It was after dinner; and he needed little persuasion to sit down by the fire in a warm corner, and take his share of the wine that was on the table.

I am afraid he is dead now. I recollect he was a jovial, ruddy, broad-faced man; that we got acquainted directly; and that we talked on all kinds of subjects, except the school, which he showed a great anxiety to avoid. "Was there any large school near?" I asked him in reference to the letter. "Oh yes," he said; "there was a pratty big'un." "Was it a good one?" I asked. "Ey!" he said, "it was as good as anoother; that was a' a matther of opinion;" and fell to looking at the fire, staring round the room, and whistling a little. On my reverting to some other topic that we had been discussing, he recovered immediately; but, though I tried him again and again, I never approached the question of the school, even if he were in the middle of a laugh, without observing that his countenance fell, and that he became uncomfortable. At last, when we had passed a couple of hours or so, agreeably, he suddenly took up his hat, and leaning over the table and looking me full in the face, said, in a low voice: "Weel, Misther, we've been very pleasant toogather, and ar'll spak' my moind tiv'ee. Dinnot let the weedur send her lattle boy to yan o' our schoolmeasthers, while there's a harse to hoold in a' Lunnun, or a gootther to lie asleep in. Ar wouldn't mak' ill words amang my neeburs, and ar speak tiv'ee quiet loike. But I'm dom'd if ar can gang to bed and not tellee, for weedur's sak', to keep the lattle boy from a 'sike scoondrels while there's a harse to hoold in a' Lunnun, or a gootther to lie asleep in!" Repeating these words with great heartiness, and with a solemnity on his jolly face that made it look twice as large as before, he shook hands and went away. I never saw him afterwards, but I sometimes imagine that I descry a faint reflection of him in John Browdie.

John Browdie is a real personage, and it has been suspected that Wackford Squeers must also have been encountered in that cold visit. There is an army of these schoolmasters in that district, and several of those, though they had the regular number of eyes, insisted that Dickens must have drawn the portrait of each—just as a learned Professor lately took the trouble of proclaiming on the house-top that *he*, and none else, must have been the "social parasite" sketched in Mr. Disraeli's last novel. But Mr. Dickens drew from a class and not from individuals. He says, "Mr. Squeers is the representative of a class, and not of an individual. Where imposture, ignorance, and brutal cupidity, are the stock in trade of a small body of men, and one is described by these characteristics, all his fellows will recognize something belonging to themselves, and each will have a misgiving that the portrait is his own." He added the emphatic declaration that "his object in calling public attention to the system would be very imperfectly fulfilled, if he did not state now in his own person, emphatically and earnestly, that Mr. Squeers and his school are faint and feeble pictures of an existing reality, purposely subdued and kept down lest they should be deemed impossible—that there are upon record trials at law in which damages have been sought as a poor recompense for lasting agonies and disfigurements inflicted upon children by the treatment of the master in these places, involving such offensive and foul details of neglect, cruelty, and disease, as no writer of fiction would have the boldness to imagine—and that, since he has been engaged upon these Adventures, he has received from private quarters far beyond the reach of suspicion or distrust, accounts of atrocities, in the perpetration of which upon neglected or repudiated children these schools have been the main instruments, very far exceeding any that appear in these pages."

In *Nicholas Nickelby*, he had the advantage of breaking up new ground. Here was a system full of abuses, equally injurious to body and mind, which no writer, whether of fact or fiction, had attempted to expose. In the public journals, liberal education and good treatment were freely promised to pupils,—or, to use the words in Mr. Squeers's own card, "Youth were boarded, clothed, booked, furnished with pocket-money, provided with all necessaries, instructed in all languages—living and dead," and so on, for twenty guineas a year. Any one could see that to fulfil this compact was impossible, yet many poor children, offspring of misfortune or vice, were exiled to such schools, often with a hope, perhaps, that they never were to return. They were the devoted victims of cupidity, ignorance, and brutality. American readers cannot realize the extent and enormity of this foul system, because it would not be allowed to exist, even for a day, in any part of their country, which, humane and liberal in all things, is especially so in the treatment and education of youth.

There was Hogarthian humor, with Hogarth's truth, too,

in the exhibition, not only of the scholastic but the domestic *menage* at Dotheboys Hall. Miss Fanny's flirtations came out in pleasant relief with the weekly doses of brimstone and treacle, while the story of poor Smike was told with a tenderness and pathos that went to the heart at once. There were varieties of character, in this tale;—and giving precedence, in courtesy if not of right, to the fair sex, we may mention Mrs. Nickleby, the very queen of garrulous, tiresome, good-hearted, soft-headed, and ridiculous English matrons; little Miss La Creevy; Mrs. John Browdie, Fanny Squeers, the severe mistress of Dotheboys Hall, and the theatrical ladies, from Mrs. Vincent Crummles and the Phenomenon, down to Henrietta Petowker and indispensable Mrs. Grudden. Here it may be mentioned, parenthetically, but not in a parenthesis, (to which some of my readers have occasionally objected,) that the scenes in the theatre at Portsmouth, in which the Crummles's company very prominently appear, are full of reality and true humor. They could only have been written by one who had been a great deal behind the curtain.

Nicholas Nickleby, the hero of the story, is an ordinary young gentleman, whom the author's own statement best characterizes:—"If Nicholas be not always found to be blameless or agreeable, he is not always intended to appear so. He is a young man of an impetuous temper and of little or no experience; and I saw no reason why such a hero should be lifted out of nature." Ralph, the uncle, is the villain of the romance. His vile death is in accord with his bad life. Contrasted with him are the Cheeryble Brothers, drawn from life, (or rather from a second-hand description, seeing that Mr. Dickens never interchanged a word with either,) and it may be said that Tim Linkinwater is worthy of them. Newman Noggs, the Marplot in the dark drama of his master's ill doing, is an almost impossible eccentric. John Browdie and Linkinwater, with their honest, truthful nature, add flavor to the narrative. The compact between Gride, Ralph, and Bray; the Sliderskew-episode; the adventures of Mr. Lillyvick, Miss Petowker, and the Kenwigs family are rather blemishes on the work. But the life and death of Smike are wonderfully touching and true. There is not so much pure fun in *Nickleby* as overflowed in *Pickwick*, but the more earnest purpose is felt, and gives a higher tone to the story.

Nickleby was completed in 1840. The conclusion, critical readers will notice, is scarcely in accordance with what the incidents had evidently led up to. Mr. Moncrieff, who had dramatized Pierce Egan's "Tom and Jerry," twenty years before, and was ever on the look-out for novels which he could "adapt" for the stage, had laid his predatory hands upon *Nickleby* before it was three-fourths written, and, framing a finale of his own, had sold it, as "a drama," to the manager of one of the inferior London theatres. The *dénouement* which he had contrived forced Dickens to make a new conclusion of the story. Perhaps to this we owe the rather impossible incident of Smike being finally presented as Ralph Nickleby's son. The last appearance of Mantalini, in a cellar, turning a mangle for a truculent Irish washerwoman, is unnatural, and out of keeping with the narrative. It may be objected, too, that no schoolmaster, least of all Squeers, would have given such a suggestive title as Dotheboys Hall to his residence. The old dramatists were addicted to it, but modern tastes does not sanction the giving surnames which indicate character. It is true that Sheridan has Sir Anthony Absolute, as a very positive father; Sir Lucius O'Trigger, as a professioned duellist; and Mrs. Malaprop, as a conversational blunderer, in "The Rivals;" while among the satirical coterie of "The School for Scandal," are persons called Backbite, Sneerwell, Candor, and Crabtree. On or off the stage this sort of nomenclature is now rarely used. Lord Frederick Verisopht and Sir Mulberry Hawk, the pigeon and the rook—may be considered as having names a trifle too suggestive.

Nicholas Nickleby when completed, like *Pickwick*, in a guinea volume, appeared with the author's name, and an engraving on steel, from his portrait by Daniel Maclise, the great painter. A *fac simile* of his very peculiar autograph was also given. This is the portrait in which Mr. Dickens is represented with long hair and little whisker. It hung, in the dining-room in Gad's Hill House, where its original was death-smitten, and was sold at auction, with his other pictures, on July 9th, in London.

In *Fraser's Magazine*, for March, 1842, Mr. Thackeray gave an account, in a free and easy manner, with a few of his own peculiar pen-and-ink drawings, of the production of "Nicholas Nickleby, ou les Voleurs de Londres," at the Ambigu-Comique Theatre, on the Boulevard, in Paris, and of a ferocious criticism upon the piece by Jules Janin,—who considered play and story as the productions of "Monseiur Dickens." Previously, however, Mr. Thackeray had seen *Nickleby* played at the Adelphi Theatre in London, with Mrs. Keeley as *Smike*, Mr. Yates as *Mantalini*, and Mr. Wilkinson as *Squeers*. The French version took many amusing liberties with the original, and opened with the "Paradis des Enfans,"—the romantic Parisian name for Dotheboys Hall. Neekolass Neeklbee, usher in this seminary, is giving a lesson to the young and lovely daughter of the Earl of Clarendon, whose estate is adjacent. Neekolass is represented as nephew of a rich London banker, who provided for him by getting him this usher's place, with about twenty-two dollars per annum. John Browdie is there, and so is Smeek, and the first act closes with Neeklbee's flogging Monsieur Squarrs, the schoolmaster, and going away, accompanied by Smeek. They go to London, where, being utterly pennyless, they stop at a first-class hotel, which Browdie, old Ralph and the Earl of Clarendon frequent. On the death of this nobleman, who must not be confounded with a late Foreign Minister of England, Smeek turns out to be successor to the coronet and estates, makes Kate Neeklbee his countess, and bestows the hand of his sister, the lady Annabella, upon Neekolass, whose pupil she had been when he was usher at Dotheboys Hall. A new incident in the story is the introduction of a gang of thieves, of whom Ralph and Squeers are commanders, whose place of rendezvous, Codger's Hall, is a great gothic hall, hidden a thousand feet below the Thames!

The French dramatists, it will be seen, deviated a good deal from the original story. Jules Janin—famous critic, then and now!—wrote an article, in the *Journal des Debats*, in which he assailed the play, as if Dickens himself had written it, and branded him as an immodest writer! Now, immodesty was the very last offence with which Dickens could honestly be charged, at any time; while, unfortunately, it cropped out, rather luxuriantly, in the contemporary compositions of his critic.

Long before "Nickleby" was completed, some unscrupulous and impudent scribbler brought out in penny weekly numbers, a new version of what he called "The Nickleby Papers, by Poz." They were stupid to a degree, but the low price was in their favor, and they had a large sale. On the completion of "Nickleby," a continuation, also by "Poz," was published. The narrative began ten years after the close of the real story, and reintroduced Squeers, who had served out his seven years' transportation to Botany Bay. He had not improved *there*, and naturally took to burglary and forgery on his return to London. He was shot, if I remember correctly, while engaged in an attempt to break into the dwelling house of Nicholas Nickleby in Devonshire. Nothing could have been more clumsily written, but the book had thousands of readers—among the non-respectables in London.

The intimation that "Boz" was the handsome young gentleman whose portrait was a frontispiece to *Nicholas Nickleby*, was information to the public, though many of them suspected that "Dickens" itself was only a *nom de plume.* In London, however, while *Pickwick* was in progress, and after Mr. Dickens had become editor of *Bentley's Miscellany*, his identity was generally known, not in literary society only, but in the most fashionable and aristocratic circles. It would have been no wonder if the young author's head had been turned by the prestige which he had gained, and the adulation which was given to him, from all quarters. London society, usually so cold and stand-off, threw open its portals for him, and it is no exaggeration to say that, from the conclusion of *Pickwick* to the close of his life, Charles Dickens was as warmly greeted and as kindly estimated there as, in his time, Scott had been. It was singular that the annalist, the champion of the poor and humble, should always have been the *enfant cheri* of the rich and mighty, and gladly received by them on terms of complete equality.

CHAPTER IX.

MASTER HUMPHREY'S CLOCK.—ITS PROPOSED OBJECT.—ILLUSTRATIONS.—THE WORKS.—AUTHOR'S CONFESSION.—MR. PICKWICK AND THE WELLERS REVIVED.—THE PRECOCIOUS GRANDSON.—OLD CUSIOSITY SHOP.—LITTLE NELL.—THOMAS HOOD.—BARNABY RUDGE.—RIOTS OF LONDON.—THE RAVEN.—LORD JEFFREY.—DINNER AT EDINBURGH.—CHRISTOPHER NORTH.—PUBLIC SPEAKING.

On the completion of *Nicholas Nickleby*, its author, full of the energy of youth excited by success, resolved to carry into execution a project which, with novelty to recommend it, he thought might elevate him still higher in public favor. In the Preface to the revised edition of his works, he says: "In April, 1840, I issued the first number of a new weekly publication, price three pence, called *Master Humphrey's Clock.* It was intended to consist, for the most part, of detached papers, but was to include one continuous story, to be resumed from time to time, with such indefinite intervals between each period of resumption as might best accord with the exigencies and capabilities of the proposed Miscellany. The original Preface, dated September, 1840, says:

When the author commenced this Work, he proposed to himself three objects:

FIRST. To establish a periodical, which should enable him to present, under one general head, and not as separate and distinct publications, certain fictions which he had it in contemplation to write.

SECONDLY. To produce these Tales in weekly numbers; hoping that to shorten the intervals of communication between himself and his readers, would be to knit more closely the pleasant relations they had held for Forty Months.

THIRDLY. In the execution of this weekly task, to have as much regard as its exigencies would permit, to each story as a whole, and to the possibility of its publication at some distant day, apart from the machinery in which it had its origin.

The characters of Master Humphrey and his three friends, and the little fancy of the Clock, were the result of these considerations. When he sought to interest his readers in those who talked, and read, and listened, he revived Mr. Pickwick and his humble friends; not with any intention of reopening an exhausted and abandoned mine, but to connect them in the thoughts of those whose favorites they had been, with the tranquil enjoyments of Master Humphrey.

It was never the author's intention to make the Members of Master Humphrey's Clock, active agents in the stories they are supposed to relate. Having brought himself in the commencement of his undertaking to feel an interest in these quiet creatures, and to imagine them in their old chamber of meeting, eager listeners to all he had to tell, the author hoped—as authors will—to succeed in awakening some of his own emotions in the bosoms of his readers. Imagining Master Humphrey in his chimney-corner, resuming, night after night, the narrative,—say, of the Old Curiosity Shop—picturing to himself the various sensations of his hearers—thinking how Jack Redburn might incline to poor Kit, and perhaps lean too favorably even towards the lighter vices of Mr. Richard Swiveller—how the deaf gentleman would have his favorite, and Mr. Miles his—and how all these gentle spirits would trace some faint reflection of their past lives in the varying current of the tale—he has insensibly fallen into the belief that they are present to his readers as they are to him, and has forgotten that like one whose vision is disordered he may be conjuring up bright figures where there is nothing but empty space.

The short papers which are to be found at the beginning of this volume were indispensable to the form of publication and the limited extent of each number, as no story of lengthened interest could be begun until "The Clock" was wound up and fairly going.

The work was of large octavo size, beautifully printed upon fine paper, and was principally illustrated by H. K. Browne and George Cattermole. The former of these was the artist of *Sunday in London, Pickwick, and Nickleby;* the latter was famous for his charming interiors and architectural designs, as well as for his figure drawings, several of which add much to the interest of *The Old Curiosity Shop* and *Barnaby Rudge.* George Cruikshank and Daniel Maclise each contributed one sketch. The engravings, on wood, were printed with the text, instead, as before, of being etched on steel and printed separately.

Master Humphrey's Clock was fashioned somewhat on the plan of the *Spectator*, *Tattler*, and *Guardian*, which, more than a century before, Addison, Steele and Swift had composed and published. The framework was written with great care, in its author's best manner. *Master Humphrey*, self-introduced to the reader, was an amiable old man, living in retirement "in a venerable suburb of London, in an old house, which in bygone days was a famous resort for merry roysterers and peerless ladies, long since departed." He is almost a recluse, "a misshapen, deformed old man," but neither churlish or cold; fond of children and beloved by them. He has a great liking for his Clock, which has stood upon the staircase at home, nigh sixty years ago, and is a quaint old thing, in a huge oaken case, curiously and richly carved. It sets the time for the neighborhood, and the barber "would sooner believe it than the Sun." By degrees, Master Humphrey has made a few choice friends—to wit: a deaf gentleman, of whose name he is ignorant; a kind-hearted old librarian and factotum, named Jack Redburn; and one Mr. Miles, a retired merchant, who places implicit faith in Redburn's capabilities.

"We are men of secluded habits," Master Humphrey says, "with something of a cloud upon our early fortunes, whose enthusiasm nevertheless has not cooled with age, whose spirit of romance is not yet quenched, who are content to ramble through the world in a pleasant dream, rather than ever waken again to its harsh realities. We are alchemists who would extract the essence of perpetual youth from dust and ashes, tempt coy Truth in many light and airy forms from the bottom of her well, and discover one crumb of comfort or one grain of good in the commonest and least regarded matter that passes through our crucible. Spirits of past times, creatures of imagination, and people of to-day, are alike the objects of our seeking, and, unlike the objects of search with most philosophers, we can ensure their coming at our command."

These four meet, once a week, in a quaint old room, where were six chairs, and have determined to fill the empty ones whenever they find two men to their mind. In the Clock-case, beneath where the steady pendulum throbs and beats with healthy action, these friends have deposited files of dusty papers, which they read at their weekly meetings.

These are of various kinds:—for example, the Giant Chronicles, related by Gog and Magog, the pride of Guildhall, London; a Murderer's Confession; a story written by Mr. Pickwick; a little imaginary correspondence; and at last, *The Old Curiosity Shop*, which has the sub-title of Personal Adventures of Master Humphrey. Of this Mr. Dickens tells us:

The first chapter of this tale appeared in the fourth number of Master Humphrey's Clock, when I had already been made uneasy by the desultory character of that work, and when, I believe, my readers had thoroughly participated in the feeling. The commencement of a story was a great satisfaction to me, and I had reasons to believe that my readers participated in this feeling too. Hence, being pledged to some interruptions and some pursuit of the original design, I cheerfully set about disentangling myself from those impediments as fast as I could ; and—that done —from that time until its completion, *The Old Curiosity Shop* was written and published from week to week, in weekly parts.

When the story was finished, in order that it might be freed from the incumbrance of associations and interruptions with which it had no kind of concern, I caused the few sheets of Master Humphrey's Clock, which had been printed in connection with it, to be cancelled ; and, like the unfinished tale of the windy night and the notary in the Sentimental Journey, they became the property of the trunk-maker and the butterman. I was especially unwilling, I confess, to enrich those respectable trades with the opening paper of the abandoned design, in which Master Humphrey described himself and his manner of life. Though I now affect to make the confession philosophically, as referring to a by-gone emotion, I am conscious that my pen winces a little even while I write these words. But it was done, and wisely done, and Master Humphrey's Clock, as originally constructed, became one of the lost books of the earth—which, we all know, are far more precious than any that can be read for love or money.

The machinery *was* clumsy and embarrassing, and Mr. Dickens acted judiciously in relieving himself from it.

One portion of it, however, was very good, though sequels of popular stories are usually inferior to the original. This portion introduced Mr. Pickwick as a candidate for one of the vacant chairs, (his qualification being a Witch story of the time of James the First,) with, in his train, three generations of the House of Weller,—namely, the old retired coachman, who maintained that "vidth and visdom always go together;" his only son, known in romantic history by the name of "Samivel," and a tender scion who acknowledges the old "whip" as grandfather.

The scene in which Mr. Pickwick, wearing his immortal black gaiters, presents himself to Master Humphrey, is in its author's best manner, and, from first to last, the individuality of the great chief of *the* Club is extremely well sustained. While the little coterie up-stairs are enjoying themselves under the shadow of the Clock, the two Wellers, with a not youthful housekeeper, who is not "a widder," and the barber-valet, meet down stairs, and their symposium is dignified with the title of "Mr. Weller's Watch." Here is a little bit of the narrative :

It was a warm evening, but the elder Mr. Weller was attired, notwithstanding, in a most capacious great coat, and had his chin enveloped in a large speckled shawl, such as is usually worn by stage-coachmen on active service. He looked very rosy and very stout, especially about the legs, which appeared to have been compressed into his top-boots with some difficulty. His broad-brimmed hat he held under his left arm, and with the fore-finger of his right hand he touched his forehead a great many times, in acknowledgment of my presence.

"I am very glad to see you in such good health, Mr. Weller," said I.

"Why, thankee sir," returned Mr. Weller, "the axle an't broke yet. We keeps up a steady pace—not too sewere but vith a moderate degree o' friction—and the consekens is that ve're still a runnin' and comes in to the time, reg'lar. —My son Samivel, sir, as you may have read on in history," added Mr. Weller, introducing his first-born.

I received Sam very graciously, but before he could say a word, his father struck in again.

"Samivel Veller, sir," said the old gentleman, "has conferred upon me the ancient title o' grandfather, vich had long laid dormouse, and wos s'posed to be nearly hex-tinct, in our family. Sammy, relate a anecdote o' vun o' them boys—that 'ere little anecdote about young Tony, sayin' as he *vould* smoke a pipe unbeknown to his mother."

"Be quiet, can't you?" said Sam, "I never see such a old magpie—never!"

"That 'ere Tony is the blessedest boy,"—said Mr. Weller, heedless of this rebuff, "the blessedest boy as ever *I* see in *my* days! of all the charmin'est infants as ever I heerd tell on, includin' them as wos kivered over by the robin red-breasts arter they'd committed sooicide with black-berries, there never was any like that 'ere little Tony. He's alvays a playin' vith a quart pot that boy is! To see him a settin' down on the door step pretending to drink out of it, and fetching a long breath artervards, and smoking a bit of fire-vood and sayin' 'Now I'm grandfather'—to see him a doin' that at two year old is better than any play as wos ever wrote. 'Now I'm grandfather!' He wouldn't take a pint pot if you wos to make him a present on it, but he gets his quart and then he says, 'Now I'm grand-father!'"

Mr. Weller was so overpowered by this picture that he straightway fell into a most alarming fit of coughing, which must certainly have been attended with some fatal result, but for the dexterity and promptitude of Sam, who taking a firm grasp of the shawl just under his father's chin, shook him to and fro with great violence, at the same time admin-istering some smart blows between his shoulders. By this curious mode of treatment Mr. Weller was finally recovered, but with a very crimson face and in a state of great ex-haustion.

"He'll do now, Sam," said Mr. Pickwick, who had been in some alarm himself.

"He'll do, sir!" cried Sam, looking reproachfully at his parent, "Yes, he *will* do one o' these days—he'll do for his-self and then he'll wish he hadn't. Did anybody ever see sich a inconsiderate old file,—laughing into conwulsions afore company, and stamping on the floor as if he'd brought his own carpet vith him and wos under a wager to punch the pattern out in a given time? He'll begin again in a minute. There—he's goin' off—I said he would!"

In fact, Mr. Weller, whose mind was still running upon his precocious grandson, was seen to shake his head from side to side, while a laugh, working like an earthquake, below the surface, produced various extraordinary appear-ances in his face, chest, and shoulders, the more alarming because unaccompanied by any noise whatever. These emotions, however, gradually subsided, and after three or four short relapses, he wiped his eyes with the cuff of his coat, and looked about him with tolerable composure.

Surely, this is quite as good as any of the scenes in *Pickwick*, in which Old Weller appeared? Sam, also, is racy—though not so talkative as he was in the old story. However, neither the public nor the author liked the interruptions, and, in a short time, the new tale went on, without them.

The *Old Curiosity Shop* is the most poetical, tender, and imaginative of Mr. Dickens's compositions. Little Nell, who is thought of by readers rather as a real than a fictitious personage, is superior to Mignon, as drawn by Goethe in "Wilhelm Meister's Apprenticeship." She is the embodiment of youth, girlish beauty, the wisdom which comes from suffering, and perfect innocence. Unfortunately, she *is*

> "Too bright and good
> For human nature's daily food."

She is an idyllic impossibility, and not "of the earth, earthy." She is only too perfect—and her death is worthy of her life. Many a tear has been drawn forth by her imaginary adventures. Mr. Dickens says of this tale: "The many friends it won me, and the many hearts it turned to me when they were full of private sorrow, invest it with an interest in my mind which is not a public one, and the rightful place of which appears to be 'a more removed ground.' I will merely observe, therefore, that, in writing the book, I had it always in my fancy to surround the lonely figure of the child with grotesque and wild but not impossible companions, and to gather about her innocent face and pure intentions, associates as strange and uncongenial as the grim objects that are about her bed when her history is first foreshadowed."

He adds, "I have a mournful pride in one recollection associated with 'Little Nell.' While she was yet upon her wanderings, not then concluded, there appeared in a literary journal, an essay of which she was the principal theme, so earnestly, so eloquently, and tenderly appreciative and of all her shadowy kith and kin, that it would have been insensibility in me, if I could have read it without an unusual glow of pleasure and encouragement. Long afterwards, and when I had come to know him well, and to see him stout of heart going slowly down into his grave, I knew the author of that essay to be Thomas Hood."

There are not so many characters in this story as are to be found in some others by the same hand, but almost every one of them *tells*. To balance monstrosity against monstrosity we have Quilp, with Sampson and Sally Brass. The grandfather and his brother stand alone. The Punch-and-Judy exhibitors are hit off to the life—and we have a warm wish in our heart for excellent Mrs. Jarley. The old schoolmaster and his favorite pupil are delicately limned. Kit and the rest of the Nubbles family, in which pretty Barbara may be included, are creatures of daily life. We shut the book with a hearty hope that, having made an out-pensioner of Mrs. Jiniwin, pretty Mrs. Quilp did lead a merry life, with her second husband, on the dead dwarf's money. Of the excellent Garlands, no praise can be too high—such people are the salt of the earth; and what may be said of Mr. Richard Swiveller? Thoughtless and careless, but tenderhearted and true, he is good foil to the wonderful little Marchioness. How splendidly he comes out, at last, when the Notary tells him, just after he had nearly lost his life in a fever, that he had fallen heir to an annuity of one hundred and fifty guineas a year, "Please God, we'll make a scholar of the Marchioness yet! And she shall walk in silk attire, and siller have to spare, or may I never rise from this bed again!" She had saved his life by nursing him through a brain-fever, and, for he had a heart in his bosom, despite of being a thoughtless, careless man, he does educate her, at a superior school, though it keeps him poor for half a dozen years. "In a word," the story runs, "Mr. Swiveller kept the Marchioness at this establishment until she was, at a moderate guess, full nineteen years of age—good-looking, clever, and good-humored; when he began to consider seriously what was to be done next. On one of his periodical visits, while he was revolving this question in his mind, the Marchioness came down to him, alone, looking more smiling, and more fresh than ever. Then it occurred to him, but not for the first time, that if she would marry him, how comfortable they might be! So Richard asked her; whatever she said, it wasn't no; and they were married in good earnest that day week, which gave Mr. Swiveller frequent occasion to remark at divers subsequent periods that there had been a young lady saving up for him after all."

Next to excellent Sam Weller, let us give our regards to Dick Swiveller.

Barnaby Rudge, the most highly-wrought, earnest, and powerful of all his works, I will not except even the impressive *Tale of Two Cities*, was the second long story which Mr. Dickens placed in "Master Humphrey's Clock." It is historical, and is more true in its details than the great majority of histories. The time was June, 1780, and the events described are the No-Popery Riots which that well-meaning, weak-minded fanatic, Lord George Gordon, may be said to have created. Dickens wrote that tale as a plea for tolerance, declaring that the Riots taught a good lesson; "that what we falsely call a religious cry is easily raised by men who have no religion, and who in their daily practice set at naught the commonest principles of right and wrong; that it is begotten of intolerance and persecution; that it is senseless, besotted, inveterate, and unmerciful; all History teaches us. But perhaps we do not know it in our hearts too well, to profit by even so humble and familiar an example as the 'No-Popery' riots of seventeen hundred and eighty." It was meant to be an argument, too, against Capital Punishment, the excess of which was notorious in these days. How London was in the hands of a drunken and infuriated mob, for several days, with terrible ruin to property and life, and how fanaticism raised a devil which it could not lay, are written in that tale:—too much with melodramatic effect, perhaps, but very powerfully. Mixed up with this is the mystery of a dreadful murder. But there is a good deal of relief. Old Willet, the landlord, and his friends are peculiar characters, and so are the locksmith, with his shrewish wife and that coquettish pocket-Venus, his daughter, Dolly Varden. Mr. Chester, the incarnation of selfishness, is a study, and directly opposite is Mr. Haredale. Simon Tappertit and the accomplished Miss Miggs go hand in-hand together, for a time, and even Dennis, the hangman, is said to be no caricature. Then Joseph Willet, whose arm was "took off in the defence of the Salwanners in America where the war is." We have pity for poor Hugh, and a kind thought for honest John Grueby. But, in the van, are Barnaby and his illustrious raven, to be known through all coming time, as well as Lance's dog, sketched by Shakespeare. Without Grip, poor made Barnaby would resemble a ship without a rudder. The two must go together. Grip evidently was one of Dickens's favorites, for a supplementary notice, in his last preface, thus disposes of him:

The raven in this story is a compound of two great originals, of whom I have been, at different times, the proud possessor. The first was in the bloom of his youth, when he was discovered in a modest retirement in London, by a friend of mine, and given to me. He had from the first, as Sir Hugh Evans says of Anne Page, "good gifts," which he improved by study and attention in a most exemplary manner. He slept in a stable—generally on horseback—and so terrified a Newfoundland dog by his preternatural sagacity, that he has been known, by the mere superiority of his genius, to walk off unmolested with the dog's dinner, from before his face. He was rapidly rising in acquirements and virtues, when, in an evil hour, his stable was newly painted. He observed the workmen closely, saw that they were careful of the paint, and immediately burned to possess it. On their going to dinner, he ate up all they had left behind, consisting of a pound or two of white lead; and this youthful indiscretion terminated in death.

While I was yet inconsolable for his loss, another friend of mine in Yorkshire discovered an older and more gifted raven at a village public house, which he prevailed upon the landlord to part with for a consideration, and sent up to me. The first act of this Sage, was, to administer to the effects of his predecessor, by disinterring all the cheese and halfpence he had buried in the garden—a work of immense labor and research, to which he devoted all the energies of his mind. When he had achieved this task, he applied himself to the acquisition of stable language, in which he soon became such an adept, that he would perch outside my window, and drive imaginary horses with great skill, all day; perhaps even I never saw him at his best, for his former master sent his duty with him, "and if I wished the bird to come out very strong, would I be so good as show him a drunken man"—which I never did, having (unfortunately) none but sober people at hand. But I could hardly have respected him more, whatever the stimulating influences of his sight might have been. He had not the least respect, I am sorry to say, for me in return, or for anybody but the cook; to whom he was attached—but only, I fear, as a Policeman might have been. Once I met him unexpectedly, about half-a-mile off, walking down the middle of the public street, attended by a pretty large crowd, and spontaneously exhibiting the whole of his accomplishments. His gravity under those trying circumstances, I never can forget, nor the extraordinary gallantry with which, refusing to be brought home, he defended himself behind a pump, until overpowered by numbers. It may have been that he was too bright a genius to live long, or it may have been that he took some pernicious substance into his bill, and thence into his maw—which is not improbable, seeing that he new-pointed the greater part of the garden-wall by digging out the mortar, broke countless squares of glass by scraping away the putty all round the frames, and tore up and swallowed, in splinters, the greater part of a wooden staircase of six steps and a landing—but after some three years he too was taken ill, and died before the kitchen fire. He kept his eye to the last upon the meat as it roasted, and suddenly turned over on his back with a sepulchral cry of "Cuckoo!"

After this mournful deprivation, I was, for a long time, ravenless. The kindness of another friend at length provided me with another raven; but he is not a genius. He leads the life of a hermit, in my little orchard, on the summit of SHAKESPEARE'S Gad's Hill; he has no relish for society; he gives no evidence of ever cultivating his mind; and he has picked up nothing but meat since I have known him —except the faculty of barking like a dog.

Barnaby Rudge, completed in 1841, was dedicated to Mr. Samuel Rogers, with a complimentary reference to his Pleasures of Memory.

Lord Jeffrey, erst so formidable, as Editor of the *Edinburgh Review*, and a great reader and admirer of Dickens, wrote to him some years after *The Old Curiosity Shop* was published, saying: "How funny that *besoin* of yours for midnight rambling on city streets, and how curious that Macaulay should have the same taste or fancy. * * I wish I had time to discuss the grounds and *extent* of my preference of your soft and tender characters to his humorous and grotesque; but I can only say now, that I am as far as possible from undervaluing the merit, and even the charm of the latter; only it is a lower and more imitable style. I have always thought Quilp and Swiveller great marvels of art; and yet I should have admired the last far less, had it not been for his redeeming gratitude to the Marchioness, and that inimitable convalescent repast, with his hand locked in hers, and her *tears* of delight. If you will only own that you are prouder of that scene than of any of his antecedent fantasticals, I shall be satisfied with the conformity of our judgments." In a subsequent letter, he wrote: "I do not consider Quilp or Dick Swiveller as at all out of nature."

In the summer of 1841, a public compliment, of a very high character, was conferred upon Mr. Dickens, by two hundred and fifty of the literati, lawyers, and other publicists in the city of Edinburgh. The Scotch are not readily influenced into enthusiasm, but when they are aroused, it is to some purpose. In her life of her father (Professor Wilson), Mrs. Gordon simply states "that he presided at a large public dinner given in honor of Charles Dickens."

I believe that Lord Jeffrey had something to do with this compliment. Early in May, he was in London, circulating among the best Whig society, and, in a letter to his old friend, Lord Cockburn, a Scottish Judge like himself, mentions the numerous invitations he was compelled to decline, adding: "To make amends, however, I have seen a great deal of Tommy Moore, who is luckily here, on a visit like my own; * * * and, above all, of Charles Dickens—with whom I have struck up what I mean to be an eternal and intimate friendship. He lives very near us here, and I often run over and sit an hour *tete-à-tete,* or take a long walk in the Park with him—the only way really to know or to be known by either man or woman. Taken in this way, I find him very amiable and agreeable. In mixed company—where he is now much sought after as a lion—he is rather reserved, etc. He has dined here, and we with him, at rather too sumptuous a dinner for a man with a family and only beginning to be rich, though selling 44,000 copies of his weekly issues of *Master Humphrey's Clock.*" The regard of Jeffrey for Dickens was "eternal and intimate" while the old critic lived, and, at various times, as will be subsequently mentioned, manifested itself in the presentation of some very good advice, personal and literary, from the aged to the youthful writer.

However the Dickens's dinner at Edinburgh originated, it took place on the 25th June, 1841, with "Christopher North" as Chairman. In a private letter written at the time, I find it recorded that "on his right sat the distinguished guest—a little, slender, pale-faced, boyish-looking individual, and perhaps the very last man in the room whom a stranger to his portrait could have picked on as being the author of Pickwick. I really was quite in pain for him; I felt as if the tremendous cheering which accompanied his entrance would overwhelm him. After dinner, one of the stewards introduced into the gallery Mrs. Dickens, accompanied by about one hundred and fifty ladies in full dinner dress; she was most loudly cheered." It was very doubtful, even on the morning of the banquet, whether, from ill health, Professor Wilson would be able to take the chair, but his energetic character and his generous enthusiasm in the cause of literature made him rise superior to mere physical weakness, and he spoke more than once, with a spirited eloquence all his own —so fervid its expression and so lofty its character. He pronounced an eulogium upon Mr. Dickens, at once discriminating and generous, adding "He is also a satirist. He satirizes human life; but he does not satirize it to degrade it. He does not wish to pull down what is high, into the neighborhood of what is low. He does not seek to represent all virtue as a hollow thing in which no confidence can be placed. He satirizes only the selfish and the hard-hearted and the cruel; he exposes, in a hideous light, the principle which, when acted upon, gives a power to men in the lowest grades to carry on a more terrific tyranny than if placed upon thrones."

After the toast had been duly honored, Mr. Dickens rose to return thanks. "Then," the letter states, "There *was* silence deep as in the tomb—not a breath stirred, or a muscle moved in that crowded room—every eye was riveted on that wonderful man—every ear painfully on the alert to catch the first tones of the voice of that mighty magician; and soft were those tones, and calm that voice, as though he were dictating to an amanuensis the next number of Humphrey's Clock. He is as happy in public speaking as in writing—nothing studied, nothing artistical; his were no written speeches, conned, and got by heart, but every sentence seemed to be suggested on the impulse of the moment. Before concluding his address, he made a few observations respecting the untimely death of his little heroine (Nelly). He said, 'When I first conceived the idea of conducting that simple story to its termination, I determined rigidly to adhere to it, and never to forsake the end I had in view. I thought what a good thing it would be if, in my little work of pleasant amusement, I could substitute a garland of fresh flowers for the sculptured horrors which disgrace the tomb. If I have put in my book anything which can fill the young mind with better thoughts of death, or soften the grief of older hearts; if I have written one word which can afford pleasure or consolation to old or young, in time of trial, I shall consider it as something achieved, which I shall be glad to look back upon in after life.' He made a very long speech, and from the commencement to the end never hesitated a moment, or misplaced a word. In the course of the evening he had to propose several toasts, and, of course, preface them with appropriate remarks, all of which were in the same happy manner, and received with an enthusiasm approaching to idolatry." One of his toasts was the health of "Christopher North, the old man of the lion-heart and sceptre-crutch." It is singular enough that, during Wilson's long connection with Blackwood's Magazine, he scarcely ever mentioned the name of Dickens. One would have thought that he would have gladly expatiated on the genius whose track was so brilliant and unexpected.

It was remarked, at the great Dickens's dinner, the first of many similar entertainments, that the two best speakers were the chairman and the guest. The latter, then in his thirtieth year, was known by his intimate friends to possess remarkable readiness and ability as a speaker, but this was the first occasion of his publicly exhibiting these gifts. He possessed to an eminent degree, that faculty of "thinking on one's legs," which, with presence of mind, and the intuitive talent for putting the best words in the proper places, constitutes good oratory if not true eloquence. Mr. Thackeray, on the other hand, was a poor speaker, who prepared a great deal beforehand, took pains to commit it to memory, delivered it with a certain fear, probably forgetting half of what he had to say when the time for speaking came, and would confusedly blunder and stammer to his own mortification and that of his friends. Mr. Dickens, for years before he died, had the reputation of being the best after-dinner speaker in England.

CHAPTER X.

VISIT TO AMERICA. — AT BOSTON. — DICKENS'S DINNER. — GEOFFREY CRAYON AND BOZ.—DICKENS AT SUNNYSIDE.— IN PHILADELPHIA.—WASHINGTON.—IN CONGRESS.

ASSURED by a warm reception in the New World, and it may be well to remember, having a purpose, besides seeing the country and the people, of endeavoring to get up a gentle pressure of the subject of Copyright, Mr. Dickens and his wife were passengers on the mail steamer which left Liverpool on the 3d, arrived at Boston on the 22d of January, and quitted New York for England on the 7th of June, 1842. During a period of four months and a half he saw several cities in New England, New York, Philadelphia, Washington, Richmond, Baltimore, Harrisburg, Pittsburgh, Cincinnati, Louisville, St. Louis, the Looking-Glass Prairie, Columbus, Sandusky, Columbus, Niagara, Canada, (Toronto, Kingston, Montreal, Quebec, and St. John's,) Lebanon, the Shaker Village, and West Point. He can scarcely be said to have seen any thing of the South, for he had but a glimpse of Richmond.

He was received at Boston with a generous and wild enthusiasm, which may be said to have hailed him in every place where his name was known, and where, in a nation of readers such as we are, was it unknown? Not only private but public hospitality was tendered to him, with the heartiest liberality. In January, 1842, the *Boston Transcript* contained this paragraph:

We are requested to state that Charles Dickens, Esq., will be at the Tremont Theatre this evening. The desire to see this popular author will, no doubt, attract a large audience. We had an hour's conversation with him last evening, and found him one of the most frank, sociable, noble-hearted gentlemen we ever met with, perfectly free from all haughtiness or apparent self-importance. His lady, too, is most beautiful and accomplished, and appears worthy to be the partner and companion of her distinguished husband. In fact, he is just such a person as we had supposed him to be, judging from his writings, which have acquired a popularity almost unprecedented in this country.

Of course the theatre was filled, just as Old Drury or Covent Garden, in London, would have been at that time, if Queen Victoria had given "a Royal bespeak" to either.

There was a Dickens's banquet at Boston on the 1st of February, at which the most notable men of literature, politics, business, and the liberal professions were present, with Mr. Josiah Quincy, Jr., in the chair. Mr. Dickens spoke at some length, and said:

There is one other point connected with the labors (if I may call them so) that you hold in such generous esteem, to which I cannot help adverting. I cannot help expressing the delight, the more than happiness, it was to me to find so strong an interest awakened on this side of the water in favor of that little heroine of mine to whom your President has made allusion, who died in her youth. I had letters about that child, in England, from the dwellers in log-huts among the morasses and swamps and densest forests and deep solitudes of the Far West. Many a sturdy hand, hard with the axe and spade and browned by the summer's sun, has taken up the pen and written to me a little history of domestic joy or sorrow, always coupled, I am proud to say, with something of interest in that little tale, or some comfort or happiness derived from it; and the writer has always addressed me, not as a writer of books for sale, resident, some four or five thousand miles away, but as a friend to whom he might freely impart the joys and sorrows of his own fireside. Many a mother—I could reckon them now by dozens, not by units—has done the like; and has told me how she lost such a child at such a time, and where she lay buried, and how good she was, and how, in this or that respect, she resembled Nell. I do assure you that no circumstance of my life has given me one-hundredth part of the gratification I have derived from this source. I was wavering at the time whether or not to wind up my Clock and come and see this country; and this decided me. I felt as if it were a positive duty, as if I were bound to pack up my clothes and come and see my friends; and even now I have such an odd sensation in connection with these things that you have no chance of spoiling me. I feel as though we were agreeing—as indeed we are, if we substitute for fictitious characters the classes from which they are drawn—about third parties, in whom we had a common interest. At every new act of kindness on your part, I say it to myself: That's for Oliver—I should not wonder if that was meant for Smike—I have no doubt that it was intended for Nell; and so became a much happier, certainly, but a more sober and retiring man than ever I was before.

A few days later he arrived in New York, which, by a mistake which even its natives frequently make, he designates "the beautiful *metropolis* of America." He had not known Paris at this time, and was struck with the vivacity and variety of our great city. Here, also, he was remarkably *fêted*, in private and in public, there being a great Dickens's Ball, as well as a great Dickens's Dinner. Washington Irving presided at the latter. Irving and Dickens first met in New York. It seems that, some months before, Geoffrey Crayon had written to Boz, expressing the delight which Little Nell had given him. At this time, Irving was fifty-eight and Dickens twenty-nine years old. Mr. Charles Lanman, of Georgetown, D. C., who had the good fortune of knowing both, truly says that Dickens's reply was minute, impetuously kind, and eminently characteristic. It begun thus: "There is no man in the world could have given me the heartfelt pleasure you have, by your kind note of the 13th of last month, [April, 1842.] There is no living writer, and there are very few among the dead, whose approbation I should feel so proud to earn. And with everything you have written upon my shelves, and in my thoughts, and in my heart of hearts, I may honestly and truly say so. If you could know how earnestly I write this, you would be glad to read it—as I hope you will be, faintly guessing at the warmth of the hand I autobiographically hold out to you over the broad Atlantic. * * I have been so accustomed to associate you with my pleasantest and happiest thoughts, and with my leisure hours, that I rush at once into full confidence with you, and fall, as it were naturally, and by the very laws of gravity, into your open arms. * * I cannot thank you enough for your cordial and generous praise, or tell you what deep and lasting gratification it has given me." There were some allusions to Irving's works, which must have pleased the older writer: "I should love to go with you, as I have gone, God knows how often—into Little Britain, and Eastcheap, and Green Arbor Court, and Westminster Abbey. I should like to travel with you, astride the last of the coaches, down to Bracebridge Hall. It would make my heart glad to compare notes with you about that shabby gentleman in the oilcloth hat and red nose, who sat in the nine-cornered back-parlor of the Mason's Arms; and about Robert Preston, and the tallow-chandler's widow, whose sitting-room is second nature to me; and about all those delightful places and people that I used to walk about and dream of in the day-time, when a very small and not over-particularly-taken-care-of-boy. * * Diedrich Knickerbocker I have worn to death in my pocket, and yet I should show you his mutilated carcass with a joy past all expression." The closing sentence is characteristic. "Do you suppose the post office clerks care to receive letters? A postman, I imagine, is quite callous. Conceive his delivering one to himself, without being startled by a preliminary double knock."

In October of that year (1841) Irving received intimation from Dickens that he was "coming to America." Irving's name was before the Senate of the United States, on the nomination of President Tyler, originating with Daniel

Webster then Secretary of State, as Ambassador to the Court of Madrid. This was as unexpected and unsolicited as it was popular and merited. With these "blushing honors thick upon him," Irving was met, for the first time, at New York. As Mr. Lanman correctly says, then it was that the two lions first met face to face; and for a few weeks, at Sunnyside, and in the delightful literary society which was a striking feature in New York life at that time, they saw as much of each other as circumstances would allow. Professor C. C. Felton, in his remarks on the death of Mr. Irving, before the Historical Society of Massachusetts, gave us some interesting recollections of this winter in New York. Among other things he said: "I passed much of the time with Mr. Irving and Mr. Dickens; and it was delightful to witness the cordial intercourse of the young man, in the flush and glory of his fervent genius, and his elder compeer, then in the assured possession of immortal renown. Dickens said in his frank, hearty manner, that from his childhood he had known the works of Irving; and that before he thought of coming to this country, he had received a letter from him, expressing the delight he felt in reading the story of Little Nell."

Mr. Lanman must permit me again to quote from his very interesting article:—"But the crowning event of the winter in question was the great dinner given to Mr. Dickens by his many admirers at the old City Hotel. I was a mere boy at the time, a Pearl street clerk, but through the kindness of certain friends the honor was granted to me of taking a look from a side door at the august array of gifted authors before they were summoned to the sumptuous table. It was but a mere glimpse that I enjoyed; but while Mr. Irving, as the presiding host, was sacrificing his sensitive nature for the gratification of his friend, and was, by breaking down in his speech of welcome, committing the only failure of his life."

Mr. Felton, in his remarks before the Massachusetts

Historical Society, after Mr. Irving's death, said, "Great and varied as was the genius of Mr. Irving, there was one thing he shrank with a comical terror from attempting, and that was *a dinner speech.*" He anticipated that he should "break down," and had prepared a manuscript speech some twelve to twenty pages long. He got through two or three sentences pretty easily, but in the next hesitated; and, after one or two attempts to go on, gave it up, with a graceful allusion to the tournament, and the troops of Knights all armed and eager for the fray; and ended with the toast, "Charles Dickens, the guest of the evening." In the newspaper reports, this speech occupied a dozen or twenty lines. Mr. Dickens own speech, in reply, was eloquent and modest.

Soon after the New York dinner, business called Mr. Irving to Washington, and Mr. Dickens made his arrangements to be there at the same time. He went on through Philadelphia, where he put up at the old United States Hotel, Chestnut street, part of which was the office of Forney's *Press*, when that paper was established in 1857. He said, in his book, Philadelphia "is a handsome city, but distractingly regular. After walking about for an hour or two, I felt that I would have given the world for a crooked street. The collar of my coat appeared to stiffen and the rim of my hat to expand, beneath its Quakerly influence. My hair shrunk into a sleek, short crop, my hands folded themselves upon my breast of their own calm accord, and thoughts of taking lodgings in Mark Lane, over against the Market-place, and of making a large fortune by speculations in corn, came over me involuntarily." He praised the water works, the hospital, the quiet, quaint old library, named after Franklin, what he saw of our society, and paid particular attention to the Eastern Penitentiary and its system of solitary confinement, which, in company with many other humane persons, he strongly condemned.

Mr. Dickens went to Washington by steamboat and there renewed his intimacy with Washington Irving. "They laughed together," Mr. Lanman says, "at the follies of the politicians, enjoyed the companionship of the great triumvirs—Webster, Calhoun and Clay—and were of course victimized at the President's receptions." On one of these occasions the honors were certainly divided between the two authors; and while we know that Mr. Dickens had no reason to complain of any want of attention on the part of the people, it is pleasant to read his comments upon the conduct of the assembled company toward Mr. Irving. "I sincerely believe," said he in his *American Notes*, "that in all the madness of American politics, few public men would have been so earnestly, devotedly and affectionately caressed as this most charming writer; and I have seldom respected a public assembly more than I did this eager throng when I saw them turning with one mind from noisy orators and officers of state, and flocking with a generous and honest impulse, round the man of quiet pursuits; proud in his promotion as reflecting back upon their country, and grateful to him with their whole hearts for the store of graceful fancies he had poured out among them."

In Washington every attention was paid to Mr. Dickens. The Hon. B. B. French, who resided in that city at the time, kept a careful diary of events, a copy of which has been kindly lent me by H. M. Keim, Esq., of Reading. From this I learn that, in March 10th, 1842, Mr. Dickens visited the House of Representatives with Mr. N. P. Tallmadge, of the Senate. Two days later, he "was in the House" nearly through its session. He was invited to a seat within the bar by some member, and occupied the self-same chair in which Lord Morpeth sat nearly every day while he was in the city. On the following Monday he was entertained with dinner at Boulanger's: Hon. John Quincy Adams and General Van Ness were invited guests. Hon. George M. Keim was president, in the room of the Hon. John Taliaferro, who was expected to preside, but was unavoidably absent from Washington, and Hon. M. St. Clair Clarke and Hon. Aaron Ward were vice presidents. The following persons made the party: Mr. Dickens, Mr. Adams, and General Van Ness as guests; General Keim, Mr. M. St. C. Clarke, General Ward, Messrs. Sumpter, Roosevelt, Irwin, Cushing and Holmes of the House of Representatives; and Messrs. Kingman, F. W. Thomas, (the author,) Bache, Rice, John Tyler, Jr., J. Howard Payne, Frailey, Keller, Dimitry, Major Harrison, Messrs. Samuel P. Walker, Robert N. Johnston, Sutton, H. G. Wheeler, Riggs, and B. B. French. * * Wit, sentiment, song-singing, story-telling, and speech-making occupied the time till eleven, when Mr. Dickens rose, and in the most feelingly beautiful manner possible, bade us, good night. The diarist warmly eulogized the guest, saying, "Dickens, by his modesty, his social powers, and his eloquence, has added to the high esteem in which I was previously induced to hold him. I believe every person present was delighted." Mr. Keim proposed Mr. Dickens's health in the following exalted terms: "Philanthropy and Genius, and a representative of both, now our guest in Washington, whom Washington himself would have rejoiced to welcome." Dickens, in reply said, "that if this were a public dinner, he supposed he would be expected to make a speech; as it was but a social party, surely no such effort would be expected of him; and when he looked about the table, and saw gentlemen whose positions in public life rendered it unavoidable that they should either speak themselves or listen to the speeches of others every day, his refraining upon this occasion must be far more acceptable, and surely possess more novelty than any remarks he might make—and he must be allowed to presume that here, in the enjoyment of a social hour, they will be happy to give their ears some rest, and he should, therefore, consider himself relieved from making a speech. He would, however, say, that like the Prince in the Arabian Tales, he had been doomed, since he arrived in this hospitable country, to make new friendships every night, and cut their heads off on the following morning. But the recollection of this night—wherever he might go—

should accompany him, and like the bright smiles of his better angel, be treasured in his mind as long as memory remains." Among the subsequent toasts were "The health of John Quincy Adams," "The City of Boston," and "The Old Curiosity Shop"—among whose *notions* are the oldest wine, the newest wit, and the best *cradle* in the United States. After the evidence our guest had of the goodness of the two former, we hope and trust they gave him the benefit of the latter. After "The Queen of Great Britain," had been drank standing, Mr. Dickens said: "Allow me to assume the character of Mr. Pickwick, and in that character to give you 'The President of the United States,'" which was also drank standing. By this time the company had apparently reached a period of very pleasurable enjoyment, for, after Mr. Caleb Cushing had responded to "Our Country and our Guest—Both in the first vigor of their youth, and both made great by the might of mind," he proposed "The Health of Mr. Pickwick." At eleven o'clock Mr. Dickens arose and said, "I rise to propose to you one more sentiment; it must be my last; it consists of two words—'Good night!' Since I have been seated at this table I have received the welcome intelligence that the news from the dear ones has come at last—that the long expected letters have arrived. Among them are certain scrawls from little beings across the ocean, of great interest to me, and I thought of them for many days past, in connection with drowned men and a noble ship, broken up and lying in fragments upon the bottom of the ocean.* But they are here, and you will appreciate the anxiety I feel to read them. Permit me, in allusion to some remarks made by a gentleman near me, to say, that every effort of my pen has been intended to elevate the masses of society; to give them the station they deserve among mankind. With that intention I com-

* The Caledonia was driven back to England by tempestuous weather, and fears were entertained that she was lost.

menced writing, and I assure you, as long as I write at all, that shall be the principal motive of my efforts. Gentlemen, since I arrived on your hospitable shore, and in my flight over your land, you have given me everything I can ask but *time*—that you cannot give me, and you are aware that I must devote some of it to myself; therefore, with the assurance that this has been the most pleasant evening I have passed in the United States, I must bid you farewell, [illegible] ce more repeat the words, Good Night!" The [illegible] t to be let off without a parting bumper, on [illegible] lan,

> "Let the toast pass,
> Drink to the lass,
> I'll warrant 'twill prove an excuse for a glass,"

for Mr. St. Clair Clarke proposed "Mrs. Dickens: May her stay amongst us be pleasant; may her return voyage be comfortable, and when she reaches her home, may she find her little ones as healthy as they surely will be happy."

After a short visit to Richmond, Mr. Dickens went to Baltimore, *viâ* Washington, and wrote a hasty note to Irving, hoping he would join him at Baltimore, adding, "What pleasure I have had in seeing and talking with you I will not attempt to say. I shall never forget it as long as I live. What *would* I give if we could have but a quiet week together! Spain is a lazy place, and its climate an indolent one. But if you ever have leisure under its sunny skies to think of a man who loves you, and holds communion with your spirit oftener, perhaps, than any other person alive—leisure from listlessness I mean—and will write to me in London, you will give me an inexpressible amount of pleasure."

Irving *did* meet him at Baltimore. In a letter, (Washington, 5th of February, 1868,) Mr. Dickens thus mentions the fact to Mr. Lanman; "Your reference to my dear friend, Washington Irving, renews the vivid impressions reawakened in my mind at Baltimore but the other day. I saw his fine face for the last time in that city. He came there from New York to pass a day or two with me before I went westward; and they were made among the most memorable of my life by his delightful fancy and genial humor. Some unknown admirer of his books and mine sent to the hotel a most enormous mint-julep, wreathed with flowers. We sat, one on either side of it, with great solemnity (it filled a respectable-sized round table), but the solemnity was of very short duration. It was quite an enchanted julep, and carried us among innumerable people and places that we both knew. The julep held out far into the night, and my memory never saw him afterwards otherwise than as bending over it with his straw with an attempted air of gravity (after some anecdote involving some wonderfully droll and delicate observation of character), and then, as his eye caught mine, melting into that captivating laugh of his, which was the brightest and best I have ever heard."

The enchanted julep was a gift from the proprietor of Guy's Hotel, Baltimore, and, "having held out far into the night," must have been on a magnificent scale, at first—large enough for Gog and Magog, were they alive, to have become mellow upon. George Cruikshank or H. L. Stephens—no inferior artist should dare to attempt it—might win additional fame by sketching the two authors, so much akin in genius and geniality, imbibing the generous, mellifluous fluid from a pitcher which, like the magic purse of Fortunatus, seemed always full!

Dickens—who can doubt it?—would have doubly enjoyed the nectarious julep had he known that, in the masque of "Comus," by John Milton, a good receipt for making it was given, more than two centuries back. The hero, son of Bacchus, is first described as

> Offering to every weary traveller
> His orient liquor in a crystal glass,
> To quench the drouth of Phœbus,

and then offers it to the lady, thus addressing her:

And first, behold this cordial Julep here,
That flames and dances in his crystal bounds,
With spirits of balm and fragrant Syrops mixed:
Not that Nepenthes, which the wife of Thone
In Egypt gave to Jove-born Helena,
Is of such power to stir up joy as this,
To life so friendly, or so cool to thirst.

The identical name, "Julep," is mentioned, then the ingredients—the balm, or *mint*, which gives the flavor; the *spirits;* the "fragrant *syrop,*" so palpably denoting the saccharine element; mixed up in, and imbibed from, a "crystal glass;" and, to crown all, the unmistakable addition of ice, which makes the mixture not only "to life so friendly," but "so *cool* to thirst" that it would actually "quench the drouth of Phœbus." However Milton's tastes may have deteriorated in old age, when he had fallen upon evil days, his early propensities were evidently genial, if not hilarious. At the age of twenty-three, when he wrote the exquisite poem of "L'Allegro," he exclaims,

Haste thee, nymphs, and bring with thee
Jest, *and youthful jollity.*

Even in "Paradise Lost," which is a serious poem, Milton was unable to refrain from an allusion to mixed liquors, for he mentioned in the most express terms, being "bound for the *port of Negus.*"

Mr. Dickens acknowledged the receipt of the Julep, in the following letter, which is carefully and proudly preserved at Guy's, South Seventh street, Philadelphia:

BARNUM'S HOTEL,
Twenty-third March, 1842.

MY DEAR SIR:—I am truly obliged to you for the beautiful and delicious mint-julep you have so kindly sent me. It's quite a mercy that I knew what it was. I have tasted it, but await further proceedings until the arrival of Washington Irving whom I expect to dine with me, *tête-a-tête;*

and who will help me to drink your health. With many thanks to you,

Dear sir,
Faithfully yours,
CHARLES DICKENS.

—— GUY, Esquire.

It is not my intention to follow Mr. Dickens from place to place, but to introduce some illustrations of his journey. The *Louisville Courier-Journal* says that when Mr. Dickens came to that city during his first visit, he stopped at the Galt House, whose landlord, Throckmorton, was a high strung Southerner of much character and influence, the intimate of Clay, Crittenden, and all the worthies. Mr. Dickens had not been stopping there long when Mr. Throckmorton visited him and offered his services in introducing him to the first families in Kentucky. "Sir, are you the publican who keeps this inn?" inquired Mr. Dickens." Yes, sir." "Then, sir, when I have need of your services I will ring for you."

A young lady of Cincinnati, who made a note of it at the time, gives this recollection of his visit to that city: "I went last evening to a party at Judge Walker's, given to the hero of the day, Mr. Charles Dickens, and, with others, had the honor of an introduction to him. M—— had gone to a concert, and we awaited her return, which made us late. When we reached the house, Mr. Dickens had left the crowded rooms, and was in the hall, with his wife, about taking his departure when we entered the door. We were introduced to him in our wrapping, and in the flurry and embarrassment of the meeting one of the party dropped a parcel, containing shoes, gloves, etc. Mr. Dickens, stooping, gathered them up and restored them with a laughing remark, and we bounded up stairs to get our things off. Hastening down again, we found him with Mrs. Dickens, seated upon a sofa, surrounded by a group of ladies, Judge Walker having requested him to delay his departure for a few moments, for the gratification of some tardy friends who had just arrived, ourselves among the number. Declining to re-enter the rooms where he had already taken leave of the guests, he had seated himself in the hall. He is young and handsome, has a mellow, beautiful eye, fine brow, and abundant hair. His mouth is large, and his smile so bright it seemed to shed light and happiness all about him. His manner is easy—negligent—but not elegant. His dress was foppish; in fact, he was over-dressed, yet his garments were worn so easily they appeared to be a necessary part of him. He had a dark coat, with lighter pantaloons; a black waistcoat, embroidered with colored flowers; and about his neck, covering his white shirt-front, was a black neckcloth, also embroidered in colors, in which were placed two large diamond pins connected by a chain; a gold watch-chain, and a large red rose in his button-hole, completed his toilet. Mrs. Dickens is a large woman, having a great deal of color, and is rather coarse; but she has a good face and looks amiable. She seemed to think that Mr. Dickens was the attraction, and was perfectly satisfied to play second, happy in the knowledge that she was his wife. She wore a pink silk dress, trimmed with a white blond flounce, and a pink cord and tassel wound about her head. She spoke but little, yet smiled pleasantly at all that was said. He appeared a little weary, but answered the remarks made to him—for he originated none—in an agreeable manner. Mr. Beard's portrait of Fagin was so placed in the room that we could see it from where we stood surrounding him. One of the ladies asked him if it was his idea of the Jew. He replied, 'Very nearly.' Another, laughingly, requested that he would give her the rose he wore, as a memento. He shook his head and said: 'That will not do; he could not give it to one; the others would be jealous.' A half dozen then insisted on having it, whereupon he proposed to divide the leaves among them. In taking the rose from his coat, either by design or accident, the leaves loosened and fell upon the floor, and amid considerable laughter the ladies stooped and gathered them. He remained some twenty minutes, perhaps, in the hall, then took his leave. I must confess to considerable disappointment in the personal of my idol. I felt that his throne was shaken, although it never could be destroyed."

After disposing of the famous julep, at Baltimore, Mr. Dickens had proceeded westward, reaching Harrisburg partly by railway and, partly, from York, by stage-coach. The mode of conveyance from Harrisburg, at that time, was by canal-boat, and an account of his voyage is given in the "American Notes." I am indebted to my friend Chief Justice Ellis Lewis, of Philadelphia, for an interesting personal reminiscence of a rencontre with Mr. Dickens, which he is so obliging as to permit me to publish:

"In the year 1842, I resided in Williamsport, Lycoming county. I had been at Philadelphia, and on arriving from that city, at Buehler's Hotel, in Harrisburg, I found quite a crowd of people in the house, and surrounding it. The news was circulated that the celebrated Charles Dickens was at the hotel. Some alleged that he had gone to the Capitol to witness the proceedings of the Legislature, then in session. There was a great desire to get a sight of this distinguished man. I confess that my own desire was to get away from the crowd, and to avoid participating in the eager anxiety which our citizens generally display to pay court to distinguished strangers from abroad. Accordingly I went immediately to the packet boat, then lying at the wharf, in the canal, although its time for starting for Williamsport had not arrived by several hours. I found, in the cabin of the boat, my old friend, Samuel R. Wood, a Quaker gentleman of Philadelphia, in company with a lady and gentleman. To these latter, my friend Wood honored me by an introduction. They were Mr. and Mrs. Charles Dickens, who had come on board the packet boat, with the same object which brought me there—to avoid the crowd and the intended display of attention. I need not say that I was much gratified with my new acquaintances.

"One circumstance," the Chief Justice adds, "made a deep impression upon my mind. It happened during our intercourse on board the Canal Packet Boat. I was much pleased with the social and genial disposition of Mr. Dickens, and was impressed with the great difference which appeared to exist, at that early time, in their lives, between the husband and wife. She was good looking, plain and courteous in her manners, but rather taciturn, leaving the burthen of the conversation to fall upon her gifted husband. In the course of conversation I told him that I had a little daughter at home who would be delighted if I could present her with his autograph, written expressly for her. He consented to give it. Our mutual friend, the good Quaker Warden of the Eastern Penitentiary, Samuel R. Wood, immediately bustled about, and prepared a sheet of foolscap, with pen and ink. Mr. Dickens took up the pen, and *commencing very close to the top of the sheet,* wrote:

'Yours faithfully, CHARLES DICKENS.'

Mr. Wood remarked 'Thee begins very close to the top of the sheet.' 'Yes,' said Mr. D., 'if I left a large blank over my name somebody might write a note or a bond over it.' 'Does thee suppose that a Judge of the Court would do such a thing?' said Mr. Wood. Mr. D. replied 'I did not intimate any thing of that kind. The paper might soon pass out of the Judge's possession, and be made use of by others. But I do not suppose that Judges of Courts in America are any better men than the Judges in England.' This autograph was written for my daughter Juliet, and was delivered to her. She is the wife of the Hon. James H. Campbell, formerly member of Congress from Schuylkill and Northumberland counties, recently American Minister to Sweden, and now residing in Philadelphia."

The practice of writing the signature quite close to the top of the paper was begun, I have heard, by Talleyrand.

Mr. Lewis adds, "Twenty-five years afterwards, Mr. Dickens again visited this country, and gave us the benefits of his own readings of many of the sketches and scenes to be found in his works. Our citizens generally called on him to pay their respects. In my feeble state of health, I was unable either to attend any of his readings, or to call on him, in order to pay my great respects to him, and to bear my testimony to his usefulness and the great benefits which, as a writer, he had rendered to the citizens of this country. I therefore sent him my card, with a short note, calling to mind our pleasant trip up the Susquehanna in the canal packet. It will serve to show his kind and genial disposition as well as the strength of his memory, to subjoin his reply to my letter. This I have accordingly done."

Mr. Dickens's letter is as follows:

WESTMINSTER HOTEL, NEW YORK,
Saturday, Eighteenth January, 1868.

MY DEAR SIR:—I have received your kind letter with sincere interest and pleasure, and I beg to thank you for it cordially. The occasion you bring back to my remembrance is as fresh and vivid as though it were of yesterday. Accept from me the accumulated good wishes of five and twenty years, and believe me, my dear sir,

Faithfully Yours,
CHARLES DICKENS.

THE HON. ELLIS LEWIS.

CHAPTER XI.

AMERICAN NOTES FOR GENERAL CIRCULATION.—PICKWICK READINGS AT A WHITE-SMITH'S.—RECEPTION OF THE NOTES IN ENGLAND.—OTHER TOURISTS.—CHANGE FOR THE NOTES.—LORD JEFFREY'S OPINION.—MARTIN CHUZZLEWIT.—CRUSADE AGAINST SELFISHNESS—ENGLISH CRITICISMS.—CHRISTMAS CAROL AND ITS FOLLOWERS.—JOURNEY TO ITALY.

"He fell at Waterloo," was the short and severe criticism of a reviewer upon a poem, which, with his accustomed facility, Scott dashed off, soon after he had visited the arena, on which, on the 18th of June, 1815, the famous and wonderful "Hundred Days" reign of the escaped prisoner of Elba, long the Dictator of Europe, closed his career in a hurricane of tumultuous strife and defeat. Scott hurried over to Belgium, after the great battle, in which the star of Napoleon set. One of the results of that visit, was a hasty poem, "The Field of Waterloo," altogether unworthy of the subject and of his own genius, which, though it sold far better than "Rokeby" or "The Lord of the Isles," was a poor performance—for Scott.

America, it must be confessed, was Dickens's Waterloo. He returned to England in the summer of 1842, and proceeded, with more rapidity than judgment, to write two volumes of "American Notes for General Circulation," which were published by Chapman & Hall, 186 Strand, London, and were in a second edition, in a few weeks, though the price was a guinea, and, besides not having illustrations, which had remarkably given almost tangible reality to his previous works, contained little more than a third of the quantity of letter-press in *Pickwick* or *Nickleby*. These, published in monthly shilling numbers, had been chiefly purchased by the middle and the working classes, but the American tour, at a high price, went almost exclusively into the hands of the "higher" classes. The public at large had to do without it, or hire it, at sixpence or a shilling for two or three days, from the circulating libraries, which had almost coined money by lending *Pickwick* and *Nickleby* at a penny per number for a day's reading. I remember when I lived in Liverpool, having a small job to be done,—the picking of a lock, in default of a lost key—and went to the lodging of a white-smith, as he was called, to engage his skill for a few minutes. I found him reading *Pickwick*, then in course of publication, to an audience of twenty persons, literally men, women, and children, and found that as they could not afford the shilling to purchase each number, out and out, they hired it, month after month, from a circulating library, which let them read it, at the rate of two pence a day. There come up before me, after a lapse of thirty-three years, the ringing merriment of that audience, "few but fitting," their thorough enjoyment of Sam Weller's quaint language, and their ready tears as the white-smith, who read with great judgment and feeling, told them of the death of the poor Chancery prisoner, in the Fleet. There was no such eager audience for the *American Notes*.

The general complaint was that the author told very little that was new about the United States. Some critics declared that the book might have been written, four-fifths of it, without Mr. Dickens having quitted his library in London. At that time, nearly thirty years ago, there had recently been published many books about America. Hamilton, Marryat, and Tyrone Power had been at work, and Frances Trollope, Fanny Kemble, and Harriet Martineau had written on the subject with great spirit and effect, as well as in a satirical and discontented vein. The female writers on America were more or less saucy, but Miss Martineau, attempting to be philosophical as well, was only heavy. Fanny Kemble was severe and flippant, complaining so bitterly of the inconveniences of travel and the deficiencies of toilet appliances at the hotels, that one might have imagined her to have been at least a Countess in her own right, instead of a "stage-actor," whom the chambermaids of the caravanserai might have seen, flashing in her mock jewelry, as tragedy-queen or comedy-heroine, on payment of a shilling at the gallery-door of a play house. Mr. Dickens, coming after her, only echoed what she had said about the mysteries and miseries of the toilette; the want of water, towels, and soap; the horror of narrow and hard beds on board steamers and canal boats; the poor breakfasts and rough dinners; the tobacco-chewing and the spitting, and so on. But what might have annoyed a woman, should have been tolerated by a man, who went travelling, accompanied by his wife, into all sorts of out-of-the-way places. He dedicated his book "to those friends in America who had left his judgment free, and who loving their country, can bear the truth when it is told good humoredly and in a kind spirit."

In fact, however, it was not so much writing his book in a satirical and dissatisfied manner, but writing it at all, which was Mr. Dickens's great mistake. With all his popularity, as a novelist, his readers did not desire to have his views of America and her society, and did not think that he was particularly qualified or called upon to present them. He would have done better if he had not written a page about America. He had fallen into the habit of looking at every thing from burlesque and grotesque points of view, like the familiar diner-out, who never allows anything to be said or done without trying to make a pun upon it. Some of his facetious passages are very good, but when he tried to be didactic and philosophical, he rarely succeeded. His remarks upon the legislature in Washington were coarse and even scurrilous;—what would *he* have said had an eminent American man of letters, say Washington Irving, have used language only half so disparaging of the British Lords and

Commons? His declaration against slavery, though he never went farther south than Virginia, was fearless and direct. His instincts as a freeman were very strong against a system which, let us all, whether of North or South, thank God is now forever ended. There are many odds and ends of description scattered throughout the "American Notes," which are in the author's best manner. It was received, in America, with a hurricane of disapprobation. Mr. Dickens was reminded, not quite fairly, that his was not a mere reception but a great ovation in the country he had "handled without gloves," and was told that he was therefore ungrateful as well as unjust. A reply, entitled "Change for American Notes," was hurried through the press, but it was feebly written, besides being illustrated, not embellished, by several portraits, apparently engraved in the infancy of the art. This had few readers in England, and has long and deservedly been forgotten. It was a memorable instance of zeal acting without discretion.

When Mr. Dickens re-published his book in 1850, in his People's edition, he did not withdraw a word of it. "Prejudiced, I am not," he said, "otherwise than in favor of the United States." In 1868, when he saw the country, after twenty-five years, during which it had worked out "a problem of the highest importance to the whole human race," be candidly confessed that he had originally taken an incorrect impression of it. His ample retractation may be said to have closed the account between the Americans and himself, leaving a handsome balance in his favor.

The English critics did not think favorably of the "American Notes," and maliciously said that Mr. Dickens appeared to have availed himself of a hint given by Mr. Weller senior, in *Pickwick*, to "have a passage ready taken for 'Merriker; and then let him come back and write a book about the 'Merrikins, as 'll pay all his expenses and more, if he blows 'em up enough." Mr. Dickens *did* accomplish one part of this prediction, for Lord Jeffrey speaks of a sale of

3000 copies, and author's profit of £1,000 within the first few months. Lord Jeffrey, on his first perusal, complimented him highly, saying, "You *have* been very tender to our sensitive friends beyond sea, and really said nothing which should give any serious offence to any moderately rational patriot among them," and declared that "the world has never yet seen a more faithful, graphic, amusing, kind-hearted narrative than you have now bestowed upon it." But later, in December 1843, when praising the *Christmas Carol*, he adds "is not this better than caricaturing American knaveries?"

To recover the prestige thus jeopardized, rather than lost, a new serial work was begun in 1843. This was *The Life and Adventures of Martin Chuzzlewit*, dedicated to Miss Burdett Coutts. As usual, this tale had a deliberate purpose underlying the adventures. The object was to expose the vice of Selfishness in various forms, and, in some instances, to exhibit its vices. In the Preface to the first edition, the author said:

> I set out, on this journey which is now concluded, with the design of exhibiting, in various aspects, the commonest of all the vices. It is almost needless to add, that the commoner the folly or the crime which an author endeavors to illustrate, the greater is the risk he runs of being charged with exaggeration; for, as no man ever yet recognized an imitation of himself, no man will admit the correctness of a sketch in which his own character is delineated, however faithfully.

Young Martin Chuzzlewit, the hero, is one of the most masterly and best sustained characters ever created by Dickens. He has many good qualities, is strong in love and friendship, is not devoid of generosity, but so intensely selfish that his sacrifices are not for love or friendship, but solely to contribute to his own comfort. Mark Tapley, who has a large share in working out this young gentleman's cure, though not without passing him through the ordeal of poverty and suffering, may be considered as his moral antipode. Mr. Pecksniff, with his children, represents falsity and pretence, hypocrisy and humbug. Directly opposed to Pecksniff is inimitable Tom Pinch, who appears as if he had been born chiefly for the purpose of being imposed upon, but comes out, at the close, rewarded and happy. His secret passion for his friend's sweetheart is most delicately developed, without being made too prominent. The Chuzzlewit family, at large, are clearly drawn and forcibly distinguished. Ruth Pinch, the little governess, who is finally converted into Mrs. John Westlock, is a "pure and perfect chrysolite," whom a monarch might have worn, proudly and gladly, next his very heart of heart. We must admit that Jonas Chuzzlewit, the chief villain of the tale, is equal, in his way to Sikes, Sir Mulberry Hawk, or Quilp, but the darker scenes in which he figures are rather obscure and involved. He believes that he has poisoned his father—which he did not. He murders Montague Tigg, who has the secret of his presumed guilt—thus committing a real crime to conceal an imaginary one. But the whole description of that fatal deed, from the commencement of the ill-omened journey in the post-chaise to his return home, with detection and suicide, is as powerful as anything written by this great master, or by any other hand. Mrs. Lupin, Mark Tapley, and young Bailey, are finely drawn, and Mrs. Todgers, who kept a boarding-house, and had a tender heart withal, could not be dispensed with. As for Sairey Gamp and Betsey Prig, to say nothing of that celebrated myth, Mrs. Harris, they have become household words. *Chuzzlewit*, dramatized under Mr. Dickens's own supervision, was played at the Lyceum Theatre, in the season of 1844, the part of the Nurse by Mr. Robert Keeley, and was very successful.

It was declared by some of the writers, that *Chuzzlewit* was inferior in style to the preceding tales. There were such expressions as "It had not been painted or papered, hadn't

Todger's, past memory of man;" "She was the most artless creature, was the youngest Miss Pecksniff;" "Nature played them off against each other; *they* had no hand in it, the two Miss Pecksniffs;" and so on. Mr. Dickens spoke of *impracticable* nightcaps, *impossible* tables and *exploded* chests of drawers, *mad* closets, *inscrutable* harpsichords, *undeniable* chins, *highly geological* home-made cakes, *remote suggestions* of tobacco lingering within a spittoon, and the *recesses* and *vacations* of a tooth-pick. Then it was complained that there was too much of the drunken humors of Jonas, and Chevy Slime, and Pecksniff, and Mrs. Gamp, and Mrs. Prig. It was noticed, but scarcely complained of, that when some of the characters had nothing else to do they indulged in kissing, such as Martin kissing Mary in the park; Mark kissing Mrs. Lupin, *ad libitum*, on the night of his return to the Blue Dragon; Pecksniff kissing Mary; Martin kissing Mary in Pecksniff's parlor; John Westlock kissing Ruth; Martin kissing Mary the third time, and so on.

When the author reviewed, or at least re-read, this book for the People's edition, he added these sentences to the Preface:

In all the tales comprised in this cheap series, and in all my writings, I hope I have taken every possible opportunity of showing the want of sanitary improvements in the neglected dwellings of the poor. Mrs. Sarah Gamp is a representation of the hired attendant on the poor in sickness. The hospitals of London are, in many respects, noble Institutions; in others, very defective. I think it not the least among the instances of their mismanagement, that Mrs. Betsy Prig is a fair specimen of a Hospital Nurse; and that the hospitals, with their means and funds, should have left it to private humanity and enterprise, in the year Eighteen Hundred and Forty-nine, to enter on an attempt to improve that class of persons.

One portion of *Chuzzlewit* gave great pain to most of its home, and raised great anger among many of its foreign readers. Without any very clear or ostensible purpose, Mr. Dickens brought his hero, with Mark Tapley as a squire, over to the United States, where, in the guise of a fictitious narrative, he repeated a good deal of what had been considered unfair and prejudiced in the *American Notes.* It is right that his own explanation, as originally published in 1850, and again in 1867, should here be given;

The American portion of this book is in no other respect a caricature than as it is an exhibition, for the most part, of the ludicrous side of the American character—of that side which is, from its very nature, the most obtrusive, and the most likely to be seen by such travellers as Young Martin and Mark Tapley. As I have never, in writing fiction, had any disposition to soften what is ridiculous or wrong at home, I hope (and believe) that the good-humored people of the United States are not generally disposed to quarrel with me for carrying the same usage abroad. But I have been given to understand, by some authorities, that there are American scenes in these pages which are violent exaggerations; and that the Watertoast Association and eloquence, for example, are beyond all bounds of belief. Now, I wish to record the fact that all that portion of Martin Chuzzlewit's American experiences is a literal paraphrase of some reports of public proceedings in the United States (especially of the proceedings of a certain Brandywine Association), which were printed in the *Times* newspaper in June and July, 1843—at about the time when I was engaged in writing those parts of the book. There were at that period, on the part of a frothy Young American party, demonstrations making of "sympathy" towards Ireland and hostility towards England, in which such outrageous absurdities ran rampant, that, having the occasion ready to my hand, I ridiculed them. And this I did, not in any animosity towards America, but just as I should have done the same thing, if the same opportunity had arisen in reference to London, or Dublin, or Paris, or Devonshire.

Miss Mitford, writing to that Irish friend to whom she had introduced Mr. Pickwick some years before, said: "I like Dickens's Christmas Carol, too, very much—not the ghostly part, of course, which is very bad; but the scenes of the clerk's family are very fine and touching." That story had been published in December, 1843, in a five shilling 16mo. volume, with a few illustrations, designed by John Leech, engraved on steel and colored. Its full title was "A Christmas Carol: In Prose. Being a Ghost Story of Christmas." Its success was immense. Once again, the great author had struck into a new vein of greatest value. Lord Jeffrey was in raptures over the new story. He wrote, "we are all charmed with your Carol, chiefly, I think, for the genuine *goodness* which breathes all through it, and is the true inspiring angel by which its genius has been awakened. The whole scene of the Cratchetts is like the dream of a beneficent angel in spite of its broad reality—and little *Tiny Tim*, in life and death almost as sweet and as touching as Nelly. And then the schoolboy scene, with that large-hearted, delicate sister, with his gall-lacking liver and milk of human-kindness for blood, and yet all so natural and so humbly and serenely happy." There were other Christmas stories, one in each of four succeeding years, but none of them were so much liked as the first. These are "The Chimes: A Goblin Story of some Bells that rang an Old Year out and a New Year in," which Jeffrey praised, though he "did not care about your twaddling Alderman [Cute] and his twaddling friends;" "The Cricket on the Hearth: A Fairy Tale of Home," which has been repeatedly dramatized, in England and America; "The Battle of Life: a Love Story;" and "The Haunted Man, and the Ghost's Bargain." Of these, only the first and third had very great success. The Cratchett Family alone would have saved any story, and little "Dot," in the other tale, contained all the elements of popularity.

In fact, the supernatural, which forms the woof of these tales, was not well managed—may have been unmanageable. Mr. Dickens thought otherwise, for he persevered in its use for several years. His own statement is:

The narrow space within which it was necessary to confine these Christmas stories when they were originally published, rendered their construction a matter of some difficulty, and almost necessitated what is peculiar in their machinery. I never attempted great elaboration of detail in the working out of characters within such limits, believing that it would not succeed. My purpose was, in a whimsical kind of masque which the good-humor of the season justified, to awaken some loving and fostering thought, never out of season in a Christian land.

Of *The Christmas Carol* there was a highly eulogistic review in *The Times*, which said, "we confess that the beauty of this 'ghost story,' and the freshness that pervaded it, took us by surprise. The spirit of the writer had manifestly grown more elastic, relieved from the pressure of former labors. His heart had helped him to work out an idea naturally suggested—it may be during a morning's walk,—not painfully and artificially forged at the author's furnace. The *Carol* was a short tale 'of the affections,' simple and truthful as one of Wordsworth's poems." The same critic was severe upon *The Chimes*, on the ground that its tendency was mischievous. It said, "it may be a painful task to pronounce a verdict of condemnation upon the labors of one who, in his time, has afforded the public very much amusement; but it is also a necessary task to warn the public of the faults and errors of a teacher universally listened to—of a writer whom popularity has invested with the qualities of a model and a guide. It is the literary tendency of the present age to write *downwards* rather than *upwards*—to adapt art to the calibre of the lowest capacities, rather than to elevate the intellect by accustoming it to nervous, healthy exercise. The class of books which formed the recreation of the leisure hours of our fathers—the light reading of their time—is to-day the mind's sole occupation. Our lightest reading is the solidest; the amusement of the mind is its business; ethics are taught by illustration and caricature; knowledge is conveyed in a joke; conversation is carried on in slang; the drama undertakes to purify the heart and understanding by burlesque, whilst the modern epic positively refuses every hero that is not drawn from the purlieus of the workhouse or the prison. Unrivalled as is the power possessed by Mr. Dickens of delineating the characters and imitating the language of the humblest section of humble life, it cannot be denied by his warmest admirers that the direction given to public taste, and the unhealthy character of our current literature, are mainly owing to a vicious though brilliant example, rewarded with extreme success, and sustained by morbid appetite." Above all, the repetition of the fairy machinery was objected to, because of "the lamentable result that attends all the repetitions of the writer. That which was at first easy and to the purpose became monstrous, overcharged, and out of place." The reviewer hit the chief blot in the story thus:

This amiable gentleman [Tackleton] fascinated the blind daughter of his journeyman [Caleb Plummer] and almost breaks her heart by courting somebody else. The journeyman is an extraordinary fellow in his way, and has brought up his child to think Tackleton a saint, and the den in which they live a palace. So, Mr. Dickens, are not the blind misled! Exquisite are the spared senses, mercifully strengthened by Providence to make amends for the one tremendous deprivation. The *fingers* of the blind read the Bible; the *ears* of the blind,—the figure is a bold one—see the friendly visitor long before you or I, even whilst his foot is lingering at the threshold. Would you have us believe that touch, feeling, hearing, remained for twenty years torpid and dead in the sensitive creature whom you have spoiled by your perversion? We tell you, and not without good warrant for the assertion, that no man living, journeyman or master, has power to stop up the avenues through which knowledge rushes to the soul of a poor innocent deprived of sight. Bertha, by your own account, had mixed in the world; she talked wisely and even profoundly on abstruse matters; she worked with her father; she knew every toy in the room, and where to seek it, and how to make it; she was in daily intercourse with those who knew the character of Tackleton and who spoke of him with freedom. And yet you ask us to believe that this young lass, all feeling and perception, never knew "that walls were blotched and bare of plaster here and there; that iron was rusting, wood rotting, paper peeling off; that sorrow and faint-heartedness were in the house; that they had a master cold, exacting and interested." If we believe you, it must be when Nature proves a liar.

In 1844, on the completion of *Martin Chuzzlewit*, Mr. Dickens, with his wife and children, two boys and two girls, proceeded to Italy, where they resided for a year. I shall take advantage of their voluntary exile, to mention a few facts concerning the illustrations to Mr. Dickens's works, and the artists who executed them.

CHAPTER XII.

RELATIONS WITH ARTISTS.—GEORGE CRUIKSHANK.—TOM AND JERRY.—HOW OLIVER TWIST WAS BROUGHT TO LONDON.—RE-PURCHASING COPYRIGHTS.—ROBERT SEYMOUR'S SKETCHES.—SUCCEEDED BY "PHIZ."—THE AUTHOR'S LAST HISTORY OF PICKWICK.—THE PALAZZO PESCHIERE IN GENOA.—KIND DEALINGS WITH AN ARTIST.—UNPUBLISHED LETTER FROM CHARLES DICKENS.

THE relations, personal as well as professional, between Charles Dickens and leading artists, were always of the most satisfactory nature. He went into general society, rather as a duty to his family and position, but his heart was with such artists, authors, and actors as were well known to and highly regarded by him.

Mr. Dickens was fortunate, at the beginning of his career, in the aid of such an artist as George Cruikshank, who designed and etched thirty-nine characteristic illustrations for the *Sketches by "Boz,"* published in 1835–6, in three volumes. Cruikshank, who is now nearly eighty years old, was about forty-three when he met Dickens, and, as an illustrator of books, was in such request that he not only obtained his own prices, but was compelled, at times, to refuse commissions. He had obtained celebrity before Dickens was born, for I have a colored caricature, from his *burin*, published in *The Scourge*, as early as the year 1808. He had an elder brother, Robert Isaac Cruikshank, who had some ability, but was a far inferior artist,—his style in fact, much resembling that of Robert Seymour, whom we shall presently meet. In 1820–1, during the trial of Queen Caroline, George Cruikshank worked with remarkable cleverness, fancy, and facility on the popular side. Such productions as "The Queen's Matrimonial Ladder," "The Queen that Jack Found," and similar squibs, were largely sold then and now are "worth their weight in gold." He was the artist, too, of Pierce Egan's "Life in London," a worthless book, full of slang and coarseness, in which were related the adventures, sprees, and varied dissipations of a brace of bucks, called Tom and Jerry, who undertook to show "life" (as they called it) to a greenhorn rejoicing in the pastoral surname of Hawthorne. There was a certain Corinthian Kate who participated in their adventures. The work, very badly written, came out in numbers, and had surprising popularity. Men and women actually dressed *after* the characters, and when the chapters were adapted to the stage, the fortune of the manager of the theatre was made in the single season of their remarkable success. Mr. Thackeray, in whose youth "Tom and Jerry" had appeared, has repeatedly referred to it in his writings.

Cruikshank, who flourishes, in a green old age, and is one of the leaders of the Temperance movement in London, was by no means a caricaturist, though he has been classed with Gilray, Bunbury, and Rowlandson. "My Sketch Book," "Points of Humor," and "Illustrations of Phrenology" were noticed with the highest praise and *in extenso*, by

Christopher North, in *Blackwood's Magazine*, and, not long before the appearance of Mr. Dickens among that "noble army of martyrs," the authors by profession, Cruikshank had designed and engraved a series of illustrations of Fielding, Smollet, and Goldsmith, in Roscoe's Novelist's Library, which gave him the highest position as what may be called a book-artist. From his boyish days, Cruikshank had been familiar with all the varieties and phases of middle life and low life in London. It was said of him that you could not name a lane or alley in the Modern Babylon, the locality of which he could not instantly describe. He was the true "guide, philosopher, and friend" for Charles Dickens, and both were the very men to produce, with pen and pencil, the "Sketches of English Life and Character," which bore the now familiar *nom de plume* of "Boz" upon the title-page.

Pickwick, which followed the *Sketches*, was not illustrated by Cruikshank, from causes to be presently stated, but while it was yet in course of serial publication, its author having become editor of *Bentley's Miscellany*, his arrangement was that Cruikshank should illustrate *Oliver Twist*, the new story which he begun in February, 1837, in that magazine. Accordingly, (also supplying a couple of engravings for Mayor Tulrumble and the Mudfog Association, which Mr. Dickens published in *Bentley**) he executed designs for *Oliver Twist*, and very effective they are. At this place properly may be introduced a curious bit of literary history.

The seventh chapter of *Oliver Twist* ends with the flight of the parish boy, from the dwelling of Mr. Sowerberry, the undertaker, and that terrible beadle, Mr. Bumble, and his

---

* The "Personal Adventures of Mr. Tulrumble," never re-published by Mr. Dickens, may be found in Petersons' editions of the *Sketches*, and "The Proceedings of the Mudfog Association" are in the present volume, not having been previously reprinted in England or America

bidding farewell to his poor little friend Dick, the parochial orphan, to whom he says, "I am running away. They beat and ill-use me, Dick; and I am going to seek my fortune some long way off, I don't know where." At the opening of the eighth chapter, however, Oliver is on his way to London; and before its close he is an inmate of Fagin the Jew, and companion of that free-and-easy young gentleman, Mr. John Dawkins (commonly known as the "Artful Dodger"), and a few other choice but youthful aspirants of the same school. When the *Quarterly Review* criticised the book, it said that Mr. Dickens had made a great mistake in not keeping Oliver Twist in the country, instead of taking him to the thieves' haunts in London, which had been described over and over again.

I have been informed that Dickens originally intended to carry out the promise of his title (*Oliver Twist; or The Parish Boy's Progress*) and to trace the life, struggles and successes of what Miss Braddon calls "a clod,"—to locate him in Kent, the county best beloved by himself, at all times, and to introduce hop-picking, and other picturesque ruralties. He changed his purpose, as we all know, and brought him to London. George Cruikshank told me how this was done.

In London, I was intimate with the brothers Cruikshank, Robert and George, but more particularly with the latter. In 1847, having called upon him one day at his house (it then was in Mydleton Terrace, Pentonville), I had to wait while he was finishing an etching for which a printer's boy was waiting. To wile away the time, I gladly complied with his suggestion that I should look over a portfolio crowded with etchings, proofs, and drawings, which lay upon the sofa. Among these, carelessly tied together in a wrap of brown paper, was a series of some twenty-five to thirty drawings, very carefully finished, through most of which were carried the now well-known portraits of Fagin, Bill Sikes and his dog, Nancy, the Artful Dodger, and Master

Charles Bates—all well known to the readers of *Oliver Twist*—and many others who were not introduced. There was no mistake about it, and when Cruikshank turned round, his work finished, I said as much. He told me that it had long been in his mind to show the life of a London thief by a series of drawings, engraved by himself, in which, without a single line of letter-press, the story would be strikingly and clearly told. "Dickens," he continued, "dropped in here one day just as you have done, and, while waiting until I could speak with him, took up that identical portfolio and ferreted out that bundle of drawings. When he came to that one which represents Fagin in the Condemned Cell, he silently studied it for half an hour, and told me that he was tempted to change the whole plot of his story; not to carry Oliver Twist through adventures in the country, but to take him up into the thieves' den in London, show what their life was, and bring Oliver safely through it without sin or shame. I consented to let him write up to as many of the designs as he thought would suit his purpose; and that was the way in which Fagin, Sikes, and Nancy were created. My drawings suggested them, rather than his strong individuality suggested my drawings."

It has been stated by Mr. Mayhew, that when Cruikshank was designing Fagin in the Condemned Cell, he made various attempts to produce the required effect of terror, hatred, and despair, but did not succeed, until, one morning, as he was sitting up in bed, gnawing his nails, as he used to do when he found himself at a nonplus, he caught a view of his own face reflected in a pier-glass opposite, and, jumping out of bed, on the moment, went to work on his sketch. He had got the position and the expression he wanted.

Before quitting *Oliver Twist,* I may mention that when Bulwer wished to purchase the interest his publisher had in two of his novels, ("Eugene Aram" and "Paul Clifford," I believe,) the question was referred to arbitration, and he had to pay £750. In the same time, and for the same purpose, Mr. Dickens purchased Mr. Bentley's share in *Oliver Twist.* This work had prosperously launched *Bentley's Miscellany* on the popular tide, and, republished in the usual three-volume edition, had sold very largely. By mutual consent, Mr. John Forster was appointed co-valuer, with Mr. William Jerdan of the *Literary Gazette,* to ascertain what Mr. Bentley's interest in the said *Oliver Twist* was worth, and they fixed the amount at £2,250, which Mr. Dickens handed over to Mr. Bentley, receiving for that large sum, a written surrender of copyright interest, and the steel plates on which George Cruikshank had etched his admirable illustrations. In both of these cases, the authors had to *pay.* In 1818, however, the case was reversed. Walter Scott obtained £12,000 for his copyright in seven of the Waverley Novels, and his share in the copyright of some of his poems. Constable, the publisher, was the person who agreed to pay this large sum, for which he gave bonds. But, in 1826, when Constable failed, the *whole* amount of these bonds not having been paid to Scott, his entire interest in the copyright reverted to him—rather according to *law* than *justice,* for he had received a large portion of the money.

Leaving George Cruikshank, we now come to another artist who, under the *sobriquet* of "Phiz" was longer and later associated with Mr. Dickens. A correspondent of the *N. Y. Tribune,* whose general accuracy I have to acknowledge, gives the following detailed account of the beginning of Mr. Dickens's long connection with Chapman & Hall, the publishers, at whose suggestion, as I have mentioned in a preceding chapter, he undertook to write the *Pickwick Papers.* It is as follows:

Early in the year 1836, Messrs. Chapman & Hall, who a few years previously were both engaged in the once famous publishing-house of Baldwin & Cradock, were established as booksellers and publishers in the Strand, London; and among their literary ventures then in preparation was a magazine to be illustrated and sold for one shilling, and to be called *The Library of Fiction.* It was to be filled with short stories and sketches by the popular authors of the day, and was under the editorial charge of Mr. Charles Whitehead, a *littérateur* of the period. In making a selection of authors who were to be requested to contribute to the work, Mr. Chapman called Mr. Whitehead's attention to the "Sketches" then being published under the signature of "Boz" in *The Monthly Magazine* and in *The Morning Chronicle,* and desired that he should be applied to for contributions. "His name is Dickens, and I know where to find him," was the editor's reply. Mr. Dickens acceded to the request, and contributed to the new serial "The Tuggs at Ramsgate," with which the initial number opened, and which was eventually contained in the collected edition of "Sketches by Boz," published by the same house. Such was Mr. Dickens's first engagement to write for the publishers with whom he was afterwards so closely connected.

Shortly before this time Mr. Seymour, whose humorous etchings of cockney life and character were then very popular, had partly arranged with Messrs Chapman & Hall for the publication of a new series of etchings of a like nature, to be accompanied by illustrative letter-press, and issued in monthly numbers at one shilling; and in view of the publication, an author of the day, whose name is known to the writer, was written to and requested to undertake the literary department of the work, but he never replied to the application. When *The Library of Fiction* was under way, Seymour called upon the publishers, and urged that his proposed work should be proceeded with at once, or if not he should be compelled to engage upon other labors he had offered to him, but which he did not so much fancy. Mr. Chapman told Seymour that as he had no reply from the author referred to, he would at once call upon Dickens, and ascertain if he would be willing to write the descriptive letter-press. He fulfilled his mission, and was gratified to find that the young author entered enthusiastically into the scheme, suggesting a modification of the plan, and promised to let him have the copy for a prospectus of the work on the following day, which promise he fulfilled. This is the visit alluded to by Mr. Dickens in his preface.

Many works had just then been issued with either the name of the author appearing on the title-page under the guise of editor, or, when they were from the pens of unknown writers, under the editorial sponsorship of well-known authors, and it was decided that the new book should follow in the wake, and it consequently appeared as "edited by Boz." The title was written out by Mr. Chapman, and was scarcely altered except in the leading word, that of "Nimrod" having, as Mr. Dickens asserts, been first proposed. A better name was soon found.

Robert Seymour was much inferior, in imagination, humor, and execution, to George Cruikshank and others. His etchings on copper or steel were coarse when not scratchy, and, for the most part, he drew his designs on stone, for the lithographer. His best productions were in the sporting line; burlesques, in which cockney sportsmen made ludicrous blunders. I remember an exception to this, which appeared long before *Pickwick*, and had great success. It was a series of designs, published monthly, in shilling duodecimo parts, with the title of "New Readings of Old Authors." They were roughly drawn and carelessly lithographed, but some of them exhibited genuine humor.

When Seymour began drawing for the *Pickwick Papers*, he was in feeble health, the result of general poverty and irregular habits; he was fond of his wife and children, but could not resist the temptation of drink. For *Pickwick*, he supplied only four engravings in all. These are: 1. Mr. Pickwick addressing the Club, in which the old gentleman, supported by Tupman, Winkle, and Snodgrass, stands upon a Windsor chair, with one hand covered by his coat-tails, while he anathemizes unfortunate Mr. Blotton—his opponent. 2. Mr. Pickwick and the pugnacious Cabman. 3. The sagacious dog, who, seeing a notice that "The gamekeeper had orders to shoot dogs found in this enclosure," turns tail, and refuses to follow a cockney sparrow-shooter into a field—this is in Seymour's best style. 4. The Dying Clown, which is a poor performance, in all respects.

Unfortunately, Mr. Seymour died by his own hand, just

at the time when it appeared as if better days were at hand. Mr Thackerary has told how, then striving to live rather by his pencil than pen, he had called on Mr. Dickens at Furnival's Inn, and, soliciting employment as artist to *Pickwick*, showed some sketches which did *not* get him the appointment. The artist who did was Mr. Hablot Knight Browne, some three years younger than Mr. Dickens, and like him, living at the time *en garçon*, "in chambers" at Furnival's Inn. He was known to Mr. Dickens, having illustrated his little work on Sunday in London, of which I have given some account in an earlier chapter. His pseudonym was "Phiz," which he retains. His first illustration in *Pickwick* was Dr. Slammer's defiance of Jingle. He illustrated most of Dickens's serial stories, issued within the familiar green covers. Author and artist suited each other exactly.

In March, 1866, Mr. Dickens was compelled, as it were, to publish a detailed account of Mr. Seymour's connection with *Pickwick*. There had been published, an edition of "Seymour's Sketches," with a memoir by Mr. Bohn. Mr. Seymour's son wrote a long letter to the *Athenæum* declaring that these were not printed from the original plates, but were imitations. He adds:

As regards "Pickwick," it is true that the original plan was to give the adventures of a club of cockney sportsmen, and the idea and title of the work was my father's, who had so far matured his plan as to show it to Mr. McLean, and afterwards to Mr. Spooner, who had some idea of publishing it, and proposed that Theodore Hook should write the letter-press. We have reason to infer, from an entry in the artist's book, that the first four plates were etched before he showed the work, and that they were afterwards re-etched, and modified, in some degree, to suit Mr. Dickens's views—which circumstance may account for the style of his letter to my father, written just after the first number appeared, where he seems to claim a share of merit in originating the design:

"15, FURNIVAL'S INN.

"MY DEAR SIR,—I had intended to write you, to say how much gratified I feel by the pains you have bestowed on our mutual friend, Mr. Pickwick, and how much to the result of your labors has surpassed my expectations. I am happy to be able to congratulate you, the publishers, and myself on the success of the undertaking, which appears to have been most complete.—Dear Sir, very truly yours,

CHARLES DICKENS."

Mr. Seymour promised, in a future letter, an account of the origin of the "Pickwick Papers." This drew the following from Mr. Dickens, also published in the *Athenæum.*

GAD'S HILL PLACE, *March* 28, 1866.

As the author of the "Pickwick Papers" (and of one or two other books), I send you a few facts, and no comments, having reference to a letter signed "R. Seymour," which in your editorial discretion you published last week.

Mr. Seymour the artist never originated, suggested, or in any way had to do with, save as illustrator of what I devised, an incident, a character (except the sporting tastes of Mr. Winkle), a name, a phrase, or a word, to be found in the "Pickwick Papers."

I never saw Mr. Seymour's handwriting, I believe, in my life.

I never even saw Mr. Seymour but once in my life, and that was within eight-and-forty hours of his untimely death. Two persons, both still living, were present on that short occasion.

Mr. Seymour died when only the first twenty-four printed pages of the "Pickwick Papers" were published; I think before the next twenty-four pages were completely written; I am sure before one subsequent line of the book was invented.

Here Mr. Dickens quoted, from the Preface to the cheap edition of the *Pickwick Papers*, published in October, 1847, that account of the origin of that work, which has already been given (pp. 63–64) in the present volume. He concludes thus:

In July, 1849, some incoherent assertions made by the

widow of Mr. Seymour, in the course of certain endeavors of hers to raise money, induced me to address a letter to Mr. Edward Chapman, then the only surviving business partner in the original firm of Chapman & Hall, who first published the "Pickwick Papers," requesting him to inform me in writing whether the foregoing statement was correct.

In Mr. Chapman's confirmatory answer, immediately written, he reminded me that I had given Mr. Seymour more credit than was his due. "As this letter is to be historical," he wrote, "I may as well claim what little belongs to me in the matter, and that is, the figure of Pickwick. Seymour's first sketch," made from the proof of my first chapter, "was of a long, thin man. The present immortal one was made from my description of a friend of mine at Richmond."

CHARLES DICKENS.

There were subsequent letters from Mr. H. G. Bohn and Mr. R. Seymour (who is a music master, not an artist), but the above closed the question, as far as Mr. Dickens was concerned.

On looking through the works of Mr. Dickens, I find that George Cruikshank illustrated the *Sketches by 'Boz;' Oliver Twist;* and the *Life of Joseph Grimaldi;* that H. K. Browne, as 'Phiz' exclusively illustrated the *Pickwick Papers, Nicholas Nickleby, Martin Chuzzlewit, Dombey and Son, The History of David Copperfield, Bleak House*, and *Little Dorrit;* that Marcus Stone illustrated *Great Expectations, A Tale of Two Cities, Pictures from Italy*, and *American Notes;* that J. Walker illustrated *Hard Times* and *Reprinted Pieces;* that H. K. Browne and George Cattermole were the artists of the *Old Curiosity Shop*, (Daniel Maclise contributing the sketch of Little Nell and the Sexton,) and *Barnaby Rudge;* and that the *Christmas Carol* and four other stories of that series, were illustrated by John Leech, Daniel Maclise, Clarkson Stanfield, and Sir Edwin Landseer. "The Mystery of Edwin Drood" is illustrated by a new artist, Mr. S. L. Fildes, to whom Mr. Dickens was attracted by a picture of his in an exhibition. In addition, as already stated, Maclise painted the portrait, a line engraving of which was the frontispiece to *Nicholas Nickleby*, when completed as a volume in 1840.

This chapter, exclusively relating to artists, may close with an instance of Mr. Dickens's kind consideration for one, with whom he was not personally acquainted. In the autumn of 1847, a friend of mine, who had spent several years in Italy, engaged in the study and practice of his art as a painter, showed me several views which he had taken of the Villa, in Genoa, where Dickens had resided in 1844-5, and which he has described so brilliantly and effectively in his *Pictures from Italy*. This was a superb residence—the Palazzo Peschiere, within the city, which he has spoken of in this glowing language, a picture in words:

There is not in Italy, they say (and I believe them), a lovelier residence than the Palazzo Peschiere, or Palace of the Fish-ponds, whither we removed as soon as our three months' tenancy of the Pink Jail at Albaro had ceased and determined.

It stands on a height within the walls of Genoa, but aloof from the town; surrounded by beautiful gardens of its own, adorned with statues, vases, fountains, marble basins, terraces, walks of orange trees and lemon trees, groves of roses and camelias. All its apartments are beautiful in their proportions and decorations; but the great hall, some fifty feet in height, with three large windows at the end, overlooking the whole town of Genoa, the harbor and the neighboring sea, affords one of the most fascinating and delightful prospects in the world. Any house more cheerful and habitable than the great rooms are, within, it would be difficult to conceive; and certainly nothing more delicious than the scene without, in sunshine or in moonlight, could be imagined. It is more like an enchanted palace in an Eastern story than a grave and sober lodging.

How you may wander on, from room to room, and never tire of the wild fancies on the walls and ceilings, as bright in their fresh coloring as if they had been painted but yesterday; or how one floor, or even the great hall which opens on eight other rooms, is a spacious promenade; or how there are corridors and bed-chambers above which we never use and rarely visit, and scarcely know the way through; or how there is a view of a perfectly different character on each of the four sides of the building; matters little. But that prospect from the hall is like a vision to me. I go back to it in fancy, as I have done in calm reality a hundred times a day; and stand there, looking out, with the sweet scents from the garden rising up about me, ina perfect dream of happiness.

There lies all Genoa, in beautiful confusion, with its many churches, monasteries and convents, pointing up into the sunny sky; and down below me, just where the roofs begin, a solitary convent parapet, fashioned like a gallery, with an iron cross at the end, where sometimes, early in the morning, I have seen a little group of dark-veiled nuns gliding sorrowfully to and fro, and stopping now and then to peep down upon the waking world in which they have no part. Old Monte Faccio, brightest of hills in good weather, but sulkiest when storms are coming on, is here, upon the left. The Fort within the walls (the good King built it to command the town, and beat the houses of the Genoese about their ears, in case they should be discontented) commands that height upon the right. The broad sea lies beyond, in front there; and that line of coast, beginning by the lighthouse, and tapering away, a mere speck in the rosy distance, is the beautiful coast road that leads to Nice. The garden near at hand, among the roofs and houses: all red with roses and fresh with little fountains: is the Aqua Sola—a public promenade, where the military band plays gaily, and the white veils cluster thick, and the Genoese nobility ride round, and round, and round, in state-clothes and coaches at least, if not in absolute wisdom. Within a stone's-throw, as it seems, the audience of the Day-Theatre sit; their faces turned this way. But as the stage is hidden, it is very odd, without a knowledge of the cause, to see their faces change so suddenly from earnestness to laughter; and odder still, to hear the rounds upon rounds of applause, rattling in the evening air, to which the curtain falls. But, being Sunday night, they act their best and most attractive plays. And now, the sun is going down in such a magnificent array of red, and green, and golden light, as neither pen nor pencil could depict; and to the ringing of the vesper bells, darkness sets in at once, without a twilight. Then, lights begin to shine in Genoa, and on the country road; and the revolving lantern out at sea there, flashing, for an instant, on this palace front and portico, illuminates it as if there were a bright moon bursting from behind a cloud; then, merges it in deep obscurity. And this, so far as I know, is the only reason why the Genoese avoid it after dark, and think it haunted.

My memory will haunt it, many nights in time to come; but nothing worse, I will engage. The same Ghost will occasionally sail away, as I did one pleasant Autumn evening, into the bright prospect, and snuff the morning air at Marseilles.

My friend the artist, whom I beg to introduce as Mr. Samuel G. Tovey, had taken a fancy to this Palace of the Fish-ponds, immediately after Dickens had left it and before the above description had appeared. He had made various sketches of it, from different points, and was never tired, he or his lively little wife, in praising the beauty of its situation, construction, prospects, terraces, garden. On my suggestion, he resolved to place his sketches, if possible, under the eye of him, who, of all men in England, was best qualified to decide upon their fidelity and effect. Accordingly, I wrote to Mr. Dickens, and subjoin his reply.

DEVONSHIRE TERRACE, *Tenth December*, 1847.

My Dear Sir:—My engagements are so very numerous just now, that I cannot have the pleasure of immediately seeing Mr. Tovey's drawings. But I have made a note of that gentleman's address, and propose calling at his studio one day towards the end of the month.

Yours Faithfully,
CHARLES DICKENS.

R. SHELTON MACKENZIE, ESQUIRE.

Faithful to his promise, Mr. Dickens soon visited Mr. Tovey's studio, and purchased two of the seven Genoese sketches,—merely asking the price, which he remarked was very low, giving a check for the amount, on the spot, taking the sketches home with him in his brougham, and asking Mr. Tovey's opinion as to the sort of frame which he thought would be most appropriate for them. In a few weeks he invited the artist and his wife to an evening party, where they had the pleasure of seeing the sketches properly mounted and placed, and the further gratification of receiving, from the author, a handsomely-bound copy of the "Pictures from Italy," with a gratifying complimentary presentation address, to the lady, in Dickens's autograph. There was kindness, as well as courtesy, in these little attentions.

CHAPTER XIII.

VISIT TO ITALY AND SWITZERLAND.—EDITORSHIP OF DAILY NEWS.—LONDON NEWSPAPERS.—PICTURES FROM ITALY.—RETURN TO SWITZERLAND.—DOMBEY AND SON.—LORD JEFFREY ON THE DEATH OF LITTLE PAUL.

MR. DICKENS went to Italy in 1844, some months after the publication of *The Christmas Carol,* and remained abroad for a year, though as I learn from one of Lord Jeffrey's letters to him, he ran over to London in November, 1844, doubtless to see *The Chimes,* his second Christmas tale, through the press. In the *Pictures from Italy,* published in 1846, is a desultory account of what he saw and thought. He went from Paris to Genoa, where he resided for some months, and made the usual tour, greatly impressed by Rome, Venice, Naples, and Milan, as well as by Vesuvius,—which obligingly happened to be in a state of eruption, so that he could not say, with Sir Charles Coldstream, " There's nothing in it,"—and affected, almost to awe, by those Cities of the Past, Herculaneum and Pompeii. It has been too much the habit, following the key-note given by a sneering reviewer in *The Times,* to undervalue Mr.

Dickens's book on Italy. Like the author of "Eothen," he discarded from the book a great mass of information and observation communicated by previous writers. Few classical allusions are to be found in it, for Mr. Dickens was not a classical scholar. But it professed to state what a plain Englishman thought of a country very celebrated through the ages, which he now first visited. He did not take a poetic view of Italy. He could not refrain, nor was that to be expected, from looking at the sunny, and even the funny, side of things; but whereas this formed the staple of his *American Notes,* it was episodal and occasional in his *Pictures from Italy.* He scarcely touched upon the historical associations of the land—living men and women, with actual manners and customs, were more in his way. Nor did he often describe scenery, though his sketch of the Palace of the Fish-ponds, which he inhabited in Genoa, has the breadth and brightness of Claude Lorraine, with the minute detail of David Teniers. As for impressive writing, commend me to the short sketch entitled, "An Italian Dream." Almost any other man would have served up, for the hundredth time, the Rialto and the Campanile, the Bridge of Sighs and the Piazzetta, the Ducal Palace and the granite columns of St. Theodore and St. Mark, but Mr. Dickens spoke of the Ocean-Rome, as if he had merely dreamed of it, took us across a shadowy Piazza and into an immaterial Cathedral, led up the Giants' Stairs, into the *piombi,* and, far below the sea-level, into the *pozzi;* and showed, as no guide-book does, the true moral sentiment associated in a freeman's mind, with Venice, the still lovely and picturesque City of the Sea.

This book, though completed in 1845, was not published then. Its contents had been reserved for a new daily journal, which Mr. Dickens projected towards the close of the year, in conjunction with Messrs. Bradbury & Evans, who as proprietors, printers, and publishers of *Punch,* had already built up a large, profitable, and increasing business.

It was resolved to establish the *Daily News*, in rivalry with *The Times*, which had gradually secured an influence, circulation, and profits which then made it "the leading journal of Europe." In the contemplated venture, the printers were to find the capital in money, and Mr. Dickens the capital in brain and prestige. At that time, perhaps there was room for a new daily morning paper in London. The *Public Ledger*, which was the oldest, had declined into a mere advertising sheet for city salesmen ; the *Morning Chronicle*, once acknowledged organ of the Whig party, had lost that position, and "dragged its slow length along;" the *Morning Post* was little more than a fashionable gazette ; the *Morning Herald* was ultra-tory, and badly written ; and the *Morning Advertiser* was simply the paper of the publicans. *The Times*, which had grown into a gigantic property, by careful management, by paying liberally for the best talent, and by establishing a *cordon literaire* of highly educated and able correspondents in foreign countries, towered far above its contemporaries. But it had played fast and loose in politics, the general impression being that it *followed* rather than *led* public opinion,—"ran with the hare and held with the hound," as the saying is. In November, 1834, on the dismissal of the Melbourne Cabinet, by William IV., *The Times* announced the fact, with the significant addition "The Queen has done it all." This was on a Saturday, but the paper, on Monday, was as Tory, in every respect, as it previously had been rampantly Liberal. At the close of 1845, when Sir Robert Peel was about abolishing the bread-tax, he was strongly supported by *The Times*, but the Liberal party, who were opposed to imposts upon food and also wished to return to office, after five years banishment from the Treasury benches, could not depend on *The Times* to aid them also in that. There was room, then, for the establishment of a first-class, liberal, morning paper, in London.

To show the difficulty of arriving at facts, I may mention the doubt as to the day when the first number of the *Daily*

News appeared, with Mr. Dickens as conductor. He had engaged a large staff of writers, reporters, and correspondents, at very liberal salaries,—for he always desired that newspaper men should be well paid. "Men of the Time" declares that the *Daily News* commenced on January 1st, 1846; the *London Review* states, "on the 21st" of that month; but a personal friend, whom I believe to be more accurate, puts the date some weeks later. It was announced that Mr. Dickens was "head of the literary department." He was decidedly liberal in politics, but by no means a political writer. Mr. John Forster, who had made a high reputation by his political and literary writings in *The Examiner*, had charge of the political department of the new journal, but Mr. Dickens was generally understood to be the editor in chief.

The *Daily News* was a full sized, well-printed, well-edited sheet,—but, in the first number was a misprint which caused it to be contemptuously regarded by that large and powerful class in London, called "city men." It was an error in the price of stocks,—this, by accidental transposing of the numerals, being quoted at 39 instead of 93. The publication of *Pictures from Italy* was begun in the second number, and shocked many of its serious readers by stating, in the first sentence, that Mr. Dickens had started from Paris "on a fine *Sunday* morning." In a short time he retired, finding it weary work, and having a new serial story in his mind, and Mr. C. W. Dilke, proprietor of the *Athenæum* since the year 1830, was installed as Manager of the *Daily News*, and without making many changes in the staff, systematized the whole concern, greatly reduced expenses, and worked a large portion of the morning publication, into an afternoon off-shoot called *The Express*, sold at a lower price than the *Sun*, *Globe*, and *Standard*, then the only evening London papers. It may be added here, that the *Daily News* continued to be published for many years, if not as a losing, scarcely as a paying concern, but, not long ago, became a penny paper, like the *Telegraph* and *Standard*, and now has a large circulation, great influence, and high character for consistent liberality.

Shortly after Mr. Dickens retired from the *Daily News*, he published the volume of *Pictures from Italy*. It was sneered at, as I have said, by a few sharp critics, but had a warm reception from the public, who noticed with satisfaction, a promise held out in the prefatory chapter. It was this: "I have likened these Pictures to shadows in the water, and would fain that I have, no where, stirred the water so roughly, as to mar the shadows. I could never desire to be on better terms with all my friends than now, when distant mountains rise, once more, in my path. For I need not hesitate to avow, that, bent on correcting a brief mistake I made, not long ago, in disturbing the old relations between myself and my readers, and departing for a moment from my old pursuits, I am about to resume them, joyfully, in Switzerland; where, during another year of absence, I can at once work out the themes I have now in my mind, without interruption; and while I keep my English audience within speaking distance, extend my knowledge of a noble country, inexpressibly dear to me."

The "mistake" he made was in becoming editor of a daily paper, and the new work was *Dombey and Son*, the publication of which was in the old monthly serial form, with the familiar and accustomed green covers. In the Preface, on the completion of the work, he bade farewell to its readers, saying: "If any of them have felt a sorrow in one of the principal incidents on which this fiction turns, I hope it may be a sorrow of that sort which endears the sharers in it, one to another. This is not unselfish in me. I may claim to have felt it, at least as much as anybody else, and I would fain be remembered kindly for my part in the experience." This is dated, at London, on the 24th of March, 1848. In the People's edition, a little later, he says:

I began this book by the lake of Geneva, and went on with it for some months in France. The association between the writing and the place of writing is so curiously strong in my mind, that at this day, although I know every stair in the little Midshipman's house, and could swear to every pew in the church in which Florence was married, or to every young gentleman's bedstead in Doctor Blimber's establishment, I yet confusedly imagine Captain Cuttle as secluding himself from Mrs. Macstinger among the mountains of Switzerland. Similarly, when I am reminded by any chance of what it was that the waves were always saying, I wander in my fancy for a whole winter night about the streets of Paris—as I really did, with a heavy heart, on the night when my little friend and I parted company for ever.

Next to the departure, or rather of the translation of Little Nell, nothing touched the public mind, with tender sympathy and pathetic sorrow, as the death of Little Paul Dombey. Lord Jeffrey, the most critical of readers, who used to apply the scalpel, with terrible effect, even to his own performances, thus wrote about this mournful, but not unexpected, event:

Oh, my dear, dear Dickens! what a No. 5 you have now given us! I have so cried and sobbed over it last night, and again this morning; and felt my heart purified by those tears, and blessed and loved you for making me shed them; and I never can bless and love you enough. Since that divine Nelly was found dead on her humble couch, beneath the snow and the ivy, there has been nothing like the actual dying of that sweet Paul, in the summer sunshine of that lofty room. And the long vista that leads us so gently and sadly, and yet so gracefully and winningly, to that plain consummation! Every trait so true, and so touching—and yet lightened by that fearless innocence which goes *playfully* to the brink of the grave, and that pure affection which bears the unstained spirit, on its soft and lambent flash, at once to its source in eternity. In reading of these delightful children, how deeply do we feel that "of such is the kingdom of Heaven;" and how ashamed of the contaminations which *our* manhood has received from the contact of the earth, and wonder how *you* should have been admitted into that pure communion, and so "presumed, an earthly guest, and drawn Empyreal air," though for our benefit and instruction. Well, I did not mean to say all this; but this I must say, and you will believe it, that of the many thousand hearts that will melt and swell over these pages, there can be few that will feel their chain so deeply as mine, and scarcely any so *gratefully*. But after reaching this climax in the fifth number, what are you to do with the fifteen that are to follow?—"The wine of life is drawn, and nothing left but the dull dregs for this poor world to brag of." So I shall say, and fear for any other adventurer. But I have unbounded trust in your resources, though I have a feeling that you will have nothing in the sequel, if indeed in your whole life, equal to the pathos and poetry, the truth and the tenderness, of the four last pages of this number, for those, at least, who feel and judge like me. I am most anxious and impatient, however, to see how you get on, and begin already to conceive how you may fulfil your formerly incredible prediction, that I should come to take an interest in Dombey himself. Now that you have got his stony heart into the terrible crucible of affliction, though I still retain my incredulity as to Miss Tox and the Major, I feel that I (as well as they) am but clay in the hands of the potter, and may be moulded at your will."

The general opinion of Dombey and Son, as a whole, was very favorable, though it was said that "Good Mrs. Brown" and her handsome daughter were too melodramatic—what would now be called "too sensational." Carker, too, was not liked, nor was it intended that readers would take him into their friendship. But the subtle villainy of his character was represented with delicate discrimination, nor, in any of these works is there any chapter more powerful than that in which are presented the escape of Carker from Dijon, after his signal discomfiture by Edith, with his rapid flight, across the Continent, from the avenging Nemesis of a wronged and violently angered husband. His death—sudden and crashing—is in thorough keeping with his bad deserts. With consummate skill, the author, who irritates us, at first, by the thorough, overpowering selfishness of Mr. Dombey, brings us into kind relations with him at the close. He comes out of suffering, purified and exalted. Mr. Dickens told his readers, long after the original publication: "Mr. Dombey undergoes no violent internal change, either in this book or in life. A sense of his injustice is within him all along. The more he represses it, the more unjust he necessarily is. Internal shame and external circumstances may bring the contest to the surface in a week, or a day; but, it has been a contest for years, and is only fought out after a long balance of victory. Years have elapsed since I dismissed Mr. Dombey. I have not been impatient to offer this critical remark upon him, and I offer it with some confidence."

In "Dombey and Son," it was noticed that the author's creative power was even more fruitful than ever. Florence Dombey is one of his finest impersonations of budding Womanhood. Edith is unpleasant, but effective. Mrs. Skewton seems as if she had been picked up at a watering place, hand-carriage, page, and all, and bodily thrown into the story. Then the scholastic Blimbers were new in fiction, but not in life. Who has not seen a Pipchin? Then, there is John Cheek, who *will* whistle snatches of merry tunes when he ought to look gloomy; and Miss Tox and Polly Toodle are from the life. There is not much in Sol Gills, of the Wooden Midshipman, or in Walter Gay, his nephew, but Toots and Susan Nipper are in wonderful contrast and accord, and he who discovered Captain Edward Cuttle, mariner, and his friend John Bunsby, master of "The Cautious Clara," surely merits all the honors of a literary ovation.

After the usual rest from labor, Mr. Dickens commenced a new story, *The Personal History of David Copperfield.* He avowed that, of all his works, this was his favorite, and it has generally been believed that his own early history has been given in its pages. In the Preface, dated October, 1850, he said:

I do not find it easy to get sufficiently far away from this

Book, in the first sensations of having finished it, to refer to it with the composure which this formal heading would seem to require. My interest in it is so recent and strong; and my mind is so divided between pleasure and regret—pleasure in the achievement of a long design, regret in the separation from many companions—that I am in danger of wearying the reader whom I love, with personal confidences, and private emotions.

Besides which, all that I could say of the Story, to any purpose, I have endeavored to say in it.

It would concern the reader little, perhaps, to know how sorrowfully the pen is laid down at the close of a two-years' imaginative task; or how an Author feels as if he were dismissing some portion of himself into the shadowy world, when a crowd of the creatures of his brain are going from him forever. Yet, I have nothing else to tell; unless, indeed, I were to confess (which might be of less moment still) that no one can ever believe this Narrative, in the reading, more than I have believed it in the writing.

It was critically reported of *David Copperfield*, that it is the most finished and natural of his works; it is more than good. The boyhood of the hero; the scene in church; the death of his mother; the story of Peggotty; poor little Em'ly; that touching love, so true, so perfect, and so delicate and pure, which the rough old fisherman has for his lost niece, cannot be surpassed. The mellow strength and mature vigor of style, the modest ingenuousness of Copperfield's relation of his progress to literature, supposed truthfully to portray Dickens's own career; the child-wife, her death, and David's final love for Agnes—all rush upon our memory, and put forward their claims to be admired. The original characters are good, and the family of Micawber form a group as original as was ever drawn by Mr. Dickens. The dark and weird character of Rosa Dartle, and the revolting one of Uriah Heap, are the only painful ones in the book. But they are full of fine touches of nature, which also illumine the dark drawing of the Murdstones. It would be easy to point out impressive scenes in this book. The most powerful is the description of the tempest and wreck at Yarmouth—a picture, in words, far grander and pure than any painting by Wilhelm Vandervelde or Claude Vernet.

There is not so much broad fun in this tale as in others by the same author, but there is more wit and intense passion. The old carrier's words, "Barkis is willing," have become a popular saying, and Micawber's hopeful "waiting for something to turn up" is as well known and as often repeated as a proverb. Perhaps, in all the wide range of his various compositions, the Micawber group is the best sustained—with the exception, perhaps, of the Wellers. Even the twins come into play to complete that family circle. And, at the close, when we read Micawber's letter from Australia, and find him doing well and honored, as magistrate, we rejoice that will and circumstance, working together, have saved him, a good and honored citizen, from what once threatened to be a total wreck.

Mr. Dickens concluded Copperfield as usual, by hinting at another work. "I cannot close this volume," he said, "more agreeably to myself, than with a hopeful glance towards the time when I shall again put forth my two green leaves once a month, and with a faithful remembrance of the genial sun and showers that have fallen on these leaves of David Copperfield, and made me happy." This new work was not begun so soon as was expected. Before *Copperfield* was finished, Mr. Dickens had established a cheap weekly periodical, with the title of *Household Words*. I slightly anticipate when I add that in consequence of a difference with his printers, Bradbury & Evans, this work was brought to a conclusion in 1859, and was succeeded by *All the Year Round*, similar in character, form, and size, also conducted by Mr. Dickens; the working editor, until a short time ago, being Mr. William Henry Wills, a brother-in-law of Messrs. W. & R. Chambers, the Edinburgh publishers, and for some years sub-editor of the *Daily News*. When ill health incapacitated Mr. Wills from further work, some short time ago, he was succeeded by Mr. Charles Dickens, junior, who is now, by his father's will, proprietor and editor of *All the Year Round.* But I am getting far ahead of the chronological arrangement of this memoir.

In September, 1853, was completed the publication of *Bleak House*, which had appeared in monthly parts, like the majority of its author's previous works. The avowed object was to expose the dilatory practice of the Chancery Courts. —In his Preface, Mr. Dickens said:

A Chancery Judge once had the kindness to inform me, as one of a company of some hundred and fifty men and women not laboring under any suspicions of lunacy, that the Court of Chancery, though the shining subject of much popular prejudice (at which point I thought the Judge's eye had a cast in my direction), was almost immaculate. There had been, he admitted, a trivial blemish or so in its rate of progress, but this was exaggerated, and had been entirely owing to the "parsimony of the public;" which guilty public, it appeared, had been until lately bent in the most determined manner on by no means enlarging the number of Chancery Judges appointed—I believe by Richard the Second, but any other King will do as well.

In contradiction to the judicial statement, was added this firm declaration by the author:

I mention here that everything set forth in these pages concerning the Court of Chancery is substantially true, and within the truth. The case of Gridley is in no essential altered from one of actual occurrence, made public by a disinterested person who was professionally acquainted with the whole of the monstrous wrong from beginning to end. At the present moment there is a suit before the Court which was commenced nearly twenty years ago; in which from thirty to forty counsel have been known to appear at one time; in which costs have been incurred to the amount of seventy thousand pounds; which is a *friendly suit;* and which is (I am assured) no nearer its termination now than when it was begun. There is another well known suit in Chancery, not yet decided, which was commenced before the close of the last century, and in which more than double the amount of seventy thousand pounds has been swallowed up in costs. If I wanted other authorities for JARNDYCE AND JARNDYCE, I could rain them on these pages, to the shame of—a parsimonious public.

Earnestness was apparent throughout *Bleak House*. The manner of telling the story was out of the common. A young lady, who can scarcely be considered as the heroine, is sometimes the narrator,—the tale being told, on other occasions, in the usual manner. Lady Dedlock is a sort of Lady Macbeth of private life, very capable of committing the murder, which another woman perpetrated. Mademoiselle Hortense, the actual criminal, is drawn with a free pencil. Boythorn and Harold Skimpole are effective, chiefly because we know the originals of their characters. The Jelleby family, we dare say, abound in most great cities; the mother having a mission,—to neglect her family and provide tracts and spelling books, warming-pans and flannels for the dusky natives of Borrioboola-Gha, on the left bank of the Niger. Mr. Turveydrop, like Micawber, is *sui generis*, and it is thought, the author had not to travel far to find him. Poor Joe, the crossing-sweeper, is a sad illustration of London civilization; the Rouncewell family are firm and true, each of them, and Mr. and Mrs. Bagnet, with their children (Woolwich, Quebec, and Malta,) would be the salt of any ordinary novel. Of Mr. Bucket, the detective, there is a little too much, but we have yet to find the reader, who does not honor, while he pities, that noble, broken gentleman, Sir Leicester Dedlock, Baronet.

As for the Smallweed coterie, they are a miserable set, and Mr. Dickens made one of his greatest mistakes in making their precious relative, Krook, perish by spontaneous combustion. He defended it, of course, as men will defend errors of judgment, and his position and precedents were strongly assailed by Mr. G. H. Lewes. Even if such deaths had occurred, the instances were so few as to be exceptional, and therefore not sufficient to work out the plot of a novel of common life.

In *Household Words*, in 1851–3, appeared "*A Child's History of England*," by Mr. Dickens, which cannot be said to have added to his reputation. It was written with great familiarity, with the view of bringing it down to the comprehension of youth;—for instance, James the First is mentioned, not with the conventional appellation of "His Majesty," but of "His Sow-ship"—which is novel, at least.

About the time *Household Words* was established, Mr. Dickens quitted Devonshire Terrace, Regent's Park, where he had resided for ten years, and entered into occupancy of Tavistock House, Tavistock Square. This was a beautiful villa, with trees and garden, in the heart of London, a mile to the east of Devonshire Terrace, which the late Mr. James Perry, proprietor and editor of *The Morning Chronicle*, had erected on land especially leased to him, by the Duke of Bedford, in acknowledgment of his journalistic services to the Whig party, some forty years before. It was separated from the street by a handsome iron railing, the growth of trees within which effectually shut out the curious public gaze. It was a splendid Mansion. In one part of it, Frank Stone, the artist, whose son illustrated *Great Expectations* and two other of Dickens's works, had his studio, I believe. Mr. Dickens occupied Tavistock House from 1850 to the summer of 1857, when he removed to Gad's Hill House, near Rochester, Kent, where he died.

CHAPTER XIV.

ORIGINALS OF FICTITIOUS CHARACTERS.—OLD WELLER AND MISS HUDDART.—MR. TRACY TUPMAN AND THE FAT BOY.—MRS. BARDELL.—MR. JUSTICE STARELEIGH.—MR. SERGEANT BUZFUZ.—DODSON AND FOGG.—MR. PERKER—POLICE MAGISTRATE FANG.—VINCENT CRUMMLES.—W. T. MONCRIEFF.—CHEERYBLE BROTHERS.—DANIEL GRANT'S DINNER-PEGS.—MRS. NICKLEBY.—SIR JOHN CHESTER.—ALDERMAN CUTE.—MR. DOMBEY.—PERCH.—SOL. GILLS.—CAPTAIN CUTTLE.—WILKINS MICAWBER.—ESTHER SUMMERSON.—MR. BOYTHORN AND LITTLE NELL.—INSPECTOR BUCKET.—CARLAVERO'S ENGLISHMAN.—MR. JULIUS SLINKTON.

THE characters in Dickens' works are to be counted, not in scores, but hundreds. It was once hoped that a day would arrive, when Dickens, following the example of Sir Walter Scott, would give his multitudinous readers some account of the sources whence he derived his incidents and drew his leading characters. Writers of fiction, all the world knows, do not invariably *invent*. Few stories have been written without some foundation in fact: few characters drawn without some prototype, however dim, in actual life. It has long been complained of Bulwer that he

"Is himself the great sublime he drew"

in "Pelham," and nearly every novelist has been charged, by some person, with having had *him* in view when writing. "They talked of me, I am sure," said *Scrub* in the play, "for they laughed consumedly." So, once upon a time, Sheridan, when visiting at a country house, wrote a sermon for a young clergyman, who was also a guest, the subject of the discourse being the sin of avarice. The sermon was duly preached in the village church, and among the congregation was a rich man, who was said to have acquired his wealth in no very honest manner, and to cling to it with remarkable tenacity. *He*, hearing the "still, small voice" within, believed that the divine had wilfully and wantonly preached *at* him, and never again favored him with a word or bow. It is much the same way with novel-readers, who fancy that they see their own likenesses, in characters drawn in ignorance of their very existence.

Old Weller, in "The Posthumous Papers of The Pickwick Club," reminds one, very much, of the admirable sketch of the Stage Coachman, with great bulk and curiously-mottled face, in Washington Irving's "Sketch Book." In other words, for I am not accusing Boz of committing plagiary upon Geoffrey Crayon, both authors drew from the same special *genus*—now extinct. The plethoric stage-coachman, who drove four-in-hand, changed horses every ten miles, and took a glass of ale at each change, has been swept away by Railwayism, just as the Indians have been driven farther and farther West by the irresistible progress of Civilization, and are now nearly extinct. When I first travelled through England, forty years ago, just before Railwayism was begun, nearly every stage-coach had a Jehu of this class.

I believe that Old Weller was drawn from an original, who used to "work" a stage-coach between London and Portsmouth, and had a brother on the same line. They passed by each other every day, for many years, without any opportunity of exchanging words—a mutual smile and knowing elevation of the whip-elbow being their only salute. When one of these rotund brothers of the whip died, the other took it to heart, and followed him in a month. This last was Dickens's man. Perhaps Dickens may have travelled with him—*I* did, before Steam became omnipotent. Mrs. Warner, the tragic actress, experienced an act of kindness from this coachman, which she related to Dickens soon after it occurred, and it may have influenced *his* coachman in *Pickwick*.

Before her marriage, Mrs. Warner, who paid a professional visit to the United States in 1852, was Miss Huddart, very much respected, on and off the boards. Her father had been an officer in the British army, and she always travelled under his escort. He was known, along the road, as "The Captain," and *she* was familiarly spoken of as "Polly Huddart." Once upon a time, she was travelling, with her father, to begin a short star-season at Portsmouth or Plymouth. Every one on that road knew father and daughter and the bulky coachman. When *he* saw their names on his "way-bill," he took care that the favorite box-seat, portion of his own vehicular throne, should be reserved for the lady, who was apt to get sick when an inside passenger, and was accustomed, by special favor, to take her seat on the outside, with the coachman. Courteous and conversational as this lady always was, and extremely handsome in these distant days, she had become an especial favorite with this particular "whip."

On the occasion I refer to, when the last stage, say twelve miles distant from their place of destination, was reached, it was discovered that Captain Huddart had suddenly died *in* the coach, his daughter then being *on* it. Of course, this caused considerable social commotion, and the corpse was taken into the inn, to await inquiry from a coroner's inquest. Poor Miss Huddart was sitting in the great parlor of the country inn, almost paralyzed by the sad and sudden shock, when the old coachman came into the room, and, seeing her unaware of his presence, said, as softly as his gruff voice would allow, "The coachman, Miss." Believing that he had come to her for his fee, and greatly annoyed at being so intruded upon at such a time, she took out her purse, pushed it over to him, as he stood by the table, and said in an angry tone, "Help yourself!" This he declined doing, but, while he was diving into the deep abysm of his breeches-pocket, in quest, as it seemed, of a huge pocket-book, plethoric as himself, huskily uttered the words, "You mistake me, Miss Huddart. All I came to say was that player-people don't always have as much money as they need, and that, in this sad fix, it will be very unkind if you don't allow me, who have known you so long on the road, to let you have whatever you may want. There's a hundred pound, or so, in this pocket-book, and if more's wanted towards burying of the old gentleman, I shall bring it with me to-morrow morning, when I come back, this same way." Then pushing a bundle of bank-notes into the poor young lady's hand, he waddled out of the room as fast as possible.

Next day and for several succeeding days, he again paid half a minute's visit to the afflicted and suddenly orphaned daughter, and after the funeral, had great pride in giving her as heretofore the box-seat with himself. She had great difficulty in coaxing him to take back the money he had placed at her disposal, but, hearing that she was to have a benefit at the theatre, he purchased box-tickets to a large amount, which he forced upon the passengers whom he drove, telling them the tragic story of the Captain's death, and invariably answering, whenever reminded that the person whom he wished to purchase a ticket, was going from the place where the lady's benefit was to be given, that "so much the better, as there would be the more room for the towns-people!" Miss Huddart was persuaded that Dickens, whom she had known from his school-days, and to whom she had particularly described this benevolent stage coachman, probably had some remembrance of him when he drew and devel oped the character of Old Weller.

Upon another passage of *Pickwick* it has been remarked that the incident it pretends to record must have been invented for the occasion, and "made out of the whole cloth." This passage occurs in the 13th chapter, in which is related part of what was done, and said, at a contested parliamentary election for the borough of Eatanswill, previous to the Reform Bill for 1832. Mr. Pickwick, who has been admitted "behind the scenes," on the famous *blue* interest, represented by the Honorable Samuel Slumkey, becomes acquainted with some of the ways by which the "free and independent electors" of the borough were induced to give their votes. Among these were, of course, the throwing open all the public houses to the electors and their friends; making electors drunk and locking them up until they were wanted to vote; distributing forty-five green silk parasols among voters' wives; hocusing the brandy-and-water of hostile voters, so that they were asleep when they ought to have been at the poll, and so on. Sam Weller caps these, as usual, with a story of his own, which has sometimes been pronounced "utterly extravagant" and improbable. It narrates how, at an election time, Old Weller had to bring a large number of out-voters from London; how some of the adverse party saw him, complimented him on his driving, shoved a twenty-pound note into his hand, with "'It's a werry bad road between this and London,' says the genl'm'n. —'Here and there it *is* a heavy road,' says my father.— ''Specially near the canal, I think,' says the gen'lm'n.— 'Nasty bit, that 'ere,' says my father.—'Well, Mr. Weller,' says the gen'l'm'n, 'you're a werry good whip, and can do what you like with your horses, we know. We're all wery fond o' you Mr. Weller, so in case you *should* have an accident when you're a bringing these here woters down, and *should* tip 'em over into the canal without hurtin' of 'em, this is for yourself,'" says he.—Also how "on the wery day as he came down with them woters, his coach *was* upset on that 'ere wery spot, and every man on 'em was turned into the canal." Here, as Sam observed, was "the hex-traordinary, and wonderful coincidence, that arter what that gen'l'm'n said, my father's coach should be upset in that wery place, and on that wery day." Now it is a parliamentary fact, proven upon oath before successive "committees appointed by the House of Commons to inquire into the existence of corrupt practices at elections for Members of Parliament," that the borough of Great Yarmouth has labored from an early period of its electoral history under the disadvantage of a bad character. Before the Reform Bill, the right of election lay in "the burgesses at large" to the number of eight hundred. Curious stories are extant of the way in which Yarmouth elections were managed in those days. A considerable number of the "burgesses at large" were non-residents, and had to be brought to Great Yarmouth at election times at the charge of the candidate, and at very heavy cost. On one occasion, it is related that a ship, chartered to convey out-burgesses from London, was detained off Yarmouth until the poll had closed, the captain having been paid by the other party to find the wind adverse. The incident of the upset of a stage-coach conveying voters which gave them a gratuitous cold bath, has been more than a tradition in Great Yarmouth for the last forty or fifty years, and is related, with variations, as a clever manœuvre, at every election held in that not immaculate borough.

A certain Mr. Winters, a middle aged young man, who used to be seen, on fine afternoons, ogling the belles, in the Ladies' Mile in Hyde Park, or at the fashionable watering places in the early autumn, had acquaintances, who insisted that he was a *fac simile* of stout and too susceptible Mr. Tracy Tupman.

The Fat Boy has been vaguely credited to the youthful and plump servant of a gate-keeper, ("he kept a pike!") in Essex, between London and Chelmsford. I have seen at least a score of his family, with and without buttons, in my time. In fact, in aristocratic houses, the Page, having next to nothing to do, generally runs into flesh, from feeding and idleness, even as ladies' lap-dogs do.

It has been asserted that Mrs. Bardell, with whom no woman, spinster, wife, or widow, has ever sympathized, she was so terribly absurd, in her designs upon Mr. Pickwick—was drawn, with a free but faithful touch, from a Mrs. Ann Ellis, who kept an eating-house near Doctors' Commons, (in

Knight-rider street, between St. Paul's church-yard and Upper Thames street,) and was comely, plump, and agreeable.

In the memorable trial, Bardell *v.* Pickwick, the presiding functionary, Mr. Justice Stareleigh, was a caricature, by no means extravagant, of Sir Stephen Gaselee, who had been a junior Judge of the Court of Common Pleas, at the time when Lord Wynford (W. D. Best) was Chief Justice of that court. He is thus described by Mr. Dickens: "Mr. Justice Stareleigh (who sat in the absence of the Chief Justice, occasioned by indisposition) was a most particularly short man, and so fat, that he seemed all face and waistcoat. He rolled in, upon two little turned legs, and having bobbed gravely to the bar, who bobbed gravely to him, put his little legs underneath his table, and his little three cornered hat upon it; and when Mr. Justice Stareleigh had done this, all you could see of him was two queer little eyes, one broad pink face, and somewhere about half of a big and very comical-looking wig." Falling asleep occasionally during the trial, confounding persons and things, and generally exhibiting a considerable amount of mental imbecility, were as characteristic of the actual Gaselee as of the imaginary Stareleigh. Mr. Dickens's own personal representation, in his Readings of the latter, is not to be forgotten by any one who witnessed it. Mr. Serjeant Buzfuz is supposed to represent Mr. Serjeant Bumpus, a blustering lawyer, who was dreaded, in those days, for the loud and insolent manner in which he bullied witnesses.

As for Messrs. Dodson & Fogg, who represent the Black Sheep of the law, no doubt it was not difficult to find their prototypes among the legal battalions of such a vast city as London, but my knowledge of their profession, in the new as well as the old world, warrants my asserting that for every one of their grade there are hundreds resembling little Mr. Perker, who was Mr. Pickwick's attorney,—of the class of educated gentlemen, intelligent, humane, thoughtful, and considerate, who conceive it their first duty to prevent the expense and suspense of litigation.

While *Oliver Twist* was in course of publication, the senior magistrate of Hatton Garden Police Office, was a certain A. S. Laing, Esq., barrister-at-law, notorious, at the time, for his discourtesy and coarseness to all persons, prisoners, policemen, witnesses, complainants, lawyers, and reporters, who came before him. At that time, Lord John Russell was Home Secretary, with direct official supervision of all the London police officers. Not only the short-comings, but the overdoings and the unwise sayings of Justice Laing, had repeatedly been severely criticised in the newspapers, but wholly without effect, for Laing held his place, and boasted that he would continue to hold it, whatever might be said or done about him. Whereupon, Charles Dickens came to the rescue. The eleventh chapter of *Oliver Twist* treats of Mr. Fang, the police magistrate, and furnished a slight specimen of his mode of administering justice. Oliver, charged with picking a handkerchief in the street, from a Mr. Brownlow's pocket, is brought before this worthy, and thus described:

Mr. Fang was a middle-sized man, with no great quantity of hair; and what he had, growing on the back and sides of his head. His face was stern, and much flushed. If he were really not in the habit of drinking rather more than was exactly good for him, he might have brought an action against his countenance for libel, and have recovered heavy damages.

The old gentleman bowed respectfully, and, advancing to the magistrate's desk, said, suiting the action to the word, "That is my name and address, sir." He then withdrew a pace or two; and, with another polite and gentlemanly inclination of the head, waited to be questioned.

Now, it so happened, that Mr. Fang was at that moment perusing a leading article in a newspaper of the morning, adverting to some recent decision of his and commending him, for the three hundred and fiftieth time, to the special and particular notice of the Secretary of State for the Home Department. He was out of temper, and he looked up with an angry scrowl.

"Who are you?" said Mr. Fang.

The old gentleman pointed with some surprise to his card.

"Officer!" said Mr. Fang, tossing the card contemptuously away with the newspaper, "who is this fellow?"

"My name, sir," said the old gentleman, speaking *like* a gentleman, and consequently in strong contrast to Mr. Fang, —"my name, sir, is Brownlow. Permit me to inquire the name of the magistrate who offers a gratuitous and unprovoked insult to a respectable man, under the protection of the bench." Saying this, Mr. Brownlow looked round the office as if in search of some person who could afford him the required information.

"Officer!" said Mr. Fang, throwing the paper on one side, "what's this fellow charged with?"

"He's not charged at all, your worship," replied the officer. "He appears against the boy, your worship."

His worship knew this perfectly well; but it was a good annoyance, and a safe one.

Before taking the oath, Mr. Brownlow was again insulted, and asked what *he* meant by trying to bully a magistrate? There is no evidence against Oliver, who faints, and thereupon is committed for three months' imprisonment with hard labor. But as witness appears a determined man, who proves the innocence of the accused, and compels Mr. Fang to discharge the boy, which he does reluctantly, at the same time suggesting that the old gentleman was himself a thief.—This appeared in *Bentley's Miscellany*, in 1837, and every one recognized the identity of Fang and Laing. The result was, that even the Home Secretary was compelled to do the same, and, as a matter of course, to remove Mr. Laing from all further official cares, duties, and emoluments. Dickens could say, in the words of Coriolanus, "Alone I did it," and he obtained no small degree of popularity by the directness and successful result of his sketch. From that day, London police magistrates have generally been impressed with the conviction that civility was what they were bound to dispense to, as well as receive from, such of the public as appeared before them.

It is obvious that, in "Nicholas Nickleby," the theatrical experience of the author, when a youth, was largely drawn upon. Had Dickens been an actor, he must have achieved fame and fortune. His *Captain Bobadil* was a personation which it was a delight to witness, a pleasure to recollect. Mr. Vincent Crummles is said to have been an English country manager, who emigrated to this country many years ago. The "literary gentleman present (at the Crummles's farewell supper) who had dramatized in his time two hundred and forty-seven novels as fast as they had come out—some of them faster than they had come out—and *was* a literary gentleman in consequence," was the late W. T. Moncrieff, who had dramatized "Tom and Jerry," and a great many other works. He was stricken with blindness long before his death, in 1857, which took place in the Charter House, in which he had been finally provided for by being appointed a Poor Brother of that charitable institution, like Colonel Newcome.

The Cheeryble Brothers, who figure so advantageously in "Nicholas Nickleby," are not mere inventions. In his preface to that work, Mr. Dickens says: "It may be right to say, that there *are* two characters in this book which are drawn from life. It is remarkable that what we call the world, which is so very credulous in what professes to be true, is most incredulous in what professes to be imaginary; and that while every day in real life it will allow in one man no blemishes, and in another no virtues, it will seldom admit a very strongly-marked character, either good or bad, in a fictitious narrative, to be within the limits of probability. For this reason they have been very slightly and imperfectly sketched. Those who take an interest in this tale will be glad to learn that the Brothers Cheeryble live; that their liberal charity, their singleness of heart, their noble nature, and their unbounded benevolence, are no creation of the author's brain; but are prompting every day (and oftenest by stealth) some munificent and generous deed in that town of which they are the pride and honor."

In a subsequent preface, Mr. Dickens appends the following paragraph to the above: "If I were to attempt to sum up the hundreds upon hundreds of letters from all sorts of people, in all sorts of latitudes and climates, to which this unlucky paragraph has since given rise, I should get into an arithmetical difficulty from which I could not easily extricate myself. Suffice it to say, that I believe the applications for loans, gifts, and offices of profit which I have been requested to forward to the originals of the Brothers Cheeryble, (with whom I never interchanged any communication in my life,) would have exhausted the combined patronage of all the lord chancellors since the accession of the House of Brunswick, and would have broken the Rest of the Bank of England."

The Cheerybles, in the tale, were William Grant & Brothers, cotton spinners and calico printers, near Manchester, and Dickens did not exaggerate the excellence of their kind disposition nor the wide range of their practical and unobtrusive benevolence. There were four brothers—William, Daniel, John and Charles—and the characteristics of the family were the strength of their fraternal affection, their benevolence and generosity, and their success in business, which furnished them with the means of exercising a seemingly unbounded hospitality and munificence. Their father was a small farmer in Morayshire, Scotland. A great flood carried away not only his cattle and his corn, but the very soil of his farm, leaving stones and gravel in its stead. The Highland spirit of Grant would not stoop to ask assistance from the wealthier members of his clan, and he engaged himself to conduct a drove of cattle to the south. Unsuspecting, as he was honest, he lent some of his money to men who cheated him out of it, and not having the means of conveying himself back to the Highlands, he accepted some humble employment at Bury. At that time the success of the Peels and Arkwrights had induced many rich men to give high premiums to printers and dyers to take their sons as apprentices, and that class of learners were found to be of little or no use to their employers.

William Grant, then about fourteen years of age, who had accompanied his father, had attracted the notice of a printer at Bury, who took him as an apprentice, and his conduct confirmed the good impression which his master had formed of him, and other calico printers had their eyes upon him as one that would make his way. When his apprenticeship was out, the Peels wished to concentrate their works, and offered him the print works at Ramsbottom. "I have no money to buy works with," said the young man. "We will trust you, and you will pay us by instalments," said they. The bargain was made, and in a few years William was in possession of the title deeds of his purchase. Previously the father and his thriving son had sent for old Mrs. Grant, her daughter, and the three other sons (Daniel, John, and Charles,) whom he took into partnership with him, and their course was one of uninterrupted prosperity. William accounted for this in these words, "Why, sir, you see that we were four brothers who never had a word of disagreement with each other, and we all worked heartily together for the common good. Then, sir, we took care never to have a bad stock, for whenever anything hung in the market we pushed it off, and tried to produce something better; and then, sir, money made money. When we had enough risks at sea to make a fair average risk, we gave over marine insurance, and saved 80,000*l.* in that way, for we had scarcely any losses. And then, sir, Providence blessed us; and the more we gave away, sir, the more God sent us." He might have included in the cause of their success, their strict integrity, which gave all who bought from them the firm assurance that they would be honorably dealt with. It was well said of them, that they had attained the rank of merchant princes without having incurred the charge of a single shabby transaction.

Charles was the first to die. Then followed the death of William, which was understood to have been very strongly felt by Daniel, who was very little younger, and with the infirmities of age growing upon him. After that time his appearance in public became less and less frequent; but there is no doubt that he continued to exercise the benevolence which was the characteristic of the family. He was likewise known as a patron of the fine arts; his collection of paintings at his houses in Manchester and at Springside were extensive, forming a gallery of art of no trifling value. He died, in March, 1855, and Mr. John Grant, of Nuttall Hall, Lancashire, then was the sole survivor of William Grant & Brothers, spinners and calico-printers. He too has passed away. The vast property of the brothers was inherited by their sons and nephews. A monument, erected on Pendle Hill, between Ramsbottom and Bury, marks the spot where the brothers, then starting in life, took a survey of a district, a great portion of which was subsequently their own by purchase. Mr. Daniel Grant chiefly lived, in his latter years, in his house, Mosley-street, Manchester. His friends, it was said, had a general invitation to take the usual one o'clock dinner with him whenever they pleased. But he never entertained more than *nine* friends. There were ten pegs in his hall, one of which was always occupied by his own broad-brim. As his friends came in, each appropriated one of the pegs. When the whole ten were thus covered, the next comer, seeing that the party was complete, left his card and compliments with the portly butler,—and went elsewhere to dine—determining, no doubt, that he would endeavor to arrive earlier, next time. All that I have heard, in their own neighborhood, about the generosity and kind feelings of William Grant and his brothers, strongly warrants me in stating that Dickens's account of their goodness and primitive oddity of manner, softened by geniality and benevolence, was scarcely too highly colored.

Some people, who remember what may be called the *inconsequence* of Mrs. John Dickens's conversation, fancy that they caught a glimpse of her in—Mrs. Nickleby!

In "Barnaby Rudge," we meet Sir John Chester, said to have been meant for the late Sir William Henry Maule, one of the Justices of the Court of Common Pleas. There are a few points of resemblance, but the sketch is not good. Maule was neither a selfish nor a heartless man. A recent editor of Lord Chesterfield's Letters to his Son suggests that Sir John Chester was a pseudonyme of the gallant Earl, who died as far back as 1773—seven years before the Gordon Riots took place.

Sir Peter Laurie, a Border Scot, who had built up a great business in London, as a saddler, and for many years had been a principal contractor for the East Indian army, was the original of Alderman Cute, in *The Chimes*. He had served as Sheriff of London and Middlesex, in 1823–4, on which occasion he was Knighted; was chosen Alderman in 1826; and was Lord Mayor of London in 1832–3. He was very *hard*, or rather *harsh*, with the poor, and had aroused Dickens's indignation by saying, one day, when he was acting magistrate at Guildhall police office, and a wretched woman of the town was before him, charged with attempting to drown herself, that he "would soon put down suicide." He carried out his intention, by committing for imprisonment and hard labor in "Bridewell," of which hospital he was President, all persons placed before him, charged with such attempt.

In "*Dombey & Son*," several characters are said to have been drawn from life. Mr. Dombey is supposed to represent Mr. Thomas Chapman, shipowner, whose offices were opposite the Wooden Midshipman. I had the honor of meeting Mr. Chapman, at dinner, (at Lough's, the sculptor,) and the rigidity of his manner was only equalled by that of his form; he sat or stood, as the case might be, bolt upright, as if he knew not how to bend—as stiff, in fact, as if he had swallowed the drawing-room poker in his youth, and had never digested it. As if to make Mr. Chapman undoubtedly identical with Dombey, we have, as messenger of the commercial house of "Dombey & Son," one Perch, actually taken from a funny little old chap named Stephen Hale, who was part clerk, part messenger, in Mr. Chapman's office. Old Sol Gills was intended for a little fellow named Norie, who kept a very small shop, in Leadenhall street, exactly opposite the office of John Chapman & Co., in which "the stock in trade comprised chronometers, barometers, telescopes, compasses, charts, maps, sextants, quadrants, and specimens of every kind of instruments used in the working of a ship's course, or the keeping of a ship's reckoning, or the prosecuting of a ship's discoveries." In front of this small shop stands a figure, carved in wood, and curiously painted, of a miniature midshipman, with a huge quadrant in his hand, as if about taking an observation. What is more, the little shop and the Wooden Midshipman may be seen, by the curious, adorning Leadenhall street to this very day. I speak of the Wooden Midshipman, as I saw him, in 1852. He may have been swept away by what is called "improvement." Captain Cuttle was one David Mainland, master of a merchantman, who was introduced to Dickens on the day when, with Thomas Chapman, Daniel Maclise, John Leech, Thomas Powell, and Samuel Rogers, he went to see Crosby Hall, Bishopgate street, the restoration of which had then (1842) been completed with great taste and skill. This is all that remains of the dwelling of Richard III., repeatedly mentioned by Shakespeare. The bay-window, or oriel, is the *chef d' œuvre* of the domestic architecture of Old London, and the stone carving is as sharp as when first cut, four centuries ago. The party, my exact informant tells me, proceeded from Crosby Hall to the adjacent London Tavern, also in Bishopgate street, where, at the proper charge of Mr. Thomas Chapman, Bathe & Breach supplied a lunch. Of the six who constituted that social party, only one survives. On that day, however, Dickens "booked" Captain Cuttle, though he did not appear in *Dombey & Son* until five years later.

In *David Copperfield*, the striking character of Wilkins Micawber, who was always waiting "for something to turn up," was believed, by many who thought themselves competent to decide, to have been the author's attempt to represent his own father! It was said that the elder Dickens knew and did not wholly disapprove of the sketch. It will be remembered by the readers of "David Copperfield," that though Mr. Micawber is represented as careless in money-matters, apt to get into debt, and addicted to get out of it by means of bills and notes-of-hand, he never says or does anything at variance with morality and probity. He is eternally waiting "for something to turn up," and shifting, as best he can, in the meantime. But he is never mean, false, nor dishonest, and it is his keen sense of the right that eventually places him in triumphant antagonism with that precious limb of the law—a disgrace to an honorable profession—Mr. Uriah Heep.

In *David Copperfield*, Mr. Traddles, the hero's youthful friend, who finally is spoken of as the next Judge, is supposed to have been intended for the late Sir T. N. Talfourd, the author's oldest and truest friend. The sketch is scarcely complimentary.

In *Bleak House* at least three characters are said to have been drawn from real life. These are Esther Sommerson, Boythorn, and Harold Skimpole. *Place aux dames!* Therefore, we begin by stating the belief, among parties who ought to have known, that Esther Sommerson, who tells so much of the story of Bleak House, is believed to bear a great resemblance to Miss Sophia Iselin, author of a volume of poems published in 1847. Her sister, a *protegée* of Charles Lamb, was married to Edward Moxon, the publisher, who, benefited largely by Samuel Roger's testamentary provision. Sophia Iselin has no cause to complain of her full length in *Bleak House.*

As for Harold Skimpole, it was admitted by Dickens that Leigh Hunt was irrepressibly in his mind when developing this selfish and unscrupulous sentimentalist, though he endeavored to make the sketch *not* like the original. Careless as to money—apparently ignorant of its value—Leigh Hunt may have been, but Harold Skimpole, in *Bleak House*, is drawn with a pen dipped in aqua fortis. In December, 1859, Mr. Dickens published a disavowal of having drawn Harold Skimpole, in *Bleak House*, from his friend Leigh Hunt. The statement first "came from America," and therefore Mr. Dickens "let the thing go by." He alluded to it in 1859, because the report had been received in England, since Leigh Hunt's death. Mr. Dickens must have had unusual ignorance of literary table-talk in England if he did not know, even while *Bleak House* was in serial publication, that literary people who knew Hunt and read Dickens, instantly recognized the former as the veritable Harold Skimpole. The identification of living Hunt with fictitious Skimpole did not *originate* in America, where it was but the echo of the English belief. The question is, was Leigh Hunt in Dickens's mind when he sketched and filled up the character of Harold Skimpole? His words, in *All the Year Round*, are as follows:

The fact is this: Exactly those graces and charms of manner which are remembered in the words we have quoted, *were remembered by the author of the work of fiction in question, when he drew the character in question.* Above all other things, that "sort of gay and ostentatious wilfulness" in the humoring of a subject, which had many a time delighted him, and impressed him as being unspeakably whimsical and attractive, was the airy quality he wanted for the man he invented. Partly for this reason, and partly (he has since often grieved to think) for the pleasure it afforded him to find that delightful manner reproducing itself under his hand, *he yielded to the temptation of too often making the character speak like his old friend.* He no more thought, God forgive him! that the admired original would ever be charged with the imaginary vices of the fictitious creature, than he has himself ever thought of charging the blood of Desdemona and Othello on the innocent Academy model who sat for Iago's leg in the picture. Even as to the mere occasional manner, he meant to be so cautious and conscientious, that he privately referred the proof sheets of the first number of that book to two intimate literary friends of Leigh Hunt (both still living), and *altered the whole of that part of the text on their discovering too strong a resemblance to his "way."*

Mr. Dickens admitted that Hunt *was* in his mind when he drew the character of Skimpole. Nay, more, Dickens admited that "he yielded to the temptation of too often making the character *speak* like his old friend;" and fancying that he had photographed the character too exactly, submitted what he had written to two literary friends of Hunt's, and altered that part of the text on their discovering that the *fictitious* was too recognizable for the *real* character. Enough was left, however, as the public discovered at once, to show that Skimpole was Hunt. Charles Dickens, instead of a denial that Harold Skimpole was Leigh Hunt, published an admission of the fact.

It is stated in John Forster's Biography of Walter Savage Landor, that the Boythorn of *Bleak House* was drawn from Landor, as Dickens knew him, in 1839,—the very year in which Landor wrote to Forster, saying, "Tell him (Dickens) that he has drawn from me more tears and more smiles than are remaining to me for all the rest of the world, real or ideal." A letter from Mr. Dickens, on first meeting Mr. Landor, says, "There was a sterling quality in his laugh, and in the roundness and fulness with which he uttered every word he spoke, and in the very fury of his superlatives, which seemed to go off like blank cannons and hurt nothing." He also describes him as grand in repose, "such a true gentleman in his manner, so chivalrously polite, his face lighted up by a smile of as much sweetness and tenderness, and it seemed as plain that he had nothing to hide, but showed himself exactly as he was, incapable of anything on a limited scale, and firing away with those blank great guns because he carried no small arms whatever; that really I could not help looking at him with equal pleasure as he sat at dinner, whether he smilingly conversed, or was led into some great volley of superlatives, or threw up his head like a blood-hound, and gave out that tremendous Ha! ha! ha!" The Landor of actual and the Boythorn of fictitious life are certainly one and undivided. If possible, the living Landor was more unnaturally original than his counterfeit presentment in the tale!

Mr. John Forster mentioning a visit which Dickens and himself paid to Walter Savage Landor, to keep the birthday of the latter, says "I think it was at the first celebration of the kind, in the first of his Bath Lodgings, 35th street, James's Square, that the fancy which took the form of Little Nell in the Curiosity Shop first dawned on the genius of its creator. No character in prose fiction was a greater favorite with Landor. He thought that, upon her, Juliet might for a moment have turned her eyes from Romeo, and that Desdemona might have taken her hair-breadth escapes to heart, so interesting and pathetic did she seem to him; and when, some years later, the circumstance I have recalled was named to him, he broke into one of those whimsical bursts of comical extravagance out of which arose the fancy of Boythorn. With tremendous emphasis he confirmed the fact, and added that he had never in his life regretted any thing so much as his having failed to carry out an intention he had formed respecting it; for he meant to have purchased that house, 35 St. James's Square, and then and there have burned it to the ground, to the end that no meaner association should ever desecrate the birth-place of Nell. Then he would pause a little, become conscious of our sense of his absurdity, and break into a thundering peal of laughter."

Some friends of Mr. John Dickens thought they recognized certain of his characteristics, as regarded Deportment, in the sketch of that eminent professor, Mr. Turveydrop. Mr. Bucket, the detective, also a character in *Bleak House*, was most probably Inspector Field, with whom Mr. Dickens was very well acquainted, for his original. It will be remembered that Mr. Dickens published several papers in which his wanderings under the protective escort of Mr. Field were pretty fully described.

There is a character in Dickens's works which is not fictitious, but cannot be passed over. Many have read the sketch, entitled "The Italian Prisoner," in *The Uncommercial Traveller*, in which a certain Giovanni Carlavero, anxious to express his gratitude to "a certain generous and gentle English nobleman," who saved his life when he was a galley-slave, for politics only, and rescued him from the hopeless horrors of an Italian dungeon, sends him, per Charles Dickens, a gigantic demijohn of wine, the very first of his little vineyard. With great difficulty this stupendous Bottle, holding some half dozen gallons, was taken to England, through Italy, France, and Germany, and was mere vinegar when it reached its address. "And the Englishman told me," the Sketch says, "with much emotion in his face and voice, that he had never tasted wine that seemed to him so sweet and sound." The person who received Carlavero's grateful offering was Lord Dudley Coutts Stuart, brother of the first Marquis of Bute. He was in the House of Commons for many years, and was the invariable advocate of liberal measures. He particularly devoted himself to the interests of the exiled Poles, who had founded an asylum in England. He died in November, 1854, aged forty-six. Dickens says: "He is dead in these days when I relate the story, and exiles have lost their best British friend."

In the story, entitled "Hunted Down,"* published in the

* "Hunted Down" was written specially for the "New York Ledger," by Mr. Dickens, for which Mr. Robert Bonner, the publisher of it, paid him one thousand pounds. It is included in no editions of the works of Charles Dickens, either in Europe or America, except those published by T. B. Peterson & Brothers, Philadelphia.

New York Ledger, in 1859, by Mr. Robert Bonner, it is evident that, as also in Bulwer's "Lucretia, or the Children of Night," the hero was taken, scarcely idealized, from Thomas Griffiths Wainewright, Charles Lamb's favorite "Janus Weathercock," of the *London Magazine*. This villain actually poisoned several persons, on whose lives heavy insurances had been effected, and succeeded in obtaining the money, in some instances. Tried and convicted of forgery, he was sent to one of the British penal colonies for life, and, after several years, died in that deserved captivity. Mr. Dickens, in one of his latest papers in *All the Year Round*, gave a detailed account of this wretch. In *Hunted Down*, his shadow is called Mr. Julius Slinkton, of the Middle Temple.

Dr. Charles Rogers, writing from Lewisham, a Kentish suburb of London, to the *Daily News*, gives an account of the origin of the name Master Humphrey's Clock, which has an air of probability. He says:—"In 1864, in the course of a tour, I arrived at the town of Barnard Castle, in the county of Durham, late on a winter evening, and put up at the principal hotel, a large old-fashioned structure, fronting the principal street. At breakfast the following morning I chanced to notice on the opposite side of the street a large clock-face, with the name Humphrey surrounding it, most conspicuously exhibited in front of a watch and clock-maker's shop. 'How odd,' I exclaimed to a gentleman seated beside me, 'here is Master Humphrey's clock!' 'Of course,' said the gentleman, 'and don't you know that Dickens resided here for some weeks when he was collecting materials for his Nicholas Nickleby, and that he chose his title for his next work by observing that big clock-face from this window?' After breakfast, I stepped across to the watchmaker, and asked him whether I had been correctly informed respecting Mr. Dickens and the clock. The worthy horologist entered into particulars. 'My clock,' said he, 'suggested to Mr. Dickens the title of his book of that name. I have a letter from him stating this, and a copy of the work, inscribed with his own hand. For some years we corresponded. I got acquainted with him just by his coming across from the hotel, as you have done this morning, and asking me to inform him about the state of the neighboring boarding-schools. Mr. Humphrey then entered into many particulars respecting the condition of these schools. Incidentally, he said, he had directed Mr. Dickens and his friend "Phiz" to the school which the two travellers afterward rendered infamous by their pen and pencil; but it was, he said, by no means the worst of those institutions. The schoolmaster had been very successful in obtaining pupils, and had become very tyrannical, and even insolent, to strangers. He received Mr. Dickens and his companion with extreme hauteur, and did not so much as withdraw his eyes from the operation of pen-making during their interview. But "Phiz" sketched him on his nail and reproduced him so exactly, that soon after the appearance of the novel the school fell off, and was ultimately deserted. Since that period the "Do-the-Boys" description of school had altogether ceased in the district. Mr. Dickens has mentioned that he took a journey to Yorkshire, in 1838, before he began to compose *Nicholas Nickleby*, and a letter in my possession, which I shall print, states that, in January in that year, he was in Darlington, which is within a dozen miles of the fine old market-town of Barnard's Castle.

CHAPTER XV.

LETTER-WRITING.—EPISTOLATORY MENDICANTS.—A NOTE FROM YORKSHIRE. — MR. EWART. — A SLOW BINDER. — MASTER HUMPHREY'S "WORKS." — TALFOURD'S POST-PRANDIAL READING. — LETTERS TO TALFOURD, FRANK STONE, AND MACKENZIE.—MAMMOTH JOURNALS.—THE MOON HOAX.—LORD NUGENT.

NOBODY who had once noticed could readily forget the peculiar handwriting of "Boz." I have known it for over thirty years, and have never seen any variation in it. It was very legible; it was a flowing hand, each line being written, almost, by one continuous action of hand and pen; it was unlike any other writing that you ever saw. The signature, too, was wholly out of the common, with that prolonged flourish under the name, finally tapering to a point, far below by what musicians would call a *dimuendō* movement. The first letter of the Christian name was written upon no apparent system, but had rarely varied; you were often puzzled to know whether it was a C or a G, and accepted it as the former, simply because it was impossible that it could have been the latter. This signature, with the flourish, ended each note or letter; but the outer address almost invariably had *Charles Dickens* on the corner, with one heavy stroke above and another underneath. As I have already noticed, the date was very explicit, giving the day of the week in full, and expressing the day of the month in *words* and not in numerals. Following the example of his father, quite a gentleman of the Old School, Mr. Dickens, in addressing a person, never used the familiar contraction "Esq.," but wrote "Esquire" in full. He generally used thick note-paper with a blue tint, and so invariably wrote in blue ink that it is reasonable to suppose that he always travelled with a bottle of that fluid in his dressing-case. During his last visit to the United States, 1867–8, his friends noticed that, as usual, his notes were written with blue ink.

His familiar friends here will acknowledge that Mr. Dickens possessed the *eloquence du billet* in no limited degree. Byron, Scott, Southey and Moore have largely exhibited his agreeable faculty in our own time. His letters overflowed with delightful badinage, were full of expression, touched a great many subjects with graceful ease and liveliness, and contained frequent passages, thrown off at the moment, which would have charmed multitudes of his readers had he chosen to reserve them for his printed pages. I have heard it said that Thomas Hood's almost habitual silence in society was caused by a fear of letting his good things escape in company, instead of their being reserved for his writings; but Dickens had none of this reticence, for he had great animal spirits, and the prodigality of his genius was apparently exhaustless.

Many of his epistles, and these the briefest, cost him a good deal. Though he waged perpetual war against those audacious, plausible, and unconquerable Ishmaelites, the professional begging-letter rogues and mendicants of London, he was constantly their victim. They beset him, in all manner of ways, with all sorts of applications, and so tende rwas this man's heart that, even when more than half suspecting that he was solicited by an old hand with a new story, he generally yielded. He was remonstrated with by some of his friends at times, and would say, with a smile, "Well, I may be taken in; but suppose this poor man's sad story were true, could I ever forgive myself for having not attended to it?" So he would write a courteous little letter, regretting that his own means, with many imperative demands on them, prevented his being as useful as he desired, but begging that his correspondent "would accept the enclosed,"—usually a five or even a ten pound Bank of England note. I have seen some of these little billets in the archives of autograph collectors (the beggars knew that a note from Charles Dickens would always obtain them a shilling or two from Mr. Waller, the autograph dealer in Fleet street), and I have heard of more. In one case, a truly deserving person whom he had thus relieved, and who lived to return the money, under improved circumstances, told me, with a sob in his voice, that Mr. Dickens, who saw him personally, had liberally relieved him as if he were receiving instead of conferring a favor. I wonder how far the actual liberality of the pietists, who presume to doubt whether Mr. Dickens "had religion," has extended, in cases like the above, to persons who sought relief from them? "What I give," said a miserly plateholder at a charity sermon,—"What *I* give, is nothing to nobody." Many persons who are "professors" can say the same, no doubt.

Here I may as well introduce some letters from Mr. Dickens,—of "no consequence," as Mr. Toots would say, but more or less characteristic.

The following letter from Mr. Dickens, written after the completion of *Pickwick* and when about half of *Oliver Twist* had appeared, in monthly instalments, requires a slight introduction. A friend of mine who was "going to the bar," as a nominal law-student in the Inner Temple, London, qualified himself, in the then usual manner, not by mastering Coke upon Littleton, or Blackstone's Commentaries, but by eating three dinners "in Hall," each term. He privately corresponded with the proprietor of *the* newspaper in his native town. While *Pickwick* was in progress, there was considerable curiosity to learn who its author was, and at Christmas, 1837, the future barrister sent some of the gossip of the clubs on that subject, which my editorial friend was only too glad to print, thoughtlessly retaining the signature. The newspaper accidentally fell into Mr. Dickens's hands. At that time (January, 1838,) he was in Yorkshire collecting materials relative to the seminaries there, of which Dotheboys Hall became the representative, in prose fiction. He wrote a note, short and sharp, dated, "Darlington, Saturday morning," (the actual time was at the close of January, 1838,) declaring that, in no one particular did the published "gossip" even approach correctness.—That Messrs. Chapman & Hall "were never persuaded with some difficulty to become the Pickwick publishers, but on the contrary first became known to me by waiting on me to propose the work; that by the Pickwick Papers alone I have *not* netted between £2,000 and £3,000; that the sketch called "Watkins Tottle" never appeared in the *Morning Chronicle;* that I am *not* now in the receipt of £3,000 a year; and that Mr. Bentley does *not* give me £1,000 a year for editing his Miscellany, and twenty guineas a sheet for what I write in it."

This note was published, in the peccant journal, and the gentleman who had figured as "London Correspondent," peradventure, after consulting some of his friends, frankly wrote to Mr. Dickens, mentioning how, without his authority or knowledge, part of one of his private letters had been printed, with his signature, and how much he regretted that his careless gossip had annoyed a writer, whom he so greatly admired. This brought the following reply, prompt and courteous:

48 Doughty Street, London,
Friday, February 16th, 1838.

Dear Sir:—I have to thank you very cordially for your letter of the twelfth, and to assure you that your explanation is quite satisfactory.

I saw the paragraph in question during a stay of a few minutes at Darlington in Yorkshire, and wrote a hasty contradiction to the editor of the newspaper in which it appeared. It certainly contained nothing ill-natured or offensive, but I felt for the moment annoyed at my private affairs being dragged before the public, and stated incorrectly in every particular.

Any impression of this kind is at once removed by your frank and manly letter, and I hasten to assure you that I care nothing for the paragraph since it has been the means of calling forth so polite and ready a communication.

I am, Faithfully Yours,
CHARLES DICKENS.

As we are "nothing, if not critical," I may mention that Mr. Dickens was mistaken in locating Darlington, "in Yorkshire,"—for the simple reason that it is in the County-Palitine of Durham. I may add that in fitness of time, the gentleman to whom this gracious letter was addressed, became a barrister-at-law, was introduced to Dickens by Serjeant Talfourd, became very intimate with him, has long been a Queen's counsel, in high practice, and is even in a fair way to a seat on the judicial bench. Mr. Dickens's autograph letter has remained in my possession, my friend not having cared to preserve it among *his* archives, while, as I had not only suggested but written his letter of apology to "Boz," I considered myself entitled to retain the reply. The letter is not without interest, from its early date, and also as it breathes the frankness and courtesy which, through life, were among its author's recognized characteristics.

To a little later period belongs the following communication, which was given to me by Mr. Serjeant Talfourd, with whom I was well acquainted. The year is omitted in the original, but can readily be ascertained from the context:

DEVONSHIRE TERRACE,
Tuesday, April the Twenty-seventh, [1840.]

MY DEAR TALFOURD:—Many thanks for the Sonnet. Do you know Ewart? I want, on behalf of an oppressed lady, to remind him of a promise he made her relative to the presentation of a petition to the House. I don't like to approach a man of his kidney, without an introduction. Can you give me one in a couple of lines?

Faithfully Always,
CHARLES DICKENS.

The Sonnet is to be found in Talfourd's Poems, and is as follows:

TO CHARLES DICKENS

ON HIS "OLIVER TWIST."

Not only with the Author's happiest praise
Thy work should be rewarded: 'tis akin
To DEEDS of men, who scorning ease to win
A blessing for the wretched, pierce the maze
Which heedless ages spread around the ways
Where fruitful Sorrow tracks its parent Sin;
Content to listen to the wildest din
Of passion, and on fellest shapes to gaze,
So they might earn the power which intercedes
With the bright world and melt it for within
Wan Childhood's squalid haunts, where basest needs
Make tyranny more bitter, at thy call
An angel face with patient sweetness sheds
For infant suffering to the heart of all.

These lines, at once vague and unintelligible, are so simply complimentary in fact, that one cannot wonder at their being merely acknowledged by their recipient. Talfourd was addicted to this mode of flattering his friends. Out of his fourteen sonnets, published in the volume which contains Talfourd's three tragedies, six are personal,—addressed to Dr. Valpy, his schoolmaster; to Macready, on his performance of "Werner"; to Macready, on the birth of his first child, in recollection of his performance of "Virginius"; to Charles Dickens; to Miss Adelaide Kemble, the singer, on her approaching retirement from the stage; and to Wordsworth, the poet, on his reception at

Oxford, in 1839, when he publicly received the honorary degree of D. C. L.

Mr. Ewart, referred to in Mr. Dickens's note, was then M. P. for Wigan. He was son of a wealthy merchant in Liverpool, and was a barrister, though he did not practice. He was an extreme Liberal and deserves to be remembered on account of an Act, introduced by him and now in successful operation, for establishing Free Libraries in a large number of towns in England and Wales. Mr. Ewart, whose death occurred recently, was a liberal, well-meaning, respectable gentleman, whom Dickens need not have been shy of approaching, upon business, "without an introduction," but this was early in his career, for he soon became familiar with Lords and Commoners who expressed their satisfaction at being introduced to *him.*

The most intimate and enduring friends whom Mr. Dickens cherished through life, were the late Mr. Serjeant Talfourd, and Mr. John Forster. Here is a playful little note to the former:

DEVONSHIRE TERRACE,
Tuesday, February Sixteen, 1841.

MY DEAR TALFOURD:—A friend of mine—a man you will say of most extraordinary tastes—wants to go into the gallery of the House of Commons next Friday. Can you give me an order for that day, and will you send it by post?

Tell Mrs. Talfourd your Nickleby and Clock are in course of binding—by the slowest man in England.

Faithfully yours,
CHARLES DICKENS.

In order to obtain admission into the House of Lords or Commons, the "Strangers' Gallery" in each being very small, it is requisite to obtain an order signed by a peer or an M. P., as the case might be—with a certainty when a debate of any interest was anticipated, that only the order-holders, who had reached the closed door of the Gallery, long before the usual hour of its being opened, had any chance of admission. It has been stated, however, that *a silver key*, in the shape of half-a-crown, slyly slipped into the janitor's unreluctant hand, was an unerring "Open Sesame" to either gallery. Talfourd being the representative of his native town of Reading, had the power of complying with his friend's request.

It appears from the following note, that the slowest bookbinder in England had done his work at last. Mr. Dickens wrote:

Monday, March Twenty-second, 1841.

MY DEAR TALFOURD:—That immortally sluggish binder has at length completed your Nickleby, which I pray you accept herewith. The two Clock volumes are in progress.

The mention of them brings me to asking a favor of you. I must have *the works* to dinner again. Will Saturday, April the Tenth, at a quarter past six, suit you? and if so, will you on that day again kindly do for me what no man can do so well, or with so much pleasure to all his hearers?

The celebration of the second volume entails these pains and penalties upon you.

With best regards to Mrs. Talfourd and to Miss E. G.,

Believe me ever,

My dear Talfourd,

Faithfully yours,

CHARLES DICKENS.

MR. SERJEANT TALFOURD.

This letter will let the public into the heart of a little secret, not quite unknown to Mr. Dickens's friends. At that early period of his career, nearly thirty years ago, he used to take the opinion of some friends, "audience fit but few," upon unpublished portions of any work then in progress. Mr. Forster, the late Mr. Robert Bell, Mr. Frank Stone, and Mr. Serjeant Talfourd, are believed to have been members of this board of private criticism, which might have been called "Friends in Council." Talfourd, who read very well, despite of a curious lisp, always did *his* part to admiration. At the date of this note, the first portion of *Master Humphrey's Clock*, containing the story in which Little Nell is embalmed, had been completed, and *Barnaby Rudge* was in course of publication.

It was declared by Douglas Jerrold, that dinner-giving is such an established institution in England, that if an earthquake were to destroy London, leaving Lord Macaulay's New Zealander sitting on the *debris* of St. Paul's, like Marius amid the ruins of Carthage, no doubt a party of the survivors, assembling on Ludgate Hill, next day, would celebrate the destructive catastrophe by a public dinner, amid the wreck of architecture. If the catastrophe had occurred when Mr. Dickens was near, assuredly he would have purchased a ticket, for, independent of thinking that the good things of life were not meant for the "unco guid" only, he was genially fond of celebrating the completion of each of his works, by a good dinner to his friends. On the occasion in question "*the works*" evidently mean certain friends of the author, to whom Talfourd was to read new and unpublished portions of the story. This, as well as I remember, was the explanation given by Mr. Talfourd, from whom I received the autograph.

What may have been written or printed on "the scrap of paper" alluded to in the following note, I do not recollect. The newspaper referred to, (published in the English town of Shrewsbury, which, by its quaint architecture and remarkably narrow and crooked streets, greatly attracted the attention of Nathaniel Hawthorne, when he visited it, in 1855,) was then edited by myself, and the lines which Mr. Dickens was pleased to praise, written on the recent death of my daughter, a child of rare beauty and rich promise:

BRODSTANS, KENT,
Monday, Twenty-third August, 1841.

DEAR SIR:—I am much obliged to you for your letter, and the scrap of paper enclosed in it. I was aware of the imposition soon after it was attempted, but had never seen the article. I can bear, like a good Christian, the not having any more of it.

Let me thank you also for the newspaper I received from you. I found some lines in its columns which afforded me very great pleasure in the perusal.

Faithfully yours,

CHARLES DICKENS.

DR. MACKENZIE.

Among the "Curiosities of Literature," in which Mr. Dickens was interested, were what are known as "Mammoth" American papers. I was able to supply him with some specimens of this gigantic class of Journalism. In a note, dated "First September, 1842," Mr. Dickens thus acknowledges the receipt of either *The New World*—or an enormous *Brother Jonathan*—which my old friend Major M. M. Noah, had sent to me from New York. Mr. Dickens wrote: "I am greatly obliged to you for your note and its accompanying Paper, which is indeed a phenomenon. The announcement you allude to [in America, of a new work by Mr. Dickens, which he had neither written nor intended to write,] had attracted my attention. We shall see a hundred others of the same family, and shall continue to see them until we die."

Mr. Dickens's recollections of *Brother Jonathan* were not pleasant. In 1842, after the first visit to the United States, the late Mr. Isaac C. Pray, previously editor of the *Boston Pearl*, was in London, conducting a cheap evening paper, so very liberal in its politics, that even the Chartists thought it went too far. By application of what is figuratively designated "oil-of palm," he obtained proof-sheets of the "American Notes" from some of the pressmen in Bradbury & Evans's printing office, and sent them to Boston, in advance of the English book, in two volumes, the selling price of which was twenty-one shillings. Mr. Dickens had made arrangements with a New York publisher for the reproduction of a fac-simile edition for America, but before the legitimate advance sheets arrived, the entire book was circulated throughout the United States, in a double number of *Brother Jonathan*, for six cents. Of course, this took the bloom from Mr. Dickens's peach. Mr. Lockhart has mentioned how, on several occasions, sheets of Sir Walter Scott's novels were surreptitiously obtained from Ballantyne's printing office, for American, French, and German publishers.

Mr. Locke's celebrated "Moon Hoax," of which I sent a copy to Mr. Dickens, greatly interested and amused him. He acknowledged it, in a brisk little note, saying that he was at work when it reached him—that he carelessly looked into it, and was attracted by the matter-of-fact character of the narrative—that he did not lay it down until he had read every line of it, and that, for the first ten minutes, he thought it really was, what it purported to be, a *bonâ fide* scientific report by Sir John Herschell, the astronomer. "Since Captain Lemuel Gulliver and Robinson Crusoe," he wrote, "there has not been any story so *very* like truth as this." I quote this sentence from Memory, having given the original letter to an autograph collector,—an indiscretion, I beg to inform all brethren of *that* craft, which I am determined never again to commit.

The following note to Frank Stone, the painter, one of Dickens's most intimate friends, was written, as the date shows, immediately after that mysterious Wednesday, in 1849, during the Epsom Races, when the Derby was won by the Flying Dutchman. The first paragraph alludes to this:

DEVONSHIRE TERRACE,
Twenty-fourth May, 1849.

MY DEAR STONE:—I "took" a good deal yesterday—but not in the way of odds. I understand from my ladies that not much was taken at Arethura's last night.

It is most annoying that on Tuesday I shall be at Aylesbury, down at old Nugent's. I come back, however, that evening, and am your man when ever you like afterward.

Yours affectionately,
CHARLES DICKENS.

FRANK STONE, Esquire.

"Old Nugent" was a younger brother of the first Duke of Buckingham and Chandos, and succeeded to an Irish Barony, in 1813. He had been M. P. for Aylesbury, near which town was his small but beautiful estate. One of his works bears the alliterative title of "Legends of the Library at Lilies, by the Lord and Lady There." Lord Nugent was fond of literary society, was hospitable on rather limited means, and was sixty years old when Mr. Dickens wrote. He died in the following year, without a direct male heir, and the title became extinct.

None of Mr. Dickens's letters, in this chapter, have been previously published. They are printed from the originals.

CHAPTER XVI.

POETRY IN PROSE. — THACKERAY'S OPINION. — RYTHMICAL LANGUAGE. — EXAMPLES FROM SOUTHEY, SHELLEY, AND DICKENS. — LITTLE NELL'S FUNERAL. — LESSON OF DEATH TO LIFE. — SMIKE'S GRAVE-STONE. — NIAGARA. — HYMN OF THE LABORERS.—A WORD IN SEASON.

It does not follow, as many think, that Poetry must consist of metre, measured language, rhyme, or rythm. There are poets, in prose as well as in verse. There is the truth, as well as the pathetic tenderness of poetry, in that short and simple verse, in the New Testament, "Jesus wept," which shows how entirely, how devotedly, the Saviour grafted our humanity upon His divinity. Many a man has unconsciously expressed the sentiments of poetry, in speech or writing. As Wordsworth put it,

Many are the Poets that are sown
By Nature; men endowed with highest gifts,
The vision and the faculty divine;
Yet wanting the accomplishment of verse,

and Byron, evidently paraphrasing these lines, puts into the mouth of Dante, the poet-sire of Italy, the following declaration:

> Many are poets who have never penned
> Their inspiration, and perchance the best;
> * * * * * * *
> Many are poets, but without the name.

On this principle, Charles Dickens undoubtedly was a poet. He has not mere passages, but scenes, full of the most sensitive, natural, and impressive poetry. "But," I have heard critics say, "he never printed them *as* poetry." My friends, whether the window through which the glory of sunlight comes to us, be circular, square, or oval, or whether it be set in the Egyptian, the Grecian, the Gothic, or the Log-cabin order of architecture, the shape of the medium does not concern us so much as the light itself does,

> As sunshine, broken in the rill,
> Though turned astray, is sunshine still,

and what light is to the material world, poetry is to the intellectual. Thackeray, who was honest with all his cynicism, acknowledged the claim of Dickens to be ranked among the poets. Mr. Hodder has recorded that, when the fifth number of *Dombey and Son*, closed with the death of Little Paul, Mr. Thackeray appeared electrified at the thought that there was one man living whose pathos could so thoroughly stir the depths of his soul, and rushing down to the office of *Punch*, where the portly editor, Mr. Mark Lemon, was correcting manuscript, dashed that fifth number down on the table, with startling vehemence, and exclaimed: "There's no writing against such power as this—one has no chance! Read that chapter describing young Paul's death: it is unsurpassed—it is stupendous!" This, a rival's praise, was perhaps the highest tribute that an author could have received.

Many other scenes in Dickens's works are not merely poetic, but constitute poetry of a high order. The storm and wreck, off Yarmouth, in *David Copperfield*, are described with epic power, and the death of Little Nell will occur to every reader. It was noticed, many years ago, that "a curious circumstance is observable in a great portion of the scenes of tragic power, pathos and tenderness contained in various parts of Mr. Dickens's works, which it is possible may have been the result of harmonious accident, and the author not even subsequently conscious of it. It is that they are written in blank verse, of irregular metre and rythm, which Southey, and Shelley, and some other poets, have occasionally adopted." In Southey's "Thalaba," for example, is this fine expression upon Night:

How beautiful is Night!
  A dewy freshness fills the silent air,
No mist obscures, nor cloud, nor speck, nor stain
  Breaks the serene of heaven.
In full orbed glory yonder Moon divine
  Rolls through the dark blue depths.
  Beneath her steady ray
  The desert circle spreads,
Like the round ocean, girdled with the sky.
  How beautiful is Night!

Shelley's "Queen Mab" opens with this stanza, in the same manner:

  How wonderful is Death,
  Death and his brother Sleep!
One, pale as yonder waning moon,
  With lips of lurid blue;
  The other, rosy as the morn
When throned on ocean's wave
  It blushes o'er the world:
Yet both so passing beautiful.

Here, from Dickens, is the description of Little Nell's funeral, which is unconsciously rythmical. It is printed, as prose, in *The Old Curiosity Shop,* and seems as if it had spontaneously ran into metre. Only two trifling words (*in* and *its*) have been omitted; *e'en* has been put for *almost,* and *gran'dames* has been put for *grandmothers.* Everything else is unchanged; not a word transposed, not even a comma altered in the punctuation; here it is, printed as poetry:

LITTLE NELL'S FUNERAL.

And now the bell—the bell
She had so often heard by night and day,
And listened to with solemn pleasure,
E'en as a living voice—
Rung its remorseless toll for her,
So young, so beautiful, so good.

Decrepit age, and vigorous life,
And blooming youth, and helpless infancy,
Poured forth—on crutches, in the pride of strength
And health, in the full blush
Of promise, in the mere dawn of life—
To gather round her tomb. Old men were there,
Whose eyes were dim
And senses failing—
Gran'dames, who might have died ten years ago,
And still been old—the deaf, the blind, the lame,
The palsied,
The living dead in many shapes and forms,
To see the closing of this early grave.
What was the death it would shut in,
To that which still could crawl and creep above it!

Along the crowded path they bore her now;
Pure as the new-fallen snow
That covered it; whose day on earth
Had been as fleeting.
Under that porch, where she had sat when Heaven
In mercy brought her to that peaceful spot,
She passed again, and the old church
Received her in its quiet shade.

Here, too, is the brief homily with which the description of the funeral closes:

DEATH'S LESSON.

Oh! it is hard to take
The lesson that such deaths will teach,
But let no man reject it,
For it is one that all must learn
And is a mighty universal Truth.
When Death strikes down the innocent and young,
For every fragile form from which
He lets the parting spirit free,
A hundred virtues rise,
In shapes of mercy, charity, and love,
To walk the world and bless it,
Of every tear
That sorrowing mortals shed on such green graves,
Some good is born, some gentle nature comes.

Akin to this, and also without the alteration of a word, is the concluding paragraph of *Nicholas Nickleby:*

SMIKE'S GRAVE-STONE.

The grass was green above the dead boy's grave,
Trodden by feet so small and light,
That not a daisy drooped its head
Beneath their pressure.
Through all the spring and summer time
Garlands of fresh flowers, wreathed by infant hands,
Rested upon the stone.

Even in the *American Notes,* rather an unlikely depository for poetic thought and expression, is a passage, upon Niagara, very much in the same manner:

NIAGARA.

I think in every quiet season now,
Still do these waters roll, and leap, and roar,
And tumble, all day long;
Still are the rainbows spanning them
A hundred feet below.
Still when the sun is on them, do they shine
And glow like molten gold.
Still when the day is gloomy do they fall
Like snow, or seem to crumble away,
Like the front of a great chalk cliff,
Or roll adown the rock like dense white smoke.

But always does this mighty stream appear
To die as it comes down.
And always from the unfathomable grave
Arises that tremendous ghost of spray
And mist which is never laid:
Which has haunted this place
With the same dread solemnity,
Since darkness brooded on the deep,
And that first flood before the Deluge—Light,
Came rushing on Creation
At the word of God.

Of actual verses written by Mr. Dickens, not much is known. In *Pickwick*, he introduced two simple lyrics, "A Christmas Carol," and "The Ivy Green," both of which were set to music and are yet occasionally sung by melodious bucolics. In the opera of "Village Coquettes," which though published seems to have dropped out of sight, were several songs—as usual, it may be presumed, mere vehicles for the music. But Mr. Dickens, an English authority states, was fond of versifying, and numerous of his productions were printed, anonymously, in different periodicals.

The *Daily News*, the London paper of which he was first editor, for a brief time, states that, on February 14th, 1846, it published the following, elicited by a speech at one of the night meetings of the wives of agricultural laborers in Wiltshire, held to petition for free trade:

THE HYMN OF THE WILTSHIRE LABORERS.

"Don't you all think that we have a great need to cry to our God to put it in the hearts of our greaseous Queen and her members of Parlerment to grant us free bread!"—*Lucy Simpkins, at Brem Hill.*

Oh God, who by Thy Prophet's hand
Did'st smite the rocky brake,
Whence water came at Thy command,
The people's thirst to slake;
Strike now, upon this granite wall,
Stern, obdurate, and high,
And let some drops of pity fall
For us who starve and die!

The God, who took a little child
  And set him in the midst,
And promised him His mercy mild,
  As, by Thy Son, Thou did'st:
Look down upon our children dear,
  So gaunt, so cold, so spare,
And let their images appear
  Where Lords and Gentry are!

Oh God, teach them to feel how we,
  When our poor infants droop,
Are weakened in our trust in Thee,
  And how our spirits stoop:
For, in Thy rest, so bright and fair,
  All tears and sorrows sleep:
And their young looks, so full of care,
  Would make Thine angels weep!

The God, who with His finger drew
  The Judgment coming on,
Write for these men, what must ensue,
  Ere many years be gone!
Oh God, whose bow is in the sky,
  Let them not brave and dare,
Until they look (too late) on high
  And see an Arrow there!

Oh God, remind them! In the bread
  They break upon the knee,
These sacred words may yet be read,
  "In memory of Me!"
Oh God, remind them of His sweet
  Compassion for the poor,
And how He gave them Bread to eat,
  And went from door to door.

The same journal has rescued the following from an Annual edited by Lady Blessington, in 1844, and written by Mr. Dickens. It is an apologue at once graceful and shrewd, somewhat in the manner of Leigh Hunt, with a little of Thomas Hood's familiar flavor. Its author entitled it:

A WORD IN SEASON.

They have a superstition in the East,
  That ALLAH written on a piece of paper
Is better unction than can come of priest,
  Of rolling incense, and of lighted taper;
Holding that any scrap which bears that name,
  In any characters, its front imprest on,
Shall help the finder through the purging flame,
  And give his toasted feet a place to rest on.

Accordingly, they make a mighty fuss
  With every wretched tract and fierce oration,
And hoard the leaves; for they are not, like us,
  A highly civilized and thinking nation;
And always stooping in the miry ways
  To look for matter of this earthly leaven,
They seldom, in their dust-exploring days,
  Have any leisure to look up to Heaven.

So have I known a country on the earth
  Where darkness sat upon the living waters,
And brutal ignorance, and toil, and dearth,
  Were the hard portion of its sons and daughters;
And yet, where they who should have ope'd the door
  Of charity and light for all men's finding,
Squabbled for words upon the altar floor,
  And rent the Book, in struggles for the binding.

The gentlest man among these pious Turks,
  God's living image ruthlessly defaces;
Their best High Churchman, with no faith in works,
  Bowstrings the virtues in the market-places.
The Christian pariah, whom both sects curse
  (They curse all other men, and curse each other),
Walks through the world not very much the worse,
  Does all the good he can, and loves his brother.

Except that the fifth line in the last stanza is curiously defective in rythm, this poem might be conceded perfect in its way. Like many other things by the same author, it was a plea for Charity and Toleration.

CHAPTER XVII.

LITTLE DORRIT.—THE CIRCUMLOCUTION OFFICE.—HARD TIMES. —TALE OF TWO CITIES.—GREAT EXPECTATIONS.—NEW CHRISTMAS STORIES.—OUR MUTUAL FRIEND.—AMENDE TO THE JEWS.—SYSTEMATIC BUSINESS HABITS.—DEALINGS WITH AMERICAN PUBLISHERS.

IN June, 1857, having been published, in the usual serial form, *Little Dorrit* was completed. It had several objects: The How-not-to-do-it system of the British government departments, all of which he closed together under the title of "The Circumlocution Office;" the discouragement given, in the shape of delay and costs, to inventors who wanted patents in the British islands; the evil effects of imprisonment for debt, particularly in the cases where the victims were wholly and hopelessly unable to discharge the claims upon them; and the homage which Society delights to pay to mere wealth, or the appearance of it, represented by such persons as Mr. Merdle or the Veneering family. The assault upon the Circumlocution Office brought the *Edinburgh Review* into the field, for the defence, this periodical, once so powerful, when it had assailed the wrong, now asserting—that the adoption of the penny postage plan, and Rowland Hill's own appointment to superintend its working, were proofs against Dickens's "rash and wholesale satire." Mr. Dickens answered, at some length, in *Household Words*, referring to the notoriety of the fact that for years *after*, as well as *before*, the penny postage scheme was established, the Post Office vehemently opposed it—that Mr. Hill was not allowed to have anything to do with its working until years after it commenced—that he was finally pressed on the Government by public opinion—and that, after all, instead of being Postmaster General, or at least Secretary, he was smuggled in as Secretary to the Postmaster, only. Lord Decimus, Mr. Tite Barnacle & Co., still remain in office. There is no occasion to be critical upon *Little Dorrit*—except to say that she is the most devoted and delightful of daughters, and that, from first to last, whether as the mendicant prisoner in the Marshalsea or the rich man in society, the character of her father is wonderfully well sustained. It is made of numerous delicate touches, each helping towards the perfecting of it.

Hard Times had previously been published in "Household Words." Every one knows Gradgrind, that man of facts; boasting Bounderby; light-eyed Bitzer; Mrs. Sparsit, who had genteel connections; excellent Sleary, the circus-man; poor Louisa Gradgrind, and Sissy Jupe, and those two tragic personages, Stephen Blackpool, who declares it "aw a muddle! fro' first to last, a muddle," and his poor friend Rachel, who, less fortunate, lived on to work and mourn. The circus scenes in this story are equal to the theatre scenes in *Nickleby*. No wonder, for Mr. James T. Fields relates of the author, "If he contemplated writing 'Hard Times,' he arranged with the master of Astley's circus to spend many hours behind the scenes with the riders and among the horses; and if the composition of the 'Tale of Two Cities' were occupying his thoughts, he could banish himself to France for two years to prepare for that great work."

The other work here referred to, the *Tale of Two Cities*, which are London and Paris, appeared in "All the Year Round." Its main idea was suggested, Mr. Dickens says, while, with his children and friends, he was acting in Mr. Wilkie Collins's drama of the "Frozen Deep." One of his hopes, he tells us, was to add something to the popular and picturesque means of understanding that terrible time, though no one can hope to add any thing to the philosophy of Mr. Carlyle's wonderful book. "The idea," he adds, "throughout its execution, has had complete possession of me; I have so far verified what is done and suffered in these pages, as that I have certainly done and suffered it all myself. Whenever any reference (however slight) is made here to the condition of the French people before or during the Revolution, it is truly made, on the faith of trustworthy witnesses." In the whole range of fiction, wide as that realm is, there is not to be found any account of the French Revolution, its causes, and its action, so truthful, so powerful as this. Had Mr. Dickens written nothing but this, so intense and so correct, the most exacting critic might say, "This is a master-piece." Mr. Richard Grant White, who has given us a reliable edition of Shakespeare, does justice to this story and pronounces it "so noble in its spirit, so grand and graphic in its style, and filled with a pathos so profound and simple, that it deserves and will surely take a place among the great serious works of imagination." The character of Sidney Carton, the castaway, who with equal simplicity and sublimity of thought and act, realizes the solemn aphorism "Greater love hath no man than this, that he lay down his life for his friend." Self-wrecked and self-devoted, this man does, in fiction, what, I do believe, knowing what sacrifices it has made, Humanity is capable of doing. I thought once, that poetical justice ought to have been exercised on the fortunes or the person of that legal brain-sucker, Mr. Stryver,—but I abandoned that idea, long since. Mosquitoes live and die, and no one thinks of their obsequies. No doubt, when Sidney Carton disappeared, Stryver, the "lion" for whom, as he had been "provider" (so naturalists call the jackal), perished for want of food. It is gratifying to think that Barrister Stryver, deprived of Carton's aid, must have sank by force of gravitation, into the ranks of the Briefless.

There were two other works, which, like this powerful French story, first appeared in "All the Year Round." These are a series of desultory papers, *de omnibus rebus et quibusdam aliis*, entitled *The Uncommercial Traveller.* Almost to the last, Mr. Dickens was occasionally contributing to this collection. The other, a tale entitled *Great Expectations*, commenced towards the close of 1860, had its scene in London and the Essex Marshes. There are some good characters here. Joe Gargery, the blacksmith, is natural to a degree,—uneducated, but a thorough gentleman in principal and action. Pumblechook is a common individual,—life-like, but unpleasant. Jaggers, the lawyer, and his clerk—that wide-a-wake Wemmick, in whose mind the propriety of realizing "portable property" is a decided principle,—are novelties, to a degree. The death of Provis, the convict, in Newgate, is in Dickens's best manner:—he died in his bed, but was liable to be hanged for having committed the terrible crime of returning from transportion. My own opinion, morally if not legally asserted, is that when Law has a hold upon a man, for offence committed, Law ought to hold him—if it can. A man's natural instinct, whether innocent or guilty, is to be unfettered in limb, uncontrolled in liberty. The custom, if a convict escape from prison, and is recaptured, is to sentence him to an additional term; if he escape from banishment, to take his life,—just as, in Venetian history, Foscari returning from Candia, whither he had been banished, makes his last escape, by death. There is an issue, between the jailer and the prisoner. It is the duty of the jailer to provide safe custody: it is the instinct, I think the *right*, of the prisoner to regain his liberty, if he can. In escaping, he but fulfils the principle of manhood, which prompts him to become free.

In his periodical, for several years, was given a Christmas number; in which, though the master's hand was occasionally observable, the greater portion was by other writers. These were variously entitled: The Wreck of the Golden Mary, A Message from the Sea, (also dramatized, by Charles Dickens and Wilkie Collins,) The Perils of Certain English

Prisoners, Tom Tiddler's Ground, A House to Let, The Haunted House, The Holly Tree Inn, Seven Poor Travellers, Mrs. Lirriper's Lodgings, Mrs. Lirriper's Legacy, Somebody's Luggage, Mugby Junction, Dr. Marigold's Prescriptions, and No Thoroughfare. The last named concluded the series, with, as a novel reason for discontinuance, the statement that the supplement had been only too successful! All of these stories are to be found in Petersons' editions, but all that Mr. Dickens has acknowledged are the portions entitled Somebody's Luggage, Mrs. Lirriper's Lodgings and Legacy, Dr. Marigold, Two Ghost Stories, The Boy at Mugby, The Seven Poor Travellers, and the Holly Tree Inn, which last includes the narrative, by Cobbs, the "Boots," of the Courtship and Elopement of Master Harry Walmer, and his little Cousin Norah. Ah, how exquisite was the author's reading of that very impossible but thoroughly romantic love-tale! Who did not, in spirit, go with that soft-hearted chambermaid, who, as she peeped through the key-hole, called out, "It's a shame to part 'em!" So it would have been, had the lovers been a dozen or fourteen years older.

The next and last completed work was *Our Mutual Friend*, also a serial. The "Postscript in lieu of Preface," is dated September 2d, 1865, and expresses a very strong opinion of the English Poor Law and its working. The object of the tale, however, was to show, in the gradually developed character of Bella Wilfer, the change, by love, from selfishness to its reverse. That young lady has some trials to bear, but they improve her. Silas Wegg is carefully drawn, and scarcely too extravagantly. The "Boffinses" are perfect in their simplicity and shrewdness. The Welfer household, too, is cleverly sketched. The Veneerings, name and all, are poor, and unworthy of the labor bestowed upon them. The Schoolmaster supplies the tragedy. Fascination Fledgeby, not at all natural, is worthy of the punishment Lammle gives him. Riah, the benevolent Jew, seems to have been introduced as an offset to Fagin, in

Oliver Twist, and under peculiar circumstances. In June, 1863, a Jewish lady, name undisclosed, complained that, in the character of Fagin, "Charles Dickens the large-hearted, whose works plead so eloquently for the oppressed of his country, has encouraged a vile prejudice against the despised Hebrew." In his reply, which enclosed a subscription to some Jewish charity, Mr. Dickens said, "Fagin, in *Oliver Twist*, is a Jew because it unfortunately was true, at the time to which that story refers, that that class of criminal almost invariably was a Jew. But surely no sensible man or woman of your persuasion can fail to observe—firstly, that all the rest of the wicked *dramatis personæ* are Christians; and, secondly, that he is called the 'Jew,' not because of his religion, but because of his race. If I were to write a story in which I described a Frenchman or a Spaniard as the 'Roman Catholic,' I should do a very indecent and unjustifiable thing; but I make mention of Fagin as the Jew because he is one of the Jewish people, and because it conveys that kind of idea of him which I should give my readers of a Chinaman by calling him a Chinese." He added, "I have no feeling towards the Jewish people but a friendly one. I always speak well of them, whether in public or in private, and bear my testimony (as I ought to do) to their perfect good faith in such transactions as I have ever had with them; and in my 'Child's History of England' I have lost no opportunity of setting forth their cruel persecutions in old times." The reply to another letter from the same lady on the 14th July, 1863, was the character of Riah, in "Our Mutual Friend," and some favorable sketches of Jewish character and the lower class published in some articles in *All the Year Round.* In acknowledgment, his fair correspondent presented him with a copy of Benisch's "Hebrew and English Bible," with this inscription:—"Presented to Charles Dickens, Esq., in grateful and admiring recognition of his having exercised the noblest quality man can possess —that of atoning for an injury as soon as conscious of having inflicted it. By a Jewess." In a letter, written at Bradford, Yorkshire, on "Friday, First March, 1867," he thanked her, saying, "the terms in which you send me that mark of your remembrance are more gratifying to me than I can possibly express to you; for they assure me that there is nothing but goodwill felt between me and a people for whom I have a real regard, and to whom I would not wilfully have given an offence or done an injustice for any worldly consideration."

Let me close this chapter, in which mention is so often made of the periodicals with which Mr. Dickens was associated for so many years, by saying that they really were *conducted* by him. For many years, he was assisted by Mr. Wills, as well as latterly by his own eldest son, now thirty years of age, and a good writer, but his own *survèillance* over his weekly was constant and thorough. A writer in *Every Saturday*, who is believed to have been Mr. James T. Fields, thus does justice to his friend:

Notwithstanding that for the last twenty-five or thirty years, Dickens has been one of the best-known and most-talked-about men in the world, he has been most curiously misunderstood on two or three points. For instance in this country it was supposed, until recently, that he had made two or three fortunes and spent them; that he was loose in money matters, and was always laboring under "pecuniary difficulties," like his own Mr. Micawber. That he realized large sums from his writings is true enough; as for the rest, nothing could be further from the facts. Dickens was a thorough business man. His precision and accuracy in all commercial matters were marvellous. In spite of his great industry, he would have failed to produce so many volumes as he has, if he had not worked with system. The same clear-headed method which guided him in his literary labors, he brought to bear in his business relations. Loose in money matters! More than one literary brother, dying, left Charles Dickens sole executor of his will, knowing that in those hands his scant estate would be stretched to the utmost to cover the wants of wife and little ones. How carefully these pathetic accounts were kept, is shown by certain private ledgers at Gad's Hill, written in that peculiar blue ink familiar to those who have had dealings with Dickens's manuscripts.

It is singular that, being "a thorough business man," Mr. Dickens should have totally misunderstood his position as author in the United States. Early in 1867, was published a letter, as from Mr. Dickens to an American publishing house, abounding in expressions of peculiar gratification at the display of their honorable dealing, in remitting to him the sum of two hundred pounds, as part profits of their edition of his works, at the same time implying that such payment was so extraordinary as to be looked upon as an isolated act of honesty on the part of American publishers. He wrote: "I think you know how high and far beyond the money's worth I esteem this act of manhood, delicacy, and honor. I have never derived greater pleasure from the receipt of money in all my life." This letter drew some comment in the papers, and also from Sampson Low, London, who stated, in a letter published in *The Pall Mall Gazette*, that he had, "as the agent of Messrs. Harper & Brothers, paid to Mr. Charles Dickens many thousands of pounds for and on account of his works, when no other publishing house had paid anything." Next, it appeared that the old Philadelphia firm of Carey, Lea & Blanchard, without any solicitation, had sent Mr. Dickens £50 for *Pickwick;* had paid £60 for advance manuscript of the latter part of *Oliver Twist;* had offered £100 for advance sheets of *Nicholas Nickleby*, which was not accepted; had paid £112 10*s*. for the *Old Curiosity Shop*, and £107 10*s*. for *Barnaby Rudge*. Mr. Dickens declined accepting for *Martin Chuzzlewit* twice as much (that is, £440,) as they had paid for the two last, so they reprinted that work, as well as *David Copperfield* and *Dombey and Son*, without any arrangement with him.

In 1851, all these stereotype plates, with their illustrations on steel and wood, then forming the only complete edition of Dickens in America, were sold to T. B. Peterson, who subsequently purchased, from Harper & Brothers, *A Tale of Two Cities, Great Expectations, Bleak House, Little Dorrit,* and *Our Mutual Friend,* for the sole continuous right to republish which in the United States, that house had paid £1,000, £1,250, £400, £250, and £1,000—making £3,900, which, added to £330, paid by Mr. Lea's house, make a total of £4,230 in gold, paid to Mr. Dickens by American publishers, before he had received £200 from the liberality of a Boston house, on their publishing a Diamond edition of his works.

Mr. Dickens subsequently acknowledged that, for *The Tale of Two Cities, Great Expectations,* and *Our Mutual Friend,* Messrs. Harper *had* paid him £3,250. Moreover, they expended over $2,000 in having sixty-four original designs made and engraved on wood for the first of these three stories; and also had twenty-seven original designs made and engraved for *Great Expectations.** The cost of this, and of purchasing the original right *exclusively* to publish in the United States, was defrayed by the Messrs. Harper, in connection with the Messrs. Peterson; who naturally considered that they had expended all this money in getting such an equivalent for copyright, in this country, as Mr. Dickens could sell. To this has to be added £1,000 paid Mr. Dickens, in 1859, by the enterprising proprietor of the *New York Ledger,* for a tale entitled "Hunted Down," which, per arrangement between Mr. Bonner and the Messrs. Peterson, is only printed in their editions of Dickens.

So, Mr. Dickens had received £5,230, in hard cash, before the £200 from Boston, which he acknowledged as if it were the *first* and *only* money he had from the United States, had reached him. He had sold an *exclusive* interest in nine of his works—which means an equitable right, as against all other American publishers—to certain firms here, but subsequently transferred *another* exclusive interest to other publishers!

---

* These original illustrations are copyrighted, and can only be had in Petersons' editions of the works of Charles Dickens.

CHAPTER XVIII.

CHARLES DICKENS'S NAMES. — ODD NAMES. — FUTILITY OF PERSONAL ARGUMENT. — RETORT ON LOCKHART. — MAKING FRIENDS.—MR. REE-ACK.—LORD CAMPBELL.—TEMPERATE HABITS. — UNDERVALUING SHAKESPEARE. — WORDSWORTH AND DICKENS.—PHILADELPHIA STREETS.—PERSONAL TASTES. —PITY FOR THE FALLEN.—TOWN AND COUNTRY.—LONGING FOR SUDDEN DEATH.—JOHN DICKENS AND SHERIDAN.—CHILDREN.—DOMESTIC TROUBLES.

MORE than a quarter of a century back, Mr. Dickens was taking a long walk in the country with a friend, and among other topics, Christian names were spoken of. The friend said, it was curious that in English history, literature, science, theology, and art, the greater number of persons who had distinguished themselves, had only a single Christian name. In literature, there were John Gower, Geoffrey Chaucer, William Shakespeare, Ben Jonson, Francis Bacon, John Milton, Samuel Butler, Andrew Marvel, John Dryden, Alexander Pope, Joseph Addison, Richard Steele, Lawrence Sterne, Henry Fielding, Samuel Richardson, Samuel Johnston, Oliver Goldsmith, William Cowper, George Crabbe, Walter Scott, Thomas Moore, William Godwin——Here he was interrupted with, "and you mean to wind up this catalogue of single-name worthies with Charles Dickens?" The friend confessed that his thought had that way tended. "I suspected so. But you must not include *my* name." Here he paused, planted himself right before his companion, waved his hand in a mock-heroic manner, and in a deep-growling voice, like the *aside* of the "first villain" in a melo-drama, on a country stage, said, "Know then that I was christened CHARLES JOHN HOUGHAM, which three names are to be found in the parish register." It was as he had said,—but long ere he became a writer, he disused two of them, and instead of CHARLES JOHN HOUGHAM DICKENS, signed plain CHARLES DICKENS, for all time.

The observation of Charles Dickens was as great, some have thought, as even his imagination. It seemed as if he noticed everything that he saw—and remembered whatever he noticed. He noted down all curious names painted over shop-windows, and was ever adding, from old Directories, to his large collection of odd patronymics.

Mr. Dickens was not a conversationalist, although he told a story well, and with humorous exaggeration. He hated argument,—indeed, he would not, or could not go into it. He used to observe, "No man but a fool was ever talked *out* of his own opinion and *into* your state of mind. Arguments are only cannon-balls, fired at a sand-bank, or water poured into a sieve—a sheer waste of time and trouble. I won't argue with a man: it is going down, on all-fours, to an obstinate dog. In emphatic cases the only argument is a punch of the head. That's a stunner!"

In general Mr. Dickens was not happy in retort; but on one occasion he decidedly turned the tables on Mr. Lockhart, the Editor of the *Quarterly Review*, in which publication, a short time previous, a very hostile criticism on one of Dickens's works had appeared. It wound up with the flattering prophecy that the author of *Nicholas Nickleby* "had gone up like a rocket, and would come down like its stick." On this particular occasion, Dickens and Lockhart chanced to meet at the Marquis of Northampton's, when some ultra-officious friend insisted on introducing the Author to his Critic, and as he did so, had the bad taste to mention the offensive prophecy. Dickens, as he cordially grasped Lockhart's hand, said:—"Well, Mr. Lockhart, I'll wait till that stick comes down, and when it does," he said with a sly twinkle in his eye, "I'll break it over your shoulders."

Lockhart laughed heartily, and they were tolerable friends ever after.

Another time, when a bilious young poet was talking disparagingly of the human race, and was abusing his fellow-creatures, Dickens gravely said across the table, "I say, old boy, what a lucky thing you and I don't belong to them! That reminds me of something I read the other day: Two men were on a platform, going to be hanged. The rope had just been placed round their necks, when a bull burst into the crowd, and began tossing the unfortunate spectators right and left, whereupon one of the criminals said to the other, 'Bill, isn't it lucky you and I are safe up here?' "

Again, when the conversation had turned upon the reconciliation of two friends, who had long been estranged, Dickens said: "Yes, quarreling is very well, but the making up is dreadful. A man who had hanged himself, but who had been cut down and resuscitated, told me he did not suffer half so much in the hanging as he did in being brought back to life."

One day, after dinner, some "mutual friend," after the death of Mr. Angus B. Reach, told Dickens that once upon a time, Thackeray had made a good hit on the clever young Scotchman's pertinacity, as regarded the pronunciation of his surname. It seemed that, at dessert, Thackeray had addressed him as "Mr. Reech," the obvious way of pronouncing the name. "No, sir," was the indignant reply, "my name is pronounced *Ree-ack*—in two syllables." Without giving any verbal reply, Thackeray politely handed his neighbor a peach, saying, "Mr. *Ree-ack*, will you allow me to help you to a *pee-ack*?" The story was neatly told, and the rewarding smile went round. "*Did* you say that?" asked Dickens. "Certainly." "And think it original?" "Of course. Perhaps *you* said it?" "No," replied Dickens, with a merry twinkle of the eye, "but I was at Lord John Russell's the other day, and, having to wait for him a few minutes, took up a book, which happened to be one of the volumes of Tom Moore's Diary. There I read, under date of 1826, I think, that Luttrell, the wit, dining next a gentleman whose father invented the small napkins or *serviettes* used, after dinner, to put finger-glasses or wine-glasses upon, addressed him as 'Mr. *Doyley*,' and was informed, rather angrily, that the real name was Deh'–Oyley, with a long rest between the elided preposition 'D' (or *de*) and the rest of the word. 'Very well,' said Luttrell, in his blandest manner, pointing to a neighboring dumpling on the table, 'May I trouble you, Mr. D'—Oyley, for a little of that D'—umpling.' So, added Dickens, turning triumphantly to Thackeray, *your* joke is at least thirty years old. *Where* did you hear of Luttrell's?" The wit protested that it was his own, and even questioned its existence in Moore. But the volume was referred to, and found to contain Luttrell's *jeu d' esprit.* Probably Thackeray had never heard of it, but the mere idea of plagiarism so much annoyed him that he did not utter ten words more during the remainder of that evening.

When *Bleak House* was ended, and all the world was laughing at the manner in which the case of Jarndyce *v.* Jarndyce was literally kicked out of the Court of Chancery, (the costs having devoured the estate,) Mr. Dickens was called on a special jury, in the Court of Queen's Bench, but the particular case did not come off, the record having been withdrawn. Lord Campbell, then Chief Justice of England, was sitting at Nisi Prius, and said, "The name of the illustrious Charles Dickens has been called on the jury, but he has not answered. If his great Chancery suit had been still going on, I certainly would have excused him, but, as that is over, he might have done us the honor of attending here, that he might have seen how we went on at common law."

Charles Lamb was very impulsive and knew it. He told my informant that he never dared to look out of a third story window, because he was afraid of being tempted to throw himself out. Once, at a funeral, he burst out into a hearty laugh—not because any ludicrous idea had been excited, but out of pure hysterics. Dickens was also very impulsive, and, when in high spirits, would do a series of odd things. In Nathaniel Hawthorne's "English Note-Book," under date, October, 1853, mention is made of his being told by a gentleman at a dinner party, "an instance of Charles Dickens' unwearibility," that during some (amateur) theatricals in Liverpool, "he acted in play and farce, spent the rest of the night making speeches, feasting, and drinking at table, and ended at seven o'clock in the morning by jumping leap-frog over the backs of the whole Company." His stock of animal spirits was large, and was to be drawn upon by society rather than by wassail. Few men, to quote an expression of Moore's respecting Sheridan, only reversing its personal application, had more rarely "passed the Rubicon of the cup."

Dickens's taste in literature was peculiar. Like Byron, he undervalued Shakespeare, saying "for a great poet he is too careless, and his finest plays are full of absurdities." He forgot that he himself, like Shakespeare, was fond of introducing *ultra-natural* situations. Nevertheless he had no appreciation of the grave-digger's scene in Hamlet, and the smothering scene in Othello. He maintained they were beneath the dignity of Tragedy, being entirely sensational and realistic, adding, "I should like to see Sheridan Knowles try such scenes upon the stage now; they would damn any play however good." His favorite poet was Tennyson, although he thought Browning still greater. He once declared in a fit of enthusiasm that he would rather have written Browning's "Blot on the Scutcheon," than any work of modern times. He once horrified Charles Knight, editor of Shakespeare, by calling Hamlet "that prosy chap," and said that "no audience could stand his dreary soliloquies unless they had known them by heart;" thus unconsciously sounding the great poet's praise. When Walter Savage Landor was praising Dickens's style and asking him where he got it, he said, " Why, from the New Testament to be sure."

Wordsworth and Dickens did not *take* to each other. Indeed, there was a mutual contempt between them, though they met only once. This was about the year 1843. Some days after the gentleman whose guest Wordsworth was, in the suburbs of London, asked the Poet, how he liked the great Novelist? Wordsworth had a great contempt for young men, and, after pursing up his lips in a fashion peculiar to him, and swinging one leg over the other, the bare flesh of his ankles appearing over his socks, slowly answered: "Why, I am not much given to turn critic on people I meet; but, as you ask me, I will candidly avow that I thought him a very talkative, vulgar young person—but I dare say he may be very clever. Mind, I don't want to say a word against him, for I have never read a line he has written." Some time after this, the same querist guardedly asked Dickens how he had liked the Poet Laureate?—"Like him? Not at all. He is a dreadful Old Ass." In short, the two authors did not assimilate at all.

On his return from his first visit to America, Dickens used to make great fun of the rectangular Philadelphia streets, and said that the worst nightmare he ever had was caused by them, when he dreamed that he was locked up in Philadelphia, without being able to get out of it. First, he ran up one street, *that* was blocked; then he turned round, and tried another, but *that* was blocked also. He continued these hopelessly unsuccessful attempts, until, at last, heart-weary and foot-sore, he sank down in such agony that he—awoke!

Dickens's personal taste in dress was always "loud." He loved gay vests, glittering jewelry, showy satin stocks, and every thing rather *prononcé*, yet no man had a keener or more unsparing critical eye for these vulgarities in others. He once gave to a friend a vest of a most gorgeous shawl-pattern. Soon after, at a party, he quizzed his friend unmercifully for his "stunning" vest, although he had on him at that very moment, its twin-brother, or sister —whichever sex vests belong to. This inability to turn the bull's eye upon himself, with the same searching fearlessness he did on others, was a defect in his idiosyncrasy; for, despite man's self-love and vanity, there exists in men a *little* self-consciousness. All of us are not blind to our own defects.

Charles Dickens had a peculiar pity for fallen women, and was as tender towards them as his fellow-moralist, Dr. Johnson, always had been—which made a keen judge of human character say, that Johnson might be a bear, but all that was rough about him was his skin. Once, in private conversation, during a ramble in the streets, Dickens said that he was sure that God looked leniently upon all vice that proceeded from human tenderness and natural passion.

Dickens's favorite county was Kent, and he loved to roam about its charming green nooks. One of the best of the Uncommercial Traveller's papers, in which the manners and customs of Tramps are described, is tinted with this Kentish coloring. Dickens was one of the few men I ever met who had an equal appreciation for the country and the town. He equally revelled in the dell and the squalid alley. Charles Lamb really had no relish for the beauties of Nature;—he preferred Ludgate Hill to Snowdon. So did Samuel Johnson; and Captain Charles Morris, the lyrist, was in earnest when he wrote the line,

"Oh, give me the sweet shady side of Pall Mall."

Wordsworth had a strong contempt for cities, but Charles Dickens loved both silent field and crowded street. A village inn was one of his beloved spots. The Tiger's Head, on the top of Highgate Hill, just opposite Mr. Gilman's house, where Coleridge spent the closing nineteen years of his life, was a great favorite of his. So was Garraway's Coffee-house, in Change Alley, Cornhill, just opposite the Royal Exchange, London, which was finally closed in April, 1866, after having been open for two hundred years! To see the intense unction with which Dickens would empty a magnum of Brown Stout, was the next thing to drinking it oneself!

The great power of Dickens, before years came on, was in his eye. When he was in Rome, he sat in the *halle de hôte*, opposite a somewhat vulgar woman, whose loudness of manners attracted his attention. Thenceforth, ever and anon he flashed upon her the "full blaze of his visual orb," which, as all who knew him must remember, was a very large one. At last, the lady cried out, in the unmistakable cockney vernacular: "Drat that man there—I wish he'd take his *heyes* (eyes) hoff my face. They're like a policeman's bull's eye!"—Such, also, was the searching glance he cast upon life.

Dickens often expressed a longing for a sudden death, and he was not the man to assert an opinion for mere word's sake. A friend has told us that walking across Kensington Gardens one day with Dickens, a thunder storm suddenly came. As the rain began to descend, the great Novelist proposed shelter beneath the trees. "No," said his heroic but timid friend, "that is too dangerous. Many people have been killed beneath trees from the effects of lightning." "Well," said Dickens, turning and looking earnestly at his friend, "of all the fears that harrass a man on God's earth, the fear of sudden death seems to me the most absurd, and why we pray against it in the Litany I cannot make out. A death by lightning most resembles the translation of Enoch." He then quoted the lines from Byron's Corsair, commencing:

> "Let him who crawls enamored of decay,
> Cling to his Couch, and sicken years away;
> Heave his thick breath, and shake his palsied head;
> Ours—the fresh turf, and not the feverish bed;
> While, gasp by gasp, he falters forth his soul,
> Ours with one pang—one bound—escapes control."

Mr. John Dickens, the author's father, was a fine specimen of the semi-Sheridan class of gentlemen who dressed well, were very liberal with other folk's money, enjoyed a joke, repeated a *bon mot* in an airy manner, and believed, with Micawber, that giving a note at hand, or accepting a promissory note for the amount of debt, interest, and costs, was a payment in full. It has been more than suspected, by those who knew him, that Mr. Turveydrop, in *Bleak House*, was a gentle quiz upon this gentleman's obvious attention to deportment. He had lived in London, during the Regency, when

"Hal was the rascalliest, sweetest young Prince,"

(Leigh Hunt's "Adonis of fifty,") considered the Prince of Wales as the veritable "glass of fashion and the mould of form," and dressed after the princely attire. He delighted in a tall collar, a stiff choker, a white vest, and patent leather boots. His hat, of the glossiest, was ever in newest fashion. He wore a belt, so tightly buckled, that it threw the blood into his face. The old gentleman was above the middle height, and stoutly built. Some who knew the late Captain James Leonard, of the New York police, and remembered Dickens senior, affirm that, though the latter was much the older, the general resemblance of figure, feature, and flush complexion was great. He was very courteous—imposingly so, like an English linendraper selling his wares. His face was always clean-shaved and ruddy. Latterly, it was a very handsome face for a man advanced in years. His wife declared that "none of the boys were half as handsome as their father." Had he inherited a fortune, he would always have been regarded as a perfect, well-looking, well-mannered gentleman. Mr. John Dickens told an anecdote well, and remembered many. Here is one which has not found its way into any Sheridaniana ;

When the Fox and Grenville Administration was formed,

on the death of Mr. Pitt, early in 1806, the office of Treasurer of the Navy was given to Richard Brinsley Sheridan, who, in and out of office, was almost always in an impecunious state. John Dickens, one of the clerks in the Navy Department, then a handsome, smart young fellow, had attracted Sheridan's attention. One day, Mr. Dickens was summoned into the Treasurer's room. Sheridan civilly invited him to be seated, and producing two important-looking letters, with the large official red seal upon each, said, " Mr. Dickens, I am going to employ you in an important mission, upon His Majesty's Service. Information has been received that certain French emissaries have been sent over to pay secret visits to our Dock yards, for the purpose of obtaining information for the enemy. You will immediately set out for Portsmouth, with these letters, and immediately on your arrival, respectively deliver them to the Port Admiral and the military officer commanding the station. On receipt of their answers, you will return to me without delay. A post-chaise and four horses will convey you through your journey, and the principal pay-clerk, (naming him,) will provide you with ample funds for defraying all expenses. I need not impress upon you the propriety of being profoundly secret, even to the gentlemen of your office. I have the pleasure of wishing you a pleasant journey." As this new King's Messenger was leaving the room, naturally elate and important, Sheridan added, "By the way, Dickens, I have just remembered that Mrs. Sheridan is on a visit at Southampton, and has expressed a desire to return. After you leave Portsmouth, you may drive round to Southampton and pick her up. Here is her address. I am sure I can rely upon your taking every care of her." Instructions were followed to the letter. The missives to Portsmouth, pooh-poohed by the authorities there, as "old Sherry's idle fancies" were officially answered, and young Dickens, who had travelled over ninety miles in a rattling post-chaise, hastened to Southampton, where he "picked up" the lady, and had the honor of escorting her to London, paying all expenses out of the Government purse. The truth, as the reader has probably suspected ere this, was, that Sheridan, having no money and wishing for his wife's return, had *invented* the French spies, and had a Navy clerk dispatched merely to bring Mrs. Sheridan a long and expensive journey, at the public cost!

Mrs. Charles Dickens had lost four or five children. Her eldest son, Charles, now over thirty years of age, was married to Miss Fanny Evans, daughter of one of the firm of Bradbury & Evans, printers, and her father-in-law died a few days after her own father. Miss Kate Dickens is wife of Mr. Charles Collins, artist-author, brother of Mr. Wilkie Collins, the novelist. There is one unmarried daughter, Miss Mary Dickens, and several other sons—including Francis Jeffrey, Walter Savage Landor, Edward Bulwer Lytton, and Alfred Tennyson Dickens.

In June, 1858, it became town-talk, everywhere, that Mr. and Mrs. Charles Dickens had separated. The following letter, from the husband, also to be viewed as the wife's statement, appeared in the newspapers, addressed to Mr. Arthur Smith:

LONDON, W. E., TAVISTOCK HOUSE, TAVISTOCK SQUARE,
Twenty-eighth May, 1858.

MY DEAR ARTHUR:—You have not only my full permission to show this, but I beg you to show it to any one who wishes to do me right, or to any one who may have been misled into doing me wrong.

Faithfully yours, C. D.

LONDON, W. E., TAVISTOCK HOUSE, TAVISTOCK SQUARE,
Tuesday, *Twenty-fifth May*, 1858.

TO ARTHUR SMITH, ESQ.:—Mrs. Dickens and I have lived unhappily together for many years. Hardly any one who has known us intimately can fail to have known that we are, in all respects of character and temperament, wonderfully unsuited to each other. I suppose that no two people, not vicious in themselves, ever were joined together who had a greater difficulty in understanding one another, or who had less in common. An attached woman servant (more friend to both of us than a servant), who lived with us sixteen years, and is now married, and who was and still is in Mrs. Dickens's confidence and mine, who had the closest familiar experience of this unhappiness in London, in the country, in France, in Italy, wherever we have been, year after year, month after month, week after week, day after day, will bear testimony to this.

Nothing has, on many occasions, stood between us and a separation but Mrs. Dickens's sister, Georgina Hogarth. From the age of fifteen she has devoted herself to our house and our children. She has been their playmate, nurse, instructress, friend, protectress, adviser, companion. In the manly consideration towards Mrs. Dickens which I owe to my wife, I will only remark of her that the peculiarity of her character has thrown all the children on some one else. I do not know—I cannot by any stretch of fancy imagine—what would have become of them but for this aunt, who has grown up with them, to whom they are devoted, and who has sacrificed the best part of her youth and life to them.

She has remonstrated, reasoned, suffered and toiled, and came again to prevent a separation between Mrs. Dickens and me. Mrs. Dickens has often expressed to her, her sense of her affectionate care and devotion in the house—never more strongly than within the last twelve months.

For some years past Mrs. Dickens has been in the habit of representing to me that it would be better for her to go away and live apart; that her always increasing estrangement was due to a mental disorder under which she sometimes labors; more, that she felt herself unfit for the life she had to lead, as my wife, and that she would be better far away. I have uniformly replied that she must bear our misfortune, and fight the fight out to the end; that the children were the first consideration; and that I feared they must bind us together in "appearance."

At length, within these three weeks, it was suggested to me by Forster that, even for their sakes, it would surely be better to reconstruct and rearrange their unhappy home. I empowered him to treat with Mrs. Dickens, as the friend of both of us for one and twenty years. Mrs. Dickens wished to add, on her part, Mark Lemon, and did so. On Saturday last Lemon wrote to Forster that Mrs. Dickens "gratefully and thankfully accepted" the terms I proposed to her. Of the pecuniary part of them I will only say that I believe they are as generous as if Mrs. Dickens were a lady of distinction, and I a man of fortune. The remaining parts of them are easily described—my eldest boy to live with Mrs. Dickens and to take care of her; my eldest girl to keep my house, both my girls and all my children, but the eldest son, to live with me in the continued companionship of their Aunt Georgina, for whom they have all the tenderest affection that I have ever seen among young people, and who has a higher claim (as I have often declared, for many years), upon my affection, respect and gratitude than anybody in this world.

I hope that no one who may become acquainted with what I write here, can possibly be so cruel and unjust as to put any misconstruction on our separation, so far. My elder children all understand it perfectly, and all accept it as inevitable.

There is not a shadow of doubt or concealment among us. My eldest son and I are one as to it all.

Two wicked persons, who should have spoken very differently of me, in consideration of earnest respect and gratitude, have (as I am told, and, indeed, to my personal knowledge) coupled with this separation the name of a young lady for whom I have a great attachment and regard. I will not repeat her name—I honor it too much. Upon my soul and honor, there is not on this earth a more virtuous and spotless creature than that young lady. I know her to be innocent and pure, and as good as my own dear daughters.

Further, I am quite sure that Mrs. Dickens, having received this assurance from me, must now believe it in the respect I know her to have for me, and in the perfect confidence I know her in her better moments to repose in my truthfulness.

On this head, again, there is not a shadow of doubt or concealment between my children and me. All is open and plain among us, as though we were brothers and sisters. They are perfectly certain that I would not deceive them, and the confidence among us is without a fear. C. D.

The "trouble" here referred to had insinuated that Mr. Dickens had been only too much attached to Miss Hogarth, his wife's sister,—who, indeed, as an inmate of their household, had given to the Dickens's children a tender care like that of a mother. *He* could not have written a stronger disclaimer, without doing the lady the great wrong of publishing her name. The public fully accepted his frank and indignant denial.

In No. 429 of *Household Words*, published on Saturday, June 12, 1858, was a notice, connected with these domestic relations, which was very impressive—by reason of its candor and simplicity. "He who excuses, accuses himself," says the wordly-wise French proverb, but the utter absence of excuse here, the mere statement of plain facts, *as* facts, had great weight with Dickens's multitudinous readers,—to be found wherever the Anglo-Saxon tongue, which he used so well, was known. This address to the readers of *Household Words*, has not hitherto been published in America, and runs thus:

PERSONAL.

Three-and-twenty years have passed since I entered on my present relations with the public. They began when I was so young, that I find them to have existed for nearly a quarter of a century.

Through all that time I have tried to be as faithful to the public as they have been to me. It was my duty never to trifle with them, or deceive them, or presume upon their favor, or do anything with it but work hard to justify it. I have always endeavored to discharge that duty.

My conspicuous position has often made me the subject of fabulous stories and unaccountable statements. Occasionally such things have chafed me, or even wounded me; but I have always accepted them as the shadows inseparable from the light of my notoriety and success. I have never obtruded any such personal uneasiness of mine, upon the generous aggregate of my audience.

For the first time in my life, and I believe for the last, I now deviate from the principle I have so long observed, by presenting myself in my own journal in my own private character, and entreating all my brethren (as they deem that they have reason to think well of me, and to know that I am a man who has ever been unaffectedly true to our common calling), to lend their aid to the dissemination of my present words.

Some domestic trouble of mine, of long-standing, on which I will make no further remark than that it claims to be respected, as being of a sacredly private nature, has lately been brought to an arrangement, which involves no anger or ill-will of any kind, and the whole origin, progress, and surrounding circumstances of which have been, throughout, within the knowledge of my children. It is amicably composed, and its details have now but to be forgotten by those concerned in it.

By some means, arising out of wickedness, or out of folly, or out of inconceivable wild chance, or out of all three, this trouble has been made the occasion of misrepresentations, most grossly false, most monstrous, and most cruel—involving, not only me, but innocent persons dear to my heart, and innocent persons of whom I have no knowledge, if, indeed, they have any existence—and so widely spread, that I doubt if one reader in a thousand will peruse these lines, by whom some touch of the breath of these slanderers will not have passed, like an unwholesome air.

Those who know me and my nature, need no assurance under my hand that such calumnies are as irreconcilable with me, as they are, in their frantic incoherence, with one another. But, there is a great multitude who know me through my writings, and who do not know me otherwise; and I cannot bear that one of them should be left in doubt, or hazard of doubt, through my poorly shrinking from taking the unusual means to which I now resort, of circulating the truth.

I most solemnly declare, then—and this I do, both in my own name and in my wife's name—that all the lately whispered rumors touching the trouble at which I have glanced, are abominably false. And that whosoever repeats one of them after this denial, will lie as wilfully and as foully as it is possible for any false witness to lie, before Heaven and earth. CHARLES DICKENS.

The separate maintenance which Mrs. Dickens received from her husband, secured to her for life, is stated at $3,000 a year. The broken tie was never reunited, but Mrs. Dickens used to often meet her sister, and the children saw their mother whenever she or they were so minded. The publishers of *Household Words* are understood to have sided with Mrs. Dickens, and to have objected, as having some proprietary share in that periodical, to the insertion in it of Mr. Dickens's address to his readers.

A considerable interval elapsed between the publication of Mr. Dickens's card in *Household Words*, and his secession from that journal. The difference between himself and publishers eventuated in a chancery suit, and the Master of the Rolls, this time avoiding delay, made a decree *in re* Bradbury & Evans *v.* Dickens and another, that the right to use the name of the periodical *Household Words*, together with the printed stock and stereotype plates of the work should be sold by auction on May 16th, 1859. This was carried into effect Hodgson's auction-room was crowded. The salesman mounted his rostrum, and set up the right "from and after the 28th day of May, instant, to publish under the said name or title, any periodical or other work, whether in continuation of the said periodical called *Household Words*, in the pleadings of this cause mentioned, or otherwise, as the purchaser shall think fit, be sold."

The first bidding was £500, and rose up to £3,550, bid by Mr. Arthur Smith, (brother of Albert Smith, the author,) to whom the auctioneer declared it was sold, although, in fact, it was known and stated in the room he only acted for Mr. Charles Dickens, who was the real purchaser. Messrs. Bradbury & Evans, Mr. Arthur Smith, Messrs. Chapman & Hall, and one or two others were the only bidders. As Mr. Charles Dickens held three-fourths of the copyright, and Messrs. Bradbury & Evans one-fourth, the purchaser had, therefore, to pay to the latter £887; but as the stereotype plates were valued at £750, and the stock at more than £200, it will be seen that the purchaser gained a clear profit on the transaction. Mr. Dickens purchased *Household Words* to discontinue it.

Immediately after the sale, Messrs. Bradbury & Evans

published a statement of their difference with Mr. Dickens, the more material portions of which is here added; partly because it bears upon the great author's literary history, and partly because his domestic trouble is mixed up in it:—

Their connection with *Household Words* ceased *against their will*, under circumstances of which the following are material:

So far back as 1836, Bradbury & Evans had business relations with Mr. Dickens, and, in 1844, an agreement was entered into, by which they acquired an interest in all the works he might write, or in any periodical he might originate, during a term of seven years. Under this agreement Bradbury & Evans became possessed of a joint, though unequal, interest with Mr. Dickens in *Household Words* commenced in 1850. Friendly relations had simultaneously sprung up between them, and they were on terms of close intimacy in 1858, when circumstances led to Mr. Dickens's publication of a statement on the subject of his conjugal differences, in various newspapers, including *Household Words* of June 12th.

The public disclosure of these differences took most persons by surprise, and was notoriously the subject of comments, by no means complimentary to Mr. Dickens himself, as regarded the taste of this proceeding. On the 17th of June, however, Bradbury & Evans learned, from a common friend, that Mr. Dickens had resolved to break off his connection with them, because this statement was not printed in the number of *Punch* published the day preceding—in other words, because it did not occur to Bradbury & Evans to exceed their legitimate functions as proprietors and publishers, and to require the insertion of statements on a domestic and painful subject, in the inappropriate columns of a comic miscellany. No previous request for the insertion of this statement had been made either to Bradbury & Evans, or to the editor of *Punch*, and the grievance of Mr. Dickens substantially amounted to this, that Bradbury & Evans did not take upon themselves, unsolicited, to gratify an eccentric wish by a preposterous action.

Mr. Dickens, with ample time for reflection, persisted in the attitude he had taken up, and in the following November, summoned a meeting of the proprietors of *Household Words*. He did not himself attend this meeting; but a literary friend of Mr. Dickens came to it as his representative, and announced there, officially, that Mr. Dickens, in consequence of the non-appearance, in *Punch*, of his statement, considered that Bradbury & Evans had shown such disrespect and want of good faith towards him, as to determine him, in so far as he had the power, to disconnect himself from them in business transactions; and the friend above mentioned, on the part of Mr. Dickens, accordingly moved a resolution dissolving the partnership, and discontinuing the work on May 28. Bradbury & Evans replied that they did not and could not believe that this was the sole cause of Mr. Dickens's altered feeling towards them; but they were assured that it was the sole cause, and that Mr. Dickens desired to bear testimony to their integrity and zeal as his publishers, but that his resolution was formed, and nothing would alter it. Bradbury & Evans repeatedly pressed Mr. Dickens's friend upon this point, but with no other result.

Thus, on this ground alone, Mr. Dickens puts an end to personal and business relations of long standing; and by an unauthorized and premature public announcement of the cessation of *Household Words*, he forced Bradbury & Evans to an unwilling recourse to the Court of Chancery to restrain him from such proceedings, thereby injuring a valuable property in which others beside himself were interested. In fact, by this mode of proceeding he inflicted as much injury as his opportunities afforded. Not having succeeded in purchasing the share of his partners at his own price, he depreciated the value of this share by all the agencies at his command. By publicly announcing (so far as the Court of Chancery permitted) his intention to discontinue the publication of *Household Words;* by advertising a second work of a similar class under his management, by producing it, and by making it as close an imitation as was legally safe of *Household Words*, while that publication was actually still issuing, and still conducted by him; he took a course calculated to reduce the circulation and impair the prospects of a common property; and if he inflicted this injury on his partners, it is no compensation to them that he simultaneously sacrificed his own interest in the publication he is about to suppress.

Household Words having been sold on the 16th inst., under a decree in Chancery, Bradbury & Evans have no further interest in its continuance, and are now free to make this personal statement, and to associate themselves in the establishment of *Once a Week*.

Mr. Dickens began the publication of *All the Year Round*, simultaneously with the cessation of *Household Words*, thus getting ahead of his competitors, who, having to prepare for an illustrated work, did not publish the first number of *Once a Week* until July 2d, 1859. It had twelve engravings, after original designs, by Leech, Tenniel, Millais, C. Keene, T. R. Macquoid, H. Rogers and T. Scott; contained articles by Charles Reade, Shirley Brooks, G. W. Dasent, Tom Taylor, G. H. Lewes, etc., and was edited by Mr. Samuel Lucas, literary critic of *The Times*, but did not succeed, though a great deal of money was spent on it; while Dickens's rival publication, without engravings, commanded, from the first, a larger circulation than its predecessor had obtained.

CHAPTER XIX.

FONDNESS FOR THEATRICALS.—AMATEUR ACTING.—LORD LYTTON'S PLAY.—QUEEN VICTORIA.—WILKIE COLLINS'S PLAYS.—CAPTAIN BOBADIL.—HANS CHRISTIAN ANDERSEN AT GAD'S HILL.—JERROLD MEMORIAL.—PUBLIC READINGS.—SECOND VISIT TO AMERICA.

FROM childhood, Charles Dickens was fond of theatres and actors. In one of his prefaces he mentions that at the early age of eight or nine, he had acted, with his brothers and sisters, in little dramas which he had himself composed. Mr. J. T. Fields, (in the *Atlantic Monthly*,) says: "He was passionately fond of the theatre, loved the lights and music and flowers, and the happy faces of the audience; he was accustomed to say that his love of the theatre never failed, and, no matter how dull the play, he was always careful while he sat in the box to make no sound which could hurt the feelings of the actors, or show any lack of attention." Actors, as well as artists, were among his best regarded friends. He was himself one of the best amateur performers in England. Before he was twenty-five years old he had two farces and an opera of his own played at St. James Theatre, London, then managed by John Braham, who, during full fifty years, was *the* great English tenor. Mr. Dickens first became known to the public as an amateur actor, by his performance, as member of a company resolved to establish a "Guild of Literature and Art," for the advantage of authors, artists and actors. On May 27th, 1851, in Devonshire House, London, took place, with the eagerly willing sanction of the Duke, a performance of singular interest. Sir E. Bulwer Lytton had written for and presented to the Guild a comedy entitled "Not so Bad as We Seem; or, Many Sides to a Character." The scenery was painted by Clarkson Stanfield, David Roberts, Telbin, Pitt, John Absalon, Grieve, and L. Haghe—some of the leading artists of the time. Here is the cast of

NOT SO BAD AS WE SEEM.

Duke of Middlesex, - - - -	Mr. Frank Stone.
Earl of Loftus, - - - - -	Mr. Dudley Costello.
Lord Wilmot, - - - - - -	Mr. Charles Dickens.
Mr. Shadowby Softhead, - - - -	Mr. Douglas Jerrold.
Mr. Hardman, - - - - - -	Mr. John Forster.
Sir Geoffrey Thornside, - - - -	Mr. Mark Lemon.
Mr. Goodenough Easy, - - - -	Mr. F. W. Topham.
Lord Le Trimmer, - - - - -	Mr. Peter Cunningham.
Sir Thomas Timid, - - - - -	Mr. Westland Marston
Colonel Flint, - - - - - -	Mr. R. H. Horne.
Mr. Jacob Tonson, - - - - -	Mr. Charles Knight.
Smart, - - - - - - - -	Mr. Wilkie Collins.
Hedge, - - - - - - - -	Mr. John Tenniel.
Paddy O'Sullivan, - - - - -	Mr. Robert Bell.
Mr. David Fallen, - - - - -	Mr. Augustus Egg.
Lucy, - - - - - - - -	Mrs. Henry Compton.
Barbara, - - - - - - - -	Miss Ellen Chaplin.
The Silent Lady of Deadman's Lane, - - - -	Mrs. Coe.

Of these eighteen characters, only the three last were

represented by professionals. Mrs. Henry Compton, pretty Miss Ellen Chaplin, and Mrs. Coe. Authors, artists, critics, editors, made up the rest. Mr. Dickens represented *Lord Wilmot*, described in the cast as "a young man at the head of the Mode more than a century ago, son to Lord Loftus," a thorough gentleman, high-born and high-bred. The time of the play, I should say, was the reign of George I., and the scene was in London. It seemed to me, when I saw the performance, (afterwards, in the provinces,) that everybody played well; though Mr. Dickens played best. Mr. John Forster, Mr. Wilkie Collins, Mr. Augustus Egg, and Mr. Douglas Jerrold ranked next; but then, Jerrold's father was a country manager, and he himself had tried to act, in the Strand Theatre, London, but failed in his own piece, "The Painter of Ghent;" a good play, too, if well acted. The character of Mr. David Fallen, who was what Washington Irving called "a poor devil author," was played, with great truth, by Mr. Charles Knight, editor of "The Pictorial Shakespeare." There was a farce, also, entitled "Mr. Nightingale's Diary," cast thus:

Mr. Nightingale, - - - - -	Mr. Dudley Costello.
Mr. Gabblewig, - - - - -	Mr. Charles Dickens.
Tip, - - - - - - - -	Mr. Augustus Egg.
Slap, - - - - - - - -	Mr. Mark Lemon.
Lithers, - - - - - - - -	Mr. Wilkie Collins.
Rosina, - - - - - - - -	Miss Ellen Chaplin.
Susan, - - - - - - - - - - -	- Mrs. Coe.

In this thorough bit of fun, Mr. Dickens eclipsed the others, and the contrast between his broad farce in the afterpiece, and his good breeding, and tone, and *ton* in the comedy, were remarkable. Nineteen years ago—only nineteen, and what changes! of eighteen persons who performed in Bulwer Lytton's comedy, there survive only Mr. John Forster, who is joint executor of Mr. Dickens, under his will; Mr. Westland Marston, author of "The Patrician's Daughter" and other dramas; Mr. R. H. Horne, poet; Mr. Charles Knight, historian and critic; Mr. Wilkie Collins, novelist; and Mr.

John Tenniel, principal artist of *Punch* :—two-thirds of that fine array of talent and generosity have passed away.

Queen Victoria sent a Royal intimation, equal to a command, that she wished this unique company of amateurs to go to Windsor Castle, and repeat the performances there, for the gratification of herself, family, and court, but received a polite intimation from Mr. Dickens, who acted as Manager, that he and his friends were private gentlemen, who could not perform in any house where they were not received on an equality with all the other guests. So, the Guild amateurs did not play in Windsor Castle. It was long before Queen Victoria forgave the frank independence of this communication,—but, a few weeks before Mr. Dickens's death, she showed her appreciation of him by personally inviting him to visit her at Windsor, and offering to confer upon him any distinction it might be in her power to bestow. He wanted none,—he had won a higher title for himself than King or Kaiser could give.

The performances of "the Guild," in the principal British cities, were popular to a degree, and the prices of admission being high, yielded a considerable addition to the Fund. In 1855, Mr. Dickens took a leading part in another performance, at Tavistock House, his own residence. Mr. Wilkie Collins had written a two-act play, entitled "The Lighthouse," in which Mr. Dickens, with his daughter and sister-in-law performed, to a select audience of friends. So much was said of it, that Mr. Dickens consented to appear in it, at Lampden House, Kensington, then inhabited by a noted, afterwards even notorious, personage—Colonel Waugh, then supposed to be a millionaire, but subsequently a bankrupt, with "no effects," against enormous liabilities, in his schedule. The play, which had a scene in the Eddystone Lighthouse, was there performed for the benefit of a charity connected with the army in the Crimea. The splendid mansion was crowded with the most brilliant company that could be assembled in London, and the following was the cast of the comedy:

Aaron Gurnock, head light-keeper, - -	Charles Dickens.
Martin Gurnock, his son, - - - -	Wilkie Collins.
Jacob Dale, third light-keeper, - - -	Mark Lemon.
Sam Finlay, a pilot, - - - -	Augustus Egg, A. R. A.
Relief of keepers, boatmen, etc.	
Shipwrecked Lady, - - - - - - -	Miss Hogarth.
Phœbe, - - - - - - - - - -	Miss Dickens.

Of the performance, a notice written by Mr. Tom Taylor next day appeared in the *London Times*, saying, "The acting of Mr. Dickens and Mr. Lemon was most admirable, not only worthy of professional actors, but of a kind not to be found save among the rarest talents. Aaron, a rough, rugged son of Cornwall, with the lines of misery deeply furrowed in his face, rendered more irritable than humble by remorse, and even inclined to bully his way through his own fears, is elaborated by Mr. Dickens with wonderful fulness of detail, so that there is not an accent, a growl, or a scowl without its distinctive significance. In a word, it was a great individual creation of a kind that has not been exhibited before. Jacob Dale, the bluff, honest, straightforward father of Phœbe, does not afford the same opportunity"—the *Times* goes on to say—"for refined variety, but his representation by Mr. Mark Lemon was a masterpiece of sturdy, thoroughly 'made-up' reality." Much praise was also bestowed upon the ladies. But the association of Miss Hogarth with these performances is said to have given great umbrage to her sister, Mrs. Dickens, and to have been one of the causes of the melancholy rupture between herself and her husband, which occurred in 1858.

Another of these performances, but earlier in time, was Ben. Jonson's "Every Man in His Humor," played at "Miss Kelly's Theatre," Soho street, with Mr. Charles Dickens as *Captain Bobadil*, Mr. Mark Lemon as *Brainworm*, Mr. John Leech as *Master Matthew*, Mr. Frank Stone as *Justice Clement*, Mr. Gilbert a'Beckett as *William*,

Mr. Douglas Jerrold as *Master Stephen*, Mr. Frederick Dickens as *Edward Knowell*, Mr. Alfred Dickens as *Thomas Cash*, and Mr. Dudley Costello as *Downright*. All of these are dead. Mr. John Forster, Mr. Horace Mayhew, Mr. Blanchard Jerrold, and Mr. Evans are the sole survivors of that little troop. Mr. Dickens's *Bobadil* was declared to have been a remarkable performance.

In 1857, another drama, by Mr. Wilkie Collins, entitled "The Frozen Deep," was privately played at Tavistock House, by Mr. Dickens and his friends. It was afterwards brought out, with the same cast, at the Gallery of Illustration on Regent street. It may be remembered that the Preface to the *Tale of Two Cities* began with the sentence, "When I was acting, with my children and friends, in Mr. Wilkie Collins's drama of The Frozen Deep, I first conceived the main idea of this story."

On the 8th of June, 1857, Mr. Douglas Jerrold breathed his last. Mr. Dickens, an old friend of his, was one of the pall-bearers at the funeral. It became known that Jerrold had not left his family well off, and Mr. Dickens got up what was called The Jerrold Memorial, in their behalf. He and his friends played "The Frozen Deep" in aid of this fund. Only a very few weeks before, he had changed his residence, from town to country,—having become owner of Gad's Hill House. His very first visitor was Hans Christian Andersen—the Dane, whom he had not seen for ten years, and who arrived on June 9th,—the day after Jerrold's death. Almost the last words of the dying man to his broken-hearted wife were "Dickens will take care of you when I am dead." He did. Mainly through his exertions, a large sum was raised, and so invested that the interest supplied her wants. Dickens read one of his Christmas Stories. "Time and labor," the good Dane writes, "were required to carry all this into effect. There were days when I saw him write and forward twenty letters; all of which he did with an eagerness and joy, as if it were child's play. The only thing that grieved me in this respect, was that it shortened and limited our intercourse; for, owing to these affairs, he had to go repeatedly to London and stay there for whole days."

He adds:

The time drew nigh when I was to bid farewell to Dickens and Gad's Hill; but previously I was to see and admire him as a great actor. The rehearsals of the dramatic performance, the proceeds of which were destined for Douglas Jerrold's widow, called us for a week to London. Dickens was to read his Christmas Carol at St. Martin's Hall, and the Adelphi Theatre contributed its mite by performing Douglas Jerrold's best plays, "The Rent Day," and "Black-eyed Susan." The most brilliant performance, however, was the play in which Dickens appeared with some of his friends and several members of his family. A new romantic drama, "The Frozen Deep," by Wilkie Collins, was to be performed. The author intended to play one of the leading parts, and Dickens the other.

It had long been the Queen's desire to see Dickens play. Her Majesty, therefore, resolved to witness one of the representations given several nights previous to the public performance, at the small theatre, "The Gallery of Illustration." The Queen, Prince Albert, the royal children, the Crown Prince of Prussia, and the King of Belgium, were present. Beside them only a few relatives of the amateur actors were admitted. From Dickens's house there were none but his wife, his mother-in-law and I.

The Gallery of Illustration had been beautifully decorated with flowers and carpets, in honor of the Queen's presence, a special *buffet* with refreshments had been arranged for the royal guests; and another for the rest of the spectators. Dickens played the *rôle* of "Richard" with wonderful impressiveness, and in a calm and natural manner, widely different from the manner in which the tragedians of England and France generally play their parts. He would have been admired and applauded even though nobody had known that he was the great novelist. Beside Dickens, his two daughters, his eldest son, his two sisters-in-law, and his brother Alfred, appeared on the stage. Wilkie Collins played the *rôle* of "Frank Aldersby."

The performance closed with the farce, "Two o'clock in

the morning," which Charles Dickens and Mark Lemon, the editor of *Punch*, played with the most rollicking and brilliant humor. Dickens was excellent, both as a tragedian and low comedian, and is doubtless one of the most talented actors of our times.

After the first performance was over, all those who had participated in it, assembled at Dickens's literary office, where a merry, merry time was had. The festival was afterwards renewed in the open air at the house of the amiable Albert Smith.

Mr. Dickens and Mr. Arthur Smith, as Joint Secretaries of the Jerrold Committee, announced that "the audited accounts show that the various performances, readings, and lectures have realized, after the payment of all expenses, a clear profit of £2,000. This sum was expended in the purchase (through trustees) of a Government annuity for Mrs. Jerrold and her unmarried daughter, with remainder to the survivor." This statement drew from Mr. William Blanchard Jerrold, who had succeeded his father in the editorship of Lloyd's Weekly Newspaper, a comment, in which he stated that he felt it due to the memory of his father to state that if the public had gathered any idea that the family stood in need of any charity they were laboring under a mistake; that his father had left behind him property to the amount of £3,000, besides an income of £100 arising from the copyright of his works; and that if any further assistance be requisite it could be supplied by the family itself. Upon these grounds, Mr. Blanchard Jerrold declined "to permit the English public to remain impressed with the idea that there was need to pass the hat around—however gracefully—in the name of Douglas Jerrold." Upon this, another London paper, *The Critic*, said: "But the hat *has* passed round, and it is not until it has been filled, and the proceeds safely invested, that Mr. Blanchard Jerrold issues his disclaimer. Surely it is rather late in the day to take this course, for it places both himself and the Remembrance Committee between the horns of a dilemma. If there were 'no need' of the fund, why was it raised? If there were 'no need,' why did not Mr. Blanchard Jerrold say so before? There are many uses to which that money could have been put other than throwing it where it was not wanted."

Immediately after having thus done so well for his dead friend's family, Mr. Dickens entered into a new line, for himself, in which he made considerable profits, and while extending his own reputation, making his works even more generally known than before. He had been "in training," for some time, for his Readings.

The first of those, I understand, had been given, some years before, at Chatham, where he had been a school-boy. Money was required for some good purpose,—educational, I think,—and a committee wrote to Mr. Dickens asking whether he would lecture for them—and on what terms. His reply was that he was very busy then, but would be disengaged before Christmas, that he would not lecture but read, and that he would not accept payment. In due time, he fulfilled this engagement, his reading—probably out of compliment to the season, being out of his *Christmas Carol*, and his success so unequivocal that it gave assurance to himself of triumph and emolument, if he were to take it up as a professional performance. After this, he read *The Carol* and *The Chimes*, on several occasions, in aid of charitable purposes. A writer in the *Round Table* fixed the scene of Mr. Dickens's first professional reading in the English Cathedral city of Peterborough, which enjoyed, at that time, a Mechanic's Institution, deeply in debt. When nearly sunk in an abysm of despair, the announcement was made that Mr. Charles Dickens had kindly consented to lecture for the institution. Mr. Dickens at that time had had no public appearance as a reader. He had occasionally been heard of as giving selections from his works to small coteries of friends or in the private saloon of some distinguished patron of art. But he had nervously shrunk from any public *debut*, unwilling, so it seemed, to weaken his reputation as a writer by any possible failure as a reader. He only stipulated that the prices of admission should be such that every mechanic, if he chose, might come to hear him, and named two shillings, a shilling, and sixpence as the limit of charge. Vain limitation!—a fortnight before the reading, every place was taken, and half a guinea and a guinea were the current rates for front-seat tickets. Our R. T. reporter goes on to say:

Dickens came down and himself superintended the arrangements, so anxious was he as to the result. At one end of the large Corn Exchange he had caused to be erected a tall pulpit of red baize, as much like a Punch and Judy show with the top taken off as anything. This was to be the reader's rostrum. It was the Christmas Carol that Mr. Dickens read; the night was Christmas Eve. As the clock struck the appointed hour, a red, jovial face, unrelieved by the heavy moustache which the novelist has since assumed, a broad, high forehead, and a perfectly Micawber-like expanse of shirt-collar and front appeared above the red baize box, and a full, sonorous voice rang out the words "*Marley-was-dead-to-begin-with,*" then paused, as if to take in the character of the audience. No need of further hesitation. The voice held all spell-bound. Its depths of quiet feeling when the ghost of past Christmases led the dreamer through the long forgotten scenes of his boyhood—its embodiment of burly good nature when old Fezziwig's calves were twinkling in the dance—its tearful suggestiveness when the spirit of Christmases to come pointed to the nettle-grown, neglected grave of the unloved man—its exquisite pathos by the death-bed of Tiny Tim, dwell yet in memory like a long-known tune. That one night's reading in the quaint little city, so curiously brought about, so ludicrous almost in its surroundings, committed Mr. Dickens to the career of a public reader; and he has since derived nearly as large an income from his readings as from the copyright of his novels. Only he signally failed to carry out his wish of making his first bow here before an uneducated audience. The vote of thanks which closed the proceedings was moved by the senior marquis of Scotland, and seconded by the heir of the wealthiest peer in England.

Mr. Edmund Yates, the novelist, has recorded that it was not until the evening of Thursday, the 29th of April, 1858, that Mr. Dickens appeared in St. Martin's Hall (now converted into the New Queen's Theatre) to give a reading for his own benefit. He prefaced this reading, with his reasons for appearing in public, saying:

Ladies and Gentlemen:—It may perhaps be known to you that, for a few years past, I have been accustomed occasionally to read some of my shorter books, to various audiences, in aid of a variety of good objects, and at some charge to myself both in time and money. It having at length become impossible in any reason to comply with these always accumulating demands, I have had definitely to choose between now and then reading on my own account, as one of my recognized occupations, or not reading at all. I have had little or no difficulty in deciding on the former course.

The reasons that have led me to it,—besides the consideration that it necessitates no departure whatever from the chosen pursuits of my life,—are three-fold: firstly, I have satisfied myself that it can involve no possible compromise of the credit and independence of literature; secondly, I have long held the opinion, and have long acted on the opinion, that in these times whatever brings a public man and his public face to face, on terms of mutual confidence and respect, is a good thing; thirdly, I have had a pretty large experience of the interest my hearers are so generous as to take in these occasions, and of the delight they give to me, as a tried means of strengthening those relations—I may almost say of personal friendship—which it is my great privilege and pride, as it is my great responsibility, to hold with a multitude of persons who will never hear my voice nor see my face. Thus it is that I come, quite naturally, to be here among you at this time; and thus it is that I proceed to read this little book, quite as composedly as I might proceed to write it, or to publish it in any other way.

From that time, until last spring, when he retired, as if he feared it might be said

> "Reluctant lags the veteran on the stage,"

Mr. Dickens was occupied several months during each year in giving his Readings,—visiting nearly every considerable city and town in England, Ireland, and Scotland, and even giving a course in Paris, which last was remarkably successful. When not before the public, who ever evinced the strongest desire even to *see* him who had, as author, contributed so greatly to their amusement, instruction, and gratification, he was much occupied in studying his readings. His consummate ability was not acquired or acquirable without great labor and perseverance. It took him three months, I have heard, to become perfect in each new scene, and I was assured, on equally good authority, that his bodily exhaustion after a night's reading was very great.

At last, many reports of his performances and successes having reached this country, and strong inducements, personal and pecuniary, having been held out to him, to visit the United States, Mr. Dickens assented, and reached Boston, in 1867.

CHAPTER XX.

SECOND VISIT TO AMERICA.—RATIONALE OF HIS READINGS.—RECEPTION AT BOSTON.—EFFECTS OF THOUGHT AND TIME.—DRAMATIC POWER.—LONG WALKS.—LIST OF SELECTIONS.—CORRESPONDENCE.—LAST READINGS IN BOSTON AND NEW YORK.—PRESS BANQUET AT DELMONICO'S.—LAST WORDS ON THE AMERICAN NOTES.—AMENDE.—DEPARTURE.

ON the 19th November, 1867, Mr. Dickens arrived in Boston, from England, the second time. In 1842, on his departure for Italy, he had been the recipient of a valedictory dinner from his friends, the Marquis of Normanby, himself a man of letters, in the chair. So, ere he went to the United States, in the winter of 1867, another farewell banquet was given to him, in London, the chairman of which was Lord Lytton, of Knebworth,—the only living writer who has closely approached, if he has not quite attained, the excellence of his friendly competitor, "Boz." There was, as usual, a great deal of speech-making. Mr. Dickens thus referred to his impending journey—and the great people whom, after a lapse of more than twenty-five years, he was about visiting:

Since I was there before, a vast and entirely new generation has arisen in the United States. Since I was there most of the best known of my books have been written and published. The new generation and the books have come together, and have kept together, until, at length, numbers of those who have so widely and constantly read me, naturally desiring a little variety in the relationship between us, have expressed a strong wish that I should read myself. (Cheers). This wish, at first conveyed to me through public channels, has gradually become enforcedly an immense accumulation of letters from individuals and associations of individuals, all expressing in the same hearty, homely, cordial, unaffected way, a kind of personal interest in me—I had almost said a kind of personal affection for me (cheers), which I am sure you would agree with me it would be dull insensibility on my part not to prize. Little by little this pressure has become so great that although, as Charles Lamb says, my household gods strike a terribly deep root, I have torn them from their places, and this day week, at this hour, shall be upon the sea. You will readily conceive that I am inspired by a national desire to see for myself the astonishing change and progress of a quarter of a century over them, to grasp the hands of many faithful friends whom I left there, to see the faces of the multitude of new friends upon whom I have never looked, and last, not least, to use my best endeavor to lay down a third cable of intercommunication and alliance between the Old World and the New. (Loud cheers). Twelve years ago, when, Heaven knows, I little thought I should ever be bound on the voyage which now lies before me, I wrote in that form of my writings which obtains by far the most extensive circulation, these words of the American nation: "I know full well, whatever little motes my beaming eyes may have descried in theirs, that they are a kind, large-hearted, generous, and great people." (Hear). In that faith I am going to see them again; in that faith I shall, please God, return from them in the spring; in that same faith to live and to die.

He remained a fortnight in Boston before he made his public appearance in that city, receiving only his immediate friends, living in his hotel in the quietest manner, and taking his daily constitutional walk, always extending to several miles,—frequently accompanied by Mr. Fields, the publisher, whom he had known for some years and greatly liked. He lived at the Parker House, and visited few houses except those of Mr. Longfellow, Professor Lowell, and Mr. Fields. Mr. Clarence Cook, of the *N. Y. Tribune*, who kept the public properly "posted" upon the great author's proceedings, thus reported:

Mr. Dickens has kept himself strictly secluded from all but one or two old and intimate friends. His rooms are at the Parker House, and there he has remained busily engaged all day in writing and study, excepting when he is engaged in taking his daily eight mile constitutional walk with Mr. Fields, the publisher, and steadily declining all the invitations to breakfast, dinner, tea, supper, parties, balls and drives that hospitable Boston pours in upon him in an unfailing stream. Most of his time is spent in the most laborious, pains-taking study of the parts he is to read. Indeed, the public has but little idea of the cost—in downright hard work of mind, body and voice—at which these readings are produced. Although Mr. Dickens has read now nearly five hundred times, I am assured, on the best authority, that he never attempted a new part in public until he has spent at least two months over it in study as faithful and searching as Rachel or Cushman would give to a new character. This study extends not merely to the analysis of the text, to the discrimination of character, to the minutest points of elocution; but decides upon the facial expression, the tone of the voice, the gesture, the attitude, and even the material surroundings of the actor, for acting it is, not reading, in the ordinary sense, at all. Mr. Dickens is so essentially an artist, that he cannot neglect the slightest thing that may serve to heighten the effect of what he has undertaken to do. And he is so conscientious, so strict in his dealings—a very Martinet in business and thorough man of affairs—that he will leave nothing undone that time and labor can do, to give to the public that pays so much for the pleasure of hearing him the full worth of its money. This is the reason why he, a man of the world, greatly delighting in society, thoroughly fitted to enjoy it himself, deliberately cuts himself off from it until his task shall be done. "I am come here," he says, "to read. The people expect me to do my best, and how can I do it if I am all the time on the go? My time is not my own, when I am preparing to read, any more than it is when I am writing a novel; and I can as well do one as the other without concentrating all my power on it till it is done."

On the second of December, 1867, the first reading was given in Boston, in the Tremont Temple. Crowds assembled in the street to have a look at him. Mr. Cook continues:

Inside the house the scene was striking enough. Few

cities anywhere could show an audience of such character. Hardly a notable man in Boston, or fifty miles about, but was there; and we doubt if in London itself Mr. Dickens ever read before such an assemblage. There was Longfellow, looking like the very spirit of Christians, with his ruddy cheeks and bright soft eyes, looking out from the crest of snow-white hair and snow-white beard. There was Holmes, looking crisp and fine, like a tight little grape-skin, full of wit instead of wine. There was Lowell, as if Sidney himself had come back, with his poet's heart smiling sadly through his poet's eyes. Here, too, was the elder Dana, now an old man of eighty, with long gray hair falling around a face bright with shrewd intelligence, as able now as thirty years ago to write "Paul Fenton; or, the Buccaneer." Running the eye over the hall, one saw other men widely known. Charles Eliot Norton, whose translation of Dante's "Viva Nuova" may well stand side by side with his master Longfellow of the grander song. There in the gallery is Edwin Whipple. Yonder is Fields, to whom all owe this great pleasure, for he suggested, urged and made this visit of Dickens easy to him. Bishop Eastburn, over on the other side, seems thankful that clergymen have yet some pleasures left. There is Poole, the librarian of the Athenæum, one of our men who knows most about books, and Samuel Elliot, the President of the Social Science, and George Green, who recently crossed blades with Bancroft. Emerson's face I could not catch. Concord is far away, and snow storms no joke to travel in. Nor did Whittier come, as was promised—Whittier, who has never, in his life, been present at an evening entertainment of any description, concert or opera, or even, strange to say, a lecture. He promised, but at the last his heart failed him, and the "good gray head that all men knew" did not bless our eyes to-night.

The first thought of those who had seen him in 1842, and remembered him as a dashing, slender, handsome young man, with a smooth face and an abundance of long, dark chestnut hair, could scarcely realize that the Reader of 1867, with grizzly moustache and beard, and evidently beginning to resemble "the bald first Cæsar," was him who, in their and his youth, was oftenest called "Boz." The flush of youth had vanished. The "purpurea juventus" was of the past, for

> "O'er that fair broad brow were wrought
> The intersected lines of thought."

Mental labor, rather than years, had changed him far more than the wearing and wearying touch of time. Still, in his attire, neat even to elegance, with the glittering watch-chain and pendant ornaments, and the flower in his button-hole (his daily companion there for thirty years), his intelligent glance around and through the audience, as if it were rapidly taking stock of them, and his own apparent cool and decided manner, as if confident that in a few minutes that eager crowd would be under his spell—all combined to render him not merely "the observed of all observers," but one of the most remarkable among the truly great men of this or of any age or country.

"Cheer after cheer broke forth," it was added, "and amid cries of welcome and clapping of innumerable kids, Dickens rose and fell and rose again in a friendly roar, tried to speak and was defeated, and returned gallantly to the charge again, but had scarcely got as far as 'Ladies,' when he was obliged to succumb; made another dash at 'Gentlemen,' and gave it up; and at last saw that one Englishman was nothing to so many Yankees, and waited smiling and bowing until they had their will and were ready to let him have his."

The Readings of that evening consisted of the *Christmas Carol* and the breach-of-promise marriage trial from *Pickwick*. The audience were alternately sobbing and laughing during the former, though their tender sympathy was oftener moved than their sense of humor—but the trial, Bardell *v.* Pickwick, was farce from first to last—only varying in its grades of fun. It was in this, that, besides introducing the numerous and well-sustained changes of intonation necessary to individualize each of the characters,

Mr. Dickens brought into play that wondrous facial mobility of feature and expression, which, in common with all great actors, he largely possessed, and effectively, because judiciously exercised. When Mr. Sergeant Buzfuz, assuming more importance than ever, rose and said, "Call Samuel Weller," there was, for a moment, a pause,

> "A sound so fine that nothing lives
> 'Twixt it and Silence,"

and then, as with one consent, a loud murmur of applause among the audience, which simultaneously broke into cheers. When he was supposed to have appeared—*supposed?* Why the man was there! attired in that identical livery, which made him wonder, when he first got into it, whether he was meant to be a footman, or a groom, or a gamekeeper, or a seedsman, or "a compo of every one on 'em." It seemed as if Sam were there, in the flesh. Then, the little Judge,—little Mr. Justice Stareleigh. At one moment, Sam Weller, in his free and easy manner, was delivering his evidence, half jestingly, yet with a secret purpose, which he carried out, of doing his best for Mr. Pickwick, and in the next, he had vanished—and the audience only saw the little Judge's rubicund and owlish face, only heard his unmistakable voice pumping up, from some unknown depths, the caution, "You must not tell us what the soldier said, unless the soldier is in court, and is examined in the usual way; it is not evidence." Hey, presto,—the Judge disappeared, and we heard Sam, *saw* Sam cheerfully answering "Werry good, my Lord." Here let me observe that the illustrations of Dickens's by "Phiz" and other artists, placing so many of the characters before *readers*, in days gone by, until they had sank deep into their memory, greatly assisted Mr. Dickens, when he acted various scenes before an audience. In consequence of these engravings, Dickens has been more read and is better understood, than any other writer:—just as the particular plays of Shakespeare, which are most popular and most intelligible to the majority of readers, are those which are frequently acted on the stage. In dramatic representation and in good illustrations, there is a Realism which greatly assists intellect and memory.

A critic, whose name I would mention if I knew it, said, of these readings, "A vast amount of hard study always preceded the reader's appearance in public. Every tone and gesture was carefully weighed. The text (an abridgment of the printed story or an extracted chapter) was arranged with the utmost pains, and frequently amended. It was partly on account of his habit of such constant toil, partly through failing health, that Mr. Dickens accepted very few of the hospitalities offered him in New York and Boston by his personal friends or the distinguished men who felt entitled to seek his acquaintance." In New York, he put up at the Westminster Hotel, and outside of his own little party, (which almost always included Mr. Osgood, of Boston, and Mr. George Dolby, his agent, a very courteous gentleman,) saw few strangers, except Mr. W. C. Bryant and Mr. J. Bigelow. In Washington, almost the only private houses he visited were those of Senator Sumner, Mr. Franklin Philp, the bookseller, and his partner, Mr. A. S. Solomon. He had come to America to get through what, no matter how pleasant its results to audiences, was actual hard labor to himself. His readings were so real, to his own mind, and so exhaustive to his system, physically and mentally, that he felt compelled to eschew all other excitements. Besides, his health was far from good, even then—though he continued his long daily walks, which, perhaps, did not tend to its improvement. In this early and long continued habit of taking a great deal of pedestrian exercise, some very striking scenes in his works are due. An English writer says, "That he was a great walker was borne witness to by much that he wrote. To the wanderings of Little Nell and her grandfather Mr. Dickens's own experiences crop up. The Punch and Judy men and the scene in the inn are manifestly photographs of people the author had met and of places where he had been. The same may be said of the account of David Copperfield's journey on foot from London to Kent, and the inimitable paper on 'Tramps,' which we are never tired of reading, could have been written by no man who had not had opportunities of closely studying the begging fraternity, their habits and modes of expression. Indeed, scattered through his works are scenes and allusions that bespeak the practice of pedestrianism, if not of humbler modes of traveling. It is hard to believe that the description of the journey in that night wagon in 'The Old Curiosity Shop,' and the morning picture, the passengers cheerless, cold, ugly and discontented, with three months' growth of hair in one night, was not a realistic sketch that grew out of Mr. Dickens's own personal experience."

His first Reading in New York was given at Steinway Hall, on December 9th, 1867, and in Philadelphia, at Concert Hall, on January 13th, 1868. He read, also, in Washington, Baltimore, St. Louis, and other places:—giving a second series, on his return north, at most of these places. His Readings in America consisted of the Christmas Carol; the Trial in Pickwick; chapters from David Copperfield, in which the Peggotty household, the experiences with Dora, the Child-wife, the wreck at Yarmouth, and the Micawber family were exhibited; Bob Sawyer's Party; the story of Little Dombey; scenes at Dotheboys Hall; Boots at the Holly-Tree Inn, or rather, the adventures of Master Henry Walmers and his infantine sweetheart, Nora; Dr. Marigold; Nicholas Nickleby, Squeers, and Smike; and Mrs. Gamp, who was companioned by the invisible, but immortal Mrs. Harris. After his return to England, he added the tragic scenes from Oliver Twist to his *répertoire*, and this reading is said to have been the most effective of all. Mr. Dickens was sensitive to criticism, which, however, was rarely adverse or ill-natured to him. There is a curious episode in his American campaign, which illustrates my belief that he cared a great deal for what the newspapers said. It was written, over the signature "Semi-Occasional," in the *Jewish Messenger*, is dated "Washington, D. C., June 27th, 1870," and is known to have emanated from one of the few gentlemen in the Capital, with whom he was intimate during his brief visit there. It reads thus:

Believing that whatever relates to that great and good man, the late Charles Dickens, has abiding interest to the English-speaking world, it is my duty, as also my pleasure, to chronicle some facts, known to a few only, of which I am personally cognizant.

It will be remembered that, when Mr. Dickens last visited this country, he gave his first "readings" in Boston, then in New York, and afterward in Philadelphia and Washington. While in Philadelphia there appeared in the *Press** of that city some extremely caustic criticisms upon his readings, which, acting upon his very sensitive disposition and bodily ills—for the neuralgia in his foot was extremely painful and irritating at times—made him nervous and somewhat downcast.

Mr. Dickens returned to New York. The sale of tickets for his readings in Washington then began, and Mr. Dolby, his agent, reported to him from day to day, the most gratifying success; when, like a flash of lightning from a cloudless sky, Mr. Dolby was almost struck dumb by the receipt of a dispatch from "The Chief," as he was in the habit of calling him, to the effect that he must stop the sale of tickets, and announce his inability to appear before the Washington public; and that a special messenger had left that morning conveying his reasons in writing! Various were the surmises of Mr. Dolby, and those whom he consulted in his perplexity; and it was finally determined to continue the sale of tickets, and await the arrival of the envoy extraordinary, bearing, as the sequel proved, his still more extraordinary dispatch.

---

* It is no violation of editorial confidence to state here that this article was written neither by Colonel Forney, proprietor and principal editor of the *Philadelphia Press*, nor by R. Shelton Mackenzie, the associate editor. Nor did it express the sentiments of either.

Like his own Micawber, the expected envoy "turned up" at the proper time, and relieved himself of a formidable envelope, in which there were eight closely-written pages in blue ink, (he always used blue ink to write with), giving his reasons why he could not perform his engagement at Washington.

It appeared that the night before he had been entertained at dinner by two or three well-known New York journalists, to whom he related, in a confiding, sympathetic spirit, how unfairly, as he believed, he had been dealt with by *The Press* of Philadelphia—whereupon he was given to understand that the probabilities were that the criticisms were not conceived in the usual spirit, but were the forerunner of a still more vigorous onslaught in Washington, where the same editor was also the proprietor of an influential paper; and all this might result in personal insult. Mr. Dickens went on to say that, at his time of life, he did not feel willing to subject himself to any such disagreeable contingency, be it ever so slight; and, therefore, he deemed it advisable to withdraw from the field, leaving Mr. Dolby to tax his inventive faculties for a good and sufficient excuse to go forth to the public.

Those who knew the Washington public and the kind-hearted editor alluded to, laughed heartily at the bug-a-boo conjured up, and assured Mr. Dolby that they would be responsible that nothing of the kind occurred, the writer of these lines promising to see Colonel Forney, and explain to him the whole story. Mr. Dolby communicated these assurances to Mr. Dickens, with which he was fully satisfied.

Colonel Forney was in due time "interviewed," and expressed his surprise and indignation at the motives attributed to him. Colonel Forney stated that it was too evident a mistake had been made, and that Mr. Dickens would be criticised when he visited Washington fairly, and without prejudice: and, so far as he was concerned, he would contribute all in his power to make his visit pleasant to him—whom he loved for his large brain and still larger heart—as he was sure it would be to the public at large.

It is quite unnecessary to add that, like another celebrated hero—though not of letters—*Veni, Vidi, Vici,* and so completely did he "conquer" prejudice—which existed only in some badly-diseased brain—that he could have read every night for a month, to crowded audiences of the *élite* of the land.

Mr. Dickens spoke frequently of his appreciation of the reception he met with, and said he thought he had *never* read to such *sympathetic* audiences as welcomed him here. He thanked the writer for the humble part he had taken in inducing him to alter his determination, and was the more pleased because of the opportunity it had afforded him to observe the changes made during the past twenty years—a change from a "city of magnificent distances" to a city of elegant buildings and still more elegant ladies.

Mr. Dickens gave two sets of Readings in Philadelphia, when Concert Hall was filled, to the extent of its utmost capacity, each night. If he had appeared in the Academy of Music, which, for such a purpose, with judicious packing, could have accommodated over four thousand persons, each able to see and hear him, it would have been filled each time.

The Washington friendly anonyme further adds that Mr. Dickens was particularly impressed with the architectural grandeur and ornamentation of our Capitol, which he considered much finer than the English House of Parliament. He had good opportunity for close observation, as, with his proverbial modesty, he preferred visiting it on a Sunday, when lionizing was impossible. It was a subject of remark that, while his companions were lounging through the stately rooms with irreverently covered heads, Mr. Dickens removed his hat with the same deference he would have exhibited before the living rulers of the earth. He made many inquiries in relation to the late rebellion, and stated that his sympathies had always been with the North.

Mr. Dickens was in Washington, on February 7th, 1868, being his fifty-sixth birth-day, "and English-like and social as he was, he had around him some choice spirits to commemorate the joyous event." The writer of the above quoted statement presented him with a set of studs and sleeve-buttons of American manufacture, as a birth-day *souvenir*. Next morning, Mr. Dickens wrote to him, saying, "I was truly touched and affected yesterday evening by the receipt of your earnest letter, and your handsome birth-day present. I shall always attach a special value, to both, and shall make a point of wearing the latter on the 7th of February, as often as the day may come round to me." His previous acknowledgment, to another Washington friend is terse and genial.

BALTIMORE,
Tuesday, Twenty-eighth January, 1868.

DEAR MR. PHILP:—Pray accept my cordial thanks for the two charming bottles, (not to mention their contents), for which I am indebted to your kind remembrance. They arrived here safely, several hours before your letter; but we were not long in divining from whom they came, and whose health we must immediately drink—and did.

I was on the point of writing to express to you my regret that I must forego the pleasure of dining with you while at Washington. That national compliment, my "true American catarrh," is infallibly brought back by every railway car I enter. It is so oppressive, and would, but for occasional rest and silence, be so incompatible with my Readings, that my only safe course is to hold to the principle I established when I left Boston, and gloomily deny myself all social recreations. I am bound to disclaim the least merit in this virtuous-looking self-denial. I retire to the cloister as discontentedly and growlingly as possible.

Believe me, faithfully, yours,
CHARLES DICKENS.

FRANKLIN PHILP, Esquire.

Mr. Dickens read with touching expression. However he may have begun, he had carefully and laboriously trained himself into reading to audiences, in a novel yet natural manner. His reading, in fact, *was subdued acting:*—rarely demonstrative, but always what is called "telling." He threw himself into each character, shifting from one to the other with dexterous and surprising rapidity. There were none of the miserable airs and graces of professional elocution, which would fain teach a different and distinct action for each word. He read as a highly cultivated gentleman might be expected to read, in a drawing-room, to ladies and gentlemen of equally high culture. Above all, he was not *stagey.* His one peculiarity, which was described in a clever *brochure* by Miss Kate Field, the title of which I cannot remember, was—that, in general, he closed each sentence with a rising inflection,—quick and sharp on the ear, like the rapid crack of a whip. This is the English habit of intonation, and he had not got rid of it. The readings had been most successful, in reputation as well as in worldly gain. Nor, great though the latter may have been, did any one begrudge it. His manner of reading was peculiar. He had the printed text always ready for instant reference,—in the event of his memory failing to supply the required word,—but it is to be supposed that constant repetition had engraved each sentence upon his mind. He took the greatest care to produce the desired effects, but left no mark of the chisel upon the carving. Mrs. Browning has made Lady Geraldine's lover, the Poet, tell how

> Poets ever fail in reading their own verses to their worth,
> For the echo in you breaks upon the words which you are speaking,
> And the chariot-wheels jar in the gate through which you drive
> them forth.

There was some of this in Coleridge, whom I have heard read, or rather repeat his poem "Love" (beginning "All thoughts, all passions, all delights,") in a sing-song manner.

At the end of his last reading in Boston, Mr. Dickens said:

LADIES AND GENTLEMEN:—My precious and general welcome in America, which can never be obliterated from my memory, began here. My departure begins here, too; for I assure you that I have never, until this moment, really felt that I am going away. In this brief life of ours, it is sad to do almost anything for the last time; and I cannot conceal it from you, that although my face will so soon be turned towards my native land and to all that make it dear, it is a sad consideration with me that in a very few moments from this time this brilliant hall and all that it contains will fade from my view for evermore. But it is my consolation, that the spirit of the bright faces, the quick perception, the ready replies, the generous allowance, and the cheering crowds that have made this place joyful to me, will remain; and you may rely upon it that that spirit will abide with me as long as I have the sense and sentiment of life. I do not say this with any reference to the private friendships that have for years and years made Boston a memorable and beloved spot to me; for such private references have no business in this place. I say it purely in remembrance of and in homage to the great public heart before me. Ladies and gentlemen, I beg most earnestly, most gratefully, and most affectionately, to bid you each and all farewell.

He took leave of his last American auditors at New York, on April 20th, 1868, in these words:

Ladies and Gentlemen:—The shadow of one word has impended over me all this evening, and the time has come at last when the shadow must fall. It is but a very short one, but the weight of such things is not measured by their length; and two much shorter words express the whole realm of our human existence. When I was reading "David Copperfield" here last Thursday night, I felt that there was more than usual significance for me in Mr. Pegotty's declaration: "My future life lies over the sea." And when I closed this book just now, I felt keenly that I was shortly to establish such an alibi as would have satisfied even the elder Mr. Weller himself. The relations which have been set up between us in this place—relations sanctioned, on my side at least, by the most earnest devotion of myself to my task—sustained by yourselves, on your side at least, by the readiest sympathy and kindliest acknowledgment, must now be broken forever. But I entreat you to believe that, in passing from my sight, you will not pass from my memory. I shall often, often recall you as I see you now, equally by my Winter fire, and the green English Summer weather. I shall never recall you as a mere public audience, but rather as a host of personal friends, and ever with the greatest gratitude, tenderness, and consideration.

Ladies and gentlemen, I beg to bid you farewell, and I pray God bless you, and God bless the land in which I have met you.

Three days before, on the evening of Saturday, April 18th, a banquet was given to him at Delmonico's, in New York, by two hundred gentlemen connected with the newspaper press and periodical literature of America. There were not merely representatives, but representative men from New York, Philadelphia, Cincinnati, Albany, Troy, Springfield, Hartford, Boston, Rochester, Washington, Chambersburg, Keokuk, Brooklyn, Camden, Toledo, Waterton, Detroit, Utica, Honesdale, Syracuse, New Jersey, Scotland and London. Mr. Horace Greeley presided, and, in reply, to his own health, the toast of the evening, Mr. Dickens said:

GENTLEMEN:—I cannot do better than take my cue from your distinguished President, and refer, in my first remarks, to his remarks, in connection with the old natural associations between you and me. When I received an invitation from a private association of working members of the Press of New York, to dine with them to-day, I accepted that compliment in grateful remembrance of a calling that was once my own, and in loyal sympathy towards a brotherhood which in spirit I have never quitted. (Applause). To the wholesome training of severe newspaper work when I was a very young man I constantly refer my first successes—(applause)—and, my sons will hereafter testify of their father that he was always steadily proud of that ladder by which he rose. (Renewed applause). If it were otherwise I should have but a very poor opinion of their father, which perhaps—upon the whole—I-have-not. (Laughter). Thus, gentlemen, under any circumstances, this company would have been exceptionally interesting and gratifying to me; but whereas I supposed that, like the fairies' pavilion of the "Arabian Nights," it would be but a mere handful, and I find it drawn out like the same elastic pavilion, capable of comprehending a multitude, so much the more proud am I of the honor of being your guest. For, you will readily believe that the more widely representative of the press in America my entertainers are, the more I must feel the good will and kindly sentiments towards me of that last institution. (Applause). Gentlemen, so much of my voice has lately been heard in the land, and I have for upwards of four hard winter months so contended against what I have been sometimes quite admiringly assured was a genuine American catarrh-(laughter) —a possession which I have throughout highly appreciated, though I might have preferred to be naturalized by any other outward or visible means—(laughter)—I say, gentlemen, so much of my voice has lately been heard in the land that I might have been contented not to trouble you any further from my present standing-point, were it not a duty with which I henceforth charge myself, not only here but on every suitable occasion whatsoever and wheresoever, to express my high and grateful sense of my second reception in America, and to bear my honest testimony to the national generosity and magnanimity. (Cheering). Also, to declare how astounded I have been by the amazing changes that I have seen around me on every side. Changes moral, changes physical; changes in the amount of land subdued and cultivated; changes in the rise of vast new cities; changes in the growth of older cities almost out of recognition; changes in the growth of the graces and amenities of life; changes in the press—without whose advancement no advancement can take place anywhere. (Applause). Nor am I, believe me, so arrogant as to suppose that in five-and-twenty years there have been no changes in me, and that I had nothing to learn and no extreme impressions to correct when I was here first. (Applause). And, gentlemen, this brings me to a point on which I have, ever since I landed here last November, observed a strict silence, though sometimes tempted to break it; and, in reference to it, I will, with your good leave, take you into my confidence now. Even the press, being human, may be sometimes mistaken or misinformed—(laughter)—and I rather think that I have, in one or two rare instances, known its information to be not perfectly correct—(laughter)—with reference to myself. (Renewed laughter). Indeed, I have now and again been more surprised by printed news that I have read of myself than by any printed news that I have ever read in my present state of existence. (Applause). Thus the vigor and perseverance with which I have for some months been "collecting materials for and hammering away at a new book on America" —(laughter)—seeing that all that time it has been perfectly well known to my publishers on both sides of the Atlantic, that I positively declared that no consideration on earth should induce me to write one. (Laughter). But what I have intended, what I have resolved upon, and this is the confidence I seek to place in you, is that on my return to England, in my own English journal, manfully, promptly, plainly in my own person to bear for the behalf of my countrymen, such testimony to the gigantic changes in this country as I have hinted at to-night. (Applause). Also to record that wherever I have been, in the smallest places equally with the largest, I have been received with unsurpassable politeness, delicacy, sweet temper, hospitality, consideration, and with unsurpassable respect for the privacy daily enforced upon me by the nature of my avocation here and the state of my health. (Applause). This testimony, so long as I live, and so long as my descendants have any legal right in my books, I shall cause to be republished as an appendix to every copy of those two books of mine in which I have referred to America. (Applause). And this I will do, and cause to be done, not in mere love and thankfulness, but because I regard it as an act of plain justice and honor. (Applause). Gentlemen, this transition from my own feelings towards, and interest in America, to those of the mass of my countrymen, seems to me but a natural one, whether or not it is so, I make it an express object. I was asked in this very city, about last Christmas time, whether an American was not at some disadvantage in England as a foreigner? The notion of an American being regarded as a foreigner at all—of his ever being thought of or spoken of in that character, was so uncommonly incongruous and absurd to me that my gravity was for a moment quite overpowered. (Applause). As soon as it was restored, I said that for years and years past I had hoped I had had as many American friends and received as many American visitors as almost any Englishman living (applause), and that my unvaried experience fortified by others was that it was enough in England to be an American to be received with the most earnest respect and recognition anywhere. Thereupon, out of half a dozen people, suddenly spoke out but two. One, an American gentleman of cultivated taste for art, who, finding himself on a certain Sunday, outside the wall of a certain historical English castle, famous for its pictures, was refused admission there according to the strict rules of the place on that day, but by merely representing that he was an American gentleman on his travels, had not only the picture-gallery but the whole castle placed at his immediate disposal. (Applause and laughter). There was a lady too, being in London, and having a great desire to see the famous reading-room of the British Museum, was assured by the English family with which she staid that it was unfortunately impossible, because the place was closed for a week, and she had only three days there. Upon that lady's going, as she assured me, alone to the gate—self-introduced as an American lady—the gate flew open as if by magic. (Laughter and applause). I am unwillingly bound to add that she certainly was young and extremely pretty. (Laughter and applause). Still the porter of that institution is of an obese habit, and to the best of my observation not very impressible. (Laughter). Now, gentlemen, I refer to these trifles as collateral assurance to you that the Englishman who shall humbly strive, as I hope to do, to be in England as faithful to America as to England herself, has no previous conception to contend against. (Applause). Points of difference there have been; points of difference there are; points of difference there probably always will be between the two great peoples; but broadcast in England is sown the sentiment that these two peoples are essentially one—(applause)—and that it rests with them to uphold the great Anglo-Saxon race to which our President has referred, and all its great achievements throughout the world. If I know anything of my countrymen, and they give me the credit of knowing something of them (voice: "good,") if I know anything of my countrymen, gentlemen, the English heart is stirred by the fluttering of these Stars and Stripes, as it is stirred by no other flag that floats, except its own. (Great applause). If I know my countrymen, in any and every relation towards America, they begin, not as Sir Anthony Absolute recommended lovers to begin, with a little aversion, but with a great liking and a profound respect, and whatever may be the sensitiveness of the moment, or the little official passion, or the little official policy, now or then, or here or there, may be, take my word for it, that the first enduring great popular consideration in England is, a generous construction of justice. Finally, gentleman, I say this, subject to your correction, I do believe that from the great majority of honest minds on both sides, there cannot be absent the conviction that it would be better for this globe to be riven by an earthquake, fired by a comet, or overrun by an iceberg, and abandoned to the artic fox and bear, than that it should present the spectacle of these two great nations, each of which has in its own way and hour, striven so hard and so successfully for freedom, ever again being arrayed the one against the other. (Great applause). Gentlemen, I cannot thank your President enough, and you enough, for your kind response to my health, and my poor remarks. But believe me, I do thank you with the utmost fervor of which my soul is capable. (Loud applause).

Speeches were also made by Messrs. Henry J. Raymond, George W. Curtis, W. H. Hurlburt, C. E. Norton, J. R. Hawley, John Russel Young, G. W. Demers, M. Halsted, E. de Leon, T. B. Thorpe, and E. L. Yeomens. It happened that Mr. Dickens, in very bad health on this occasion, had to retire before all the twelve regular toasts had been given and replied to. He heard Mr. G. W. Curtis, however, and declared, after his return to England, that *his* speech was the best he had ever heard. That part of Mr. Dickens's own address, in which he may be said to have retracted extreme opinions formed in his first visit to this country, and hastily expressed by him, was received with equal satisfaction by those who read and those who heard it.

On the 22d of April, Mr. Dickens returned to England in the mail steamer, to which he was escorted by "troops of friends." In May, he again set foot on his native soil.

CHAPTER XXI.

RETURN TO ENGLAND.—IN HARNESS.—A NEW READING.—DINNER AT LIVERPOOL.—DANGEROUS ILLNESS.—GRAVE-SIDE SPEECH-MAKING.—GAD'S HILL HOUSE.—MISS CLARKE AT TAVISTOCK HOUSE.—HANS CHRISTIAN ANDERSEN.—FRANKLIN PHILP.—HABITS OF WORK.—LONG WALKS.—M. FECHTER.—CLOSE OF 1869.

THE return of Mr. Dickens to England, in May, 1868, was welcomed by his countrymen. His neighbors, chiefly small farmers and laborers in the vicinity of Gad's Hill, made a demonstration which, for England, where the practice is to repress the expression of emotion, was considered rather remarkable. They raised a floral arch, underneath which he entered into his own little territory. It was rumored that he had realized £30,000 by his readings in America,—which, most probably, was an exaggeration, as guess-work estimates generally are. That he had done well was undeniable. For some months after his return, he did little more than give increased personal superintendence to *All The Year Round.* The declining health of Mr. Wills, the sub-editor of that weekly, rendered this very necessary. He had been training his eldest son to take a leading part in the management of the publication, and now duly installed him as Mr. Wills's successor. Nor did the young man fall short of the paternal estimate of his ability and steadiness. At the same time, Mr. Dickens reserved to himself, for the most part, what may be designated the critical dealing with authors, their proposed subjects, their manuscripts. He saw them personally, or corresponded with them. Generally, he had to write from twelve to twenty missives a day, on subjects connected with his weekly. For the most part these were all from his own pen. Sometimes, when the pressure upon his time was considerable, he would pencil down the heads of his letter, another hand would reduce these into epistolatory shape, which after he had read and approved of, he would complete by his signature,—that peculiar well-known specimen of eccentric calligraphy. He wrote some short papers, (they are collected in the present volume) in which his old manner was well preserved. He had almost resolved to give no more readings in England, but, yielding to strong and general solicitations,—more particularly made by members of the theatrical profession, whose opportunities of hearing him had necessarily been few,—announced a farewell course. The skilled elocution and dramatic talent with which he illustrated the creations of his fancy, bestowing fresh animation on the characters, and bringing out more vividly both the pathos and the fun, had rendered the readings extremely popular; and additional interest was imparted to them by the personal tie established between the reader and his audiences. The new series was announced to take place in St. James's Hall, London, and Mr. Dickens's agents intimated that "any announcement made in connection with these Farewell Readings will be strictly adhered to and considered final; and that on no consideration whatever will Mr. Dickens be induced to appoint an extra night in any place in which he shall have been once announced to read for the last time."

On October 20th, 1868, in London, he read a selection of scenes from "David Copperfield," and finished with a glimpse of Mrs. Gamp. The readings from that autobiographical story comprised the introduction of Steerforth to the Peggotty household, on the night of little Emily's betrothal to Ham; the dinner party at David's chambers in London, at which symposium Mr. and Mrs. Micawber appear to such characteristic advantage; the loves of David and Dora, with a glimpse at the queer domestic economy of their wedded life; and the storm at Yarmouth, ending with the stirring description of the wreck and death of Ham Peggotty and the man who had wronged him. This final episode and culmination of the tale was preceded by a short narrative of the meeting between David Copperfield and Emily's uncle, when the latter tells the story of his wanderings through France in sorrowful quest of the poor girl. The delight of his audience was manifest in all parts of the hall, silence being more strongly indicative of appreciation than applause.

The pressure of friends, and of friendly critics, who thought, to use a familiar term, that he never "had let himself out" in his personations—never given full play to his dramatic genius—prevailed, at last. Mr. Edmund Yates says: "That wish has now been realized. When Mr.

Dickens called round him some half-hundred of his friends and acquaintances, on whose discrimination and knowledge of public audiences he had reliance, and when, after requesting their frank verdict on the experiment, he commenced the new reading, 'Sikes and Nancy,' until, gradually warming with excitement, he flung aside his book and acted the scene of the murder, shrieked the terrified pleadings of the girl, growled the brutal savagery of the murderer, brought looks, tones, gestures simultaneously into play to illustrate his meaning, there was no one, not even of those who had known him best or who believed in him most, but was astonished at the power and the versatility of his genius." The individuality of each character was rendered with almost astonishing power. The conclusion was a climax of surpassing force. We are told, "throughout the entire scene of the murder, from the entrance of Sikes into the house until the catastrophe, the silence was intense; the old phrase 'a pin might have been heard to drop,' might have been legitimately employed. It was a great study to watch the faces of the people,—eager, excited, intent,—permitted for once in a life-time to be natural, forgetting to be British, and cynical and unimpassioned. The great strength of this feeling did not last into the concluding five minutes. The people were earnest and attentive; but the wild excitement so seldom seen amongst us died as Nancy died, and the rest was somewhat of an anti-climax." This was the only one of Mr. Dickens's Readings which was not given in America. In fact, he had not studied it out until after his return home.

The farewell readings were given in "the provinces," during the winter of 1868 and the spring of 1869. Their popularity was, if possible, greater than before—the crowning success in America had re-acted in England. In Liverpool, where he was always a great favorite, advantage was taken of his presence to give him a grand dinner, in St. George's Hall. Mr. Dickens had been invited to stop with his friend, Dr. Muspratt, the eminent chemist, during his visit to Liverpool, but could not be induced to violate his invariable rule to forego social visiting during his professional labors.

The last public compliment conferred upon Mr. Dickens was on the 10th of April, 1869, when a banquet was given to him, by the merchants of Liverpool, in their magnificent St. George's Hall. The chair was occupied by Mr. Dover, Mayor of Liverpool. Among the guests were Lords Dufferin and Houghton, W. Hepworth Dixon, Mark Lemon, Anthony Trollope, G. A. Sala, and M. Alphonse Esquiros, a liberal French author, formerly a member of the Corps Legislatif, but exiled by the *coup d' état* of December 2d, 1850. The speech of the evening was to this effect:

MR. MAYOR, LADIES, AND GENTLEMEN, although I have become so well accustomed of late to the sound of my own voice in this neighborhood as to hear it with perfect composure (laughter), the case is, believe me, very, very different in respect of those overwhelming voices of yours. As Professor Wilson once confided to me in Edinburgh, that I had not the least idea from hearing him in public what a magnificent speaker he found himself to be when he was quite alone (laughter), so you can form no conception, from the specimen before you, of the eloquence with which I shall thank you, again and again, in some of the innermost moments of my future life (loud cheers). Often and often, then, God willing, my memory will recall this brilliant scene, and will repeople and reilluminate

> This banquet-hall deserted—
> Its lights all fled, its garlands dead,
> And all but I departed;

and faithful to this place in its present aspect will preserve and mark it exactly as it stands—not one man's seat empty, not one woman's fair face absent, while life and memory abide in me (cheers). Mr. Mayor, Lord Dufferin in his speech, so affecting to me, so eloquently uttered, and so rapturously received, made a graceful and gracious allusion to the immediate occasion of my present visit to your noble city. It is no homage to Liverpool, based upon a moment's untrustworthy enthusiasm, but it is a solid fact, built upon the rock of experience, that when I first made up my mind, after considerable deliberation, systematically to meet my readers in large numbers, face to face, and try to express myself to them through the breadth of life, Liverpool stood foremost amongst the great places out of London to which I looked with eager confidence and pleasure (cheers). And why was this? Not merely because of the reputation of its citizens for a generous estimation of the arts; not merely because I had unworthily filled the chair of its great self-educational institution long ago (hear, hear); not merely because the place had been a home to me since the well-remembered winter day when its blessed roofs and steeples dipped into the Mersey behind me on the occasion of my first sailing away to see my generous friends across the Atlantic (hear, and applause), seven-and-twenty years ago; not for any of these considerations, but because it had been my happiness to have an opportunity of testing the spirit of its people. I had asked Liverpool for its help towards the worthy preservation of Shakespeare's house (applause); on another occasion, I had ventured to address Liverpool in the names of Leigh Hunt, and Sheridan Knowles (applause); on still another occasion I had addressed it in the cause of the brotherhood and sisterhood of letters and the kindred arts; and on each and all the response had been unsurpassable, instantaneous, open-handed and munificent. Mr. Mayor, ladies, and gentlemen, if I may venture to take a small illustration of my present position from my own peculiar craft, I would say that there is this objection in writing fiction to giving a story an autobiographical form, that, through whatever dangers the narrator may pass, it is clear, unfortunately, to the reader, beforehand, that he must have gone through them somehow (laughter), else he could not have lived to tell the tale (renewed laughter and applause). Now, in speaking fact, when the fact is associated with such honors as these with which you have enriched me, there is this singular difficulty in the way of returning thanks, that the speaker must infallibly come back to himself through whatsoever oratorical disasters he may languish on the road (laughter). Let me, therefore—let me, then, take the plainer and simple, middle course of dividing my subject equally between myself and you (applause). Let me assure you that whatever you have accepted with pleasure, either by word of pen or by word of mouth, from me, you have greatly improved in the acceptance (laughter, and hear, hear). As the gold is said to be doubly and trebly refined which has seven times passed through the furnace, so the fancy may be said to become more and more refined each time it passes through the human heart (loud applause). You have, and you know you have, brought to the consideration of me that quality in yourselves without which I should have but beaten the air. Your earnestness has stimulated mine, your laughter has made me laugh, and your tears have overflowed my eyes (loud applause). All that I can claim for myself in establishing the relations which exist between us is constant fidelity to hard work. My literary brethren about me, of whom I am so proud to see so many (applause), know very well how true it is, in all art, that what seems the easiest done is oftentimes the most difficult to do, and that the smallest good may come of the greatest pains—much as it occurred to me at Manchester, the other day, as I saw the sensitive touch of Mr. Whitworth's wonderful measuring machine, though Heaven and its maker only knew how much previous hammering and firing were required to bring it out. My companions in arms know thoroughly well, and I think it is right that the public should know too, that in our careful toil and trouble, and in our steady striving after excellence, not after any little gifts misused by fits and starts, lies our highest duty at once to our calling, to one another, to ourselves, and to you (applause). Ladies and gentlemen, before sitting down I find I have to clear myself of two very unexpected accusations (hear, hear). The first is the most singular charge preferred against me by my old friend Lord Houghton, that I have been somewhat unconscious of the merits of the House of Lords (laughter). Now, ladies and gentlemen, seeing that I have had some few not altogether obscure or unknown personal friends in that assembly; seeing that I had some little association with and knowledge of a certain obscure peer little known in England by the name of Lord Brougham (renewed laughter); seeing that I regard with some admiration and affection another obscure peer wholly unknown in literary circles, called Lord Lytton (continued laughter); seeing also that I had for some years some slight admiration for the extraordinary judicial properties and amazingly acute mind of a certain Lord Chief Justice, popularly known by the name of Lord Cockburn (loud applause and laughter); and also seeing that there is no man in England whom I respect more in his public capacity, whom I love more in his private capacity, or from whom I have received more remarkable proofs of his honor and love of literature, than another obscure nobleman called Lord Russell (renewed applause and laughter); taking these things into consideration I was rather amazed by my noble friend's accusation. When I asked him, on his sitting down, what amazing devil possessed him to make this charge, he replied that he had never forgotten the days of Lord Verisopht (laughter). Then, ladies and gentlemen, I understood it all, because it is a remarkable fact that in the days when that depreciative and profoundly unnatural character was invented, there was no Lord Houghton in the House of Lords (loud laughter and applause). There was in the House of Commons a rather indifferent member called Richard Monckton Milnes (continued laughter). Ladies and gentlemen, to conclude (cries of "No," and "Go on,")—for the present (laughter). To conclude, I close with the other charge of my noble friend; and here I am more serious, and I may be allowed, perhaps, to express my seriousness in half-a-dozen plain words When I first took literature as my profession in England I calmly resolved within myself that, whether I succeeded or whether I failed, literature should be my sole profession (hear, hear, and applause). It appeared to me at that time that it was not so well understood in England as it was in other countries that literature was a dignified profession (hear, hear), by which any man might stand or fall (hear, and applause). I made a compact within myself that in my person literature should stand by itself, of itself, and for itself (hear, hear); and there is no consideration upon earth which would induce me to break that bargain (hear, and loud applause). Ladies and gentlemen, finally, allow me to thank you for your great kindness, and for the touching earnestness with which you have drank my health. I should have thanked you with all my heart if it had so unfortunately happened that for many sufficient reasons I lost my heart between half-past six and half-past seven o'clock to-night (loud and prolonged cheering).

I have given the above in full, as the last speech of any importance made by Mr. Dickens, and conveying a fair idea of his manner. The playful allusion to the House of Lords, was elicited bv a querulous observation, in a previous speech by Lord Houghton, that Mr. Dickens had dealt rather harshly, in his writings, with the British peerage,—into which body Lord H. had himself been elevated only half a dozen years ago. A well-known expression of the late Earl Gray was "I will stand by my order," and Lord Houghton, formerly Mr. R. M. Milnes, who has published several volumes of verses, besides editing Keats' Poems, was huffed at Mr. Dickens' small respect for the aristocracy. As it happened, the only person supposed to be connected in the works of "Boz," with that august body, was Lord Frederick Verisopht, for whom the reader must feel pity rather than dislike. Mr. Dickens showed his readiness of retort, in his improvised reply to Lord Houghton's unexpected charge.

Mr. Dickens proposed a toast towards the close of the proceedings. He said:

GENTLEMEN—for I address myself solely to you—the nature of the toast I am about to propose cannot, I think, be better or more briefly expressed than in a short quotation from Shakespeare, slightly altered:

SCENE.—A Banquet Hall, Thunder—of admiration. Lightning—of eyes.

Banquo.—What are these,
So sparkling, and so bright in their attire
That look not like the inhabitants o' the earth,
And yet are on 't?

(loud laughter and applause). Sir, these are the "Lancashire Witches," (applause). Pondering this turn in my mind just now, and looking around this magnificent hall, I naturally pondered also on the legend of its patron saint. It is recorded of St. George that he was even more devoted to love and beauty than the other Six Champions of Christendom, (laughter and applause); and I, his loyal imitator and disciple, have moulded myself completely upon him in looking around me here.

How happy could I be with either
Were t'other dear charmer away,

is a sentiment that was first put in writing some few ages after St. George's time. But I have a profound conviction that he would have written it if he could but have projected himself into this occasion, (laughter). However, he was much better employed in killing the dragon, (cries of "Oh,") O, yes, much better employed in killing the dragon, who would have devoured the lady; and he was much better employed still in marrying the lady and enslaving himself by freeing her. The legend, as I remember, goes on to relate that the accursed brood of dragons after that time retired to inaccessible solitudes, and was no more seen except on especial occasions, (laughter). Now it appeared to me that if any of these dragons should yet be lingering in retirement, and if they should have any virtue and bewitching sixth sense, or the slightest notion of the havoc that will be wrought amongst St. George's descendants by this assembly of glowing beauty here to-night, then the dragon race is even with St. George's at last, and is most terribly avenged, (laughter and applause). Gentlemen, I give you "The Ladies."

On the 22d of April, 1869, when Mr. Dickens was to have given a reading in "proud Preston," he was suddenly taken ill. Mr. Beard, his medical attendant, was summoned from London, and, in conjunction with Dr. Charles Watson, issued this document: "We certify that Mr. Charles Dickens has been seriously unwell through excessive exhaustion and fatigue of body and mind, consequent upon his public readings and long and frequent railway journeys. In our judgment, Mr. Dickens will not be able, with safety to himself, to resume his readings for several months to come."

Mr. Dickens was to have presided at the Newsvendors' Dinner, on April 26th, but his son stated that, although his father had been seriously indisposed, there was no cause for alarm. It was true that he would be prevented, for some time, from appearing in the capacity of a public "reader," but he would still be enabled to attend to his literary duties, which would be continued as heretofore.

He retired to his residence, at Gad's Hill, Kent, settling down to his country life, and laying the foundation of a new story,—"*The Mystery of Edwin Drood.*"

In August 1869, a request was made that Mr. Dickens would deliver an address, on the completion of the Leigh Hunt Memorial, (a bust) in Kensal Green Cemetery, but declined. His note to Mr. Ollier says, "I am very sensible of the feeling of the committee towards me; and I received their invitation (conveyed through you) as a most acceptable mark of their consideration. But I have a very strong objection to speech-making beside graves. I do not expect or wish my feelings in this wise to guide other men; still, it is so serious with me, and the idea of ever being the subject of such a ceremony myself is so repugnant to my soul, that I must decline to officiate."

On the 30th of the same month, the third day after the celebrated Oxford and Harvard boat-race, he attended at the dinner given, in the Crystal Palace, at Sydenham, by the London Rowing Club, to the contending crews, and said that he had been permitted to propose the toast of the evening, namely, "The Health of the Oarsmen of the Harvard and Oxford Universities." Oxford (he said) was only represented by one member, Mr. Willan, who in spite of difficulties, in spite of family inconvenience, was present. Oxford had given up her position to Harvard in the toast; indeed, she seemed glad to offer any advantage or triumph to Harvard whatever, except the advantage and triumph of beating her. It is not long since a book appeared in America, giving the lives of ninety-five gentlemen of Harvard University who entered the American Army during the Civil War and who died in that cause. Not less to be admired, not less to be honored, were that set of gentlemen who had come over here to challenge the Oxford crew, the flower of English oarsmen. They had lost, but it was no dishonor to them to have been beaten by the best crew that England could put forth. He proposed "The Health of Harvard and Oxford," which was acknowledged by Mr. Willan and Mr. Lyman, respectively. Mr. Dickens had attended, that day, against medical advice,—his excuse being that the subject being as much American as English, he felt himself bound in honor to be present.

Gad's Hill House, which very much resembles an American country-mansion, two-story high, with what are called "dormer windows" in the roof, had a roomy hall in the centre, and two bow or oriel windows, one over the other, on each side. It has a comfortable, old-fashioned look, was surrounded by fine trees of many years growth, and its lawn, nicely laid out, looks very pretty from the road. The only objection to the house is that it is too near the road,—probably, this was no defect in its owner's eyes, for he was fond of standing at his front door, leaning against one of the pilasters, and chatting to his children, grand-children and friends. He was a social man, and delighted to see happy faces, to hear joyous voices. Hans Christian Andersen, as I have previously stated, was a guest at Gad's Hill, in June 1857—nearly a year before the cloud fell, in all men's view, upon his domestic life. A few days before his death, Mr. Dickens had invited Andersen to repeat his visit this autumn.

Five-and-twenty years ago, Mr. Serjeant Talfourd, who was warmly attached to Dickens, frankly told him that he would be a richer man, as well as a better author, by retreating from the entanglements and expenses of a London life. He suggested a residence—such as Dickens since had at Gad's Hill—within a convenient distance of London. This would avoid Sunday dinner-parties and the extravagances, dissipations, and temptations of a London life, and also give him more leisure to think, and a clearer head to work with.

A friend of Dickens, who knew him from childhood, and dearly loved him to the last, wrote to me, a few years ago, saying, "There does not live a larger-hearted or a better-minded man than Dickens. He is liberal to a fault. He allowed his wife's relations to hang upon him, to infest his house, and to drain his purse for years. The great fault of his character is ostentation. With all his sagacity, Dickens is eternally afraid of being *slighted.* He never seems to be at ease—not even in his own house. His restless eye wanders, like a comet in a cage, beating the bars of his eyelashes to escape. He has always seemed to me as if he had something *on* his mind as well as *in* it. He danced the tight-rope of display for years. He has now carried out the plan suggested to him by Talfourd, and also by Lord Jeffrey, and lives out of London, but near enough to enjoy it, when he pleases. A more truly genial man than Dickens does not live. He likes to see others enjoy themselves, while Thackeray seems to care only for enjoying himself. One constantly hears of kind actions done by Dickens. In the possession of a good heart, as well as vast genius, I think that Dickens very closely resembles Walter Scott."

It is well-known, now, that even when a school-boy, Dickens admired the house at Gad's Hill. In mature manhood, when he accidentally heard the place was in the market, he purchased it. He expended a good deal upon improvements. In June, 1857, when he entered into possession, he still had Tavistock House as a town residence, being compelled to retain it until his lease had run out, or he had given sufficient "notice to quit," or something of the sort.

Mrs. L. K. Lippincott, (then Miss Clarke,) has lately written in the *N. Y. Tribune*, her recollections of a dinner at Mr. Dickens's in June 1852. She says, "I have in my mind still a perfectly distinct picture of the bright, elegant interior of Tavistock House, and of its inmates—of my host himself, then in his early prime—of Mrs. Dickens, a plump, rosy, English, handsome woman, with a certain air of absent-mindedness, yet gentle and kindly—Miss Hogarth, a very lovely person, with charming manners—and the young ladies, then *very* young—real English girls, fresh and simple, and innocent-looking as English daisies. I was received in the library. Mr. Dickens—how clearly he stands before me now, with his frank, encouraging smile and the light of welcome in his eyes!—was then slight in person, and rather pale than otherwise. The symmetrical form of his head, and the fine, spirited bearing of the whole figure, struck me at once—then the hearty *bonhomie*, the wholesome sweetness of his smile; but more than anything else, the great beauty of his eyes."

Miss Clarke questioned Mr. Dickens very closely about his modes of study and writing, and he answered her frankly and patiently: "I asked," she reports, "if certain characters which I pointed out, generally esteemed very peculiar and eccentric, if not positively unnatural and impossible, were not altogether beings of the mind, pure creatures of his own fancy; and he said explicitly that the most fantastic and terrible of his characters were the most real—the 'unnatural' were the natural—the 'exaggerations' were just those strange growths, those actual human traits he had copied most faithfully from life. Sam Weller, whom everybody recognized as an acquaintance, was not a real but quite an imaginary personage, he said—was only the representative of a class." She observed the exquisite order and nicety of his study-table, and asked him if he actually did his every-day work there. "Oh, yes," he said, "I sit here and write, through almost every morning." "Does the spirit always come upon you at once?" "No—sometimes," he answered, "I have to coax it; sometimes I do little else than draw figures or make dots on the paper, and plan and dream till perhaps my time is nearly up. But I always sit here, for that certain time." She asked whether, in case the flow of inspiration did not come till near the hour for lunch, or exercise, he left that seat when the hour struck, or remained? "I go at once," he said, "hardly waiting to complete a sentence. I could not keep my health otherwise. I let nothing deprive me of my tramp." Lastly, came an inquiry, which shows that the lady had thought the matter over closely. "I asked," she says, "if the mental work did not go on as he walked, and he said he supposed it always did in some degree, especially when he was alone, yet that he thought he saw almost all that was to be seen in his walks about London and Paris—indeed everywhere he went; that he had trained his eye and ear to let nothing escape him; that he had received most valuable suggestions and hints of character in that way."

This is a point on which much depended. It has long been my belief that the long walks in which Mr. Dickens systematically indulged, as if to compensate for labor of the mind by fatigue of the body, may have been injurious. Say that he was writing a book, he would work at it from nine to half-past twelve or one; at the exact moment, he would lay down his pen, scarcely waiting to finish the sentence. He would start on a three hours walk—usually without a companion. And, all through that long and solitary walk, even while his eyes saw and his ears heard all that passed before him, a continuous and severe mental process must have been going on. It would have been next to an impossibility for an author, and *such* an author, when he rose from his writing-table, to have dismissed all thought about the work he was composing. He *must* be thinking of it, as he walked, and thus, though he sought to gain quiet of mind at the expense of toil of body, he really was continuing the intellectual toil. It may be doubted whether Mr. Dickens's long walks were for the benefit of mind or body.

Hans Christian Andersen, quick and comprehensive in his observation, wrote: "When in London, Charles Dickens lives in Tavistock House. A grated gate separates the yard and garden from the lively street. In the rear of the house extends a larger garden, with several lawns and tall trees, and imparts a rural appearance to the whole in the midst of smoking and dusty London. In the passage leading from the street to the garden there hung paintings and copper-plates; here stood Dickens's marble bust, life-like, young, and handsome, and the doors to the bed-chambers and dining-rooms were surmounted by Thorwaldsen's bas-reliefs of Night and Day. On the first floor was a large library, with a fire-place and writing-table, and in the large room opening upon the garden, Dickens and his family and friends amused themselves in winter by performing plays. The kitchen is in the basement, and the bed-rooms are on the upper floor. When I came to London, I was quartered in a pleasant room opening upon the garden, whence I saw, above the trees, the Tower of London loom up or disappear, according to the clearness of the weather. It was a long way from here to the centre of business-life."

The proper address of Gad's Hill House was "Higham -by-Rochester, Kent." This is a station on the railroad to Rochester, and is scarcely two miles from Mr. Dickens's house. Andersen continued:

Now there lies on the broad high road Dickens's villa, whose turret, with the gilded weathercock, I had already descried from afar, above the tops of the trees. It was a fine, new house, with red walls and four bow-windows, and a jutting entrance supported by pillars, in the gable a large window. A dense hedge of cherry-laurel surrounded the house, in front of which extended a neat lawn, and on the opposite side rose two mighty cedars of Lebanon, whose crooked branches spread their green fan over another large lawn surrounded by ivy and wild vines, the hedge being so dense and dark that no sunbeam was able to penetrate it.

As soon as I stepped into the house, Dickens came to meet me, kindly and cordially. He looked somewhat older than he did when he bade me farewell ten years ago, but that was, perhaps, in part owing to the beard which he now wore; his eyes still sparkled as they had done at that time, the same smile played round his lips, and his dear voice sounded as sweet and pleasant, nay, more so than formerly. Dickens was now in the prime of life, still so youthful, so active, so eloquent, so rich in the most pleasant humor, through which his sterling kind-heartedness always beamed forth. As he stood before me in the first hour, so he was and remained during all the weeks which I passed in his company, merry, good-natured, and full of charming sympathy.

In the room where we assembled with some of the children

round the breakfast table, it was quiet and pleasant, and Sundaylike; a wealth of roses surrounded the large windows on the outside, and the view extended over the garden, the beautiful fields beyond the hedges, and the hills bordering the horizon, in the rear of Rochester. An excellent portrait of Cromwell hung over the fire-place, and among the other paintings adorning the walls all around, there was one which attracted my attention particularly. It represented a caléche, in which were seated two young ladies, absorbed in reading a book, whose pages were headed "Bleak House." The little groom, seated in the box behind, bent forward, and furtively read also in the book. A few birds in cages sung the more merrily the more animated the conversation grew in the dining-room.

During the meal, Dickens took the seat of the head of the family at the upper end of the table, and, according to the English custom, said a short prayer after he had seated himself; my seat was by his side during the whole of my visit.

Dickens then had no less than nine children, two grown daughters, Mary and Kate, and seven sons: Charles, Walter Savage Landor, Francis Jeffrey, Alfred Tennyson, Sidney Smith, Henry Fielding, and Edward Lytton Bulwer. The two eldest and the two youngest were at home; the other three came on a visit from Boulogne, in France, where they were at a boarding school. It was vacation time, and I saw them climb in the branches of the large cedar trees, or play at cricket with their other brothers and their father, all of them in shirt-sleeves, on the large meadow close to the garden; the ladies sat in the tall grass under the trees, peasant children peeped over the hedge, and Turk, the watch dog, who was fastened all night, had now been delivered from his chain and led the life of a free dog, while his long chain and his kennel were left to a big, old raven, who no doubt considered himself a relative to the Raven in "Barnaby Rudge," which, though stuffed, still existed, and was to be seen in the house.

When I arrived at Gad's Hill the family had not yet been two weeks at their new country-seat; both the environs and all the drives were new to them. Meanwhile I myself soon found out the most attractive points, and to one of them, the summit of Gad's Hill, I conducted Dickens and his family. Our way led across the broad highroad on which, opposite to Dickens's villa, there lies a tavern, on the faded sign of which Falstaff and Prince Henry, and on the reverse a scene from the *Merry Wives of Windsor* are represented. From the tavern a ravine, between live hedges led up to a group of peasant houses, all two-storied, and their walls beautifully clad with vine and creepers; long, neat, white curtains hung in the windows; the highest house was watched by an old blind dog, cows and sheep were grazing on the meadows, and on this highest point there rose an obelisk. The whole monument was cracked, and the first gust of wind might upset it. The inscription was no longer distinctly legible, but we saw that the monument had been erected in honor of an excellent country gentleman who had died many, many years ago. Inasmuch as I was the first to lead Dickens to this point, he afterwards called the place, jocosely, "Hans Christian Andersen's monument."

We enjoyed here a panoramic view of the country, as beautiful as it was extensive. The north of Kent is justly called the garden of England. The scenery is similar to that of Denmark, though more luxuriant and richer. The eye sweeps over green meadows, yellow cornfields, forests, peat moors, and, when the weather is clear, one may see the North Sea in the distance. The landscape, it is true, does not present a lake, but you behold everywhere the Thames, whose silver thread is meandering for many miles through the green grounds. We still found, on the summit of the hill, traces of the ancient intrenchments from the time of the Romans. We went up there many an evening, and sat down in a circle on the grass, and gazed at the setting sun, whose beams were reflected in the bends of the Thames, pouring over the river a golden lustre, on which the vessels stood forth like dark silhouettes. From the chimneys of the country houses all around, rose blue smoke; the crickets were chirping, and the whole scene presented a lively picture of peace, heightened by the sweet sound of the evening bells. A bowl of claret, adorned with a bouquet of brown field flowers, passed around our circle. The moon rose, round, large and red, until she shone in silvery lustre, and filled me with the fancy that all this was but a beautiful Midsummer night's dream in the land of Shakespeare; and yet it was more; it was reality. I sat by Dickens's side, and saw and heard him enjoy to the utmost the charming evening which, as it was reflected in his soul, was sure to be used by him for a new, glorious creation of his wonderful imagination.

This was Gad's Hill House, in 1857. Let us take a later view. Mr. Franklin Philp, of Washington, who was on very intimate terms with Mr. Dickens, has allowed a portion of his diary to be published, containing his impressions of Gad's Hill. He had been a guest of the great novelist:

July 25, 1869. Went to Charing Cross Station at 10.40, met Dickens there, (by appointment), accompanied Mr. Dickens; his daughter; his sister-in-law; Miss Stone, (sister of Marcus Stone, the artist); Charles Kent, editor of *The Sun;* to Higham, by rail—gentlemen walked up to Gad's Hill—ladies sent on in carriage. On arrival, (half-past twelve), commenced with "cider cup," which had previously been ordered to be ready for us—delicious cooling drink—cider, soda water, sherry, brandy, lemon peel, sugar and ice, flavored with an herb called borage, all judiciously mixed. Lunch at one o'clock, completed by a liqueur which Dickens said was "peculiar to the house." From two to half-past five we were engaged in a large open meadow at the back of the house, in the healthful and *intellectual* employment of playing "Aunt Sally," and rolling balls on the grass; at half-past three, interval for "cool brandy and water;" at half-past six o'clock we dined—young Charles Dickens, and a still younger Charles Dickens, (making three generations), having arrived in the meantime—dinner faultless, wines irreproachable; nine to ten, billiards; ten to eleven, music in the drawing-room; eleven, "hot and rebellious liquors," delightfully compounded into punches; twelve, to bed.

The house is a charming old mansion, a little modernized; the lawn exquisitely beautiful, and illuminated by thousands of scarlet geraniums; the estate is covered with magnificent old trees, and several "Cedars of Lebanon" I have never seen equalled. In the midst of a small plantation, across the road opposite the house, approached by a tunnel from the lawn under the turnpike road, is a French chalet, sent to Dickens as a present in ninety-eight packing cases! Here Mr. Dickens does most of his writing, where he can be perfectly quiet and not disturbed by anybody. I need scarcely say that the house is crowded with fine pictures, *original* sketches for his books, choice engravings, etc.; in fact, one might be amused for a month in looking over the objects of interest, which are numerous and beautiful.

Inside the hall are portions of the scenery painted by Stanfield for the "Frozen Deep," the play in which Dickens and others performed for the benefit of Douglas Jerrold's family, written by Wilkie Collins. Just as you enter, in a neat frame, written and illuminated by Owen Jones, is the following:

THIS HOUSE,

GAD'S HILL PLACE,

stands on the summit of Shakespeare's Gad's Hill, ever memorable for its association, in his noble fancy, with Sir John Falstaff.

"But, my lads, my lads, to-morrow morning by four o'clock, early at Gad's Hill. There are pilgrims going to Canterbury with rich offerings, and traders riding to London with fat purses. I have visors for all; you have horses for yourselves."

In the dining-room hangs Frith's original picture of Dolly Varden, and Maclise's portrait of Dickens when a young man; also Cattermole's wonderful drawings, illustrating some of Dickens's most touching scenes, besides several exquisite works by Marcus Stone, (who illustrated "Our Mutual Friend,") David Roberts, Calderon, Stanfield, and others.

My bed-room was the perfection of a sleeping apartment—the view across the Kentish Hills, with a distant peep of the Thames, charming; the screen, shutting off the dressing-room from the bed-room, is covered with proof-impressions (neatly framed) of the illustrations to "Our Mutual Friend," and other works; in every room I found a table covered with writing materials, headed note paper and envelopes, cut quill pens, wax, matches, sealing wax, and all scrupulously neat and orderly.

There are magnificent specimens of Newfoundland dogs on the grounds, such animals as Landseer would love to paint. One of them, Bumble, seems to be the favorite with Dickens. They are all named after characters in his works.

Dickens, at home, seems to be perpetually jolly, and enters into the interests of games with all the ardor of a boy. Physically (as well as mentally) he is immensely strong, having quite regained his wonted health and strength. He is an immense walker, and never seems to be fatigued. He breakfasts at eight o'clock; immediately after answers all the letters received that morning, writes until one o'clock, lunches, walks twelve miles, (every day), dines at six, and passes the evening entertaining his numerous friends.

He told me, when a boy his father frequently took him for a walk in the vicinity of Gad's Hill, and he always had a desire to become some day the owner of the house in which he now resides.

In August, 1869, so runs the story, a party of excursionists, from Chatham, had been spending the day in the vicinity of Gad's Hill, when on their return in the evening, they fell in with a couple of dancing bears, which were going through their performances in the road in front of Mr. Dickens's house. The enjoyments of the day having had their customary effects on the excursionists, one of the men, more elated than his companions, insisted on joining the bears in their performances, and dancing with them, the keepers in vain attempting to prevent him. At length with the intention of causing him to desist, the keeper removed the muzzle of one of the bears, but this failed to stop the dance. By this time a great crowd had assembled, when Mr. Dickens, seeing the serious turn matters were assuming, appeared on the scene, and himself assisted in remuzzling the bear, at the same time good-humoredly addressing the crowd and restoring peace between the enraged keepers of the bears and the author of the too serious frolic.

After Mr. Dickens returned to England, in 1868, he wrote three magazine articles for American magazines: for "Our Young Folks," the *Holiday Romance*, and for the Atlantic Monthly, a story entitled *George Silverman's Explanation*, and a paper introducing Mr. Fechter, the player, to the American public, before whom he was about appearing. He was a warm admirer of Mr. Fechter, and M. Paul Feval has related upon *no* authority, a remarkable anecdote of the actor's having incurred a debt of £3,000 by his mismanagement of the Lyceum Theatre, in London ; of Dickens having paid this money for him without being asked ; and of the actor's delight at finding himself thus freed from a heavy embarrassment. Mr. Dickens was impulsive and generous, but having the future of a large family to care for, it may be very much doubted whether he ever committed the pecuniary folly thus imputed to him by his French admirer. Except in romances, and those of the wildest character, men of letters, however rich and well-disposed, do not make presents of three thousand pounds to their histrionic friends !

Towards the close of 1869, Mr. Dickens resumed his Readings in London, and prepared for the press the "Religious Opinions of his friend, the Rev. Chauncey Hare Townshend," who had bequeathed him a handsome legacy on condition that he would edit his literary remains. By this time, too, the plot of *Edwin Drood* had been blocked out and part of the tale written.

CHAPTER XXII.

FAREWELL READINGS.—MYSTERY OF EDWIN DROOD.—VISITS QUEEN VICTORIA.—HONORS DECLINED.—SPEECH AT ROYAL ACADEMY.—ILL HEALTH.—THE LAST WEEK.—CLOSING CORRESPONDENCE.—HIS CHRISTIAN BELIEF AND HOPE.—APOPLEXY.—DEATH.—GRIEF FROM THRONE TO COTTAGE.—BURIAL IN WESTMINSTER ABBEY.—DEAN STANLEY'S SERMON ON CHARLES DICKENS IN WESTMINSTER ABBEY.

It was announced, early in 1870, that Mr. Dickens had so far completed a new work, that its first monthly number, "between green leaves," would be published in April; only, it was to be completed in twelve instead of twenty parts. He brought his Readings to a final close. On the evening of March 15th, 1870, he appeared for the last time before an audience which included intellect as well as fashion, and which had then as little thought as himself that they heard him for the last time.

> "The last! the last! Oh, by that little word,
> How many thoughts are stirred."

In the few sentences which he spoke, ere he retired forever from public view, were these:

> I have thought it well, at the full flood-tide of your favor, to retire upon those older associations between us, which date from much further back than these, and henceforth to devote myself exclusively to the art that first brought us together. Ladies and gentlemen, in but two short weeks from this time, I hope that you may enter, in your own houses, on a new "Series of Readings," at which my assistance will be indispensable; but from these garish lights I vanish now for evermore, with a heartfelt, grateful, respectful, and affectionate farewell.

The new serial, illustrated by a new artist (Mr. S. L. Fildes), caused a great deal of discussion. The general opinion on the portion of *The Mystery of Edwin Drood* already published, is not overpoweringly favorable. One-half of the work is completed. Its author was engaged in composition on the very day that he was death-smitten. He had labored, more than on any former work, to obtain complete success. So anxious was he to be accurate, that he sought out Sir John Bowring, who had been British Ambassador to China, and also Governor of Hong Kong, and made particular inquiries from him as to the manner, extent, and effects of opium smoking in that country. But he appears to have been haunted by a dread of failure. He wrote and re-wrote, revised and corrected, made excisions and additions, and, always addicted, like Burke and Canning, to a course of proof-reading which ofttimes almost remodelled the text, almost broke the compositors' hearts by the number and variety of his corrections. It might almost be said:

> "His trembling hand had lost the ease
> Which marks security to please."

The Muse, it seemed, was coy, at last, and refused to be won as freely as of yore. He was afraid, too, that he had allowed the "mystery" of his hero to be too readily guessed at. He continued his long walks, now rather of duty than of pleasure, and had lost much of the strength and activity which had distinguished him. He did not walk with ease—the elastic spring which had carried him forward at the rate of over four miles to the hour, without pause or rest, had departed.

At this time, a circumstance occured which greatly gratified him. Queen Victoria had obtained a right to have her name placed upon the roll of "Royal and Noble Authors," by her publishing a volume concerning the "Early Days of Albert, the late Prince Consort." The late General Grey, private secretary to the Queen, had prepared this volume for the press, and the fact of its being a Royal work awakened interest in its favor, and curiosity. Early in 1870 the Queen presented a copy of it to Mr. Dickens, with the modest autographic inscription, "from the humblest to the most distinguished author of England." This was meant to be complimentary, and was accepted as such by Mr. Dickens, who acknowledged it in a manly, courteous letter. Soon after, Queen Victoria wrote to him, requesting that he would do her the favor of paying her a visit at Windsor. He accepted, and passed a day, very pleasantly, in his Sovereign's society It is said that they were mutually pleased, that Mr. Dickens caught the royal lady's particular humor, that they chatted together in a very friendly manner, that the Queen was never tired of asking questions about certain characters in his books, that they had almost a *tête-á-tête* luncheon, and that, ere he departed, the Queen pressed him to accept a baronetcy (a title which descends to the eldest son), and that, on his declining, she said "At least, Mr. Dickens, let me have the gratification of making you one of my Privy Council." This, which gives the personal title of "Right Honorable," he also declined—nor, indeed, did Charles Dickens require a title to give him celebrity. The Queen and the author parted, well pleased with each other. The newspapers reported that a peerage had been offered and declined—but even newspapers are not invariably correct. Mr. Dickens presented his Royal Mistress with a handsome set of all his works, and, on the very morning of his death, a letter reached Gad's Hill, written by Mr. Arthur Helps, by her desire, acknowledging the present, and describing the exact position the books occupied at Balmoral—so placed that she could see them before her when occupying the usual seat in her sitting-room. When this letter arrived, Mr. Dickens was still alive, but wholly unconscious. What to him, at that time, was the courtesy of an earthly sovereign?

The death of Mr. Daniel Maclise, R. A., one of the most distinguished among British artists, which took place in April of 1870, was a great blow to Mr. Dickens. The fame of artist and author had been of contemporary growth. There was little difference in their ages, and their friendship had lasted, without a cloud over it, for more than thirty years. No doubt Mr. Dickens was shocked as well as grieved by this sudden blow.

The last words spoken by Charles Dickens in public were characteristic of the man. The annual exhibition of the Royal Academy, in London, always opens on the first Monday in May, when there invariably is a splendid banquet, with the President in the chair, in the principal saloon, the walls of which are then covered with paintings, as yet unseen by the public at large. This is called the Private-view Dinner, and those whom the Academicians entertain, represent royalty, and the aristocracy of title, office, wealth, and intellect. Mr. Thackeray and Mr. Dickens were always warmly welcomed and highly honored guests: it was expected, also, that they would speak. At the last of these banquets, on Saturday, 29th of April, 1870, Mr. Dickens was present. One of the finest paintings in the exhibition was by Daniel Maclise, R. A., whose sudden death, such a short time before, had painfully impressed his colleagues and friends. This picture, entitled "The Earls of Desmond and Ormond," was one of the Irish subjects Maclise so much liked, and equals most of his previous productions in design, coloring, and expression, but is said by the critics to be rather deficient in execution, as if the painter had got tired of his work, and sent it away without giving it the last touches which do so much. Maclise had twice refused the Presidency of the Royal Academy, and was an honor to the institution. Mr. Dickens concluded an excellent speech (the oration of the day, though evidently extempore), in a very impressive manner, as follows:

Since I first entered the public lists, a very young man indeed, it has been my constant fortune to number among my nearest and dearest friends members of the Royal Academy who have been its grace and pride. They have so dropped from my side one by one that I already begin to feel like the Spanish monk of whom Wilkie tells, who had grown to believe that the only realities around him were the pictures which he loved, and that all the moving life he saw, or ever had seen, was a shadow and a dream. For many years I was one of the two most intimate friends and most constant companions of the late Mr. Maclise. Of his genius in his chosen art I will venture to say nothing here, but of his prodigious fertility of mind and wonderful wealth of intellect, I may confidently assert that they would have made him, if he had been so minded, at least as great a writer as he was a painter. The gentlest and most modest of men, the freest as to his generous appreciation of young aspirants, and the frankest and largest-hearted as to his peers, incapable of a sordid or ignoble thought, gallantly sustaining the true dignity of his vocation, without one grain of self-assertion, wholesomely natural at the last as at the first, "in wit a man, in simplicity a child;" no artist, of whatsoever denomination, I make bold to say, ever went to his rest leaving a golden memory more pure from dross, or having devoted himself with a truer chivalry to the art-goddess whom he worshipped.

On the 15th of May, 1870, declining to accept an invitation to the Theatrical Fund Dinner, Mr. Dickens thus addressed Mr. Buckstone, the actor and manager:

SUNDAY, 15*th May*, 1870.

MY DEAR BUCKSTONE:—I send a duplicate of this note to the Haymarket, in case it should miss you out of town. For a few years I have been liable, at wholly uncertain and incalculable times, to a severe attack of neuralgia in the foot, about once in the course of a year. It began in an injury to the finer muscles or nerves, occasioned by over-walking in the deep snow. When it comes on I cannot stand, and can bear no covering whatever on the sensitive place. One of these seizures is upon me now. Until it leaves me, I could no more walk into St. James's Hall than I could fly in the air. I hope you will present my duty to the Prince [of Wales] and assure his Royal Highness that nothing short of my being (most unfortunately) disabled for the moment would have prevented my attending, as trustee of the Fund, at the dinner, and warmly expressing my poor sense of the great and inestimable service his Royal Highness renders to a most deserving institution by so kindly commending it to the public. Faithfully yours always,

CHARLES DICKENS.

This seems to have been the first intimation to the public of his ill health. The complaint, a severe description of neuralgia, had severely afflicted him in America.

On Thursday, June 2d, Mr. Dickens was in London, and "assisted" at some private theatricals, which seemed to give him much gratification, as usual. One of the performers was young Mr. Power, a son of Tyrone Power, the actor, who was lost in the "President." As he had left his family badly off, Mr. Dickens had exerted himself, very successfully, to obtain from the public a pecuniary provision for them. Young Mr. Power is engaged in business, in Albemarle street, London, and, as might be expected, has a devoted regard for his benefactor. As they were coming out of the place of performance, Mr. Dickens put down his open palm upon his companion's shoulder, and answered a question with the words, "I think you are very much improved in your performance. But, I must tell you that you never can become a great actor, and I recommend you by all means, not to give up business for the stage." As he was leaving, Mr. Power asked him when he again expected to be in London? "Not for some time," he said. "I am tired. I want rest—*rest*," pronouncing the last word in a lingering tone. Mr. John E. McDonough received this anecdote from Mr. Power himself. Next day Mr. Dickens wrote this letter, in which it will be observed that he again mentions his complaint and its cause:

GAD'S HILL PLACE, HIGHAM-BY-ROCHESTER, KENT,
Friday, 3rd June, 1870.

Mr. Charles Dickens sends his compliments to Messrs. Pulvermacher and Co., and begs to say he wishes to try a Voltaic Band across his right foot, as a remedy against what he supposes to be neuralgia there, (originating in overwalking in deep snow,) to which he is occasionally liable. Mr. Dickens writes on the recommendation of Mrs. Bancroft, who assures him that she has derived great relief from a similar complaint from the use of one of these Bands. If Messrs. Pulvermacher and Co. will be so good as send him one, he will remit a cheque for its cost by return of post, and will give it the fairest trial.

On Saturday, June 4th, having allowed some friends to have a féte champetre on his grounds, he visited them for about ten minutes, and then returned to his library, saying that he was not very well and had a great deal to do. Every day, at this time, he wrote some portion of *Edwin Drood.* At this time, too, he examined the books, accounts, and vouchers of *All the Year Round.* He had, just before, executed a codicil to his will, written for him by his lawyer, but copied out in his own handwriting. This instrument bequeathed *All the Year Round* to his eldest son, Charles.

On Tuesday he walked into Rochester, next day was Wednesday, 8th of June, 1870. Mr. Dickens wrote some pages of *Edwin Drood* and several letters. One to Messrs.

Pulvermacher & Co., enclosing a Post-office order for the Voltaic Band, ordered on the 3rd, and safely received. It concluded thus:—"It," the P. O. order, "has been obtained by mistake for a shilling or two more than the right amount. They can, if they please, return the balance in postage-stamps." Next, which shows how little he anticipated any early termination to his labors and life, a note to Mr. Holdsworth, manager of "All the Year Round," who had been connected with Mr. Dickens for a quarter of a century, was dated that day before his death (June 8th) and asked him to purchase at "one of those Great Queen Street shops"—who knew so well as Dickens about London brokers and their wares?—a writing-slope for Gad's Hill, such as he had in use at the office. On that same day, Mr. Dickens wrote this note:

GAD'S HILL PLACE, HIGHAM-BY-ROCHESTER, KENT,
Wednesday, the Eighth of June, 1870.

MY DEAR KENT:—To-morrow is a very bad day for me to make a call, as, in addition to my usual office business, I have a mass of accounts to settle. But I hope I may be ready for you at three o'clock. If I can't be—why, then I shan't be. You must really get rid of those opal enjoyments. They are too overpowering:

These violent delights have violent ends.

I think it was the father of your church who made the wise remark to a young gentleman who got up early (or stayed out late) at Verona. Ever affectionately,

CHARLES DICKENS.

To CHARLES KENT, Esq.

The *Athenæum*, which published the above, says, "the 'opal enjoyments' refer to the tints of the sky." Mr. Charles Kent, one of the most accomplished journalists and critics in London, is the author of a poem of great merit, entitled "Alatheia," of which a second edition was lately published. On Thursday, June 9th, when he called to keep the appointment, Mr. Dickens was lying, in his dining-room, within three hours of his death.

There was yet another letter, written and sent, on that fatal 8th of June. Some busy person, who signed "J. M. M.," had written to Mr. Dickens, suggesting that a passage in the 10th chapter of *Edwin Drood* was likely to wound the religious sensibilities of many of his admirers. The passage most probably is the following, in reference to Mr. Crisparkle:

> Into this herbaceous penitentiary, situated on an upper staircase landing—a low and narrow whitewashed cell, where bunches of dried leaves hung from rusty hooks in the ceiling, and were spread out upon shelves, in company with portentious bottles—would the Reverend Septimus submissively be led, like the highly popular lamb who has so long and unresistingly been led to the slaughter, and there would he, unlike that lamb, bore nobody but himself.

It is difficult to see how any sensible person could put such a strained interruption upon this passage, as to fancy it irreligious. Mr. Dickens thus answered it:

GAD'S HILL PLACE, HIGHAM-BY-ROCHESTER, KENT,
Wednesday, the 8th June, 1870.

DEAR SIR:—It would be quite inconceivable to me—but for your letter—that any reasonable reader could possibly attach a scriptural reference to a passage in a book of mine, reproducing a much-abused social figure of speech, impressed into all sorts of service, on all sorts of inappropriate occasions, without the faintest connection of it with its original source. I am truly shocked to find that any reader can make the mistake. I have always striven in my writings to express veneration for the life and lessons of our Saviour; because I feel it; and because I rewrote that history for my children—every one of whom knew it from having it repeated to them, long before they could read, and almost as soon as they could speak. But I have never made proclamation of this from the house-tops.

Faithfully yours, CHARLES DICKENS

This statement, perhaps the last he ever wrote, ought to settle the *questio vexata* of Mr. Dickens's Christianity.

On that same day, Wednesday, June 8th, after Mr. Dickens had sat down to dinner, about 6 o'clock, Miss Hogarth, the only person then present, observing an unusual expression in his face, and his eyes suffused in tears, said she feared that he was ill, and proposed to send or telegraph for medical assistance. He answered, rather feebly, "No, no, no; I have got the toothache, and shall be well presently." Almost in the same breath he desired that the window be closed. Immediately, he sank into a state of insensibility, from which he never rallied, never recovered. Mr. Frank Beard, his regular medical attendant in London was telegraphed for, and arrived at Gad's Hill that evening. Dr. Steele, of the adjacent village of Strood, who regularly attended the family when they were in the country, was also there, and remained until midnight. From the first, Mr. Beard saw that the attack must terminate speedily and fatally. For his own satisfaction, and that of the family, he summoned Dr. Russell Reynolds, who also pronounced the case hopeless. On Thursday morning, June 9th, Mr. Charles Dickens, Junior, arrived in London, from another part of the country, proceeded to Gad's Hill without delay, and was present at his father's death, which took place in the dining-room, at about a quarter past six P. M. There were also present, of the family, the author's two daughters and Miss Hogarth. From the moment of his attack, Mr. Dickens never uttered a word, never appeared conscious. There was not any Coroner's inquest, the medical men expressly and positively declaring that the immediate cause was apoplexy—an effusion of blood on the brain—his system having been overstrained, and the result one which was only staved off twelve months before, when he was induced to obey his doctor's injunctions and to suspend his readings in public. He was 58 years, 4 months, and 3 days old.

The first intimation of his illness, of his danger, was

published in a late edition of *The Globe*, an evening paper,—the statement being that he had been smitten by paralysis. The intelligence caused general anxiety, that evening. On the morrow, particulars of his seizure and death, were published in all the morning papers throughout the British Islands, and on the Continent. He was lamented by all. It was generally said, in London, that the great heart of England had not sustained such a shock since the death of the Princess Charlotte of Wales and her infant son, in November, 1817,—when, from the inhabitants of the palace to those of the hovel, every one wore some badge of mourning. The intelligence was known throughout the United States, by noon, on the same day, and the afternoon papers, with equal energy and talent, not merely gave extended sketches of his personal and professional career, but presented sound estimates of his character as an author and a man:—two Philadelphia evening papers particularly distinguished themselves in this respect. Next day, every morning paper had biographies of Charles Dickens, and suitable comments upon his life and death. The tone and execution of these articles were most creditable to the American press. Mr. Dickens knew—none better—that for every one reader he had at home, he had fifty in this country, and that he was more thoroughly understood here than even on his own soil.

When the news of his death reached Queen Victoria, she sent a telegram to Gad's Hill House, expressing her deep sorrow. Other members of the royal family, of the nobility, of all ranks and classes did the same. A national loss had been sustained, and, in that hour of sorrow, the country spoke as with one voice. The dead man had been, in his works, an inmate in every household. He had never written to set class against class; he had ever been the champion of the poor, the oppressed—and the afflicted. It was one consolation that, though he had not lived in a parsimonious manner, though his purse was ever open for benevolent purposes, he had left ample provision for his family.* It had been intended that, in pursuance with his oft expressed wish, his mortal remains should be deposited at Rochester, in the shadow of the fine old Cathedral—the Cloisterham of his last, and unfinished story. Preparations were made for doing this; but *The Times*, on June 11th, suggested that Westminster Abbey, the British Pantheon of England, was the proper place of sepulture for England's great author. By a coincidence of thought, which is not inexplicable, the same suggestion was made in the *Washington Chronicle*, of the same day. Mr. Gladstone eagerly sustained the suggestion, the Dean of Westminster also approving of it. Mr.

---

* The *Athenæum*, apparently making the statement on authority, said, "The ample provision which Charles Dickens made for his family consists of some £43,000, invested in public securities, half the value of the copyright of the great novelist's books, estimated at £20,000, his modest house at Gad's Hill, together with its contents, and the interest in *All the Year Round*, bequeathed to his eldest son. Mr. Dickens was at all times a munificent and free-handed man, and never made the attainment of wealth a first object." The pictures, drawings, and objects of art and *vertu* in Gad's Hill House, were disposed of, in Christie, Manson & Wood's auction-rooms, on Saturday, July 9th. The articles, of more interest than value, were thus announced:—"The pictures comprise the celebrated portrait of Mr. Dickens, painted in 1839, by D. Maclise, R. A.; three splendid pictures, illustrating 'The Frozen Deep,' painted by Clarkson Stanfield, R. A.; 'Dolly Varden' and 'Kate Nickleby,' two charming works, by W. P. Frith, R. A.; 'Dotheboys Hall,' an exquisite work of T. Webster, R. A.; 'Pickwick and Mrs. Bardell,' by C Leslie, R. A.; 'The Simoon,' by D. Roberts, R. A.; 'A Girl at a Waterfall,' a very beautiful work of D. Maclise, R. A.; 'Hide and Seek,' and 'The Letter,' by P. H. Calderon, A. R. A.; Portrait of Mr. Dickens in 'Used Up,' by A. Egg, A. R. A.; 'Tilda Price,' by Frank Stone, A. R. A.; 'The Novel' and 'The Play,' by R. Hannah; 'Miss F.'s Aunt,' by W. Gale. The Drawings include 'The Britannia,' the vessel in which Mr. Dickens first went to America, by C. Stanfield, R. A.; also, 'The Land's End,' and 'The Logan Rock,' by the same artist;

Dickens had directed, in his will, that his funeral should be "unostentatious, and strictly private," and that his friends should not make him "the subject of any monument, memorial, or testimonial whatever." His family, weighing these words, came to the conclusion that neither their letter nor spirit would be violated by a private interment in Poets' Corner, Westminster Abbey. Here, from the *London Times* of Wednesday, June 15th, 1870, is a semi-official account of the funeral:

Charles Dickens rests in the Abbey Church of St. Peter at Westminster. The funeral of the great novelist was celebrated at an early hour yesterday morning, in Poets' Corner, with as much privacy as could have been secured for it in

---

'Little Nell's Home,' and 'Little Nell's Grave,' two master-pieces by G. Cattermole, illustrating 'The Old Curiosity Shop;' 'Little Nell and her Grandfather,' and 'Barnaby Rudge and his Mother,' by F. W. Topham; 'Beauvais Cathedral,' by S. Prout; a very fine Flower Piece, by W. Hunt; an illustration to 'The Cotter's Saturday Night,' by Sir D. Wilkie, R. A.; and several other interesting works, many of which were presented by the artists; also the Silver Pickwick Ladles, with characters from the work, presented by the Publishers; Bronzes, old Nankin blue and white, richly enamelled Pekin Porcelain, Parisian Clock and Candelabra, and a variety of decorative objects and plaster casts, and other interesting relics." The friends of the deceased, and other patrons of literature and art, were numerous at that sale. "Dolly Varden," for which Mr. Dickens had paid £20 to Mr. Frith, the painter, brought £1,050. The portrait of Mr. Dickens, by Maclise, painted in 1839, brought £693. Forty pictures, exclusive of fifteen drawings, realized nearly £8,000. "Grip," (the veritable raven of *Barnaby Rudge,*) stuffed, in a glass case, went for £126. The entire proceeds were £9,410, or thrice as much as the intrinsic value of the objects. The Gad's Hill House property was advertised to be sold by auction, "in two lots," on Friday, August 5th. It consisted of a house and twenty-six acres of land. Charles Dickens, jun., was the purchaser for £8,600.

any little village church in Kent, or even in Wales or Cornwall. A grave had been dug during the night, and we believe that we are right in asserting that, besides the Dean and Canons, hardly a member of the Cathedral body on Monday evening was aware of the intended arrangement. It appears that some days ago the Dean sent a communication to the family of Mr. Dickens to the effect that, if it was desired by themselves or by the public that he should be buried in the Abbey, he would do all in his power to facilitate the arrangements; and also that on Monday, suggesting that the Abbey was the fitting resting-place for such a man, he repeated the offer in terms more distinct. Most fortunately, it was found, upon opening Mr. Dickens's will, that, although his instructions were explicit in forbidding all pomp and show, and all that "mockery of woe" which undertakers are at such pains to provide, he had named no place of burial; and therefore his executors felt that it was open to them to concur with the national wish, if they could only insure secrecy as to place and time. This was arranged satisfactorily on Monday, and at an early hour on Tuesday morning the body was conveyed, almost before any one was stirring, in a hearse from Gad's Hill to one of the railway stations of the London, Chatham, and Dover line, whence it was forwarded to London by a special train, which reached the Charing Cross station punctually at nine o'clock. In a few minutes more the hearse, which was plainness in itself, was on its way down Whitehall to the Abbey, followed by the mourning coaches, and we believe that not a single person of the many scores who must have met the gloomy cavalcade as it slowly passed along, was aware that that hearse was conveying to its last resting place all that was mortal of Charles Dickens.

A few minutes before half-past nine the hearse and mourning coaches—the latter, three in number—entered Dean's Yard, and the body was carried through the cloisters to the door of the nave, where it was met by the Dean, the two Canons in residence, Canon Jennings and Canon Nepean, and three of the Minor Canons. The choir were not present, and indeed, for the most part, were unaware that a grave had been opened in the Abbey, and that the sounds of the Burial Service were about to be heard there once more, more than half a year having passed by since the last funeral—that of Mr. Peabody. The service was most impressively read by the Dean, all but the Lesson, which was read by the Senior Canon. There was no anthem, no chanted psalm, no hymn, not even an intoned response or "Amen;" but the organ was played at intervals during the mournful ceremony. The earth was cast into the grave by the Clerk of the Works; the service ended, the mourners, thirteen in number, gathered round the grave to take a last look at the coffin which held the great novelist's remains, and to place wreaths of *immortelles* and other flowers upon the coffin-lid, and the service was at an end.

The coffin was of plain but solid oak, and it bore the plain and simple inscription:

CHARLES DICKENS.

BORN FEBRUARY 7TH, 1812.

DIED JUNE 9TH, 1870.

His grave, which is only between five and six feet deep, is situated about a yard or a yard and a half from the southern wall of Poets'-corner; the spot was selected by the Dean from among the few vacant spaces in that transept. Shakespeare's marble effigy looked yesterday into his open grave; at his feet are Dr. Johnson and David Garrick; his head is by Addison and Handel, while Oliver Goldsmith, Rowe, Southey, Campbell, Thompson, Sheridan, Macaulay, and Thackeray, or their memorials, encircle him; and "Poets' Corner," the most familiar spot in the whole Abbey, has thus received an illustrious addition to its peculiar glory. Separated from Dickens's grave by the statues of Shakespeare, Southey, and Thompson, and close by the door to "Poets' Corner," are the memorials of Ben Johnson, Dr. Samuel Butler, Milton, Spenser, and Gray; while Chaucer, Dryden, Cowley, Mason, Shadwell, and Prior are hard by, and tell the bystander, with their wealth of great names, how

"These poets near our princes sleep,
And in one grave their mansion keep."

The grave, by direction of the Dean, was left open as long as the Abbey was open yesterday; and, as the news spread about London, many visitors went to "Poets' Corner" during the afternoon to take a last sad look at the coffin of Charles Dickens; but it was understood that the grave would be closed during the course of the evening, and that it was the intention of the Dean to preach a funeral sermon upon the career and character of the great writer, whose ashes have been laid in the Abbey, on Sunday next.

In the first mourning coach were Mr. Charles Dickens, jun., Mr. Harry Dickens, Miss Dickens and Mrs. Charles Collins.

In the second coach, Miss Hogarth, Mrs. Austen (Mr. Dickens's sister), Mrs. Charles Dickens, jun., and Mr. John Forster.

In the third coach, Mr. Frank Beard, Mr. Charles Collins, Mr. Ouvry, Mr. Wilkie Collins, and Mr. Edmund Dickens.

The grave was visited, during the short time it remained open, by thousands of persons of all ranks. Mr. John E. McDonough, of Philadelphia, who had arrived in London on the day after Mr. Dickens's death, was among the crowd which visited Poets' Corner on the afternoon of the interment. "I went there," he has told us, "with a friend. Part of the pavement had been removed, but the flags were to be immediately replaced. A slight barrier of cord or line was fenced all round the grave, which was filled with flowers—not bouquets, but single rosebuds and geraniums. On inquiry, I was told that every person, male and female, who visited the grave that day, and wore a flower—an English habit which Mr. Dickens himself always favored—had thrown it, as if by some instinctive feeling, into the grave of the greatest author of our time. My friend and myself silently exchanged looks, and *our* flowers were reverently cast amid the heap already in the grave. It was a very solemn and imposing, and I might say, affecting scene."

The Very Rev. Arthur Penrhyn Stanley, D.D., who was appointed Dean of Westminster, in January, 1864, on the promotion of Dr. Trench to the Archbishopric of Dublin, and through whose influence with the family of Mr. Dickens, the remains of the great author were deposited in Poets' Corner, Westminster Abbey, is son of the late Bishop of Norwich, was educated at Rugby School, by the celebrated Dr. Arnold, and obtained the highest honors, in Classics and Theology, during his University course at Oxford. His life of Dr. Arnold, published in 1844, is considered a model biography, and he has published many other literary works, historical and religious. He is now fifty-five years old, is beloved and honored for his tolerance and talent, and, to the regret of the Church of England, has more than once refused a mitre. His sermon, "preached in Westminster Abbey, June 19th, 1870, (the First Sunday after Trinity,) being the Sunday following the funeral of Charles Dickens," was published by Macmillan & Co., London, with the intimation that "preached under the pressure of a temporary indisposition, which prevented it from being heard except by comparatively few, it is printed at the request of some of those who have since desired to read it." The Dean's voice was so low, from illness, that Mr. McDonough heard only an occasional sentence. Exactly opposite the pulpit, and so near to it, as to be within ear-shot, sat Mr. Tennyson, the poet. A little to his left was Mr. Wilkie Collins, in feature, but not in bulk, very like the late Secretary Stanton. In the present volume this sermon is given in full, as a tribute of the highest value, from one well qualified to bestow it, to the moral character of the writings, the pure life, and the comprehensive Christianity, of Charles Dickens.

THE FUNERAL SERMON.

St. Luke xv. 3; xvi. 19–21.

He spake this Parable. . . . . .

There was a certain rich man, which was clothed in purple and fine linen, and fared sumptuously every day:

And there was a certain beggar named Lazarus, which was laid at his gate, full of sores,

And desiring to be fed with the crumbs which fell from the rich man's table: moreover the dogs came and licked his sores.

There are some passages of Scripture which, when they are read in the services of the Sunday, almost demand a special notice from their extraordinary force and impressiveness. Such is the Parable of the Rich Man and Lazarus, read as the Gospel of this day. There are some incidents of human life which almost demands a special notice from the depth and breadth of the feelings which they awaken in the heart of the congregation. Such was the ceremony which, on Tuesday last, conveyed to his grave, within these walls, a lamented and gifted being, who had for years delighted and instructed the generation to which he belonged. And if the Scripture of the day and the incident of the week direct our minds to the same thoughts, and mutually illustrate each other, the attraction is irresistible, and the moral which each supplies is doubly enforced.

Let me then draw out these lessons in what I now propose to say.

1. I will speak first of the *form* of instruction which we are called upon to notice in the Gospel of this Sunday. It is not only like most of our Lord's instructions, a Parable, but it is, as it were, a Parable of the Parables. It is the last of a group which occurs in the 15th and 16th chapters of St. Luke, where the story is taken in each case, not as in the other Gospels, from inanimate or irrational creatures, but from the doings and characters of men. First comes the story of the Good Shepherd, with all its depth of tenderness; then the story of the Indefatigable Searcher, with all its depth of earnestness; then the story of the Prodigal Son, with all its depth of pathos; then the story of the Unjust Steward, with all its depth of satire; and, last of all, comes the story of the Rich Man and the Poor Man, drawn not merely from the mountain side, or the dark chamber, or the tranquil home, or the accountant's closet, but from the varied stir of human enjoyment and human suffering in the streets and alleys of Jerusalem. It is a tale of real life—so real that we can hardly believe that it is not history. Yet it is, nevertheless, a tale of pure fiction from first to last. Dives and Lazarus are as much imaginary beings as Hamlet or as Shylock; the scene of Abraham's bosom and of the rich man in Hades is drawn not from any literal outward truth, or ancient sacred record, but from the popular Jewish conceptions current at the time. This Parable is, in short, the most direct example which the Bible contains of the use, of the value of the sacredness of fictitious narrative. There are doubtless many other instances in the Sacred Records. There is the exquisite parable of the

Talking Trees in the Book of Judges; there is the sublime drama of the Patriarch and his Friends in the Book of Job; there is the touching and graceful picture of Jewish family life in the Book of Tobit, from which our Church selects some of its most striking precepts, and which, in its Homilies, is treated as if inspired directly by the Holy Ghost. All these are instances where moral lessons are conveyed by the invention of characters which either never existed at all, or, if they existed, are made to converse in forms of speech entirely drawn from the inspired imagination of the sacred writer. But the highest sanction to this mode of instruction is that given us in this Parable by our Lord Himself. This, we are told, was His ordinary mode of teaching; He stamped it with His peculiar mark. "Without a parable,"* without a fable, without an invented story of this kind, He rarely opened His lips. He, the Example of examples, the Teacher of teachers, "taught His disciples† many things by parables." Through this parabolic form some of His gravest instructions have received a double life. If we were to ask for the most perfect exposition of the most perfect truth respecting God and man, which the world contains, it will be found not in a Discourse, or a Creed, or a Hymn, or even a Prayer, but in a Parable—a story—one of those which I have already cited—the Parable of the Prodigal Son.

I have dwelt on this characteristic of the Gospel teaching because it is well that we should see how the Bible itself sanctions a mode of instruction which has been, in a special sense, God's gift to our own age. Doubtless His "grace is "manifold,"‡—in the original expression, many colored. In various ages it has assumed various forms—the divine flame of poetry, the far-reaching gaze of science, the searching analysis of philosophy, the glorious page of history, the burning eloquence of speaker or preacher, the grave address of moralist or divine. These all we have had in ages past; their memorials are around us here. These all we have in their measure, some more, some less, in the age in which we live. But it is perhaps not too much to say, that in no age of the world, and in no country of the world, has been developed on so large a scale, and with such striking effects as in our own, the gift of "speaking in parables;" the gift of addressing mankind through romance and novel and tale and fable. First and far above all others came that great-

* Matt. xiii. 34. † Mark iv. 2. ‡ 1 Pet. iv. 10.

est of all the masters of fiction—the glory of Scotland—whose romances refreshed and exalted our childhood as they still refresh and exalt our advancing years—as, would to God that they still might continue to refresh and exalt the childhood and the manhood of the coming generation. He rests not here. He rests beside his native Tweed. But long may his magic spell charm and purify the ages which yet shall be! Long may yonder monument of the Scottish Duke, whom he has immortalized in one of his noblest works, keep him forever in our memory, as, one by one, the lesser and later lights which have followed in that track where he led the way, are gathered beneath its overshadowing marble. It is because one of those bright lights has now passed from amongst us—one in whom this generation seemed to see the most vivid exemplification of this heaven-sent power of fiction, that I would thus speak of it, for a few moments, in its most general aspect.

There was a truth—let us freely confess it—in the old Puritan feeling against an exaggerated enjoyment of romances, as tending to relax the fibre of the moral character. That was a wholesome restraint which I remember in my childhood—which kept us from revelling in tales of fancy till the day's work was over, and thus impressed upon us that the reading of pleasant fictions was the holiday of life, and not its serious business. It is this very thing which, as it constitutes the danger of fictitious narratives, constitutes also their power. They approach us at times when we are indisposed to attend to anything else. They fill up those odd moments of life which exercise, for good or evil, so wide an effect over the whole tenor of our course. Poetry may enkindle a loftier fire—the Drama may rivet the attention more firmly—Science may open a wider horizon—Philosophy may touch a deeper spring—but no works are so penetrating, so pervasive, none reach so many homes, and attract so many readers, as the romance of modern times. Those who read nothing else, read eagerly the exciting tale. Those whom sermons never reach, whom history fails to arrest, are reached and arrested by the fictitious characters, the stirring plot, of the successful novelist. It is this which makes a wicked novel more detestable than almost any other form of wicked words or deeds. It is this which gives even to a foolish or worthless novel a demoralizing force beyond its own contemptible demerits. It is this which makes a good novel—pure in style, elevating in thought, true in sentiment—one of the best of boons to the Christian home and to the Christian state.

O vast responsibility to those who wield this mighty engine—mighty it may be, and has been, for corruption, for debasement, for defilement; mighty also it may be, mighty it certainly has been, in our English novels (to the glory of our country be it spoken), mighty for edification and for purification, for giving wholesome thoughts, high aspirations, soul-stirring recollections. Use these wonderful works of genius as not abusing them; enjoy them as God's special gifts to us—only remember that the true Romance of Life is Life itself.

2. But this leads me to the further question of the special form which this power assumed in him whose loss the country now deplores with a grief so deep and genuine as to be itself a matter for serious reflection. What was there in him which called forth this wide-spread sympathy? What is there in this sympathy and in that which created it, worthy of our religious thoughts on this day?

I profess not here to sit in judgment on the whole character and career of this gifted writer. That must be left for posterity to fix in its proper niche amongst the worthies of English literature.

Neither is this the place to speak at length of those lighter and more genial qualities, such as made his death, like that of one who rests beside him, almost "an eclipse of the "gaiety of nations." Let others tell elsewhere of the brilliant and delicate satire, the kindly wit, the keen and ubiquitous sense of the ludicrous and grotesque. "There is a time to "laugh, and there is a time to weep." Laughter is itself a good, yet there are moments when we care not to indulge in it. It may even seem hereafter, as it has sometimes seemed to some of our age, that the nerves of the rising generation were, for the time at least, unduly relaxed by that inexhaustible outburst of a humorous temper, of a never-slumbering observation, in the long unceasing flood of drollery and merriment which, it may be, brought out the comic and trivial side of human life in too strong and startling a relief.

But even thus, and even in this sacred place, it is good to remember that, in the writings of him who is gone, we have had the most convincing proof that it is possible to have moved old and young to inextinguishable laughter without the use of a single expression which could defile the purest, or shock the most sensitive. Remember this, if there be any who think that you cannot be witty without being wicked—who think that in order to amuse the world and awaken the interest of hearers or readers, you must descend to filthy jests, and unclean suggestions, and debasing scenes. So may have thought some gifted novelists of former times; but so thought not, so wrote not (to speak only of the departed) Walter Scott, or Jane Austen, or Elizabeth Gaskell, or William Thackeray: so thought not, and so wrote not, the genial and loving humorist whom we now mourn. However deep into the dregs of society his varied imagination led him in his writings to descend, it still breathed an untainted atmosphere. He was able to show us, by his own example, that even in dealing with the darkest scenes and the most degraded characters, genius could be clean, and mirth could be innocent.

3. There is another point, yet more peculiar and special, on which we may safely dwell, even in the very house of God, even beside the freshly laid grave. In that long series of stirring tales, now for ever closed, there was a profoundly serious—nay, may we not say, a profoundly Christian and Evangelical truth,—of which we all need to be reminded, and of which he was, in his own way, the special teacher.

It is the very same lesson which is represented to us in the Parable of this day. "There was a certain rich man, "which was clothed in purple and fine linen, and fared "sumptuously every day. And there was a certain beggar "named Lazarus, which was laid at his gate, full of sores, and "desiring to be fed with the crumbs which fell from the rich "man's table. Moreover, the dogs came and licked his "sores." It is a picture whose every image is expressive, and whose every image awakens thoughts that live for ever. It is true that an Oriental atmosphere hangs around it—the Syrian purple, the fine linen of Egypt, the open banqueting hall, the beggar in the gateway, the dogs prowling about the city. But the spirit of the Parable belongs to the West as well as to the East. The contrast, the inequality of deserts, on which it insists, meets us in the streets of London, no less than in the streets of Jerusalem; and the moral which the Parable intends that we should draw from that contrast is the very same which in his own peculiar way is urged upon us, with irresistible force, throughout the writings of our lost preceptor. Close beside the magnificence, the opulence, the luxury of this great metropolis, is that very neighbor—those very neighbors—whom the Parable describes. The Rich Man has no name in the Scripture; but the Poor Man has a name in the Book of God, and he has a name given him, he has many names given him, in the tales in which the departed has described the homes and manners of our poor brethren. "Lazarus"—the "help of God"—the noble name which tells us that God helps those who help themselves—is the very prototype of those outcasts, of those forlorn, struggling, human beings, whose characters are painted by him in such vivid colors that we shrink from speaking of them here, even as we should from speaking of persons yet alive —whose names are such familiar household words that, to mention them in a sacred place, seems almost like a desecration. It is of this vast outlying mass of unseen human suffering that we need constantly to be reminded. It is this contrast between things as they are in the sight of God, and things as they seem in the sight of man, that so easily escapes us all in our busy civilization. It is the difficulty of seeing this, of realizing this, which made a Parable like that of the Rich Man and Lazarus so vital a necessity for the world when it was first spoken. But He who spake as never man spake saw, with His far-seeing glance, into our complicated age as well as into His own. What was needed then is still more needed now; and it is to meet this need that our dull and sluggish hearts want all the assistance which can be given by lively imagination, by keen sympathy, by the dramatic power of making things which are not seen be as even though they were seen. Such were the gifts wielded with pre-eminent power by him who has passed away.

It was the distinguishing glory of a famous Spanish saint, that she was "the advocate of the absent." That is precisely the advocacy of the Divine Parable in the Gospels—the advocacy of these modern human Parables, which in their humble measure represent its spirit—the advocacy of the absent poor, of the neglected, of the weaker side, whom not seeing we are tempted to forget. It was a fine trait of a noble character of our own times, that, though full of interests, intellectual, domestic, social, the distress of the poor of England, he used to say, "pierced through his happiness and haunted him day and night." It is because this susceptibility is so rare, so difficult to attain, that we ought doubly to value those who have the eye to see, and the ear to hear, and the tongue to speak, and the pen to describe, those who are not at hand to demand their own rights, to set forth their own wrongs, to portray their own sufferings. Such was he who lies yonder. By him that veil was rent asunder which parts the various classes of society. Through his genius the rich man, faring sumptuously every day, was made to see and feel the presence of the Lazarus at his gate. The unhappy inmates of the workhouse, the neglected children in the dens and caves of our great cities, the starved and ill-used boys in remote schools, far from the observation of men, felt that a new ray of sunshine was poured on their dark existence—a new interest awakened in their forlorn and desolate lot. It was because an unknown friend had pleaded their cause with a voice which rang through the palaces of the great, as well as through the cottages of the poor. It was because, as by a magician's wand, those gaunt figures and strange faces had been, it may be sometimes, in exaggerated forms, made to stand and speak before those who hardly dreamed of their existence.

Nor was it mere compassion that was thus evoked. As the same Parable which delineates the miseries of the outcast Lazarus tells us also how, under that external degradation, was nursed a spirit fit for converse with the noble-minded and the gentle-hearted in the bosom of the Father of the Faithful,—so the same master-hand which drew the sorrows of the English poor, drew also the picture of the unselfish kindness, the courageous patience, the tender thoughtfulness, that lie concealed behind many a coarse exterior, in many a rough heart, in many a degraded home. When the little workhouse boy wins his way, pure and undefiled, through the mass of wickedness in the midst of which he passes—when the little orphan girl brings thoughts of heaven into the hearts of all around her, and is as the very gift of God to the old man whose desolate life she cheers—when the little cripple not only blesses his father's needy home, but softens the rude stranger's hardened conscience—there is a lesson taught which touches every heart, which no human being can feel without being the better for it, which makes that grave seem to those who crowd around it as though it were the very grave of those little innocents whom he had thus created for our companionship, for our instruction, for our delight and solace. He labored to tell us all, in new, very new, words, the old, old story that there is even in the worst of capacity for goodness—a soul worth redeeming, worth reclaiming, worth regenerating. He labored to tell the rich, the educated, how this better side was to be found and respected even in the most neglected Lazarus. He labored to tell the poor no less, to respect this better part in themselves, to remember that they also have a call to be good and just, if they will but hear it. If by any such means he has brought rich and poor nearer together, and made Englishmen feel more nearly as one family, he will not assuredly have lived in vain, nor will his bones in vain have been laid in this home and hearth of the English nation.

4. There is one more thought that this occasion suggests. In the parable of the Rich Man and Lazarus, besides the pungent, pathetic lessons of social life which it impresses upon us, is also conveyed, beyond any other part of the Gospels, the awful solemnity of the other world. "If they hear not Moses and the prophets, neither "will they be persuaded though one rose from the dead." So also on this day there is impressed upon us a solemnity, before which the most lively sallies of wit, the most brilliant splendors of genius wax faint and pale, namely, the solemnity of each man's individual responsibility, in each man's life and death. When on Tuesday last we stood by that open grave, in the still deep silence of the summer morning, in the midst of the vast, solitary space, broken only by that small band of thirteen mourners, it was impossible not to feel that there was something more sacred, more arresting than any earthly fane however bright, or than any historic mausoleum however august—and that was the return of the individual human soul into the hands of its Maker.

As I sit not here in judgment on the exact place to be allotted in the roll of history to that departing glory, neither do I sit in judgment on that departing spirit. But there are some farewell thoughts which I would fain express.

Many, many are the feet which have trodden and will tread the consecrated ground around that narrow grave; many, many are the hearts which both in the Old and in the New World are drawn towards it, as towards the resting-place of a dear personal friend; many are the flowers that have been strewed, many the tears shed, by the grateful affection of "the poor that cried, and the fatherless, "and those that had none to help them." May I speak to these a few sacred words which perhaps will come with a new meaning and a deeper force, because they come from the lips of a lost friend—because they are the most solemn utterance of lips now for ever closed in the grave. They are extracted from "the will of Charles Dickens, dated "May 12, 1869," and they will be heard by most here present for the first time. After the emphatic injunctions respecting "the inexpensive, unostentatious, and strictly private "manner" of his funeral, which were carried out to the very letter, he thus continues: "I direct that my name be in-"scribed in plain English letters on my tomb. . . I "conjure my friends on no account to make me the "subject of any monument, memorial, or testimonial what-"ever. I rest my claims to the remembrance of my country "upon my published works, and to the remembrance of my "friends upon their experience of me in addition thereto. I "commit my soul to the mercy of God through our Lord "and Saviour Jesus Christ; and I exhort my dear chil-"dren humbly to try to guide themselves by the teaching "of the New Testament in its broad spirit, and to put no "faith in any man's narrow construction of its letter here "or there."

In that simple but sufficient faith he lived and died; in that faith he bids you live and die. If any of you have learnt from his works the value, the eternal value of generosity, purity, kindness, unselfishness, and have learnt to show these in your own hearts and lives, these are the best monuments, memorials, and testimonials of the friend whom you loved, and who loved, with a rare and touching love, his friends, his country, and his fellowmen:—monuments which he would not refuse, and which the humblest, the poorest, the youngest have it in their power to raise to his memory.

CHAPTER XXIII.

PURITY OF HIS WRITINGS.—VARIETY OF SUBJECTS AND CHARACTERS.—ABSENCE OF EGOTISM AND CYNICISM.—COMPARED WITH THACKERAY.—WILL HIS WRITINGS LIVE?—HIS DOMESTIC LIFE.—HIS BROAD CHRISTIANITY.—THE CAIAPHAS OF PLYMOUTH CHURCH.—TRIBUTES FROM THE PULPIT.—CHARLES DICKENS'S LAST WORDS, AND THEIR GREAT LESSON.

BELIEVING that the world has been made brighter and better by the writings and life of Charles Dickens, I can have no hesitation in briefly delineating his character, as Author and as Man. In the whole range, vast as it is, which constitutes the common literature, the rich treasury, of America and England, not to speak of the numerous languages into which they have been translated, there are no purer books than those written by Charles Dickens. There is no line in them which the most scrupulous parent, the most tender husband, the most sensitive lover, the most fastidious guardian could desire to keep back from the eye of Maidenhood or Womanhood. There are no other works, in the language, so well adapted for all classes and all ages. They may be taken up, at any place or time, and the reader will be gratified by the entertainment they supply, the moral lesson which they teach:

> Age cannot wither them, nor custom stale
> *Their* infinite variety.

No writer has more completely, or more successfully, appealed to the emotional and sympathetic part of human nature. It is doubtful, as he glanced from gay to grave, whether his lively humor or his tender pathos was most to be admired. Whatever vein he indulged in, for the time, he avoided cynicism. Hence, we laugh *with*, instead of *at*, his comic characters, taking Pickwick, and Sam Weller, and Wilkins Micawber, and Mr. Toots, and Dick Swiveller, and Captain Cuttle, (that truest of all rough gentlemen,) to our heart, and feeling all the better for having met, and known, and loved them. I do not intend to place Dickens by the side of Thackeray, because it is wearying work to try and discover unlike likenesses which do not exist, but would ask the reader to remember how differently he was impressed by the first works of both. Vanity Fair is a great work, which no man could have written, so severe is even its hilarity, unless he had been world-weary and *blasé*. The Pickwick Papers are the evident production of a very young man, who, up to that time, had rather glanced *at* the world than moved *in* it. Vanity Fair was as palpably written by a person who had circulated freely through society, in various countries; who had been scathed in the passage; and who poured out upon paper,

The stinging of a heart the world had stung.

Dickens was entering life, at the age of twenty-three, as he has told us, when he began to write Pickwick, and after the publication of a few sketches, had to draw mainly upon his imagination for the characters and the action of his story. Before he had gone half way through it, a purpose filled his mind, and, what was begun as a burlesque upon Cockney sportsmen, struck a heavy blow at the then unbridled license of advocates in English Courts of law, and so thoroughly besieged that great citadel of Wrong and Oppression, the Fleet Prison, that, in a few years, it was "put down" (as Alderman Cute would have said) by public opinion, embodied in an Act of Parliament. Dickens lived to see imprisonment for debt abolished in England, and to hear all men say, "*You* have done this."

Thackeray, not much older than Dickens, had been a magazine-writer, a man of all work, for at least sixteen years before the appearance of Vanity Fair. He had begun life as a gay "young man upon town," by burning the candle at both ends, at home and abroad, until his twenty thousand pounds was gone. Then he set to work, and, being highly educated and very talented, obtained a living and made reputation. Vanity Fair, which he produced at an age when Dickens had written his best things—or most of them—was very successful, as it deserved to be. Only a man of genius could have invented and sustained Beckey Sharpe. Had he written only that one story, Thackeray would have ranked as successor to the author of Tom Jones. Yet, admiring Vanity Fair as I do, and reading it enjoyably through, at least once a year, (paying the same compliment to Robinson Crusoe, Gil Blas, the Vicar of Wakefield, Ivanhoe, and the Caxton novels,) I close it with a lowered opinion of human nature. I also read Pickwick, every now and then, and though I do not find in it that thorough knowledge of "life" possessed by Thackeray, (its purchase-money being his glorious youth and the twenty thousand pounds, already named as his inheritance,) I find myself in good humor with "all the world and the rest of mankind." You read Dickens without, so to say, finding a bitter taste on the mind, after it. The flavor of the fusil oil is very strong on the mind, after reading Thackeray. Both writers, let me add, were genial, honorable, benevolent men, and warmly attached to each other.

It is to be especially noted, as showing the idiosyncrasy of each author, that, whereas Mr. Thackeray was perpetually bringing himself, in his books, before the reader, Mr. Dickens rarely alluded to himself, his experiences or opinions, in any of his numerous works of fiction.

Besides remarkable power and wonderful fertility of invention, Charles Dickens had a joyous temperament grafted upon a generous mind. When he wrote of the household virtues, of toleration, of practical charity, of fair humanity, his words had effect, for there was no "sham" in them. His kindliness of heart was almost as great as his genius. How remarkable and original *that* was, I need not point out. But genius without ballast has often been wrecked. In him, it was accompanied by skill, good sense, a well-balanced mind, and a strong purpose of doing good. His infinite variety equalled that of Shakespeare, and it is very possible that the readers of another century, now only thirty years distant, may give Mr. Dickens a place even above that occupied by the Swan of Avon. The world is steadily becoming realistic, methinks, and bids fair to prefer the tales of Dickens to the plays of Shakespeare.

It is universally known that his political opinions were strongly liberal. He was no mere partisan, however. At any time he pleased, during the last twenty-five years, Charles Dickens might have had a seat in the House of Commons. Any of the London boroughs would have been proud and glad if he had consented to be its representative. At least twenty other constituencies, throughout the British Islands, would have voted him their member by acclamation. Numerous offers to this effect were made to him, and declined. He had resolved, at the beginning of his career, to devote himself to literature, wholly and solely, and, as the years rolled on, bringing him increase of power and influence upon the public mind, he believed, more than ever, that abuses were to be laid bare, wrongs righted, and reforms effected, rather by his written than his spoken words. In the House of Commons, with all his earnestness and eloquence, he would have been only one in a crowd—though most probably a distinguished one. From first to last, he relied on the Press, to work out all his public purposes, and was right in doing so. Besides, had he become a Member of Parliament, we should have had comparatively little from his pen.

This brings me to the last point which I design to notice: Will Dickens live? I would answer in the affirmative. Future ages will regard his writings as photographs of middle and lower class life in England during the Victorian era, which had extended to thirty-four years when he died. In other novels of that period, aristocratic society is sketched, rather wearily ; but it may be safely assumed that after all, only a few, by Bulwer and Thackeray, will be read in the twentieth century, and these as rarely as the prose fictions of Fielding, Smollett, Richardson, and Goldsmith—the very writers who led Dickens, when a child, into the fair realm of romance—are read now. Dickens is so fresh, so kindly, so picturesque, so true, that his works must live, as Hogarth's do, pictures of the era which produced him.

Dramatist, actor, orator, and thorough man of the world as he was, he realizes the idea of an universal genius more than any other writer who ever lived. In whatever profession it might have pleased him to cast himself, he must have succeeded. Eminently social and domestic, he exercised a liberal hospitality, and though he lived well, as his means allowed, avoided excesses :—with a constant burthen of work upon his mind for five-and-thirty years, to say nothing of other occupations, it was impossible that he could have been what is called a free liver. It is said that he never lost a friend, that he never made an enemy. Of him it might be truly said

> He kept
> The whiteness of his soul, and so men o'er him wept.

He was the life and soul of the domestic circle, and, in a preceding chapter, I have recorded, in a statement signed by himself, and endorsed by his wife and eldest son, that the resolution to have a divided household, came from *her*. True, she stood aloof from the husband of her youth, the father of her children, at the last sad hour, and she was not present when all that was mortal of him was deposited, with the remains of some of the greatest men of his nation, in the hallowed fane of Westminster :—but, let not *her* coldness, or carelessness, or anger, be imputed as *his* offence.

There is yet one point, which I fain would have avoided.

It has been insinuated and declared, by one or two "religious" journalists and in two or three pulpits, that Mr. Dickens was not even a Christian. On Friday, June 10th, when Charles Dickens was only twenty-five hours dead, a person, whose status is that of a Deacon in Plymouth Church, Brooklyn, arose, at a meeting there, (I take the report of the *N. Y. Tribune,*) "and said that no man had ever written in the English language and gained as much popularity as Charles Dickens. But what troubled *him* was the question, *Was Dickens a Christian man?* He could not make an answer." I am unable to see what justification, either in charity or religion, this Pharisee, or any other, had for putting a question which did not concern *him.* The Caiaphas of that Brooklyn Synagogue, instead of bidding his Deacon mind his own business, and look to his own soul, said, "Whether he [Mr. Dickens] was a Christian man in the experimental term God only knew." He added that, in his writings, Mr. Dickens had considerably patronized drink:—did he ever read the warning against it, in *The Tale of Two Cities,* in the example of Sydney Carton? Then, this modern Caiaphas said: "I recollect hearing my father say of Bishop Heber, after having read his life, that he doubted whether he was a Christian." Bishop Heber, the great poet-preacher, who wrote the famous Missionary Hymn, beginning "From Greenland's icy mountains," died in the service of God, in India. It would have been as well to have left *him* alone; or, if it were thought necessary to "point a moral" from the dead, mention might have been made of the Rev. Lyman Beecher, D.D., who, as McClintock & Strong's Cyclopædia of Biblical Literature tells us, was charged by some of his brother Calvanists with *heresy,* and brought to trial on that charge, in 1835. There are multitudes, too, who, seeing how another member of this family has made Incest and Adultery, "familiar to the ear as household words," by a posthumous slander upon poor Lord Byron and his sister, naturally entertain "great doubts" as to *her* Christian faith and character.

While I write these lines, wondering at

> The rarity
> Of Christian charity
> Under the sun,

I am presented with the announcement of a forthcoming Life of Christ, written by Charles Dickens for his own children, and used by him for teaching them the great lessons of Faith, Atonement and Redemption. I remember that he is denounced only by those who, in Swift's words, "have just enough religion to make them hate, and not enough to make them love one another;" that when in this country, in 1868, when he was asked what was his object in writing, he answered, "It is to show that all men may be saved;" that, he was eulogized, as a good man and a Christian, by clergymen of various persuasions in New York, Boston and other American cities; that, in England, where he was still better known, the same justice was rendered to him, the Dean of Westminster preaching his funeral sermon, and, on that same evening, in the same pulpit, the Bishop of Manchester, saying, "He preached—not in a church nor from a pulpit, but in a style and fashion of his own—a gospel, a cheery, joyous, gladsome message, which the people understood, and by which they could hardly help being bettered; it was the gospel of kindliness, of brotherly love, of sympathy in the widest sense of the word, of humanity. I am sure I have felt in myself the healthful influence of his teaching. Possibly we might not have been able to subscribe to the same creed in relation to God, but I think we should have subscribed to the same creed in relation to man. He who has taught us our duty to our fellow-men better than we knew it before, who knew so well to weep with them that weep, and to rejoice with them that rejoice, who has shown, with all his knowledge of the dark corners of the earth, how much sunshine may rest upon the lowliest lot, who had such evident sympathy with suffering, such a love of innocence, such a natural instinct of purity, that there is not a page of the thousands he has written which might not be put into the hands of a little child, may be regarded by those who recognize the diversity of the gifts of the Spirit as a teacher sent from God. He would surely have been welcomed as a fellow-laborer in the common interests of humanity by him who asked the question, 'If a man love not his brother whom he hath seen, how can he love God whom he hath not seen?'"

Lastly, I read the broad and hopeful words of his last will and testament.

"I commit my soul to the mercy of God through our Lord and Saviour Jesus Christ; and I exhort my dear children humbly to try to guide themselves by the teaching of the New Testament in its broad spirit, and to put no faith in any man's narrow construction of its letter here or there."

Musing on the broad principles of Christianity which, as with his dying breath, this great and good man so plainly laid down, I feel their truth and beauty, which Dean Stanley so deeply felt, when he told the congregation in Westminster Abbey, "IN THAT SIMPLE BUT SUFFICIENT FAITH HE LIVED AND DIED; IN THAT FAITH HE BIDS YOU LIVE AND DIE."

THOMAS GRIFFITHS WAINEWRIGHT.

(JANUS WEATHERCOCK,) THE POISONER.

BY CHARLES DICKENS.

ONE of those pleasant winter evenings, when fires burn frosty blue, and hearts grow warmer as the weather grows colder. It is an evening soon after the ascent to the throne of his Most Gracious Majesty King George the Fourth.

A pleasant, merry, and highly intellectual party are dining at the house of the publishers of that clever periodical, the *London Magazine,* in Waterloo Place, to celebrate the new proprietorship. The cloth has been removed, the glasses sparkle in the light of the wax-candles, the wine glows ruby and topaz in the fast-revolving decanters, the oranges gleam golden, the crystalized fruits glitter with jewelled frost, the chestnuts, tight in their leather jackets, are hoarding their warm floury meal for the palates of poets and thinkers, puns are flashed in the air like fireworks, smart sayings are darting past like dragon-flies, even the gravest faces glow and brighten. A ring of brilliants the party resembles, for there is no one round the well-spread table but has a name in the world of letters or in the world of fashion. There is Charles Lamb, now busy with his *Elia,* the finest essays ever written—a little grave man in black, but with the face of a genius; Hazlitt is glorying in a Titian, upon which he is expatiating; Thomas Hood, with a face like that of an invalid Plato, is watching for a pun like a fly-fisher waiting for his cast. The Rev. H. Cary (the translator of Dante,) the mildest and gentlest of men, is explaining a passage of the Inferno to that fine, vigorous Scotch poet, Allan Cunningham the sculptor. Mr. Procter (Barry Cornwall), in his own kind, cheery way, is defending a fine passage in Ben Jonson from the volatile flippancy of the art-critic and gay dilettante of the magazine,—to wit, *Janus Weathercock*, otherwise Thomas Griffiths Wainewright.

He is a fop and a dandy, but is clever, has a refined taste, and is the kindliest and most light-hearted creature in the world. He has run through one fortune, has been in some dragoon regiment, and no doubt distinguished himself against the French—if he ever met them. He is on the wrong side of thirty, and records his military career by that exquisitely blue undress military coat he wears, all braided and befrogged down the front. His cravat is tied to a nicety. His manner most gallant, insinuating, and winning. His face, however, is by no means that of the mere dandy. His head is massive, and widens at the back. His eyes are deeply set in their orbits. His jaw is square and solid. He seldom looks the person he talks to full in the face. He has his hair curled every morning (a stray ringlet or so left free), and slightly stoops. His expression is at once repelling and fascinating.

He is ubiquitous. Go to the Park, and you observe him in his phaeton, leaning out with his cream-colored gloves and his large turned-down wristbands conspicuous over the splashboard. Go to old Lady Fitzrattle's ball the same evening, and you will see the fascinating creature with the belle of the evening, gracefully revolving in the waltz. In the club library he is conspicuous; at the supper-party he is the merriest and the gayest. He has fortunately left us portraits of himself both at the coffee-house and at home.

Let us see the charming man at nine o'clock on a November evening, 1822. The diners at George's Coffee-house, 213 Strand, then the great resort of Kentish lawyers and men from the Temple, are all gone but three,—two young barristers in the last box but one from the fire, and next to them a fashionably dressed man with the exquisite cravat, the square jaw, and the deep-set eyes, that we at once recognize. George's was famous for its soups and wines, and Mr. Wainewright has dined luxuriously, A bottle of the rarest wine he has sipped away with supercilious pleasure. He now holds to the candle, in an affected manner, displaying carefully his white jewelled fingers, a little glass of eau de vie de Dantzig, and is languidly watching the little flakes, or, as he would call them, "aureate particles," float and glimmer in the oily and glutinous fluid like scales of goldfish. The voices in the next box catch his ear; he listens. The one Templar is reading to the other with unction an article by Janus Weathercock in the last *London Magazine.*

"Soothed into that desirable sort of self-satisfaction so necessary to the bodying out those deliciously voluptuous ideas perfumed with languor which occasionally swim and undulate like gauzy clouds over the brain of the most cold-blooded men, we put forth one hand to the folio which leant against a chair by the sofa-side, and at haphazard extracted thence Lancret's charming Repas :

> 'A summer party in the greenwood shade,
> With wine prepared and cloth on herbage laid,
> And ladies' laughter coming through the air.'
>
> *Rimini.*

This completed the charm."

The gay writer listens with half-turned head, gloating over every word, inhaling slowly the incense so delicious to his vanity, taking care, however, that the waiter is not looking. Again they are talking about it.

First Voice: "How glowing! how exquisite! how *recherché!* how elegant! how full of the true West-end manner! A fine mind that young fellow has. O, he'll do."

Second Voice: "Don't like it. Flashy assumption. Mere amateur stuff. By the by, when does that case of Badger versus Beaver come on, Jones? Isn't to-day the 15th?"

"Low creature; debased nature," thinks Janus. "Upon my honor, these coffee-houses are getting mere haunts for the inferior classes. The 15th, eh? So it is. Why, that's the day I promised to write my article for the *London.* I must be off to Turnham Green."

Let us follow the delight of society to the White Horse, and take a seat beside him in the two-horse stage till it stops at the door of Linden House, Mr. Wainewright's elegant residence. His wife meets him at the door, and with her come dancing out, radiant with almost an exuberance of life, Phœbe and Madeleine, the two blooming daughters by a second husband of his wife's mother. They kiss him, they pet him, they load him with playful caresses, for he is their idol: they admire his genius, they love him as their nearest and dearest relation. Laughingly he frowns in assumed anger, and pleads the occupations of a popular author and a great critic. He breaks at last from their pretty siren wiles, and locks himself in his sanctum. It is a luxurious den. We can sketch it in almost Mr. Wainewright's own coxcombical words.

He strips off his smart tight-waisted befrogged coat, in which he so exquisitely masquerades as the retired officer of dragoons, and, in his own airy way, tosses on an easy, flowered, rustling chintz dressing-gown, gay with pink ribbons. He lights a new elegantly gilt French lamp, the ground glass globe of which is painted with gay flowers and gaudy butterflies. He then hauls forth languidly, as if the severity of the labor almost exhausted him, "portfolio No. 9," and nestles down into the cushioned corner of "a Grecian couch;" stroking "our favorite tortoise-shell cat" into a sonorous purr. He next, by a tremendous effort, contrives to ring the bell by the fireside. A smiling "Venetian-shaped" girl enters, and places on the table "a flask of as rich Montepulciano as ever voyaged from fair Italy," then, after contemplating his elegant figure in a large glass, placed with a true artistic sense opposite the chimney mirror, with a fresh exertion he pours out "a full cut glass" of wine with one hand, and strokes the cat with the other.

The sheet of glass returns sharp-cut photographs of a gay carpet, the pattern of which consists of garlands of flowers, a cast of the Venus de Medicis, (for Mr. Wainewright is an artist,) a Tomkinson piano, some Louis Quinze novels and tales, bound in French "marroquin," with tabby silk linings, some playful volumes choicely covered by Rogers, Payne, and Charles Lewis, some azaleas teeming with crimson blossoms, standing on a white marble slab, and a large peaceful Newfoundland dog also. A fine Damascus sabre hung against the wall, (dragoons again,) an almost objectionable picture by Fuseli, that gay old bachelor at Somerset House, (a friend of the eminently popular and accomplished art-critic,) and last, but not least of all, the exquisite man of the world himself, full of heart, full of soul, and bathed in the Correggio light of the aforesaid elegantly gilt French lamp.

At last the insufferable fop begins, and after one glance at the yellow ceiling, and one desultory smiling peep at some curious white crystals, probably filbert salt, in a secret drawer of his inlaid writing-desk, he pens the following sublime bit of euphuism, worthy, indeed, of the age of Keepsakes:

"This completed the charm. We immersed a well-seasoned prime pen into our silver inkstand three times, shaking off the loose ink again lingeringly, while, holding the print fast in our left hand, we perused it with half-shut eyes, dallying awhile with our delight. Fast and faster came the tingling impetus, and this running like quicksilver from our sensorium to our pen, we gave the latter one conclusive dip, after which we rapidly dashed off the following description *couleur de rose.*"

A little later this bright butterfly of fashion informs his enraptured world in the *London Magazine* that he has bought a new horse, and secured a new book:—

"I have nothing more in the way of news, except that I have picked up a fine copy of Bochius's Emblems, (you know the charming things by Bonasone,) first edition; Boulogne, 1555. Capital condition, in blue French morocco, by De Rome, for whom I still retain some small inkling of affection, in spite of the anathemas of the Rev. T. F. Dibdin. Also, a new horse, (Barbary sire and Arabian dam,) with whose education I occupy nearly all my mornings, though I have considerable doubts whether I shall push it beyond the *military manege.*"

This exulting egotism, this delight in bindings, is characteristic of the man, as also is the graceful allusion in the last line to the writer's military achievements, (disgracefully ignored by Napier.)

Later in his career Wainewright fell foul of that wise thinker and profound critic, William Hazlitt, who also wrote for the *London*, laughing to scorn, "spitefully entreating," and hugely condemning his dramatic criticism. Hazlitt, the most inflammable of old bachelors, praised the Miss Dennetts' dancing; Janus derided them as little unformed creatures, great favorites with "the Whitechapel orders;" cried "Faugh!" when Hazlitt visited the Coburg and Surrey Theatres; and sneered when his great rival praised Miss Valancy, "the bouncing Columbine at Astley's and them there places,—as his barber informs him." All this shows the vanity and shallow temerity, the vulgar and impertinent superciliousness of the pseudo critic. He got a bludgeon-blow on the head for it, however, from Hazlitt, who then left him to flutter his hour and to pass away in his folly.

When Hazlitt left the *London Magazine*, about 1825, Janus Weathercock ceased to delight the world also, but he still rattled at parties, still drove in the Park, and flashed along the Row on his Arab horse "Contributor;" he still bought well-bound books, pictures, and hot-house plants, and still expended his affections on his cat. Honest Charles Lamb, guileless as a child, lamented "kind, light-hearted Janus," the tasteful dandy, the gay sentimentalist of the boudoir. Fine generous natures like Othello are prone to trust Iago. One of those gentlemen who are mean enough to get their bread by professional literature, and yet affect to despise their business, Wainewright must have felt the loss of his liberal monthly salary, for he had expensive tastes, and a knack of getting through money.

Say some eight or ten years after the delightful dinner in Waterloo Place, this fine nature (true Sèvres of the rarest clay) was living in his own luxurious cosey way (books, wine, horses, pictures, statues, hot-house plants, Damascus sabre, tortoise-shell cat, elegantly gilt French lamp and all) at Linden House, Turnham Green, remarkable for its lime-trees, on the pretty heart-shaped leaves of which the gay artist probably lavished a thousand fancies. Only once had those rose-leaves fallen since the house and pleasant grounds had belonged to Wainewright's uncle, a Dr. Griffith, a comfortable, well-to-do man, who had, for many years, edited a monthly publication. His death occurred after a very short illness, and during a visit paid him by Mr. Wainewright and his wife, who was there confined of her first, and, as it proved, her only child. It was not exactly apoplexy, nor was it heart-disease; but then even doctors are sometimes puzzled by organic complications. One thing is certain, it was mortal, and Dr. Griffiths died under proper medical care, and watched by the most affectionate of relatives. Wainewright gained some property by his uncle's death; lamented him tearfully, and spent the money smilingly. Bills soon began, however, to be left unpaid, servants' wages were delayed, credit was occasionally refused, Turnham Green bakers and butchers dared to talk about Linden House, and people who "made much of themselves, but did not do the right thing, not what yer may call the right thing."

Things were not going altogether comfortable with a man who must have his wine, his cigars, his eau de vie de Dantzig, all the new books and prints, and must dress "in the style, you know."

The fact must come out: Wainewright was a monster egotist, and not accustomed to starve either his tastes or his appetites. He must have money for champagne and bread, Marc Antonio's prints and meat. As well be starved as have his cutlet without truffles. Poverty's iron walls were closing in upon him closer and closer, but he shrugged his shoulders, buttoned tighter his befrogged coat, pawned his rings, and got on well enough.

Linden House must have been a peculiarly unhealthy place, for about this time Mrs. Abercrombie, Wainewright's wife's mother, died there also, after a very short illness,—something in the brain or heart, probably. Mrs. Abercrombie had married a second time a meritorious officer, and left two daughters, Helen Frances Phœbe and Madeleine, beautiful girls, just reaching womanhood. The poor orphans, having only ten pounds a year granted them by the Board of Ordnance for their father's services, (these must have been small indeed not to deserve more,) were invited to his pleasant, luxurious, but decidedly unhealthy house, by Mr. Wainewright, their step-sister's husband, in the most kind and generous manner, dear creature!

Helen Frances Phœbe Abercrombie, the eldest of the girls, attained the age of twenty-one on the 12th of March, 1830, a very short time after coming to Turnham Green, and within a few days of this event, the oddest caprice entered into Mr. Wainewright's mind. He proposed to insure her life to a very large amount for the short period of two or three years. Such an arrangement is, however, the commonest thing in the world with persons either permanently or temporarily embarrassed. Such insurances are often used as securities for bills of exchange or for loans, where the lender is especially cautious. There was nothing singular about it. It did not the least matter that Miss Abercrombie was almost penniless, and without expectations of any kind, except a trifling possibility under a settlement.

One pleasant morning in March a trip to the city was

suggested as quite a divertisement, an agreeable opportunity of observing the habits and customs of "those strange city people." Mr. Wainewright was jauntier and more *dégagé* than ever, in his tight fashionable befrogged coat, as he guided his wife and the beautiful girl,—his temporary ward,—their ribbons fluttering brightly in the March wind, through the defiles and labyrinths of the busy city. His whims and fancies about insurance offices were delightful in their careless gayety. It was quite an adventure for the ladies. It was singular, though, that Mr. Wainewright, embarrassed as he was, should venture on a speculation that involved a large annual payment for interest, and yet seemed to promise no pecuniary return. It might be a chivalrous risk of some kind or other, the innocent and playful girl probably thought, and she would not care to inquire further into a business she did not profess to understand. It cost her nothing; she was only too glad to gratify the whim of her kind kinsman, and to lend herself to his mysterious, but, no doubt, well-planned and well-intended business arrangement.

So, on the 28th, sixteen days after coming of age, Miss Abercrombie went to the Palladium Insurance Office with Mr. and Mrs. Wainewright, and insured her life for three thousand pounds for three years. The object of the insurance was stated to be (whether correctly or not) to enable the young lady's friend to recover some property to which she was entitled. The life was pre-eminently good, and the proposal was accepted. On the 20th of April Mrs. Wainewright and Miss Abercrombie went to the office to pay the first year's premium, and receive the policy. On or about the same day, a similar insurance for three thousand pounds, but this for two years only, was effected with the Eagle Insurance Office, and the premium for one year and the stamp duty duly paid by Miss Abercrombie in her young sister's presence.

In the following October four more policies were effected:

with the Provident for one thousand pounds, with the Hope for two thousand pounds, with the Imperial for three thousand pounds, and with the Pelican for the largest amount usually permitted,—namely, five thousand pounds,—each for the period of two years; making altogether insurances to the amount of eighteen thousand pounds. The premiums paid, together with the stamps, amounted to more than two hundred and twenty pounds; and yet, in case of Miss Abercrombie living more than three years, all these payments would be lost.

Lost they would be, who could doubt. The actuary at the Provident described her as "a remarkably healthy, cheerful, beautiful young woman, whose life was one of a thousand." Old secretaries, smiling over their spectacles, must have felt as if a sunbeam had glanced across the room, and have sighed to think that, if a full insurance had been effected, fifty years hence, that same Miss Abercrombie might enter the room still hearty and vigorous to pay her annual interest, when they were long ago gone, and their very tombstones were effaced by rain and wind.

Still all this insuring was odd, too, for Mr. Wainewright was deeply in debt. Shabby truculent men behind grated doors in Cursitor street were speaking irreverently of him; dirty Jew-faced men at the bar of the Hole-in-the-Wall in Chancery Lane discussed him and were eager to claw his shoulder. He spent more than ever, and earned less. His literary friends, Lamb and Reynolds, seldom saw him now. His artist friends, Fuseli the fiery and Stothard the gentle, Westall and Lawrence, seldom met him. A crisis was coming to the man with elegant tastes. In August he had given a warrant of attorney and a bill of sale of his furniture at Linden House; both of these had become absolute, and seizure was impending. "The Jew fellows" could only be scared away (from the elegant gilt lamp, the books, and prints) till the 20th or 21st of December.

At some offices scruples, too, began to arise, which it was

not found easy to silence. At the Imperial, it was suggested to Miss Abercrombie, by Mr. Ingall, the actuary, that, "as she only proposed to make the insurance for two years, he presumed it was to secure some property she would come into at the expiration of that time;" to which Mrs. Wainewright replied—

"Not exactly so; it is to secure a sum of money to her sister, which she will be enabled to do by other means if she outlives that time; but I don't know much about her affairs; you had better speak to her about it."

On which Miss Abercrombie said, "That is the case."

By what means the ladies were induced to make these statements, can scarcely even be guessed. The sum of eighteen thousand pounds did not yet bound the limits of speculation, for, in the same month of October, a proposal to the Eagle to increase the insurance by the addition of two thousand pounds was made and declined; and a proposal to the Globe for five thousand, and a proposal to the Alliance for some further sum, met a similar fate. At the office of the Globe, Miss Abercrombie, who, as usual, was accompanied by Mrs. Wainewright, being asked the object of the insurance, replied that "she scarcely knew; but that she was desired to come there by her friends, who wished the insurance done." On being further pressed, she referred to Mrs. Wainewright, who said: "It is for some money matters that are to be arranged; but ladies don't know much about such things;" and Miss Abercrombie answered a question whether she was insured in any other office, in the negative. At the Alliance, she was more severely tested by the considerate kindness of Mr. Hamilton, who, receiving the proposal, was not satisfied by her statement that a suit was depending in Chancery which would probably terminate in her favor, but that if she should die in the interim the property would go into another family, for which contingency she wished to provide. The young lady, a little irritated at the questions, said, rather sharply, "I supposed that what you had to inquire into was the state of my health, not the object of the insurance;" on which Mr. Hamilton, with a thoughtful look, said—

"A young lady, just such as you are, miss, came to this very office two years ago to effect an insurance for a short time; and it was the opinion of the company *she came to her death by unfair means.*"

Poor Miss Abercrombie replied: "I am sure there is no one about me who could have any such object."

Mr. Hamilton said, gravely, "Of course not;" but added, "that he was not satisfied as to the object of the insurance; and unless she stated in writing what it was, and the directors approved it, the proposal could not be entertained." The ladies retired; and the office heard no more of the proposal nor of Miss Abercrombie, till they heard she was dead, and that the payment of other policies on her life was resisted.

Early in that month Wainewright left the house with the leaf-stripped trees, the very unhealthy house, and took furnished lodgings at Mr. Nicoll's, a tailor, in Conduit street, to which he was accompanied by his wife, his child, and those two beautiful, affectionate girls, his half-sisters, Phœbe and Madeleine Abercrombie. Books, sabre, elegant French lamp, portfolios, and desk with the mysterious little eccentric drawer with the especial salt for filberts.

There was still a little more law business for Phœbe; the artistic mind remarked one morning in his playful, delighted way, "Would the dear girl be kind enough to keep in profile for one moment? Exquisite! Yes, there was a will to be made to benefit dear Madeleine in case of any unforeseen circumstance." Phœbe no doubt carolled out a laugh, and expressed a horror "of those dusty old lawyers." On that same day, the 13th, Miss Abercrombie called on a solicitor named Lys, to whom she was a stranger, to attest the execution of a will she desired to make, as she was going abroad; he complied, and she executed a will in favor of her sister Madeleine, making Mr. Wainewright its executor. On the 14th, having obtained a deed of assignment from the office of the Palladium, she called on another solicitor named Kirk, to whom she was also a stranger, to perfect for her an assignment of the policy of that office to Mr. Wainewright. This the solicitor did by writing in ink over words pencilled by Mr. Wainewright, and witnessing his signature.

That same evening (as a reward, perhaps) the two sisters went to the play, as they had done the evening before, accompanying their kind relations, Mr. and Mrs. Wainewright. Whatever bailiffs may be watching the gay and volatile creature in the befrogged coat, he has no idea of stinting his amusements. Providence is hard on your delightful and fashionable men, who earn little and spend much.

The play is delightful, the pathos pierces, the farce convulses the pleasant party of four. After the play they have an oyster-supper, and Mr. Wainewright is gayer and wittier than ever. In the night, however, Miss Phœbe is taken ill, evidently having caught cold from walking home that long way from Drury Lane or Covent Garden two nights in the wet and wind. There is great regret in the house, and frequent kind inquiries at her door from Mr. Wainewright. She gets up to dinner, but in a day or two, the cold not lifting, Dr. Locock is sent for. Mrs. Wainewright and Madeleine are with her constantly. Mr. Wainewright, who is clever in these things, as in everything else, prescribes her a black draught before the doctor is sent for. The doctor is kind and sympathizing, thinks little of the slight derangement, and prescribes the simplest remedies. On the seventh day of her indisposition, Mr. Wainewright, impatient of the doctor's remedies, prescribes her a powder, which she took willingly in jelly. She was decidedly better, and was no longer wandering; she was so much better in fact, that Mr. Wainewright, great in spirits, and full of sentiment, sympathy, and artistic feeling, told his wife to put on her bonnet and come for a walk sketching, while dear Phœbe had some sleep. That was about twelve o'clock. At two, Phœbe was taken violently ill with convulsions. She appeared in great agony, became delirous, and struggled violently.

Dr. Locock, who had been previously consulted about insurance certificates, was instantly sent for, and came. The fit had then subsided, but there was pressure on the brain. She said, "O doctor! I am dying. These are the pains of death. I feel I am. I am sure so." The doctor said, "You'll be better by and by." She cried, "My poor mother! O my poor mother!" Dr. Locock left, and she had a fit, and grasped the hand of one of the servants. When Dr. Locock left, she lay quiet, and said she thought she heard a little boy coming along the room, and that he ought not to be there, and she burst into tears and convulsions.

A servant who had lived twenty years with Dr. Griffiths, and had known Mr. Wainewright since he was a child, instantly sent for Messrs. King and Nicholson, apothecaries. A Mr. Hanks came and saw Miss Abercrombie in the convulsion fit. She had said to Dr. Locock, "Doctor, I was gone to heaven, but you have brought me back to earth." Hanks gave her some medicine while Dr. Locock was there. The convulsions got better, and the doctors went away. Soon after they were gone, the convulsions came on again, and at four o'clock she died.

Who can paint the horror and agony of Mr. and Mrs. Wainewright when they returned and found the beautiful girl, with the exquisite profile, only a day or two ago so bright and full of life, so arch, so graceful,—dead.

Dr. Locock, leaving the house in which he was now useless, with a sad face and heart, met Mr. Wainewright returning gay and light-hearted, perhaps humming a fashionable tune. He appeared much shocked and astonished at the sad news, and asked what was the cause of death. Dr. Locock replied, "*Mischief in the brain,*" and proposed to examine the head, to which Wainewright immediately assented. On the next day the skull was opened by Hanks, and they found what witness believed was a quite sufficient cause of death,—a considerable quantity of water on the lower part of the brain, pressing upon the upper part of the spinal marrow. Witness thought the effusion caused the convulsion, and that the convulsion caused death. Oysters had often produced similar effects upon irritable constitutions. Wet feet had perhaps rendered the constitution weak and susceptible.

There was a further examination two days afterwards. The contents of the stomach were minutely examined. There was no appearance of anything sufficient to account for death, except water at the base of the brain. There were a few points in which the bloodvessels were much more injected with blood than usual, an appearance often seen in those who die suddenly. Violent vomiting would account for this. The doctors observed a few little specks on the coat of the stomach, but that was all.

This distressing and sudden death changed matters, and gave a new and quite unexpected significancy to that mysterious insurance business. Eighteen thousand pounds now became payable to the elegant, needy, and somewhat desperate man; part of the money as executor for Phœbe; two of the policies being assigned to himself, with a secret understanding that they were for the benefit of Madeleine.

Unchristian suspicions soon arose, degrading, as Mr. Wainewright remarked, only to those who entertained them. Exasperated by the loss which, by the dear girl's distressing death, they had incurred, all the insurance offices meanly and criminally refused payment. The crisis came, but Wainewright was too poor to stay and press his legal claims, and therefore stealthily retired to the friendly asylum of France, where urbanity always reigns, and claret is delightfully cheap; where the air is ever sunny, and meat is lean, but not dear. He there resided, gay as ever, for several years.

After many delays, occasioned chiefly by proceedings in equity, the question of the validity of the policies was tried in the Court of Exchequer, before Lord Abinger, on the 29th of June, 1835, in an action by Mr. Wainewright, as the executor of Miss Abercrombie, on the imperial policy of three thousand pounds. Extraordinary as were the circumstances under which the defence was made, it rested, says Mr. Serjeant Talfourd, on a narrow basis, on the mere allegation that the insurance was not, as it professed to be, that of Miss Abercrombie for her own benefit, but the insurance of Mr. Wainewright, effected at his cost for some purpose of his own, and on the falsehood of representations she had been induced to make in reply to inquiries as to insurances in other offices. The cause of her death, if the insurance was really hers, was immaterial.

Lord Abinger, always wishing to look at the pleasant side of things, refused to enter into the cause of death, and intimated that the defence had been injured by a darker *suggestion.*

Sir William Follett appeared for the plaintiff, and the Attorney-General, Sir F. Pollock, and Mr. Thesiger for the defendant. The real plaintiff was not Mr. Wainewright, but Mr. Wheatley, a respectable bookseller, who had married the sister of the deceased. The jury, partaking of the judge's disinclination to attribute the most dreadful guilt to a plaintiff on a nisi prius record, and perhaps scarcely perceiving how they could discover for the imputed fraud an intelligible motive without it, were unable to agree, and were discharged without giving a verdict. It was clear to every one there had been foul play.

The cause was tried again, before the same judge, on the 3d of December following, when the counsel for the defence, following the obvious inclination of the bench, avoided the fearful charge, and obtained a verdict for the office without hesitation, sanctioned by Lord Abinger's proffered approval to the jury. In the meantime, says Mr. Serjeant

Talfourd, Mr. Wainewright, leaving his wife and child in London, had acquired the confidence and enjoyed the hospitality of the members of an English family residing in Boulogne.

While he was thus associated, a proposal was made to the Pelican office to insure the life of his host for five thousand pounds: which, as the medical inquiries were satisfactorily answered, was accepted. The office, however, received only one premium, for the life survived the completion of the insurance only a few months: falling after a very short illness, and, singularly enough, with symptoms not unlike those of Dr. Griffiths, Mrs. Abercrombie, and poor Phœbe. The world is full of coincidences.

And here we feel compelled to throw off our mask, to turn suddenly on the delight of the boudoirs and salons of May Fair, and shaking him by the throat, proclaim him as a A POISONER,—one of the most cruel, subtle, and successful secret murderers since the time of the Borgias. It is now well known that he wore a ring in which he always carried strychnine, crystals of the Indian nux vomica, half a grain of which blown into the throat of a rabbit kills it dead in two minutes; a poison almost tasteless, difficult of discovery, and capable of almost infinite dilution. On the night the Norfolk gentleman in difficulties at Boulogne died, Wainewright had insisted on making his friend's coffee, and passed the poison into the sugar. The poisoner had succeeded before this in winning the affections of his friend's daughter, and gaining a supreme influence in the house.

A friend of the writer's, at a visit to this Norfolk gentleman's house in Caroline Place, Mecklenburgh Square, London, long before his murder, was arrested in mistake for Wainewright, who, at that very time, was serenading with a Spanish guitar in the garden of the square. He was eventually seized opposite the house of his friend Van Holst, a pupil of Fuseli's.

Wainewright, obtaining the insurance, left Boulogne, and

became a needy wanderer in France, but being brought under the notice of the correctional police for passing under a feigned name, was arrested. In his possession was found the vegetable poison called strychnine, a fact which, though unconnected with any specific charge, increased his liability to temporary restraint, and led to a six months' incarceration in Paris. After his release he ventured to revisit London, when, in June, 1837, soon after his arrival, he was met in the street by Forester, the police-officer who had identified him in France, and was committed for trial for forgery.

July 5th, 1837, (seven years after the death of Miss Abercrombie,) Wainewright, then forty-two years old, "a man of gentlemanly appearance, wearing moustachios," was tried at the Central Criminal Court for forging certain powers of attorney to sell out two thousand two hundred and fifty-nine pounds' worth of Bank Stock, which had been settled on him and his wife at their marriage. This was a capital offence at that time, but the Bank not wishing to shed blood, Wainewright at first declared himself not guilty, but eventually pleaded guilty, by advice of his lawyer, to two of the minor indictments out of the five, and was therefore only transported for life.

The moment the chief insurance offices found that Wainewright was under sentence of transportation for forgery, they determined to open negotiations with the villain, and get from him certain confessions necessary to their interests: little doubting that he would make them "for a consideration." He made them readily enough when he had struck his bargain. At this time he was confined in Newgate (modern prison discipline had not then found its way into that jail) in a cell with a bricklayer and a sweep: in which polite company he was actually recognized through a strange chance, by Mr. Proctor and Mr. Macready, visiting the prison with the Conductor of Bentley's Miscellany. When the agent of the insurance offices had extracted from the ruffian all that he wanted to know, that gentleman said, in conclusion: "It would be quite useless, Mr. Wainewright, to speak to you of humanity or tenderness, or laws human or Divine; but does it not occur to you, after all, that, merely regarded as a speculation, crime is a bad one? See where it ends. I talk to you in a shameful prison, and I talk to a degraded convict." Wainewright returned, twirling his moustache: "Sir, you city men enter on your speculations, and take the chances of them. Some of your speculations succeed, some fail. Mine happen to have failed; yours happen to have succeeded; that is the difference, sir, between my visitor and me. But I'll tell you one thing in which I have succeeded to the last. I have been determined through life to hold the position of a gentleman. I have always done so. I do so, still. It is the custom of this place that each of the inmates of a cell shall take his morning's turn of sweeping it out. I occupy a cell with a bricklayer and a sweep. But by G— they never offer me the broom!"

On the same occasion, or on another similar occasion in the same place, being asked how he could find it in his heart to murder the trusting girl who had so confided in him, (meaning Miss Abercrombie,) he reflected for a moment, and then returned, with a cool laugh: "Upon my soul I don't know,—unless it was that her legs were too thick."

A more insupportable scoundrel never troubled this earth. He had kept a diary. The insurance offices, by the masterly stroke of sending to a French inn where he had lived, paying the bill he had left unpaid and demanding the effects he had left there, obtained possession of it. Description of this demoniacal document cannot be attempted, but it contained a kind of index to the details of his various crimes, set forth with a voluptuous cruelty and a loathesome exultation worthy of the diseased vanity of such a masterpiece of evil.

In the meantime, says Mr. Talfourd, in his version of the affair, proceedings were taken on behalf of Miss Abercrombie's sister by her husband, Mr. Wheatley, to render the insurances available for her benefit, which induced the prisoner to revengefully offer communications to the insurance offices which might defeat a purpose entirely foreign to his own, and which he hoped might procure him, through their intercession, a mitigation of the more painful severities incident to his sentence. In this expectation he was miserably disappointed. For though, in pursuance of their promise, the directors of one of the offices made a communication to the Secretary of State for the Home Department, the result, instead of a mitigation, was an order to place him in irons, and to send him to his place of punishment in the Susan, a vessel about to convey three hundred convicts.

In Newgate the gay-hearted creature was sublime. He asserted himself as a poet, a philosopher, and a martyr. He claimed for himself "a soul whose nutriment is love, and its offspring art, music, divine song, and still holier philosophy." When writing even from the hold of the convict-ship to complain of his being placed in irons, he said: "They think me a desperado. *Me! the companion of poets, philosophers, artists, and musicians,* a desperado! You will smile at this. No: I think you will *feel* for the man, educated and reared as a gentleman, now the mate of vulgar ruffians and country bumpkins."

In 1842, the dandy convict was admitted as inpatient of the General Hospital in Hobart Town, where he remained some years. Whilst an inmate of the hospital he forwarded to the Governor, Sir Eardley E. Wilmot, the following memorial. It is too characteristic of the man not to be given. The gilt had all gone now. The Governor's minute on the memorial is very laconic,—"A. T. L. (ticket-of-leave) would be contrary to Act of Parlt. T. L. refused. *3d class wages received?*—E. E. W."

"To His Excellency, Sir John Eardley Wilmot, Bart., Lieut.-Governor of Van Diemen's Land, &c., &c.,

"The humble petition of T. Griffiths Wainewright, praying the indulgence of a ticket-of-leave.

"To palliate the boldness of this application he offers the statement ensuing: That *seven* years past he was arrested on a charge of forging and acting on a power of attorney to sell stock *thirteen years previous.* Of which (though looking for little credence) he avers his entire innocence. He admits a knowledge of the actual committer, gained though, some years after the fact. Such, however, were their relative positions, that to have disclosed it would have made him infamous where any human feeling is manifest. Nevertheless, by his counsel's direction, he entered the plea NOT *Guilty*, to allow him to adduce the '*circonstance attenuante*,' viz., that the money (£5,200) appropriated was, without quibble, *his own*, derived from his parents. An hour before his appearing to plead he was trepanned (through the just but deluded Governor of Newgate) into withdrawing his plea, by a promise, in such case, of a punishment merely nominal. The same *purporting* to issue from y[e] *Bank Parlor*, but in fact from the agents of certain *Insurance Companies* interested to a heavy amount (£16,000) in compassing his legal non-existence. He pleaded guilty—and was forthwith hurried, stunned with such ruthless perfidy, to the hulks at Portsmouth, and thence in *five days* aboard the *Susan*, sentenced to Life in a land (to him) a moral sepulchre. As a ground for your mercy he submits with great deference his foregone condition of life during forty-three years of freedom. A *descent*, deduced, through family tradition and *Edmondson's Heraldry*, from a stock not the least honored in Cambria. Nurtured with all appliances of ease and comfort,—schooled by his relative, the well-known philologer and bibliomaniac, Chas. Burney, D. D., brother to Mdme. D'Arblay, and the companion of COOKE. Lastly, such a modest competence as afforded the *mental* necessaries of Literature, Archæology, Music, and the Plastic Arts; while his pen and brush introduced him to the notice and friendship of men whose fame is European.

"The Catalogues of Somerset House Exhibitions, the

Literary Pocket-Book, indicate his earlier pursuits, and the MS. left behind in Paris attest at least his industry. Their titles imply the objects to which he has, *to this date*, directed all his energies :—'A Philosophical Theory of Design, as concerned with the Loftier Emotions, showing its deep action on Society, drawn from the Phidean-Greek and early Florentine Schools,' (the result of seventeen years' study,) illustrated with numerous plates, executed with conscientious accuracy, in one vol. atlas folio. 'An Æsthetic and Psychological Treatise on the Beautiful; or the Analogies of Imagination and Fancy, as exerted in Poesy, whether Verse, Painting, Sculpture, Music, or Architecture;' to form four vols. folio, with a profusion of engravings by the first artists of Paris, Munich, Berlin, Dresden, and Wien. 'An Art-Novel,' in three vols., and a collection of 'Fantasie, Critical Sketches, &c., selected partly from *Blackwood*, the *Foreign Review*, and the *London Magazine*.' All these were nearly ready for, *one* actually at *press*. Deign, your Excellency! to figure to yourself my *actual* condition during seven years; without *friends, good name*, (the breath of life) or *art*, (the fuel to it with *me*,) tormented at once by memory and ideas struggling for outward form and realization, barred up from increase of knowledge, and deprived of the exercise of profitable or even of *decorous* speech. Take pity, your Excellency! and grant me the power to shelter my eyes from Vice, in her most revolting and sordid phase, and my ears from a jargon of filth and blasphemy that would outrage the cynism (*sic*) of Parny himself. Perhaps this clinging to the lees of a vapid life may seem as *base, unmanly*, arguing rather a plebeian, than a liberal and gentle descent. But, your Excellency! the wretched *Exile* has a child!—and *Vanity* (sprung from the praise of Flaxman, *Charles Lamb*, Stothard, Rd. Westall, *Delaroche, Cornelius*, Lawrence, and the god of his worship, FUSELI) whispers that the *follower of the Ideal might* even yet achieve another reputation than that of a *Faussaire*. Seven years of steady demeanor may in *some* degree promise that no indulgence shall ever be abused by your Excellency's miserable petitioner,

"T. G. WAINEWRIGHT."

Discharged from the hospital, the elegant-mannered poisoner, his dress with no style at all about it now, his spelling rather wandering, and his bearing less refined than it used to be, set up as an artist at Hobart Town, where sketches by him still exist. His conversation to lady-sitters was often indelicate. A writer in a Melbourne paper, 6th July, 1841, says of this dangerous and abandoned wretch (we must use plain words for him now): "He rarely looked you in the face. His conversation and manners were winning in the extreme; he was never intemperate, but nevertheless of grossly sensual habit, and an opium-eater. As to moral character, he was a man of the very lowest stamp. He seemed to be possessed by an ingrained malignity of disposition, which kept him constantly on the very confines of murder, and he took a perverse pleasure in traducing persons who had befriended him. There is a terrible story told of his savage malignity towards a fellow-patient in the hospital, a convict, against whom he bore a grudge. The man was in a state of collapse,—his extremities were already growing cold. Death had him by the throat. Wainewright's snakish eyes kindled with unearthly fire. He saw at once the fatal sign. He stole softly as a cat to the man's pallet, and hissed his exultation into his dying ear,—

"'You are a dead man, you.—In four-and-twenty hours your soul will be in hell, and my arms will be up to that (touching his elbow) in your body, dissecting you.'"

Such was the ingrained and satanic wickedness of this triple murderer. Twice this delight of society attempted to poison people who had become obnoxious to him. Even in that polluted corner of the world the man was dreaded, hated, and shunned. No chance homicide had imbrued his hands, but a subtle series of cowardly and atrocious crimes. His sole friend and companion was a cat, for which he evinced an extraordinary and sentimental affection. He had always been fond of cats. In 1852, this gentlemanly and specious monster was struck down in a moment, as with a thunderbolt, by apoplexy. He had survived his victims sixteen years.

Perhaps no blacker soul ever passed from a body than passed the day that Wainewright the poisoner went to his account. Well, says Mr. Serjeant Talfourd:

"Surely no contrast presented in the wildest romance between a gay cavalier, fascinating Naples or Palermo, and the same hero detected as the bandit or demon of the forest, equals that which time has unveiled between what Mr. Wainewright seemed and what he was."

It is this monster whom Lord Lytton has immortalized in his powerful novel of Lucretia.

ABOARD SHIP.

BY CHARLES DICKENS.

My journeys as Uncommercial Traveller for the firm of Human Interest Brothers have not slackened since I last reported of them, but have kept me continually on the move. I remain in the same idle employment. I never solicit an order, I never get any commission, I am the rolling stone that gathers no moss,—unless any should by chance be found among these Samples.

Some half a year ago, I found myself in my idlest, dreamiest and least accountable condition altogether, on board ship, in the harbor of the city of New York, in the United States of America. Of all the good ships afloat, mine was the good steamship RUSSIA, CAPTAIN COOK, Cunard Line, bound for Liverpool. What more could I wish for?

I had nothing to wish for but a prosperous passage. My salad-days, when I was green of visage and sea-sick, being gone with better things (and worse,) no coming event cast its shadows before.

I might, but a few moments previously, have imitated Sterne, and said, "'And yet, methinks, Eugenius'—laying my forefinger wistfully on his coat sleeve thus—'and yet methinks, Eugenius, 'tis but sorry work to part with thee, for what fresh fields . . . . my dear Eugenius . . . . can be fresher than thou art, and in what pastures new shall I find Eliza—or call her, Eugenius, if thou wilt, Annie,'"—I say I might have done this; but Eugenius was gone, and I hadn't done it.

I was resting on a skylight on the hurricane-deck, watching the working of the ship very slowly about, that she might head for England. It was high noon on a most brilliant day in April, and the beautiful bay was glorious and glowing. Full many a time, on shore there, had I seen the snow come down, down, down, (itself like down,) until it lay deep in all the ways of men, and particularly as it seemed in my way, for I had not gone dry-shod many hours for months. Within two or three days last past had I watched the feathery fall setting in with the ardor of a new idea, instead of dragging at the skirts of a worn-out winter, and permitting glimpses of a fresh young spring. But a bright sun and a clear sky had melted the snow in the great crucible of nature, and it had been poured out again that morning over sea and land, transformed into myriads of gold and silver sparkles.

The ship was fragrant with flowers. Something of the old Mexican passion for flowers may have gradually passed into North America, where flowers are luxuriously grown and tastefully combined in the richest profusion; but be that as it may, such gorgeous farewells in flowers had come on board, that the small officer's cabin on deck, which I tenanted, bloomed over into the adjacent scuppers, and banks of other flowers that it couldn't hold, made a garden of the unoccupied tables in the passenger's saloon. These delicious scents of the shore, mingling with the fresh airs of the sea, made the atmosphere a dreamy, an enchanting one. And so, with the watch aloft setting all the sails, and with the screw below revolving at a mighty rate, and occasionally giving the ship an angry shake for resisting I fell into my idlest ways and lost myself.

As, for instance, whether it was I, lying there, or some other entity even more mysterious, was a matter I was far too lazy to look into. What did it signify to me if it were I—or to the more mysterious entity—if it were he? Equally as to the remembrances that drowsily floated by me,—or by him,—why ask when, or where, the things happened? Was it not enough that they befell at some time, somewhere?

There was that assisting at the Church service on board another steamship, one Sunday, in a stiff breeze. Perhaps on the passage out. No matter. Pleasant to hear the ship's bells go, as like church-bells as they could; pleasant to see the watch off duty mustered, and come in; best hats, best Guernseys, washed hands and faces, smoothed heads. But then arose a set of circumstances so rampantly comical, that no check which the gravest intentions could put upon them would hold them in hand. Thus the scene. Some seventy passengers assembled at the saloon tables. Prayer-books on tables. Ship rolling heavily. Pause. No minister. Rumor has related that a modest young clergyman on board has responded to the captain's request that he will officiate. Pause again, and very heavy rolling

Closed double doors suddenly burst open, and two strong stewards skate in, supporting minister between them. General appearance as if somebody picked up, drunk and incapable, and under conveyance to station-house. Stoppage, pause, and particularly heavy rolling. Stewards watch their opportunity, and balance themselves, but cannot balance minister; who, struggling with a drooping head and a backward tendency, seems determined to return below, while they are as determined that he shall be got to the reading-desk in mid-saloon. Desk portable, sliding away down a long table, and aiming itself at the breasts of various members of the congregation. Here the double doors, which have been carefully closed by other stewards, fly open again, and worldly passenger tumbles in, seemingly with Pale Ale designs: who, seeking friends, says "Joe!" Perceiving incongruity, says "Hullo! Beg yer pardon!" and tumbles out again. All this time the congregation have been breaking up into sects,—as the manner of congregations often is,—each sect sliding away by itself, and all pounding the weakest sect which slid first into the corner. Utmost point of dissent soon attained in every corner, and violent rolling. Stewards at length make a dash; conduct minister to the mast in the centre of the saloon, which he embraces with both arms; skate out; and leave him in that condition to arrange affairs with flock.

There was another Sunday, when an officer of the ship read the service. It was quiet and impressive, until he fell upon the dangerous and perfectly unnecessary experiment of striking up a hymn. After it was given out, we all arose, but everybody left it to somebody else to begin. Silence resulting, the officer (no singer himself) rather reproachfully gave us the first line again, upon which a rosy pippin of an old gentleman, remarkable throughout the passage for his cheerful politeness, gave a little stamp with his boot, (as if he were leading off a country dance,) and blithely warbled us into a show of joining. At the end of the first verse we became, through these tactics, so much refreshed and encouraged, that none of us, howsoever unmelodious, would submit to be left out of the second verse; while as to the third we lifted up our voices in a sacred howl that left it doubtful whether we were the more boastful of the sentiments we united in professing, or of professing them with a most discordant defiance of time and tune.

"Lord bless us," thought I, when the fresh remembrance of these things made me laugh heartily, alone in the dead water-gurgling waste of the night, what time I was wedged into my birth by a wooden bar, or I must have rolled out of it, "what errand was I then upon, and to what Abyssinian point had public events then marched? No matter as to me. And as to them, if the wonderful popular rage for a plaything (utterly confounding in its inscrutable unreason) had not then lighted on a poor young savage boy, and a poor old screw of a horse, and hauled the first off by the hair of his princely head to 'inspect' British volunteers, and hauled the second off by the hair of his equinnie tail to the Crystal Palace, why so much the better for all of us outside Bedlam!"

So, sticking to the ship, I was at the trouble of asking myself would I like to show the grog distribution in "the fiddle" at noon, to the Grand United Amalgamated Total Abstinence Society. Yes, I think I should. I think it would do them good to smell the rum, under the circumstances. Over the grog, mixed in a bucket, presides the boatswain's mate, small tin can in hand. Enter the crew, the guilty consumers, the grown-up Brood of Giant Despair, in contradistinction to the Band of youthful angel Hope. Some in boots, some in leggins, some in tarpaulin overalls, some in frocks, some in pea-coats, a very few in jackets, most with sou'-wester hats, all with something rough and rugged round the throat; all dripping salt water where they stand; all pelted by weather, besmeared with grease, and blackened by the sooty riggings.

Each man's knife in its sheath in his girdle, loosened for dinner. As the first man, with a knowingly kindled eye, watches the filling of the poisoned chalice, (truly but a very small tin mug, to be prosaic,) and tossing back his head, tosses the contents into himself, and passes the empty chalice and passes on, so the second man, with an anticipatory wipe of his mouth on sleeve or neck-kerchief, bides his turn, and drinks and hands, and passes on. In whom, and in each, as his turn approaches, beams a knowingly kindled eye, a brighter temper, and a suddenly awakened tendency to be jocose with some shipmate. Nor do I even observe that the man in charge of the ship's lamps, who in right of his office has a double allowance of poisoned chalices, seems thereby vastly degraded, even though he empties the chalices into himself, one after the other, much as if he were delivering their contents at some absorbent establishment in which he had no personal interest. But vastly comforted I note them all to be, on deck presently, even to the circulation of a redder blood in their cold blue knuckles; and when I look up at them lying out on the yards, and holding on for life among the beating sails, I cannot for *my* life see the justice of visiting on them—or on me—the drunken crimes of any number of criminals arraigned at the heaviest of Assizes.

Abetting myself in my idle humor, I closed my eyes and recalled life on board of one of those mail packets, as I lay, part of that day, in the Bay of New York O! The regular life began—mine always did, for I never got to sleep afterwards—with the rigging of the pump while it was yet dark, and washing down of the decks. Any enormous giant at a prodigious hydropathic establishment, conscientiously undergoing the Water Cure in all its departments, and extremely particular about cleaning his teeth, would make those noises. Swash, splash, scrub, rub, toothbrush, bubble, swash, splash, bubble, toothbrush, splash, splash, bubble, rub. Then the day would break, and, descending from my berth by a graceful ladder composed of half-opened drawers beneath it, I would reopen my outer dead-light and my inner sliding window, (closed by a watchman during the Water Cure,) and would look out at the long-rolling, lead-colored, white topped waves over which the dawn, on a cold winter morning, cast a level, lonely glance, and through which the ship fought her melancholy way at a terrific rate. And now lying down again, awaiting the season for broiled ham and tea, I would be compelled to listen to the voice of conscience, —the Screw.

It might be, in some cases, no more than the voice of Stomach, but I called it in my fancy by the higher name. Because it seemed to me that we were all of us, all day long, endeavoring to stifle the Voice. Because it was under everybody's pillow, everybody's plate, everybody's campstool, everybody's book, everybody's occupation. Because, we pretended not to hear it, especially at meal-times, evening whist, and morning conversation on deck; but it was always among us in an under monotone, not to be drowned in pea soup, not to be shuffled with cards, not to be diverted by books, not to be knitted into any pattern, not to be walked away from. It was smoked in the weediest cigar, and drunk in the strongest cocktail; it was conveyed on deck at noon with limp ladies, who lay there in their wrappers until the stars shone; it waited at table with the stewards; nobody could put it out with the lights. It was considered (as on shore) ill-bred to acknowledge the Voice of conscience. It was not polite to mention it. One squally day an amiable gentleman in love gave much offence to a surrounding circle, including the object of his attachment, by saying of it, after it had goaded him over two easy-chairs and a skylight, "Screw!"

Sometimes it would appear subdued. In fleeting moments, when bubbles of champagne pervaded the nose, or when there was "hot pot" in the bill of fare, or when an old dish we had had regularly every day was described in that official document by a new name,—under such excitements, one would almost believe it hushed. The ceremony of washing plates on deck, performed after every meal by a circle as of ringers of crockery triple-bob majors for a prize, would keep it down. Hauling the reel, taking the sun at noon, posting the twenty-four hours run, altering the ship's time by the meridian, casting the waste food overboard, and attracting the eager gulls that followed in our wake; these events would suppress it for a while. But the instant any break or pause took place in any such diversion, the Voice would be at it again, importuning us to the last extent. A newly married young pair, who walked the deck affectionately some twenty miles per day, would, in the full flush of their exercise, suddenly become stricken by it, and stand trembling, but otherwise immovable, under its reproaches.

When this terrible monitor was most severe with us was when the time approached for our retiring to our dens for the night. When the lighted candles in the saloon grew fewer and fewer. When the deserted glasses with spoons in them grew more and more numerous. When waifs of toasted cheese and strays of sardines fried in batter slid languidly to and fro in the table-racks. When the man who always read had shut up his book and blown out his candle. When the man who always talked had ceased from troubling. When the man who was always medically reported as going to have delirium tremens, had put it off till to-morrow. When the man who every night devoted himself to a midnight smoke on deck, two hours in length, and who every night was in bed within ten minutes afterwards, was buttoning himself up in his third coat for his hardy vigil. For then, as we fell off one by one, and entering our several hatches, came into a peculiar atmosphere of bilge-water and Windsor soap, the voice would shake us to the centre. Woe to us when we sat down on our sofa watching the swinging candle forever trying and retrying to stand upon his head, or our coat upon its peg imitating us as we appeared in our gymnastic days by sustaining itself horizontally from the wall, in emulation of the lighter and more facile towels! Then would the Voice especially claim us for its prey, and rend us all to pieces.

Lights out, we in our berths, and the wind rising, the Voice grows angrier and deeper. Under the mattress and under the pillow, under the sofa, and under the washing-stand, under the ship and under the sea, coming to arise from the foundations under the earth with every scoop of the great Atlantic, (and O, why scoop so!) always the Voice. Vain to deny its existence in the night season; impossible to be hard of hearing; Screw, Screw, Screw. Sometimes it lifts out of the water, and revolves with a whir, like a ferocious firework,—except that it never expends itself, but is always ready to go off again; sometimes it seems to be aguish and shivers; sometimes it seems to be terrified by its last plunge, and has a fit which causes it to struggle, quiver, and for an instant stop. And now the ship sets in rolling, as only ships so fiercely screwed through time and space, day and night, fair weather and foul, *can* roll.

Did she ever take a roll before like that last? Did she ever take a roll before like this worse one that is coming now? Here is the partition at my ear down in the deep on the lee side. Are we ever coming up again together? I think not; the partition and I are so long about it that I really do believe we have overdone it this time. Heavens, what a scoop! What a deep scoop, what a hollow scoop, what a long scoop! Will it ever end, and can we bear the heavy mass of water we have taken on board, and which has let loose all the table furniture in the officers' mess, and has beaten open the door of the little passage between the purser and me, and is swashing about, even there and even here? The purser snores reassuringly, and, the ship's bells striking, I hear the cheerful "All's well!" of the watch musically given back the length of the deck, as the lately diving partition, now high in air, tries (unsoftened by what we have gone through together) to force me out of bed and berth.

"All's well!" Comforting to know, though surely all might be better. Put aside the rolling and the rush of water, and think of darting through such darkness with such velocity. Think of any other similar object coming in the opposite direction!

Whether there may be an attraction in two such moving bodies out at sea, which may help accident to bring them into collision? Thoughts, too, arise (the Voice never silent all the while, but marvellously suggestive) of the gulf below; of the strange unfruitful mountain ranges and deep velleys over which we are passing; of monstrous fish, midway; of the ship's suddenly altering her course on her own account, and with a wild plunge settling down, and making *that* voyage, with a crew of dead discoverers. Now, too, one recalls an almost universal tendency on the part of passengers to stumble at some time or other in the day, on the topic of a certain large steamer making this same run, which was lost at sea and never heard of more. Everybody has seemed under a spell, compelling approach to the threshold of the grim subject, stoppage, discomfiture, and pretence of never having been near it. The boatswain's whistle sounds! A change in the wind, hoarse orders issuing, and the watch very busy. Sails come crashing home overhead, ropes (that seem all knot) ditto; every man engaged appears to have twenty feet, with twenty times the average amount of stamping power in each. Gradually the noise slackens, the hoarse cries die away, the boatswain's whistle softens into the soothing and contented notes, which rather reluctantly admit that the job is done for the time, and the Voice sets in again.

Thus come unintelligible dreams of up hill and down hill, and swinging and swaying, until consciousness revives of atmospherical Windsor soap and bilge-water, and the Voice announces that the giant has come for the Water Cure again.

Such were my fanciful reminiscences as I lay, part of that day, in the Bay of New York O! Also, as we passed clear of the Narrows and got out to sea; also, in many an idle hour at sea in sunny weather. At length the observations and computations showed that we should make the coast of Ireland to-night. So I stood watch on deck all night to-night, to see how we made the coast of Ireland.

Very dark, and the sea most brilliantly phosphorescent. Great way on the ship, and double look-out kept. Vigilant captain on the bridge, vigilant first officer looking over the port side, vigilant second officer standing by the quarter-master at the compass, vigilant third officer posted at the stern-rail with a lantern. No passengers on the quiet decks, but expectation everywhere nevertheless. The two men at the wheel, very steady, very serious, and very prompt to answer orders. An order issued sharply now and then, and echoed back; otherwise, the night drags slowly, silently, and with no change.

All of a sudden, at the blank hour of two in the morning, a vague movement of relief from a long strain expresses itself in all hands; the third officer's lantern twinkles, and he fires a rocket, and another rocket. A sullen, solitary light is pointed out to me in the black sky yonder. A change is expected in the light, but none takes place. "Give them two more rockets, Mr. Vigilant." Two more, and a blue light burnt. All eyes watch the light again. At last a little toy sky-rocket is flashed up from it, and, even as that small streak in the darkness dies away, we are telegraphed to Queenstown, Liverpool and London, and back again under the Ocean to America.

Then up come the half-dozen passengers who are going ashore at Queenstown, and up comes the Mail Agent in charge of the bags, and up come the men who are to carry the bags into the Mail Tender that will come off for them out of the harbor. Lamps and lanterns gleam here and there about the decks, and impeding bulks are knocked away with handspikes, and the port-side bulwark, barren but a moment ago, bursts into a crop of heads of seamen, stewards, and engineers.

The light begins to be gained upon, begins to be alongside, begins to be left astern. More rockets, and, between us and the land, steams beautifully the Inman steamship, City of Paris, for New York, outward bound. We observe with complacency that the wind is dead against her (it being *with* us), and that she rolls and pitches. (The sickest passenger on board is the most delighted by this circumstance.) Time rushes by, as we rush on, and now we see the light in Queenstown Harbor, and now the lights of the Mail Tender coming out to us. What vagaries the Mail Tender performs on the way, in every point of the compass, especially in those where she has no business, and why she performs them, heaven only knows! At length she is seen plunging within a cable's length of our port broadside, and is being roared at through our speaking-trumpets to do this thing, and not to do that, and to stand by the other, as if she were a very demented Tender indeed. Then, we slackening amidst a deafening roar of steam, this much-abused Tender is made fast to us by hawsers, and the men in readiness carry the bags aboard, and return for more, bending under their burdens, and looking just like the pasteboard figures of the Miller and his Men in the Theatre of our boyhood, and comporting themselves almost as unsteadily. All the while the unfortunate Tender plunges high and low, and is roared at. Then the Queenstown passengers are put on board of her, with infinite plunging and roaring, and the Tender gets heaved up on the sea to that surprising extent that she looks within an ace of washing aboard of us, high and dry. Roared at with contumely to the last, this wretched Tender is at length let go, with a final plunge of great ignominy, and falls spinning into our wake.

The Voice of Conscience resumed its dominion as the day climbed up the sky, and kept by all of us passengers into port; kept by us as we passed other light-houses and dangerous Islands off the coast, where some of the officers, with whom I stood my watch, had gone ashore in sailing ships in fogs (and of which by that token they seemed to have quite an affectionate remembrance), and past the Welsh coast, and past the Cheshire coast, and past everything and everywhere lying between our ship and her own special dock in the Mersey. Off which, at last, at nine of the clock on a fair evening early in May, we stopped, and the Voice ceased. A very curious sensation, not unlike having my own ears stopped, ensued upon that silence; and it was with a no less curious sensation that I went over the side of the good Cunard ship Russia, (whom Prosperity attend through all her voyages!) and surveyed the outer hull of the gracious monster that the Voice had inhabited. So, perhaps, shall we all, in the spirit, one day survey the frame that held the busier Voice from which my vagrant fancy derived this similitude.

A SMALL STAR IN THE EAST.

BY CHARLES DICKENS.

I HAD been looking, yesternight, through the famous Dance of Death, and to-day the grim old woodcuts arose in my mind with the new significance of a ghastly monotony not to be found in the original. The weird skeleton rattled along the streets before me, and struck fiercely, but it was never at the pains of assuming a disguise. It played on no dulcimer here, was crowned with no flowers, waved no plume, minced in no flowing robe or train, lifted no wine-cup, sat at no feast, cast no dice, counted no gold. It was simply a bare, gaunt, famished skeleton, slaying its way along.

The borders of Ratcliffe and Stepney, eastward of London, and giving on the impure river, were the scene of this uncompromising Dance of Death, upon a drizzling November day. A squalid maze of streets, courts, and alleys of miserable houses to let out in single rooms. A wilderness of dirt, rags, and hunger. A mud-desert chiefly inhabited by a tribe from whom employment has departed, or to whom it comes but fitfully and rarely. They are not skilled mechanics in any wise. They are but laborers. Dock-laborers, water-side laborers, coal-porters, ballast-heavers, such like hewers of wood and drawers of water. But they have come into existence, and they propagate their wretched race.

One grizzly joke alone, methought, the skeleton seemed to play off here. It had stuck Election Bills on the walls, which the wind and rain had deteriorated into suitable rags. It had even summed up the state of the poll, in chalk, on the shutters of one ruined house. It adjured the free and independent starvers to vote for Thisman and vote for Thatman: not to plump, as they valued the state of parties and the national prosperity (both of great importance to them, I think!), but, by returning Thisman and Thatman, each naught without the other, to compound a glorious and immortal whole. Surely the skeleton is nowhere more cruelly ironical in the original monkish idea!

Pondering in my mind the far-seeing schemes of Thisman and Thatman, and of the public blessing called Party for staying the degeneracy, physical and moral, of many thousands (who shall say how many?) of the English race; for devising employment useful to the community, for those who want but to work and live; for equalizing rates, cultivating waste lands, facilitating emigration, and above all things, saving and utilizing the oncoming generations, and thereby changing ever-growing national weakness into strength; pondering in my mind, I say, these hopeful exertions, I turned down a narrow street to look into a house or two.

It was a dark street with a dead wall on one side. Nearly all the outer doors of the houses stood open. I took the first entry and knocked at a parlor door. Might I come in? I might, if I plased, Sur.

The woman of the room (Irish) had picked up some long strips of wood, about some wharf or barge, and they had just now been thrust into the otherwise empty grate to make two iron pots boil. There was some fish in one, and there were some potatoes in the other. The flare of the burning wood enabled me to see a table and a broken chair or so, and some old cheap crockery ornaments about the chimneypiece. It was not until I had spoken with the woman a few minutes that I saw a horrible brown heap on the floor in a corner, which, but for previous experience in this dismal wise, I might not have suspected to be "the bed." There was something thrown upon it, and I asked what that was.

" 'Tis the poor craythur that stays here, Sur, and 'tis very bad she is, and 'tis very bad she's been this long time, and 'tis better she'll never be, and 'tis slape she does all day, and 'tis wake she does all night, and 'tis the lead, Sur."

"The what?"

"The lead, Sur. Sure 'tis the lead-mills, where the women gets took on at eighteen pence a day, Sur, when they makes applicaytion early enough and is lucky and wanted, and 'tis lead-poisoned she is, Sur, and some of them gits lead-poisoned soon and some of them gits lead-poisoned later, and some but not many niver, and 'tis all according to the constitooshun, Sur, and some constitooshuns is strong and some is weak, and her constitooshun is lead-poisoned bad as can be Sur, and her brain is coming out at her ear, and it hurts her dreadful, and that's what it is and niver no more and niver no less, Sur."

The sick young woman moaning here, the speaker bent over her, took a bandage from her head, and threw open the back door to let in the daylight upon it from the smallest and most miserable back-yard I ever saw.

"That's what cooms from her, Sur, being lead-pisoned, and it cooms from her night and day the poor sick craytur, and the pain of it is dreadful, and God he knows that my husband has walked the sthreets these four days being a laborer and is walking them now and is ready to work and no work for him and no fire and no food but the bit in the pot, and no more than ten shillings in a fortnight, God be good to us, and it is poor we are and dark it is and could it is indeed!"

Knowing that I could compensate myself thereafter for my self-denial, if I saw fit, I had resolved that I would give nothing in the course of these visits. I did this to try the people. I may state at once that my closest observation could not detect any indication whatever of an expectation that I would give money; they were grateful to be talked to about their miserable affairs, and sympathy was plainly a comfort to them; but they neither asked for money in any case, nor showed the least trace of surprise or disappointment or resentment at my giving none.

The woman's married daughter had by this time come down from her room on the floor above, to join in the conversation. She herself had been to the lead-mills very early that morning to be "took on," but had not succeeded. She had four children, and her husband, also a water-side laborer and then out seeking work, seemed in no better case as to finding it, than her father. She was English and by nature of a buxom figure and cheerful. Both in her poor dress and in her mother's there was an effort to keep up some appearance of neatness. She knew all about the sufferings of the unfortunate invalid, and all about the lead-poisoning, and how the symptoms came on, and how they grew,—having often seen them. The very smell when you stood inside the door of the works was enough to knock you down, she said, yet she was going back again to get "took on." What could she do? Better be ulcerated and paralyzed for eighteen pence a day, while it lasted, than see the children starve.

A dark and squallid cupboard in this room, touching the back door and all manner of offence, had been for some time the sleeping-place of the sick young woman. But the nights being now wintry, and the blankets and coverlets "gone to the leaving shop," she lay all night where she lay all day, and was lying then. The woman of the room, her husband, this most miserable patient, and two others, lay on the one brown heap together for warmth.

"God bless you, sir, and thank you!" were the parting words from these people,—gratefully spoken too,—with which I left this place.

Some streets away, I tapped at another parlor door on another ground-floor. Looking in, I found a man, his wife, and four children, sitting at a washing stool by way of table, at their dinner of bread and infused tea-leaves. There was a very scanty cinderous fire in the grate by which they sat, and there was a tent bedstead in the room with a bed upon it and a coverlet. The man did not rise when I went in, nor during my stay, but civilly inclined his head on my pulling off my hat, and in answer to my inquiry whether I might ask him a question or two, said "Certainly." There being a window at each end of this room back and front, it might have been ventilated; but it was shut up tight, to keep the cold out and was very sickening.

The wife, an intelligent quick woman, rose and stood at her husband's elbow, and he glanced up at her as if for help. It soon appeared that he was rather deaf. He was a slow simple fellow of about thirty.

"What was he by trade?"

"Gentleman asks what are you by trade, John?"

"I am a boiler-maker;" looking about him with an exceedingly perplexed air, as if for a boiler that had unaccountably vanished.

"He ain't a mechanic, you understand, sir," the wife put in, "he's only a laborer."

"Are you in work?"

He looked up at his wife again. "Gentleman says are you in work, John?"

"In work!" cried this forlorn boiler-maker, staring aghast at his wife, and then working his vision's way very slowly round to me; "Lord, no!"

"Ah! He ain't indeed!" said the poor woman, shaking her head, as she looked at the four children in succession, and then at him.

"Work!" said the boiler-maker, still seeking that evaporated boiler, first in my countenance, then in the air, and then in the features of his second son at his knee, "I wish I *was* in work! I haven't had more than a day's work to do these three weeks."

"How have you lived?"

A faint gleam of admiration lighted up the face of the

would-be boiler-maker, as he stretched out the short sleeve of his threadbare canvas jacket, and replied, pointing her out, " On the work of the wife."

I forgot where boiler-making had gone to, or where he supposed it had gone to; but he added some resigned information on that head, coupled with an expression of his belief that it was never coming back.

The cheery helpfulness of the wife was very remarkable She did slop-work; made pea-jackets. She produced the pea-jacket then in hand, and spread it out upon the bed—the only piece of furniture in the room on which to spread it. She showed how much of it she made, and how much was afterward finished off by the machine. According to her calculation at the moment, deducting what her trimming cost her, she got for making a pea-jacket tenpence halfpenny, and she could make one in something less than two days.

But, you see, it come to her through two hands, and of course it didn't come through the second hand for nothing. Why did it come through the second hand at all? Why, this way. The second hand took the risk of the given-out work, you see. If she had money enough to pay the security deposit—call it two pounds—he could get the work from the first hand, and so the second would not have to be deducted for. But, having no money at all, the second hand came in and took its profit, and so the whole worked down to tenpence halfpenny. Having explained all this with great intelligence, even with some little pride, and without a whine or murmur, she folded her work again, sat down by her husband's side at the washing-stool, and resumed her dinner of dry bread. Mean as the meal was, on the bare board, with its old gallipots for cups, and what not other sordid makeshifts; shabby as the woman was in dress, and toning down toward the Bosjesman color, with want of nutriment and washing, there was positively a dignity in her, as the family anchor just holding the poor shipwrecked boiler-maker's bark. When I left the room, the boiler-maker's eyes were slowly turned towards her, as if his last hope of ever seeing again that vanished boiler lay in her direction.

These people had never applied for parish relief but once; and that was when the husband met with a disabling accident at his work.

Not many doors from here, I went into a room on the first floor. The woman apologized for its being in "an untidy mess." The day was Saturday, and she was boiling the children's clothes in a saucepan on the hearth. There was nothing else into which she could have put them. There was no crockery, or tinware, or tub, or bucket. There was an old gallipot or two, and there was a broken bottle or so, and there were some broken boxes for seats. The last small scraping of coals left was raked together in a corner of the floor. There were some rags in an open cupboard, also on the floor. In a corner of the room was a crazy old French bedstead, with a man lying on his back upon it in a ragged pilot jacket, and rough oilskin fantail hat. The room was perfectly black. It was difficult to believe, at first, that it was not purposely colored black, the walls were so begrimed.

As I stood opposite the woman boiling the children's clothes,—she had not even a piece of soap to wash them with,—and apologizing for her occupation, I could take in all these things without appearing to notice them, and could even correct my inventory. I had missed, at the first glance, some half a pound of bread in the otherwise empty safe, an old red ragged crinoline hanging on the handle of the door by which I had entered, and certain fragments of rusty iron scattered on the floor, which looked like broken tools and a piece of stove-pipe. A child stood looking on. On the box nearest to the fire sat two younger children; one a delicate and pretty little creature whom the other sometimes kissed.

This woman, like the last, was wofully shabby, and was

degenerating to the Bosjcsman complexion. But her figure, and the ghost of a certain vivacity about her, and the spectre of a dimple in her cheek, carried my memory strangely back to the old days of the Adelphia Theatre, London, when Mrs. Fitzwilliam was the friend of Victorine.

"May I ask you what your husband is?"

"He's a coal-porter, sir,"—with a glance and a sigh towards the bed.

"Is he out of work?"

"O yes, sir, and work's at all times very, very scanty with him, and now he's laid up."

"It's my legs," said the man upon the bed. "I'll unroll 'em." And immediately began.

"Have you any older children?"

"I have a daughter that does the needle-work, and I have a son that does what he can. She's at her work now, and he's trying for work."

"Do they live here?"

"They sleep here. They can't afford to pay more rent, and so they come here at night. The rent is very hard upon us. It's rose upon us too, now,—sixpence a week,—on account of these new changes in the law, about the rates, We are a week behind; the landlord's been shaking and rattling at that door frightful; he says he'll turn us out. I don't know what's to come of it."

The man upon the bed ruefully interposed: "Here's my legs. The skin's broke, besides the swelling. I have had a many kicks, working, one way and another."

He looked at his legs (which were much discolored and misshapen) for awhile, and then appearing to remember that they were not popular with his family, rolled them up again, as if they were something in the nature of maps or plans that were not wanted to be referred to, lay hopelessly down on his back once more with his fantail hat over his face, and stirred not.

"Do your eldest son and daughter sleep in that cupboard?"

"Yes," replied the woman.

"With the children?"

"Yes. We have to get together for warmth. We have little to cover us."

"Have you nothing by you to eat but the piece of bread I see there?"

"Nothing. And we had the rest of the loaf for our breakfast, with water. I don't know what's to come of it."

"Have you no prospect of improvement?"

"If my eldest son earns anything to-day, he'll bring it home. Then we shall have something to eat to-night, and may be able to do something towards the rent. If not, I don't know what's to come of it."

"This is a sad state of things."

"Yes, sir, it's a hard, hard life. Take care of the stairs as you go, sir—they're broken—and good day, sir!"

These people had a moral dread of entering the workhouse, and received no out-of-door relief.

In another room, in still another tenement, I found a very decent woman with five children,—the last, a baby, and she herself a patient of the parish doctor,—to whom, her husband being in the hospital, the Union allowed for the support of herself and family, four shillings a week and five loaves. I suppose when Thisman, M.P., and Thatman, M.P., and the public blessing Party, lay their heads together in course of time, and come to an equalization of Rating, she may go down the Dance of Death to the tune of sixpence more.

I could enter no other houses for that one while, for I could not bear the contemplation of the children. Such heart as I had summoned to sustain me against the miseries of adults failed me when I looked at the children. I saw how young they were, how hungry, how serious and still. I thought of them, sick and dying in those lairs. I could think of them dead without anguish; but to think of them so suffering and so dying quite unmanned me.

Down by the river's bank in Ratcliffe, I was turning upward by a side street, therefore, to regain the railway, when my eyes rested on the inscription across the road, "East London Children's Hospital." I could scarcely have seen an inscription better suited to my frame of mind, and I went across and went straight in.

I found the Children's Hospital established in an old sail-loft or storehouse, of the roughest nature, and on the simplest means. There were trap-doors in the floors where goods had been hoisted up and down; heavy feet and heavy weights had started every knot in the well-trodden planking; inconvenient bulks and beams and awkward staircases perplexed my passage through the wards. But I found it airy, sweet, and clean. In its seven-and-thirty beds I saw but little beauty, for starvation in the second or third generation takes a pinched look; but I saw the sufferings both of infancy and childhood tenderly assuaged; I heard the little patients answering to pet playful names, the light touch of a delicate lady laid bare the wasted sticks of arms for me to pity; and the claw-like little hands, as she did so, twined themselves lovingly around her wedding-ring.

One baby mite there was as pretty as any of Raphael's angels. The tiny head was bandaged for water on the brain, and it was suffering with acute bronchitis too, and made from time to time a plaintive, though not impatient or complaining, little sound. The smooth curve of the cheeks and of the chin was faultless in its condensation of infantine beauty, and the large bright eyes were most lovely. It happened, as I stopped at the foot of the bed, that these eyes rested upon mine with that wistful expression of wondering thoughtfulness which we all know sometimes in very little children. They remained fixed on mine, and never turned from me while I stood there. When the utterance of that plaintive sound shook the little form, the gaze still remained unchanged. I felt as though the child implored me to tell the story of the little hospital in which it was sheltered to any gentle heart I could address. Laying my world-worn hand upon the little unmarked clasped hand at the chin, I gave it a silent promise that I would do so.

A gentleman and lady, a young husband and wife, have bought and fitted up this building for its present noble use, and have quietly settled themselves in it as its medical officers and directors. Both have had considerable practical experience of medicine and surgery; he, as house-surgeon of a great London Hospital; she, as a very earnest student, tested by severe examination, and also as a nurse of the sick poor during the prevalence of cholera.

With every qualification to lure them away, with youth and accomplishments and tastes and habits that can have no response in any breast near them, close begirt by every repulsive circumstance inseparable from such a neighborhood, there they dwell. They live in the hospital itself, and their rooms are on its first floor. Sitting at their dinner-table, they could hear the cry of one of the children in pain. The lady's piano, drawing-materials, books, and other such evidences of refinement, are as much a part of the rough place as the iron bedsteads of the little patients. They are put to shifts for room, like passengers on board ship. The dispenser of medicines (attracted to them, not by self-interest, but by their own magnetism and that of their cause) sleeps in a recess in the dining-room, and has his washing apparatus in the sideboard.

Their contented manner of making the best of the things around them, I found so pleasantly inseparable from their usefulness! Their pride in this partition that we put up ourselves, or in that partition that we took down, or in that other partition that we moved, or in the stove that was given us for the waiting-room, or in our nightly conversion of the little consulting-room into a smoking-room. Their admiration of the situation, if we could only get rid of its one objectionable incident, the coal-yard at the back! "Our hospital carriage, presented by a friend, and very useful."

That was my presentation to a perambulator, for which a coach-house had been discovered in a corner down stairs, just large enough to hold it. Colored prints, in all stages of preparation for being added to those already decorating the wards, were plentiful; a charming wooden phenomenon of a bird, with an impossible top-knot, who ducked his head when you set a counter weight going, had been inaugurated as a public statue that very morning; and trotting about among the beds, on familiar terms with all the patients, was a comical mongrel dog, called Poodles. This comical dog, (quite a tonic in himself) was found characteristically starving at the door of the Institution, and was taken in and fed, and has lived here ever since. An admirer of his mental endowments has presented him with a collar bearing the legend, "Judge not Poodles by external appearances." He was merrily wagging his tail on a boy's pillow when he made this modest appeal to me.

When this Hospital was first opened, in January of the present year, the people could not possibly conceive but that somebody paid for the services rendered there; and were disposed to claim them as a right, and to find fault if out of temper. They soon came to understand the case better, and have much increased in gratitude. The mothers of the patients avail themselves very freely of the visiting rules; the fathers often on Sundays. There is an unreasonable (but still, I think, a touching and intelligible) tendency in the parents to take a child away to its wretched home if on the point of death. One boy who had been thus carried off on a rainy night, when in a violent state of inflammation, and who had been afterwards brought back, had been recovered with exceeding difficulty; but he was a jolly boy, with a specially strong interest in his dinner when I saw him.

Insufficient food and unwholesome living are the main causes of disease among these small patients. So nourishment, cleanliness, and ventilation are the main remedies.

Discharged patients are looked after and invited to come and dine now and then ; so are certain famishing creatures who were never patients. Both the lady and the gentleman are well acquainted, not only with the histories of the patients and their families but with the characters and circumstances of great numbers of their neighbors ; of these they keep a register. It is their common experience that people, sinking down by inches into deeper and deeper poverty, will conceal it, even from them, if possible, unto the very last extremity.

The nurses of this Hospital are all young,—ranging, say, from nineteen to four-and-twenty. They have, even within these narrow limits, what many well-endowed Hospitals would not give them, a comfortable room of their own in which to take their meals. It is a beautiful truth, that interest in the children and sympathy with their sorrows bind these young women to their places far more strongly than any other consideration could. The best skilled of the nurses came originally from a kindred neighborhood, almost as poor, and she knew how much the work was needed. She is a fair dressmaker. The Hospital cannot pay her as many pounds in the year as there are months in it, and one day the lady regarded it as a duty to speak to her about her improving her prospects and following her trade. "No," she said ; she could never be so useful or so happy elsewhere any more ; she must stay among the children. And she stays. One of the nurses, as I passed her, was washing a baby-boy. Liking her pleasant face, I stopped to speak to her charge : a common, bullet-headed, frowning charge enough, laying hold of his own nose with a slippery grasp, and staring very solemnly out of a blanket. The melting of the pleasant face into delighted smiles as this young gentleman gave an unexpected kick, and laughed at me, was almost worth my previous pain.

An affecting play was acted in Paris years ago, called The Children's Doctor. As I parted from my Children's

Doctor now in question, I saw in his easy black necktie, in his loose buttoned black frock-coat, in his pensive face, in the flow of his dark hair, in his eyelashes, in the very turn of his mustache, the exact realization of the Paris artist's ideal as it was presented on the stage. But no romancer that I know of has had the boldness to prefigure the life and home of this young husband and young wife in the Children's Hospital in the East of London.

I came away from Ratcliffe by the Stepney railway station to the terminus at Fenchurch street. Any one who will reverse that route may retrace my steps.

A LITTLE DINNER IN AN HOUR.

BY CHARLES DICKENS.

IT fell out on a day in this last autumn that I had to go down from London to a place of seaside resort, on an hour's business, accompanied by my esteemed friend Bullfinch. Let the place of seaside resort be, for the nonce, called Namelesston.

I had been loitering about Paris in very hot weather, pleasantly breakfasting in the open air in the garden of the Palais Royal or the Tuileries, pleasantly dining in the open air in the Elysian Fields, pleasantly taking my cigar and lemonade in the open air on the Italian Boulevard towards the small hours after midnight. Bullfinch—an excellent man of business—had summoned me back across the Channel, to transact this said hour's business at Namelesston, and thus it fell out that Bullfinch and I were in a railway carriage together on our way to Namelesston, each with his return ticket in his waistcoat pocket.

Says Bullfinch: "I have a proposal to make. Let us dine at the Temeraire."

I asked Bullfinch, Did he recommend the Temeraire? Inasmuch as I had not been rated on the books of the Temeraire for many years.

Bullfinch declined to accept the responsibility of recommending the Temeraire, but on the whole was rather sanguine about it. He "seemed to remember," Bullfinch said, that he had dined well there. A plain dinner, but good. Certainly not like a Parisian dinner (here Bullfinch obviously became the prey of want of confidence), but of its kind very fair.

I appealed to Bullfinch's intimate knowledge of my wants

and ways to decide whether I was usually ready to be pleased with any dinner, or—for the matter of that—with anything that was fair of its kind and really what it claimed to be. Bullfinch doing me the honor to respond in the affirmative, I agreed to ship myself as an Able Trencherman on board the Temeraire.

"Now, our plan shall be this," says Bullfinch, with his forefinger at his nose. "As soon as we get to Namelesston, we'll drive straight to the Temeraire, and order a little dinner in an hour. And as we shall not have more than enough time in which to dispose of it comfortably, what do you say to giving the house the best opportunities of serving it hot and quickly by dining in the coffee-room?"

What I had to say was, Certainly. Bullfinch (who is by nature of a hopeful constitution) then began to babble of green geese. But I checked him in that Falstaffian vein, urging considerations of time and cookery.

In due sequence of events we drove up to the Temeraire and alighted. A youth in livery received us on the doorstep. "Looks well," said Bullfinch, confidentially. And then aloud, "Coffee-room!"

The youth in livery (now perceived to be mouldy) conducted us to the desired haven, and was enjoined by Bullfinch to send the waiter at once, as we wished to order a little dinner in an hour. Then Bullfinch and I waited for the waiter until, the waiter continuing to wait in some unknown and invisible sphere of action, we rang for the waiter; which ring produced the waiter, who announced himself as not the waiter who ought to wait upon us, and who didn't wait a moment longer.

So Bullfinch approached the coffee-room door, and melodiously pitching his voice into a bar where two young ladies were keeping the books of the Temeraire, apologetically explained that we wished to order a little dinner in an hour, and that we were debarred from the execution of our inoffensive purpose by consignment to solitude.

Hereupon one of the young ladies rang a bell which reproduced—at the bar this time—the waiter who was not the waiter who ought to wait upon us; that extraordinary man, whose life seemed consumed in waiting upon people to say that he would'nt wait upon them, repeated his former protest with great indignation, and retired.

Bullfinch, with a fallen countenance, was about to say to me "This won't do," when the waiter who ought to wait upon us left off keeping us waiting at last. "Waiter," said Bullfinch, piteously, "we have been a long time waiting." The waiter who ought to wait upon us laid the blame upon the waiter who ought not to wait upon us, and said it was all that waiter's fault.

"We wish," said Bullfinch, much depressed, "to order a little dinner in an hour. What can we have?"

"What would you like to have, gentlemen?"

Bullfinch, with extreme mournfulness of speech and action, and with a forlorn old fly-blown bill of fare in his hand which the waiter had given him, and which was a sort of general manuscript index to any Cookery-Book you please, moved the previous question.

We could have mock-turtle soup, a sole, curry, and roast duck. Agreed. At this table by this window. Punctually in an hour.

I had been feigning to look out of this window; but I had been taking note of the crumbs on all the tables, the dirty table-cloths, the stuffy, soupy, airless atmosphere, the stale leavings everywhere about, the deep gloom of the waiter who ought to wait upon us, and the stomach-ache with which a lonely traveller at a distant table in a corner was too evidently afflicted. I now pointed out to Bulfinch the alarming circumstance that this traveller had *dined*. We hurriedly debated whether, without infringement of good breeding, we could ask him to disclose if he had partaken of mock-turtle, sole, curry, or roast duck? We decided that the thing could not be politely done, and that we had set our own stomachs on a cast, and they must stand the hazzard of the die.

I hold phrenology, within certain limits, to be true; I am much of the same mind as to the subtler expressions of the hand; I hold physiognomy to be infallible; though all these sciences demand rare qualities in the student. But I also hold that there is no more certain index to personal character than the condition of a set of casters is to the character of any hotel. Knowing, and having often tested this theory of mine, Bullfinch resigned himself to the worst, when, laying aside any remaining veil of disguise, I held before him in succession the cloudy oil and furry vinegar, the clogged cayenne, the dirty salt, the obscene dregs of soy, and the anchovy sauce in a flannel waistcoat of decomposition.

We went out to transact our business. So inspiriting was the relief of passing into the clean and windy streets of Namelesston from the heavy and vapid closeness of the coffee-room of the Temeraire, that hope began to revive within us. We began to consider that perhaps the lonely traveller had taken physic, or done something injudicious to bring his complaint on. Bullfinch remarked he thought the waiter who ought to wait upon us had brightened a little when suggesting curry; and although I knew him to have been at that moment the express image of despair, I allowed myself to become elevated in spirits. As we walked by the softly lapping sea, all the notabilities of Namelesston, who are forever going up and down with the changelessness of the tides, passed to and fro in procession. Pretty girls on horseback, and with detested riding-masters; pretty girls on foot; mature ladies in hats,—spectacled, strong-minded, and glaring at the opposite or weaker sex. The Stock Exchange was strongly represented, Jerusalem was strongly represented, the bores of the prosier London clubs were strongly represented. Fortune-hunters of all denominations were there, from hirsute insolvency in a curricle to closely bottoned-up swindlery in doubtful boots, on the sharp look-out for any likely young gentleman disposed to play a game at billiards round the corner. Masters of languages, their lessons finished for the day, were going to their homes out of sight of the sea; mistresses of accomplishments, carrying small portfolios, likewise tripped homeward; pairs of scholastic pupils, two and two, went languidly along the beach, surveying the face of the waters as if waiting for some Ark to come and take them off. Spectres of the George the Fourth days flitted unsteadily among the crowd, bearing the outward semblance of ancient dandies, of every one of whom it might be said, not that he had one leg in the grave, or both legs, but that he was steeped in the grave to the summit of his high shirt-collar, and had nothing real about him but his bones. Alone stationary in the midst of all the movements, the Namelesston boatmen leaned against the railings and yawned, and looked out to sea, or looked at the moored fishing-boats and at nothing. Such is the unchanging manner of life with this nursery of our hardy seamen, and very dry nurses they are, and always wanting something to drink. The only two nautical personages detached from the railing were the two fortunate possessors of the celebrated monstrous unknown barking-fish, just caught (frequently just caught off Namelesston,) who carried him about in a hamper, and pressed the scientific to look in at the lid.

The sands of the hour had all run out when we got back to Temeraire. Says Bullfinch then to the youth in livery, with boldness: "Lavatory!"

When we arrived at the family vault with a sky-light, which the youth in livery presented as the Institution sought, we had already whisked off our cravats and coats; but finding ourselves in the presence of an evil smell, and no linen but two crumpled towels newly damp from the countenances of two somebody elses, we put on our cravats and coats again, and fled unwashed to the coffee-room.

There, the waiter who ought to wait upon us had set forth

our knives and forks and glasses on the cloth whose dirty acquaintance we had already had the pleasure of making, and whom we were pleased to recognize by the familiar expression of its stains. And now there occurred the truly surprising phenomenon that the waiter who ought not to wait upon us swooped down upon us, clutched our loaf of bread, and vanished with the same.

Bullfinch with distracted eyes was following this unaccountable figure "out at the portal," like the Ghost in Hamlet, when the waiter who ought to wait upon us jostled against it, carrying a tureen.

"Waiter!" said a severe diner, lately finished, perusing his bill through his eye-glass.

The waiter put down our tureen on a remote side table, and went to see what was amiss in this new direction.

"This is not right, you know, waiter. Look here. Here's yesterday's sherry, one and eightpence, and here we are again, two shillings. And what does Sixpence mean?"

So far from knowing what sixpence meant, the waiter protested that he didn't know what anything meant. He wiped the prespiration from his clammy brow, and said it was impossible to do it—not particularizing what—and the kitchen was so far off.

"Take the bill to the bar, and get it altered," said Mr. Indignation Cocker: so to call him.

The waiter took it, looked intensely at it, didn't seem to like the idea of taking it to the bar, and submitted, as a new light upon the case, that perhaps sixpence meant six pence.

"I tell you again," said Mr. Indignation Cocker, "here's yesterday's sherry—can't you see it?—one and eightpence, and here we are again, two shillings. What do you make of one and eightpence and two shillings?"

Totally unable to make anything of one and eightpence and two shillings, the waiter went out to try if anybody else could; merely casting a helpless backward glance at Bullfinch, in acknowledgment of his pathetic entreaties for our soup-tureen. After a pause, during which Mr. Indignation Cocker read a newspaper, and coughed defiant coughs, Bullfinch rose to get the tureen, when the waiter reappeared and brought it: dropping Mr. Indignation Cocker's altered bill on Mr. Indignation Cocker's table as he came along.

"It's quite impossible to do it, gentlemen," murmured the waiter; "and the kitchen is so far off."

"Well. You don't keep the house; it's not your fault, we suppose. Bring some sherry."

"Waiter!" From Mr. Indignation Cocker, with a new and burning sense of injury upon him.

The waiter, arrested on his way to our sherry stopped short, and came back to see what was wrong now.

"Will you look here? This is worse than before. *Do* you understand? Here's yesterday's sherry one and eightpence, and here we are again two shillings. And what the devil does Ninepence mean?"

This new portent utterly confounded the waiter. He wrung his napkin, and mutely appealed to the ceiling.

"Waiter, fetch that sherry," says Bullfinch, in open wrath and revolt.

"I want to know," persisted Mr. Indignation Cocker, "the meaning of Ninepence. I want to know the meaning of sherry one and eightpence yesterday, and of here we are again two shillings. Send somebody."

The distracted waiter got out of the room under pretext of sending somebody, and by that means got our wine. But the instant he appeared with our decanter, Mr. Indignation Cocker descended on him again.

"Waiter!"

"You will now have the goodness to attend to our dinner, waiter," says Bullfinch, sternly.

"I am very sorry, but it's quite impossible to do it, gentlemen," pleaded the waiter; and the kitchen —"

"Waiter!" said Mr. Indignation Cocker,— "Is," resumed the waiter, "so far off, that—"

"Waiter!" persisted Mr. Indignation Cocker, "send somebody."

We were not without our fears that the waiter rushed out to hang himself, and we were much relieved by his fetching somebody,—in gracefully flowing skirts and with a waist,—who very soon settled Mr. Indignation Cocker's business.

"Oh!" said Mr. Cocker, with his fire surpassingly quenched by this apparition. "I wish to ask about this bill of mine, because it appears to me that there's a little mistake here. Let me show you. Here's yesterday's sherry one and eightpence, and here we are again two shillings, And how do you explain ninepence.

However, it was explained in tones too soft to be overheard, Mr. Cocker was heard to say nothing more than "Ah-h-h! Indeed! Thank you! Yes," and shortly afterwards went out a milder man.

The lonely traveller with the stomach-ache had all this time suffered severely; drawing up a leg now and then, and sipping hot brandy and water with grated ginger in it. When we tasted our (very) mock, turtle soup, and were instantly seized with some disorder simulating apoplexy, and occasioned by the surcharge of the nose and brain with lukewarm dish-water holding in solution sour flour poisonous condiments, and (say) seventy-five per cent. of miscellaneous kitchen stuff rolled into balls, we were inclined to trace the disorder to that source. On the other hand, there was a silent anguish upon him too strongly resembling the results established within ourselves by the sherry, to be discarded from alarmed consideration. Again: we observed him, with terror, to be much overcome by our sole's being aired in a temporary retreat close to him, while the waiter went out (as we conceived) to see his friends. And when the curry made its appearance he suddenly retired in great disorder.

In fine, for the uneatable part of this little dinner (as contradistinguished from the undrinkable) we paid only seven shillings and sixpence each. And Bullfinch and I agreed unanimously, that no such ill-served, ill-appointed, ill-cooked nasty little dinner could be got for the money any where else under the sun. With that comfort to our backs, we turned them on the dear old Temeraire, the charging Temeraire, and resolved (in the Scottish dialect) to gang nae mair to the flabby Temeraire.

MR. BARLOW.

BY CHARLES DICKENS.

A GREAT reader of good fiction at an unusually early age, it seems to me as though I had been born under the superintendence of the estimable but terrific gentleman whose name stands at the head of my present reflections. The instructive monomaniac, Mr. Barlow, will be remembered as the tutor of Master Harry Sanford and Master Tommy Merton. He knew everything, and didactically improved all sorts of occasions, from the consumption of a plate of cherries to the contemplation of a starlight night. What youth came to without Mr. Barlow, was displayed, in the history of Sanford and Merton, by the example of a certain awful Master Mash. This young wretch wore buckles and powder, conducted himself with insupportable levity at the theatre, had no idea of facing a mad bull single-handed (in which I think him less reprehensible, as remotely reflecting my own character), and was a frightful instance of the enervating effects of luxury upon the human race.

Strange destiny on the part of Mr. Barlow, to go down to posterity as childhood's first experience of a Bore! Immortal Mr. Barlow, boring his way through the verdant freshness of ages!

My personal indictment against Mr. Barlow is one of many counts. I will proceed to set forth a few of the injuries he has done me.

In the first place, he never made, or took, a joke. This insensibility on Mr. Barlow's part not only cast its own gloom over my boyhood, but blighted even the sixpenny jest-books of the time. For, groaning under a moral spell constraining me to refer all things to Mr. Barlow, I could not choose but ask myself in a whisper when tickled by a printed jest "What would *he* think of it? What would *he* see in it?" The point of the jest immediately became a sting, and stung my conscience. For, my mind's eye saw him stolid, frigid, perchance taking from its shelf some dreary Greek book and translating at full length what some dismal sage said (and touched up afterwards, perhaps for publication), when he banished some unlucky joker from Athens.

The incompatibility of Mr. Barlow with all other portions of my young life but himself, the adamantine inadaptability of the man to my favorite fancies and amusements, is the thing for which I hate him most. What right had he to bore his way into my Arabian Nights? Yet he did. He was always hinting doubts of the veracity of Sindbad the Sailor. If he could have got hold of the Wonderful Lamp, I knew he would have trimmed it, and lighted it, and delivered a lecture over it on the qualities of sperm oil, with a glance at the whale fisheries. He would so soon found out—on mechanical principles—the peg in the neck of the Enchanted Horse, and would have turned it the right way in so workmanlike a manner, that the horse could never have got any height into the air, and the story couldn't have been. He would have proved, by map and compass, that there was no such kingdom as the delightful kingdom of Casgar, on the frontiers of Tartary. He would have caused the hypocritical young prig, Harry, to make an experiment,—with the aid of a temporary building in the garden and a dummy,—demonstrating that you couldn't let a choked Hunchback down an eastern chimney with a cord, and leave him upright on the hearth to terrify the Sultan's purveyor.

The golden sounds of the overture to the first metropolitan pantomime I remember, were alloyed by Mr. Barlow. Click, click, ting, ting, bang, bang, weedle, weedle, weedle, Bang! I recall the chilling air that passed across my frame and cooled my hot delight, as the thought recurred to me: "This would never do for Mr. Barlow!" After the curtain drew up, dreadful doubts of Mr. Barlow's considering the costumes of the Nymphs of the Neb la as being sufficiently opaque, obtruded themselves on my enjoyment. In the Clown I perceived two persons; one, a fascinating unaccountable creature of a hectic complexion, joyous in spirits though feeble in intellect with flashes of brilliancy; the other, a pupil for Mr. Barlow. I thought how Mr. Barlow would secretly rise early in the morning, and butter the pavement for *him*, and, when he had brought him down, would look severely out of his study window and ask *him* how he enjoyed the fun.

I thought how Mr. Barlow would heat all the pokers in the house and singe him with the whole collection, to bring him better acquainted with the properties of incandescent iron, on which he (Barlow) would fully expatiate. I pictured Mr. Barlow's instituting a comparison between the clown's conduct at his studies,—drinking up the ink, licking his copy-book, and using his head for blotting-paper,--and that of the already mentioned young Prig of Prigs, Harry, sitting at the Barlovian feet sneakingly pretending to be in a rapture of useful knowledge. I thought how soon Mr. Barlow would smooth the clown's hair down, instead of letting it stand erect in three tall tufts; and how, after a couple of years or so with Mr. Barlow, he would keep his legs close together when he walked, and would take his hands out of his big loose pockets, and wouldn't have a jump left in him.

That I am particularly ignorant what most things in the universe are made of, and how they are made, is another of my charges against Mr. Barlow. With the dread upon me of developing into a Harry, and with the further dread upon me of being Barlowed if I made inquiries, by bringing down upon myself a cold shower bath of explanations and experiment, I forebore enlightenment in my youth, and became, as they say in melodramas, "the wreck you now behold." That I consorted with idlers and dunces, is another of the melancholy facts for which I hold Mr. Barlow responsible. That Pragmatical Prig, Harry, became so detestable in my sight, that he being reported studious in the South, I would have fled idle to the extremest North. Better to learn misconduct from a Master Mash than science and statistics from a Sandford! So I took the path which, but for Mr. Barlow, I might never have trodden. Thought I with a shudder, "Mr. Barlow is a bore, with an immense constructive power of making bores. His prize specimen is a bore. He seeks to make a bore of me. That Knowledge is Power I am not prepared to gainsay; but, with Mr. Barlow, Knowledge is Power to bore." Therefore I took refuge in the Caves of Ignorance, wherein I have resided ever since, and which are still my private address.

But the weightiest charge of all my charges against Mr. Barlow is, that he still walks the earth in various disguises, seeking to make a Tommy of me, even in my maturity. Irrepressible instructive monomaniacs, Mr. Barlow fills my life with pitfalls, and lies hiding at the bottom to burst out upon me when I least expect him.

A few of these dismal experiences of mine shall suffice.

Knowing Mr. Barlow to have invested largely in the Moving Panorama trade, and having on various occasions identified him in the dark with a long wand in his hand, holding forth in his old way (made more appalling in this connection, by his sometimes cracking a piece of Mr. Carlyle's own Dead Sea Fruit in mistake for a joke), I systematically shun pictorial entertainment on rollers. Similarly, I should demand responsible bail and guaranty against the appearance of Mr. Barlow, before committing myself to attendance at any assemblage of my fellow-creatures where a bottle of water and a note-book were conspicuous objects. For in either of those associations, I should expressly expect him. But such is the designing natüre of the man, that he steals in where no reasoning precaution or provision could expect him. As in the following case:—

Adjoining the Caves of Ignorance is a country town. In this country town the Mississippi Momuses, nine in number, were announced to appear in the Town Hall for the general delectation, this last Christmas week. Knowing Mr. Barlow to be unconnected with the Mississippi, though holding republican opinions, and deeming myself secure, I took a stall. My object was to hear and see the Mississippi Momuses in what the bills described as their "National Ballads, Plantation Break-Downs, Nigger Part-Songs, Choice Conundrums, Sparkling Repartees, &c." I found the nine dressed alike, in the black coat and trousers, white waistcoat, very large shirt front, very large shirt collar, and very large white tie and wristbands, which constitute the dress of the mass of the African race, and which has been observed by travellers to prevail over a vast number of degrees of latitude. All the nine rolled their eyes exceedingly, and had very red lips. At the extremities of the curve they formed seated in their chairs, were the performers on the Tambourine and Bones. The centre Momus, a black of Melancholy aspect (who inspired me with a vague uneasiness for which I could not then account), performed on a Mississippi instrument closely resembling what was once called in this Island a hurdy-gurdy.

The Momuses on either side of him had each another instrument peculiar to the Father of Waters, which may be likened to a stringed weather-glass held upside down. There were likewise a little flute, and a violin. All went well for a while and we had had several sparkling repartees exchanged between the performers on the tambourine and bones, when the black of melancholy aspect, turning to the latter, and addressing him in a deep and improving voice as "Bones, sir," delivered certain grave remarks to him concerning the juveniles present, and the season of the year; whereon I perceived that I was in the presence of Mr. Barlow,—corked!

Another night—and this was in London—I attended the representation of a little comedy. As the characters were life-like (and consequently not improving), and as they went upon their several ways and designs without personally addressing themselves to me, I felt rather confident of coming through it without being regarded as Tommy; the more so, as we were clearly getting close to the end. But I deceived myself. All of a sudden, and apropos of nothing, everybody concerned came to a check and halt, advanced to the footlights in a general rally to take dead aim at me, and brought me down with a moral homily, in which I detected the dread hand of Barlow.

Nay, so intricate and subtle are the toils of this hunter, that on the very next night after that, I was again entrapped, where no vestige of a springe could have been apprehended by the timidest. It was a burlesque, that I saw performed; an uncomprising burlesque, where everybody concerned, but especially the ladies, carried on at a very considerable rate indeed. Most prominent and active among the corps of performers was what I took to be (and she really gave me very fair opportunities of coming to a right conclusion) a young lady, of a pretty figure. She was dressed as a picturesque young gentleman, whose pantaloons had been cut off in their infancy, and she had very neat knees, and very neat satin boots. Immediately after singing a slang song and dancing a slang dance, this engaging figure approached the fatal lamps, and, bending over them, delivered in a thrilling voice a random Eulogium on, and Exhortation to pursue, the Virtues. "Great Heaven!" was my exclamation. "Barlow!"

There is still another aspect in which Mr. Barlow perpetually insists on my sustaining the character of Tommy, which is more unendurable yet, on account of its extreme aggressiveness. For the purposes of a Review or newspaper, he will get up an abstruse subject with infinite pains, will Barlow, utterly regardless of the prince of midnight oil, and indeed of everything else, save cramming himself to the eyes.

But mark. When Mr. Barlow blows his information off, he is not contented with having rammed it home and discharged it upon me, Tommy, his target, but he pretends that he was always in possession of it, and made nothing of it,—that he imbibed it with his mother's milk,—and that I, the wretched Tommy, am most abjectly behindhand in not having done the same. I ask, why is Tommy to be always the foil of Mr. Barlow to this extent? What Mr. Barlow had not the slightest notion of himself, a week ago, it surely cannot be any very heavy backsliding in me not to have at my fingers' ends to-day! And yet Mr. Barlow systematically carries it over me with a high hand, and will tauntingly ask me in his articles whether it is possible that I am not aware that every schoolboy knows that the fourteenth turning on the left in the steppes of Russia will conduct to such-and-such a wandering tribe? With other disparaging questions of like nature. So, when Mr. Barlow addresses a letter to any journal as a volunteer correspondent (which I frequently find him doing), he will previously have gotten somebody to tell him some tremendous technicality, and will write in the coolest manner: "Now, Sir, I may assume that every reader of your columns, possessing average information and intelligence, knows as well as I do that"—say that the draught from the touch-hole of a cannon of such a calibre bears such a proportion in the nicest fractions to the draught from the muzzle; or some equally familiar little fact. But whatever it is, be certain that it always tends to the exaltation of Mr. Barlow, and the depression of his enforced and enslaved pupil.

Mr. Barlow's knowledge of my own pursuits, I find to be so profound, that my own knowledge of them becomes as nothing. Mr. Barlow (disguised and bearing a feigned name, but detected by me) has occasionally taught me, in a sonorous voice, from end to end of a long dinner-table, trifles that I took the liberty of teaching him five-and-twenty years ago. My closing article of impeachment against Mr. Barlow, is, that he goes out to breakfast, goes out to dinner, goes out everywhere high and low, and that he WILL preach to me, and that I CAN'T get rid of him. He makes of me a Promethean Tommy, bound; and he is the vulture that gorges itself upon the liver of my uninstructed mind.

ON AN AMATEUR BEAT.

BY CHARLES DICKENS.

It is one of my fancies that even my idlest walk must always have its appointed destination. I set myself a task before I leave my lodging in Covent Garden on a street expedition, and should no more think of altering my route by the way, or turning back and leaving a part of it unachieved, than I should think of fraudulently violating an agreement entered into with somebody else. The other day, finding myself under this kind of obligation to proceed to Limehouse, I started punctually at noon, in compliance with the terms of the contract with myself to which my good faith was pledged.

On such an occasion, it is my habit to regard my walk as my Beat, and myself as a higher sort of Police Constable doing duty on the same. There is many a Ruffian in the streets whom I mentally collar and clear out of them, who would see mighty little of London, I can tell him, if I could deal with him physically.

Issuing forth upon this very Beat, and following with my eyes three hulking garotters on their way home,—which home I could confidently swear to be within so many yards of Drury Lane, in such a narrowed and restricted direction (though they live in their lodging quite as undisturbed as I in mine),—I went on duty with a consideration which I respectfully offer to the new Chief Commissioner,—in whom I thoroughly confide as a tried and efficient public servant. How often (thought I) have I been forced to swallow, in Police reports, the intolerable stereotyped pill of nonsense how that the Police Constable informed the worthy magistrate how that the associates of the Prisoner did at that present speaking dwell in a street or court which no man dared go down, and how that the worthy magistrate had heard of the dark reputation of such street or court, and how that our readers would doubtless remember that it was always the same street or court which was thus edifyingly discoursed about, say once a fortnight.

Now, suppose that a Chief Commissioner sent round a circular to every Division of Police employed in London, requiring instantly the names in all districts of all such much-puffed streets or courts which no man durst go down; and suppose that in such circular he gave plain warning: "If those places really exist, they are a proof of Police inefficiency which I mean to punish; and if they do not exist, but are a conventional fiction, then they are a proof of lazy tacit Police connivance with professional crime, which I also mean to punish"—what then? Fictions or realities, could they survive the touchstone of this atom of common sense? To tell us in open court, until it has become as trite a feature of news as the great gooseberry, that a costly Police system such as was never before heard of, has left in London, in the days of steam and gas and photographs of thieves and electric telegraphs, the sanctuaries and stews of the Stuarts! Why, a parity of practice, in all departments, would bring back the Plague in two summers, and the Druids in a century!

Walking faster under my share of this public injury, I overturned a wretched little creature who, clutching at the rags of a pair of trousers with one of its claws, and at its ragged hair with the other, pattered with bare feet over the muddy stones. I stopped to raise and succor this poor weeping wretch, and fifty like it, but of both sexes, were about me in a moment, begging, tumbling, fighting, clamoring, yelling, shivering in their nakedness and hunger. The piece of money I had put into the claw of the child I had overturned, was clawed out of it, and was again clawed out of that wolfish gripe, and again out of that, and soon I had no notion in what part of the obscene scuffle in the mud, of rags and legs and arms and dirt the money might be. In raising the child, I had drawn it aside out of the main thoroughfare, and this took place among some wooden hoardings and barriers and ruins of demolished buildings, hard by Temple Bar.

Unexpectedly from among them emerged a genuine Police Constable, before whom the dreadful brood dispersed in various directions, he making feints and darts in this direction and in that, and catching nothing. When all were frightened away, he took off his hat, pulled out a handkerchief from it, wiped his heated brow, and restored the handkerchief and hat to their places, with the air of a man who had discharged a great moral duty,—as indeed he had, in doing what was set down for him. I looked at him, and I looked about at the disorderly traces in the mud, and I thought of the drops of rain and the footprints of an extinct creature, hoary ages upon ages old, that geologists have identified on the face of a cliff; and this speculation came over me: If this mud could petrify at this moment, and could lie concealed here for ten thousand years, I wonder whether the race of men then to be our successors on the earth could, from these or any marks, by the utmost force of the human intellect, unassisted by tradition, deduce such an astounding inference as the existence of a polished state of society that bore with the public savagery of neglected children in the streets of its capital city and was proud of its power by sea and land, and never used its power to seize and save them.

After this, when I came to the Old Bailey and glanced up it towards Newgate, I found that the prison had an inconsistent look. There seemed to be some unlucky inconsistency in the atmosphere that day, for though the proportions of St. Paul's Cathedral, are very beautiful, it had an air of being somewhat out of drawing, in my eyes. I felt as though the cross were too high up, and perched upon the intervening golden ball too far away.

Facing eastward, I left behind me Smithfield and Old Bailey,—fire and fagot, condemned Hold, public hanging, whipping through the city at the carttail, pillory, branding-iron, and other beautiful ancestral landmarks, which rude hands have rooted up, without bringing the stars quite down upon us as yet,—and went my way upon my Beat, noting how oddly characteristic neighborhoods are divided from one another, hereabout, as though by an invisible line across the way. Here, shall cease the bankers and the money-changers; here, shall begin the shipping interest and the nautical-instrument shops; here, shall follow a scarcely perceptible flavoring of groceries and drugs; here, shall come a strong infusion of butchers; now small hosiers shall be in the ascendant; henceforth everything exposed for sale shall have its ticketed price attached. All this as if specially ordered and appointed.

A single stride at Houndsditch Church, no wider than sufficed to cross the kennel at the bottom of the Canongate, which the Debtors in Holyrood Sanctuary were wont to relieve their minds by shipping over, as Scott relates, and standing in delightful daring of Catchpoles on the free side,—a single stride, and everything is entirely changed in grain and character. West of the stride, a table, or a chest of drawers on sale shall be of mahogany and French-polished; East of the stride, it shall be of deal, smeared with a cheap counterfeit resembling lip-salve. West of the stride, a penny loaf or bun shall be compact and self-contained; East of the stride, it shall be of a sprawling and splay-footed character, as seeking to make more of itself for the money. My Beat lying round by Whitechapel Church, and the adjacent Sugar Refineries,—great buildings, tier upon tier, that have the appearance of being nearly related to the Dock-Warehouses at Liverpool,—I turned off to my right, and passing round the awkward corner on my left, came suddenly on an apparition familiar to London streets afar off.

What London peripatetic of these times has not seen the woman who has fallen forward, double, through some affection of the spine, and whose head has of late taken a turn to one side, so that it now droops over the back of one of her arms at about the wrist? Who does not know her staff, and her shawl, and her basket, as she gropes her way along, capable of seeing nothing but the pavement, never begging, never stopping, forever going somewhere on no business? How does she live, whence does she come, whither does she go, and why? I mind the time when her yellow arms were naught but bone and parchment. Slight changes steal over her, for there is a shadowy suggestion of human skin on them now. The Strand may be taken as the central point about which she revolves in a half-mile orbit. How comes she so far East as this? And coming back too! Having been how much further? She is a rare spectacle in this neighborhood. I receive intelligent information to this effect from a dog,—a lop-sided mongrel with a foolish tail, plodding along with his tail up, and his ears pricked, and displaying an amiable interest in the ways of his fellow-men,—if I may be allowed the expression. After pausing at a porkshop, he is jogging Eastward like myself, with a benevolent countenance and a watery mouth, as though musing on the many excellencies of pork, when he beholds this doubled-up bundle approaching. He is not so much astonished at the bundle (though amazed by that), as at the circumstance that it has within itself the means of locomotion. He stops, pricks his ears higher, makes a slight point, stares, utters a short, low growl, and glistens at the nose,—as I conceive with terror. The bundle continuing to approach, he barks, turns tail, and is about to fly, when, arguing with himself that flight is not becoming in a dog, he turns, and once more faces the advancing heap of clothes. After much hesitation it occurs to him that there may be a face in it somewhere. Desperately resolving to undertake the adventure and pursue the inquiry, he goes slowly up to the bundle, goes slowly round it, and coming at length upon the human countenance down there where never human countenance should be, gives a yelp of horror, and flies for the East India Docks.

Being now in the Commercial-road district of my Beat, and bethinking myself that Stepney Station is near, I quicken my pace that I may turn out of the road at that point, and see how my small Eastern Star is shining.

The Children's Hospital, to which I gave that name, is in full force. All its beds occupied. There is a new face on the bed where my pretty baby lay, and that sweet little child is now at rest forever. Much kind sympathy has been here, since my former visit, and it is good to see the walls profusely garnished with dolls. I wonder what Poodles may think of them, as they stretch out their arms above the bed, and stare, and display their splendid dresses. Poodles has a greater interest in the patients. I find him making the round of the bed, like a house-surgeon, attended by another dog,—a friend,—who appears to trot about with him in the character of his pupil dresser. Poodles is anxious to make me known to a pretty little girl, looking wonderfully healthy, who has had a leg taken off for cancer of the knee. A difficult operation, Poodles intimates, wagging his tail on the counterpane, but perfectly successful, as you see, dear Sir! The patient, patting Poodles, adds with a smile: "The leg was so much trouble to me, that I am glad it's gone." I never saw anything in doggery finer than the deportment of Poodles, when another little girl opens her mouth to show a peculiar enlargement of the tongue. Poodles (at that time on a table, to be on a level with the occasion) looks at the tongue (with his own sympathetically out), so very gravely and knowingly, that I feel inclined to put my hand in my waistcoat pocket, and give him a guinea, wrapped in paper.

On my Beat again, and close to Limehouse Church, its termination, I found myself near to certain "Lead Mills." Struck by the name, which was fresh in my memory, and finding, on inquiry, that these same Lead Mills were identical with those same Lead Mills of which I made mention when I first visited the East London Children's Hospital and its neighborhood, as Uncommercial Traveller, I resolved to have a look at them.

Received by two very intelligent gentlemen, brothers, and partners with their father in the concern, and who testified every desire to show their Works to me freely, I went over the Lead Mills. The purport of such works is the conversion of Pig Lead into White Lead. This conversion is brought about by the slow and gradual effecting of certain successive chemical changes in the lead itself. The processes are picturesque and interesting,—the most so, being the burying of the lead, at a certain stage of preparation, in pots, each pot containing a certain quantity of acid besides, and all the pots being buried in vast numbers, in layers, under tan, for some ten weeks.

Hopping up ladders and across planks and on elevated perches until I was uncertain whether to liken myself to a Bird, or a Bricklayer, I became conscious of standing on nothing particular, looking down into one of a series of large cocklofts, with the outer day peeping in through the chinks in the tiled roof above. A number of women were ascending to, and descending from, this cockloft, each carrying on the upward journey a pot of prepared lead and acid, for deposition under the smoking tan. When one layer of pots was completely filled, it was carefully covered in with planks, and those were carefully covered with tan again, and then another layer of pots was begun above; sufficient means of ventilation being preserved through wooden tubes. Going down into the cockloft then filling, I found the heat of the tan to be surprisingly great, and also the odor of the lead and acid to be not absolutely exquisite, though I believe not noxious at that stage. In other cocklofts where the pots were being exhumed, the heat of the steaming tan was much greater, and the smell was penetrating and peculiar. There were cocklofts in all stages; full and empty, half filled and half emptied; strong, active women were clambering about them busily; and the whole thing had rather the air of the upper part of the house of some immensely rich old Turk, whose faithful Seraglio were hiding his money because the Sultan or the Pasha was coming.

As is the case with most pulps or pigments, so in the instance of this White Lead, processes of stirring, separating, washing, grinding, rolling, and pressing succeed. Some of these are unquestionably inimical to health, the danger arising from inhalation of particles of lead, or from contact between the lead and the touch, or both. Against these dangers, I found good respirators provided (simply made of flannel and muslin, so as to be inexpensively renewed, and in some instances washed with scented soap), and gauntlet gloves, and loose gowns. Everywhere, there was as much fresh air as windows, well placed and opened, could possibly admit. And it was explained that the precaution of frequently changing the women employed in the worst parts of the work (a precaution originating in their own experience or apprehension of its ill effects) was found salutary. They had a mysterious and singular appearance with the mouth and nose covered, and the loose gown on, and yet bore out the simile of the old Turk and the Seraglio all the better for the disguise.

At last this vexed white lead having been buried and resuscitated, and heated, and cooled, and stirred, and separated, and washed, and ground, and rolled, and pressed, is subjected to the action of intense fiery heat. A row of women, dressed as above described, stood, let us say, in a large stone bakehouse, passing on the baking-dishes as they were given out by the cooks, from hand to hand, into the ovens. The oven or stove, cold as yet, looked as high as an ordinary house, and was full of men and women on temporary footholds, briskly passing up and stowing away the dishes. The door of another oven or stove, about to be cooled and emptied, was opened from above, for the Uncommercial countenance to peer down into. The Uncommercial countenance withdrew itself, with expedition and a sense of suffocation from the dull-glowing heat and the overpowering smell. On the whole, perhaps the going into these stoves to work when they are freshly opened, may be the worst part of the occupation.

But I made it out to be indubitable that the owners of these lead mills honestly and sedulously try to reduce the dangers of the occupation to the lowest point.

A washing-place is provided for the women (I thought there might have been more towels), and a room in which they hang their clothes, and take their meals, and where they have a good fire-range and fire, and a female attendant to help them, and to watch that they do not neglect the cleansing of their hands before touching their food. An experienced medical attendant is provided for them, and any premonitory symptoms of lead-poisoning are carefully treated. Their tea-pots and such things were set out on tables ready for their afternoon meal, when I saw their room, and it had a homely look. It is found that they bear the work much better than men; some few of them have been at it for years, and the great majority of those I observed were strong and active. On the other hand it should be remembered that most of them are very capricious and irregular in their attendance.

American inventiveness would seem to indicate that before very long White Lead may be made entirely by machinery. The sooner, the better. In the meantime, I parted from my two frank conductors over the mills, by telling them that they had nothing there to be concealed, and nothing to be blamed for. As to the rest, the philosophy of the matter of lead-poisoning and work-people seems to me to have been pretty fairly summed up by the Irish woman whom I quoted in my former paper: "Some of them gits lead-pisoned soon, and some of them gets lead-pisoned later, and some, but not many, niver, and 't is all according to the constitooshun, Sur, and some constitooshuns is strong and some is weak."

Retracing my footsteps over my Beat, I went off duty.

A FLY-LEAF IN A LIFE.

BY CHARLES DICKENS.

Once upon a time (no matter when), I was engaged in a pursuit (no matter what), which could be transacted by myself alone; in which I could have no help; which imposed a constant strain on the attention, memory, observation and physical powers; and which involved an almost fabulous amount of change of place and rapid railway travelling. I had followed this pursuit through an exceptionally trying winter in an always trying climate, and had resumed it in England after but a brief repose. Thus it came to be prolonged until, at length—and, as it seemed, all of a sudden—it so wore me out that I could not rely, with my usual cheerful confidence, upon myself to achieve the constantly recurring task, and began to feel (for the first time in my life) giddy, jarred, shaken, faint, uncertain of voice and sight and tread and touch, and dull of spirit. The medical advice I sought within a few hours, was given in two words: "Instant rest." Being accustomed to observe myself as curiously if I were another man, and knowing the advice to meet my only need, I instantly halted in the pursuit of which I speak, and rested.

My intention was, to interpose, as it were, a fly-leaf in the book of my life, in which nothing should be written from without for a brief season of a few weeks. But some very singular experiences recorded themselves on this same fly-leaf, and I am going to relate them literally. I repeat the word: literally.

My first odd experience was of the remarkable coincidence between my case, in the general mind, and one Mr. Merdle's as I find it recorded in a work of fiction called Little Dorrit. To be sure, Mr. Merdle was a swindler, forger, and thief, and my calling had been of a less harmful (and less remunerative) nature, but it was all one for that.

Here is Mr. Merdle's case :—

"At first, he was dead of all the diseases that ever were known, and several brand-new maladies invented with the speed of Light to meet the demand of the occasion. He had concealed a dropsy from infancy, he had inherited a large estate of water on the chest from his grandfather, he had had an operation performed upon him every morning of his life for eighteen years, he had been subject to the explosion of important veins in his body after the manner of fireworks, he had had something the matter with his lungs, he had had something the matter with his heart, he had had something the matter with his brain. Five hundred people who sat down to breakfast entirely uninformed on the whole subject, believed before they had done breakfast, that they privately and personally knew Physician to have said to Mr. Merdle, 'You must expect to go out, some day, like the snuff of a candle;' and that they knew Mr. Merdle to say to Physician, 'A man can die but once.' By about eleven o'clock in the forenoon, something the matter with the brain, became the favorite theory against the field; and by twelve the something had been distinctly ascertained to be 'Pressure.'

"Pressure was so entirely satisfactory to the public mind, and seemed to make every one so comfortable, that it might have lasted all day but for Bar's having taken the real state of the case into Court at half-past nine. Pressure, however, so far from being overthrown by the discovery, became a greater favorite than ever. There was a general moralizing upon Pressure in every street. All the people who had tried to make money and had not been able to do it, said, There you were! You no sooner began to devote yourself to the pursuit of wealth, than you got Pressure. The idle people improved the occasion in a similar manner. See, said they, what you brought yourself to by work, work, work! You persisted in working, you overdid it, Pressure came on, and you were done for! This consideration was very potent in many quarters, but nowhere more so than among the young clerks and partners who had never been in the slightest danger of overdoing it. These, one and all declared, quite piously, that they hoped they would never forget the warning as long as they lived, and that their conduct might be so regulated as to keep off Pressure, and preserve them, a comfort to their friends, for many years."

Just my case—if I had only known it—when I was quietly basking in the sunshine in my Kentish meadow!

But while I so rested, thankfully recovering every hour, I had experiences more odd than this. I had experiences of spiritual conceit, for which, as giving me a new warning against that curse of mankind, I shall always feel grateful to the supposition that I was too far gone to protest against playing sick lion to any stray donkey with an itching hoof. All sorts of people seemed to become vicariously religious at my expense. I received the most uncompromising warning that I was a Heathen; on the conclusive authority of a field preacher, who, like the most of his ignorant and vain and daring class, could not construct a tolerable sentence in his native tongue or pen a fair letter. This inspired individual called me to order roundly, and knew in the freest and easiest way where I was going to, and what would become of me if I failed to fashion myself on his bright example, and was on terms of blasphemous confidence with the Heavenly Host. He was in the secrets of my heart and in the lowest soundings of my soul—he!—and could read the depths of my nature better than his A B C, and could turn me inside out like his own clammy glove. But what is far more extraordinary than this—for such dirty water as this could alone be drawn from such a shallow and muddy source—I found from the information of a beneficed clergyman, of whom I never heard and whom I never saw, that I had not, as I rather supposed I had, lived a life of some reading, contemplation and inquiry; that I had not studied, as I rather supposed I had, to inculcate some Christian lessons in books;

that I had never tried, as I rather supposed I had, to turn a child or two tenderly towards the knowledge and love of our Saviour; that I had never had, as I rather supposed I had had, departed friends, or stood beside open graves; but that I had lived a life of "uninterrupted prosperity," and that I needed this "check overmuch," and that the way to turn it to account was to read these sermons and these poems enclosed, and written and issued by my correspondent! I beg it may be understood that I relate facts of my own uncommercial experience, and no vain imaginings. The documents in proof lie near my hand.

Another odd entry on the fly-leaf, of a more entertaining character, was the wonderful persistency with which kind sympathizers assumed that I had injuriously coupled with the so suddenly relinquished pursuit those personal habits of mine most obviously incompatible with it, and most plainly impossible of being maintained, along with it. As all that exercise, all that cold bathing, all that wind and weather, all that uphill training—all that everything else, say, which is usually carried about by express trains in a portmanteau and hatbox, and partaken of under a flaming row of gaslights in the company of two thousand people. This assuming of a whole case against all fact and likelihood struck me as particularly droll, and was an oddity of which I certainly had had no adequate experience in life until I turned that curious fly-leaf.

My old acquaintances the begging-letter writers came out on the fly-leaf, very piously indeed. They were glad, at such a serious crisis, to afford me another opportunity of sending that post-office order. I needn't make it a pound, as previously insisted on; ten shillings might ease my mind. And Heaven forbid that they should refuse, at such an insignificant figure, to take a weight of the memory of an erring fellow-creature! One gentleman of an artistic turn (and copiously illustrating the books of the Mendicity Society), though it might soothe my conscience in the tender respect of gifts misused, if I would immediately cash up in aid of his lowly talent for original design—as a specimen of which he enclosed me a work of art, which I recognized as a tracing from a woodcut originally published in the late Mrs. Trollope's book on America, forty or fifty years ago. The number of people who were prepared to live long years after me, untiring benefactors to their species, for fifty pounds apiece down, was astonishing. Also, of those who wanted bank-notes for stiff penitential amounts, to give away—not to keep on any account.

Divers wonderful medicines and machines insinuated recommendations of themselves in the fly-leaf that was to have been so blank. It was specially observable that every prescriber, whether in a moral or physical direction, knew me thoroughly—knew me from head to heel, in and out, through and through, upside down. I was a glass piece of general property, and everybody was on the most surprisingly intimate terms with me. A few public institutions had complimentary perceptions of corners in my mind, of which, after considerable self-examination, I have not discovered any indication. Neat little printed forms were addressed to those corners, beginning with the words: "I give and bequeath."

Will it seem exaggerative to state my belief that the most honest, the most modest, and the least vainglorious of all the records upon this strange fly-leaf, was a letter from the self-deceived discoverer of the recondite secret "how to live four or five hundred years?" Doubtless it will seem so, yet the statement is not exaggerative by any means, but is made in my serious and sincere conviction. With this, and with a laugh at the rest that shall not be cynical, I turn the fly-leaf and go on again.

A PLEA FOR TOTAL ABSTINENCE.

BY CHARLES DICKENS.

ONE day this last Whitsuntide, at precisely eleven o'clock in the forenoon, there suddenly rode into the field of view commanded by the windows of my lodging, an equestrian phenomenon. It was a fellow-creature on horseback dressed in the absurdest manner. The fellow-creature wore high boots, some other (and much larger) fellow-creature's breeches, of a slack-baked doughy color and a baggy form, a blue shirt, whereof the skirt or tail was puffily tucked into the waistband of the said breeches, no coat, a red shoulder-belt, and a demi-semi-military scarlet hat with a feathered ornament in front, which to the uninstructed human vision had the appearance of a moulting shuttlecock. I laid down the newspaper with which I had been occupied, and surveyed the fellow-man in question, with astonishment. Whether he had been sitting to any painter as a frontispiece for a new edition of Sartor Resartus; whether "the husk or shell of him," as the esteemed Herr Teufelsdroch might put it, were founded on a jockey, on a circus, on General Garibaldi, on cheap porcelain, on a toy-shop, on Guy Fawkes, on Wax-Work, on Gold Digging, on Bedlam, or on all, were doubts that greatly exercised my mind. Meanwhile my fellow-man stumbled and slided, excessively against his will, on the slippery stones of my Covent Garden street, and elicited shrieks from several sympathetic females, by convulsively restraining himself from pitching over his horse's head. In the very crisis of these evolutions, and indeed at the trying moment when his charger's tail was in a tobacconist's shop, and his head anywhere about town, this cavalier was joined by two similar portents, who, likewise stumbling and sliding, caused him to stumble and slide the more distressingly. At length this Gilpinian triumvirate effected a halt, and, looking northward, waved their three right hands as commanding unseen troops to Up, guards, and at 'em. Hereupon a brazen band burst forth, which caused them to be instantly bolted with to some remote spot of earth in the direction of the Surrey Hills.

Judging from these appearances that a procession was under way, I threw up my window, and, craning out, had the satisfaction of beholding it advancing along the street. It was a Teetotal procession, as I learnt from its banners, and was long enough to consume twenty minutes in passing. There were a great number of children in it, some of them so very young in their mothers' arms as to be in the act of practically exemplifying their abstinence from fermented liquors, and attachment to an unintoxicating drink, while the procession defiled. The display was on the whole, pleasant to see, as any good-humored holiday assemblage of clean, cheerful, and well-conducted people should be. It was bright with ribbons, tinsel, and shoulder-belts, and abounded in flowers, as if those latter trophies had come up in profusion under much watering. The day being breezy, the insubordination of the large banners was very reprehensible. Each of these being borne aloft on two poles and stayed with some half-dozen lines, was carried, as polite books in the last century used to be written, by "various hands," and the anxiety expressed in the upturned faces of those officers—something between the anxiety attendant on the balancing art, and that inseparable from the pastime of kite-flying, with a touch of the angler's quality in landing his scaly prey—much impressed me. Suddenly, too, a banner would shiver in the wind, and go about in the most inconvenient manner. This always happened oftenest with such gorgeous standards as those representing a gentleman in black corpulent with tea and water, in the laudable act of summarily reforming a family feeble and pinched with beer. The gentleman in black distended by wind would then conduct himself with the most unbecoming levity, while the beery family, growing beerier, would frantically try to tear themselves away from his ministration. Some of the inscriptions accompanying the banners were of a highly determined character, as "We never, never will give up the temperance cause," with similar sound resolutions rather suggestive to the profane mind of Mrs. Micawber's "I never will desert Mr. Micawber," and of Mr. Micawber's retort, "Really, my dear, I am not aware that you were ever required by any human being to do anything of the sort."

At intervals a gloom would fall on the passing members of the procession, for which I was at first unable to account. But this I discovered, after a little observation, to be occasioned by the coming on of the Executioners,—the terrible official beings who were to make the speeches by and by,—who were distributed in open carriages at various points of the cavalcade. A dark cloud and a sensation of dampness, as from many wet blankets, invariably preceded the rolling on of the dreadful cars containing these Headsmen, and I noticed that the wretched people who closely followed them, and who were in a manner forced to contemplate their folded arms, complacent countenances, and threatening lips, were more overshadowed by the cloud and damp than those in front. Indeed, I perceived in some of these so moody an implacability towards the magnates of the scaffold, and so plain a desire to tear them limb from limb, that I would respectfully suggest to the managers the expediency of conveying the Executioners to the scene of their dismal labors by unfrequented ways and in closely titled carts next Whitsuntide.

The procession was composed of a series of smaller processions, which had come together, each from its own metropolitan district. An infusion of Allegory became perceptible when patriotic Peckham advanced. So I judged, from the circumstance of Peckham's unfurling a silken banner that fanned heaven and earth with the words "The Peckham Life-Boat." No boat being in attendance, though life, in the likeness of "a gallant, gallant crew," in nautical uniform followed the flag, I was led to meditate on the fact that Peckham is described by geographers as an inland settlement with no larger or nearer shore line than the towing-path of the Surrey Canal, on which stormy station I had been given to understand no Life-Boat exists. Thus I deduced an allegorical meaning, and came to the conclusion that if patriotic Peckham picked a peck of pickled poetry, this *was* the peck of pickled poetry which patriotic Peckham picked.

I have observed that the aggregate procession was on the whole pleasant to see. I made use of that qualified expression with a direct meaning, which I will now explain. It involves the title of this paper, and a little fair trying of Teetotalism by its own tests.

There were many people on foot, and many people in vehicles of various kinds. The former were pleasant to see, and the latter were not pleasant to see: for the reason that I never, on any occasion or under any circumstances, have beheld heavier over-loading of horses than in this public show. Unless the imposition of a great van laden with from ten to twenty people on a single horse be a moderate tasking of the poor creature then the Temperate use of horses was immoderate and cruel. From the smallest and lightest horse to the largest and heaviest, there were many instances in which the beast of burden was so shamefully overladen, that the Society for the Prevention of Cruelty to Animals have frequently interposed in less gross cases.

Now, I have always held that there may be, and that there unquestionably is, such a thing as Use without Abuse, and that therefore the Total Abolitionists are irrational and wrong-headed. But the procession completely converted me. For so large a number of the people using draught-horses in it were clearly unable to use them without Abusing them, that I perceived Total Abstinence from Horseflesh to be the only remedy of which the case admitted. As it is all one to Teetotallers whether you take half a pint of beer or half a gallon, so it was all one here whether the beast of burden were a pony or a cart-horse. Indeed, my case had the special strength that the half-pint quadruped underwent as much suffering as the half-gallon quadruped. Moral: Total Abstinence from Horseflesh through the whole length and breadth of the scale. This Pledge will be in course of administration to all Teetotal processionists, not pedestrians, at the publishing office of ALL THE YEAR ROUND, on the first day of April, One Thousand Eight hundred and Seventy.

Observe a point for consideration. This procession comprised many persons, in their gigs, broughams, tax-carts, barouches, chaises, and what not, who were merciful to the dumb beasts that drew them, and did not overcharge their strength. What is to be done with those unoffending persons? I will not run amuck and vilify and defame them, as Teetotal tracts and platforms would most assuredly do, if the question were one of drinking instead of driving; I merely ask what is to be done with them? The reply admits of no dispute whatever. Manifestly, in strict accordance with Teetotal Doctrines, THEY must come in, too, and take the Total Abstinence from Horseflesh Pledge. It is not pretended that those members of the procession misused certain auxiliaries which in most countries and all ages have been bestowed upon man for his use, but it is undeniable that other members of the procession did. Teetotal mathematics demonstrate that the less includes the greater; that the guilty include the innocent, the blind the seeing, the deaf the hearing, the dumb the speaking, the drunken the sober. If any of the moderate users of draught-cattle in question should deem that there is any gentle violence done to their reason by these elements of logic, they are invited to come out of the procession next Whitsuntide, and look at it from my window.

FULL REPORT

OF THE FIRST MEETING OF THE MUDFOG ASSOCIATION FOR THE ADVANCEMENT OF EVERYTHING.

BY CHARLES DICKENS.

WE have made the most unparalleled and extraordinary exertions to place before our readers a complete and accurate account of the proceedings at the late grand meeting of the Mudfog Association, holden in the town of Mudfog; it affords us great happiness to lay the result before them, in the shape of various communications received from our able, talented, and graphic correspondent, expressly sent down for the purpose, who has immortalized us, himself, Mudfog, and the association, all at one and the same time. We have been, indeed, for some days unable to determine who will transmit the greatest name to posterity; ourselves, who sent our correspondent down; our correspondent, who wrote an account of the matter; or the association, who gave our correspondent something to write about. We rather incline to the opinion that we are the greatest man of the party, inasmuch as the notion of an exclusive and authentic report originated with us; this may be prejudice: it may arise from a prepossession on our part in our own favor. Be it so. We have no doubt that every gentleman concerned in this mighty assemblage is troubled with the same complaint in a greater or less degree; and it is a consolation to us to know that we have at least this feeling in common with the great scientific stars, the brilliant and extraordinary luminaries, whose speculations we record.

We give our correspondent's letters in the order in which they reached us. Any attempt at amalgamating them into one beautiful whole, would only destroy that glowing tone, that dash of wildness, and rich vein of picturesque interest, which pervade them throughout.

"*Mudfog, Monday night, seven o'clock.*

"WE are in a state of great excitement here. Nothing is spoken of, but the approaching meeting of the association. The inn-doors are thronged with waiters anxiously looking for the expected arrivals ; and the numerous bills which are wafered up in the windows of private houses, intimating that there are beds to let within, give the streets a very animated and cheerful appearance, the wafers being of a great variety of colors, and the monotony of printed inscriptions being relieved by every possible size and style of hand-writing. It is confidently rumored that Professors Snore, Doze, and Wheezy have engaged three beds and a sitting-room at the Pig and Tinder-Box. I give you the rumor as it has reached me ; but I cannot, as yet, vouch for its accuracy. The moment I have been enabled to obtain any certain information upon this interesting point, you may depend upon receiving it."

"*Half-past seven.*

"I HAVE just returned from a personal interview with the landlord of the Pig and Tinder-box. He speaks confidently of the probability of Professors Snore, Doze, and Wheezy taking up their residence at his house during the sitting of the association, but denies that the beds have been yet engaged; in which representation he is confirmed by the chambermaid,—a girl of artless manners, and interesting appearance. The boots denies that it is at all likely that Professors Snore, Doze, and Wheezy will put up here; but I have reason to believe that this man has been suborned by the proprietor of the Original Pig, which is the opposition hotel. Amidst such conflicting testimony it is difficult to arrive at the real truth; but you may depend upon receiving authentic information upon this point the moment the fact is ascertained. The excitement still continues. A boy fell through the window of the pastrycook's shop at the corner of the High-street about an hour ago, which has occasioned much confusion. The general impression is, that it was an accident. Pray Heaven it may prove so!"

"*Tuesday, noon.*

"At an early hour this morning the bells of all the churches struck seven o'clock; the effect of which, in the present lively state of the town, was extremely singular. While I was at breakfast, a yellow gig, drawn by a dark grey horse, with a patch of white over his right eyelid, proceeded at a rapid pace in the direction of the Original Pig stables; it is currently reported that this gentleman has arrived here for the purpose of attending the association, and, from what I have heard, I consider it extremely probable, although nothing decisive is yet known regarding him. You may conceive the anxiety with which we are all looking forward to the arrival of the four o'clock coach this afternoon.

"Notwithstanding the excited state of the populace, no outrage has yet been committed, owing to the admirable discipline and discretion of the police, who are nowhere to be seen. A barrel-organ is playing opposite my window, and groups of people, offering fish and vegetables for sale, parade the streets. With these exceptions everything is quiet, and I trust will continue so."

"*Five o'clock.*

"It is now ascertained beyond all doubt that Professors Snore, Doze and Wheezy will *not* repair to the Pig and Tinder-box, but have actually engaged apartments at the Original Pig. This intelligence is *exclusive;* and I leave you and your readers to draw their own inferences from it. Why Professor Wheezy, of all people in the world, should repair to the Original Pig in preference to the Pig and

Tinder-box, it is not easy to conceive. The professor is a man who should be above all such petty feelings. Some people here, openly impute treachery and a distinct breach of faith to Professors Snore and Doze; while others, again, are disposed to acquit them of any culpability in the transaction, and to insinuate that the blame rests solely with Professor Wheezy. I own that I incline to the latter opinion; and, although it gives me great pain to speak in terms of censure or disapprobation of a man of such transcendent genius, and acquirements, still I am bound to say, that if my suspicions be well founded, and if all the reports which have reached my ears be true, I really do not well know what to make of the matter.

"Mr. Slug, so celebrated for his statistical researches, arrived this afternoon by the four o'clock stage. His complexion is a dark purple, and he has a habit of sighing constantly. He looked extremely well, and appeared in high health and spirits. Mr. Woodensconse also came down in the same conveyance. The distinguished gentleman was fast asleep on his arrival, and I am informed by the guard that he had been so, the whole way. He was, no doubt, preparing for his approaching fatigues; but what gigantic visions must those be, that flit through the brain of such a man, when his body is in a state of torpidity!

"The influx of visitors increases every moment. I am told (I know not how truly) that two post-chaises have arrived at the Original Pig within the last half-hour; and I myself observed a wheelbarrow, containing three carpet-bags and a bundle, entering the yard of the Pig and Tinder-box no longer ago than five minutes since. The people are still quietly pursuing their ordinary occupations; but there is a wildness in their eyes, and an unwonted rigidity in the muscles of their countenances, which shows to the observant spectator that their expectations are strained to the very utmost pitch. I fear, unless some very extraordinary arrivals take place to-night, that consequences may arise from this popular ferment, which every man of sense and feeling would deplore."

"Twenty minutes past six.

"I HAVE just heard that the boy who fell through the pastrycook's window last night, has died of the fright. He was suddenly called upon to pay three and sixpence for the damage done, and his constitution, it seems, was not strong enough to bear up against the shock. The inquest, it is said, will be held to-morrow."

"Three-quarters past seven.

"PROFESSORS Muff and Nogo have just driven up to the hotel door; they at once ordered dinner with great condescension. We are all very much delighted with the urbanity of their manners, and the ease with which they adapt themselves to the forms and ceremonies of ordinary life. Immediately on their arrival they sent for the head-waiter, and privately requested him to purchase a live dog,—as cheap a one as he could meet with,—and to send him up after dinner, with a pie-board, a knife and fork, and a clean plate. It is conjectured that some experiments will be tried upon the dog to-night; if any particulars should transpire I will forward them by express."

"Half-past eight.

"THE animal has been procured. He is a pug-dog, of rather intelligent appearance, in good condition, and with very short legs. He has been tied to a curtain-peg in a dark room, and is howling dreadfully."

"Ten minutes to nine.

"THE dog has just been rung for. With an instinct which would appear almost the result of reason, the sagacious animal seized the waiter by the calf of the leg when he approached to take him, and made a desperate, though ineffectual resistance. I have not been able to procure admission to the apartment occupied by the scientific gentlemen; but, judging from the sounds which reached my ears when I stood upon the landing-place just now, outside the door, I should be disposed to say that the dog had retreated growling beneath some article of furniture, and was keeping the professors at bay. This conjecture is confirmed by the testimony of the ostler, who, after peeping through the keyhole, assures me that he distinctly saw Professors Nogo on his knees, holding forth a small bottle of prussic acid, to which the animal, who was crouched beneath an arm-chair, obstinately declined to smell. You cannot imagine the feverish state of irritation we are in, lest the interests of science should be sacrificed to the prejudices of a brute creature, who is not endowed with sufficient sense to foresee the incalculable benefits which the whole human race may derive from so very slight a concession on his part."

"*Nine o'clock.*

"THE dog's tail and ears have been sent down stairs to be washed; from which circumstance we infer that the animal is no more. His forelegs have been delivered to the boots to be brushed, which strengthens the supposition."

"*Half after ten.*

"MY feelings are so overpowered by what has taken place in the course of the last hour and a half, that I have scarcely strength to detail the rapid succession of events which have quite bewildered all those who are cognizant of their occurrence. It appears that the pug-dog mentioned in my last was surreptitiously obtained,—stolen, in fact,—by some person attached to the stable department, from an unmarried lady resident in this town. Frantic on discovering the loss of her favorite, the lady rushed distractedly into the street, calling in the most heart-rending and pathetic manner upon the passengers to restore her, her Augustus,—for so the deceased was named, in affectionate remembrance of a former lover of his mistress, to whom he bore a striking personal resemblance, which renders the circumstance additionally affecting. I am not yet in a condition to inform you what circumstances induced the bereaved lady to direct her steps to the hotel which had witnessed the last struggles of her *protegé.* I can only state that she arrived there, at the very instant when his detached members were passing through the passage on a small tray. Her shrieks still reverberate in my ears! I grieve to say that the expressive features of Professor Muff were much scratched and lacerated by the injured lady; and that Professor Nogo, besides sustaining several severe bites, has lost some handfuls of hair from the same cause. It must be some consolation to these gentlemen to know that their ardent attachment to scientific pursuits has alone occasioned these unpleasant consequences; for which the sympathy of a grateful country will sufficiently reward them. The unfortunate lady remains at the Pig and Tinder-box, and up to this time is reported in a very pecarious state.

"I need scarcely tell you that this unlooked-for catastrophe has cast a damp and gloom upon us in the midst of our exhilaration; natural in any case, but greatly enhanced in this, by the amiable qualities of the deceased amimal, who appears to have been much and deservedly respected by the whole of his acquaintance."

"*Twelve o'clock.*

"I TAKE the last opportunity before sealing my parcel to inform you that the boy who fell through the pastrycook's window is not dead, as was universally believed, but alive and well. The report appears to have had its origin in his mysterious disappearance. He was found half an hour since on the premises of a sweet-stuff maker, where a raffle had been announced for a second-hand seal-skin cap and a tambourine; and where—a sufficient number of members not having been obtained at first—he had patiently waited until the list was completed. This fortunate discovery has in some degree restored our gayety and cheerfulness. It is proposed to get up a subscription for him without delay.

"Everybody is nervously anxious to see what to-morrow will bring forth. If any one should arrive in the course of the night, I have left strict directions to be called immediately. I should have sat up, indeed, but the agitating events of this day have been too much for me.

"No news yet, of either of the Professors Snore, Doze, or Wheezy. It is very strange!"

"*Wednesday afternoon.*

"ALL is now over: and, upon one point at least, I am at length enabled to set the minds of your readers at rest. The three professors arrived at ten minutes after two o'clock, and, instead of taking up their quarters at the Original Pig, as it was universally understood in the course of yesterday that they would assuredly have done, drove straight to the Pig and Tinder-box, where they threw off the mask at once, and openly announced their intention of remaining. Professor Wheezy *may* reconcile this very extraordinary conduct with *his* notions of fair and equitable dealing, but I would recommend Professor Wheezy to be cautious how he presumes too far upon his well-earned reputation. How such a man as Professor Snore, or, which is still more extraordinary, such an individual as Professor Doze, can quietly allow himself to be mixed up with such proceedings as these, you will naturally inquire. Upon this head, rumor is silent; I have my speculations, but forbear to give utterance to them just now."

"*Four o'clock.*

"THE town is filling fast; eighteenpence has been offered for a bed and refused. Several gentlemen were under the necessity last night of sleeping in the brick-fields, and on the steps of doors, for which they were taken before the magistrates in a body this morning, and committed to prison as vagrants for various terms. One of these persons I understand to be a highly-respectable tinker, of great practical skill, who had forwarded a paper to the president of Section D, Mechanical Science, on the construction of pipkins with copper bottoms and safety-valves, of which report speaks highly. The incarceration of this gentleman is greatly to be regretted, as his absence will preclude any discussion on the subject.

"The bills are being taken down in all directions, and lodgings are being secured on almost any terms. I have heard of fifteen shillings a week for two rooms, exclusive of coals and attendance, but I can scarcely believe it. The excitement is dreadful. I was informed this morning that the civil authorities, apprehensive of some outbreak of popular feeling, had commanded a recruiting sergeant and two corporals to be under arms; and that, with the view of not irritating the people unnecessarily by their presence, they had been requested to take up their position before daybreak in a turnpike, distant about a quarter of a mile from the town. The vigor and promptness of these measures cannot be too highly extolled.

"Intelligence has just been brought me, that an elderly female, in a state of inebriety, has declared in the open street her intention to 'do' for Mr. Slug. Some statistical returns compiled by that gentleman, relative to the consumption of raw spirituous liquors in this place, are supposed to be the cause of the wretch's animosity. It is added, that this declaration was loudly cheered by a crowd of persons who had assembled on the spot; and that one man had the boldness to designate Mr. Slug aloud by the opprobrious epithet of 'Stick-in-the-mud!' It is earnestly to be hoped that now, when the moment has arrived for their interference, the magistrates will not shrink from the exercise of that power which is vested in them by the constitution of our common country."

"*Half-past ten.*

"THE disturbance, I am happy to inform you, has been completely quelled, and the ringleader taken into custody. She had a pail of cold water thrown over her, previous to being locked up and expresses great contrition and uneasiness. We are all in a fever of anticipation about to-morrow; but, now that we are within a few hours of the meeting of the association, and at last enjoy the proud consciousness of having its illustrious members amongst us, I trust and hope everything may go off peaceably. I shall send you a full report of to-morrow's proceedings by the night coach."

"*Eleven o'clock.*

"I OPEN my letter to say that nothing whatever has occurred since I folded it up."

"*Thursday.*

"THE sun rose this morning at the usual hour. I did not observe anything particular in the aspect of the glorious planet, except that he appeared to me (it might have been a delusion of my heightened fancy) to shine with more than common brilliancy, and to shed a refulgent lustre upon the town, such as I had never observed before. This is the more extraordinary, as the sky was perfectly cloudless, and the atmosphere peculiarly fine. At half-past nine o'clock the general committee assembled, with the last year's president in the chair. The report of the council was read; and one passage, which stated that the council had corresponded with no less than three thousand five hundred and seventy-one persons, (all of whom paid their own postage,) on no fewer than seven thousand two hundred and forty-three topics, was received with a degree of enthusiasm which no effort could suppress. The various committees and sections having been appointed, and the mere formal business transacted, the great proceedings of the meeting commenced at eleven o'clock precisely. I had the happiness of occupying a most eligible position at that time, in

"SECTION A.—ZOOLOGY AND BOTANY.

"GREAT ROOM, PIG AND TINDER-BOX.

"PRESIDENT—PROFESSOR SNORE. VICE-PRESIDENTS—

"PROFESSORS DOZE AND WHEEZY.

"The scene at this moment was particularly striking. The sun streamed through the windows of the apartments, and tinted the whole scene with its brilliant rays, bringing out in strong relief the noble visages of the professors and scientific gentlemen, who, some with bald heads, some with red heads, some with brown heads, some with grey heads, some with black heads, some with block heads, presented a *coup-d'œil* which no eye-witness will readily forget. In front of these gentlemen were papers and inkstands; and round the room, on elevated benches extending as far as the forms could reach, were assembled a brilliant concourse of those lovely and elegant women for which Mudfog is justly acknowledged to be without a rival in the whole world. The contrast between their fair faces and the dark coats and trousers of the scientific gentlemen I shall never cease to remember while Memory holds her seat.

"Time having been allowed for a slight confusion, occasioned by the falling down of the greater part of the platforms, to subside, the president called on one of the secretaries to read a communication entitled, 'Some remarks on the industrious fleas, with considerations on the importance of establishing infant schools among that numerous class of society; of directing their industry to useful and practical ends; and of applying the surplus fruits thereof, towards providing for them a comfortable and respectable maintenance in their old age.'

"The Author stated, that, having long turned his attention to the moral and social condition of these interesting animals, he had been induced to visit an exhibition in Regent street, London, commonly known by the designation of 'The Industrious Fleas.' He had there seen many fleas, occupied certainly in various pursuits and avocations, but occupied, he was bound to add, in a manner which no man of well-regulated mind could fail to regard with sorrow and regret. One flea, reduced to the level of a beast of burden, was drawing about a miniature gig, containing a particularly small effigy of his Grace the Duke of Wellington; while another was staggering beneath the weight of a golden model of his great adversary Napoleon Bonaparte. Some brought up as mountebanks and ballet-dancers, were performing a figure-dance (he regretted to observe, that, of the fleas so employed, several were females); others were in training, in a small card-board box, for pedestrians,—mere sporting characters—and two were actually engaged in the cold-blooded and barbarous occupation of duelling; a pursuit from which humanity recoiled with horror and disgust. He suggested that measures should be immediately taken to employ the labor of these fleas as part and parcel of the productive power of the country, which might easily be done by the establishment among them of infant schools and houses of industry, in which a system of virtuous education, based upon sound principles, should be observed, and moral precepts strictly inculcated. He proposed that every flea who presumed to exhibit, for hire, music or dancing, or any species of theatrical entertainment, without a license, should be considered a vagabond, and treated accordingly; in which respect he only placed him upon a level with the rest of mankind. He would further suggest that their labor should be placed under the control and regulation of the State, who should set apart from the profits, a fund for the support of superannuated or disabled fleas, their widows and orphans. With this view, he proposed that liberal premiums should be offered for the three best designs for a general almshouse; from which—as insect architecture was well known to be in a very advanced and perfect state—we might possibly derive many valuable hints for the improvement of our metropolitan universities, national galleries, and other public edifices.

"The President wished to be informed how the ingenious gentleman proposed to open a communication with fleas generally, in the first instance, so that they might be thoroughly imbued with a sense of the advantages they must necessarily derive from changing their mode of life, and apply themselves to honest labor. This appeared to him, the only difficulty.

"The Author submitted that this difficulty was easily overcome, or rather that there was no difficulty at all in the case. Obviously the course to be pursued, if her Majesty's government could be prevailed upon to take up the plan, would be, to secure at a remunerative salary the individual to whom he had alluded as presiding over the exhibition in Regent street at the period of his visit. That gentleman would at once be able to put himself in communication with the mass of the fleas, and to instruct them in pursuance of some general plan of education, to be sanctioned by Parliament, until such time as the more intelligent among them were advanced enough to officiate as teachers to the rest.

"The President and several members of the section highly complimented the author of the paper last read, on his most ingenious and important treatise. It was determined that the subject should be recommended to the immediate consideration of the council.

"Mr. Wigsby produced a cauliflower somewhat larger than a chaise-umbrella, which had been raised by no other artificial means than the simple application of highly carbonated soda-water as manure. He explained that by scooping out the head, which would afford a new and delicious species of nourishment for the poor, a parachute, in principle something similar to that constructed by M. Garnerin, was at once obtained: the stalk of course being kept downwards. He added that he was perfectly willing to make a descent from a height of not less than three miles and a quarter; and had in fact already proposed the same to the proprietors of the Vauxhall Gardens, who in the handsomest manner at once consented to his wishes, and appointed an early day next summer for the undertaking; merely stipulating that the rim of the cauliflower should be previously broken in three or four places to ensure the safety of the descent.

"The PRESIDENT congratulated the public on the *grand gala* in store for them, and warmly eulogized the proprietors of the establishment alluded to, for their love of science, and regard for the safety of human life, both of which did them the highest honor.

"A Member wished to know how many thousand additional lamps the royal property would be illuminated with, on the night after the descent.

"MR. WIGSBY replied that the point was not yet finally decided; but he believed it was proposed, over and above the ordinary illuminations, to exhibit in various devices eight millions and a half of additional lamps.

"The Member expressed himself much gratified with this announcement.

"MR. BLUNDERUM delighted the section with a most interesting and valuable paper 'on the last moments of the learned pig,' which produced a very strong impression upon the assembly, the account being compiled from the personal recollections of his favorite attendant. The account stated in the most emphatic terms that the animal's name was not Toby, but Solomon; and distinctly proved that he could have no near relatives in the profession, as many designing persons had falsely stated, inasmuch as his father, mother, brothers and sisters, had all fallen victims to the butcher at different times. An uncle of his, indeed, had with very great labor been traced to a sty in Somers Town; but as he was in a very infirm state at the time, being afflicted with measles, and shortly afterwards disappeared, there appeared too much reason to conjecture that he had been converted into sausages. The disorder of the learned pig was originally a severe cold, which, being aggravated by excessive trough indulgence, finally settled upon the lungs, and terminated in a general decay of the constitution. A melancholy instance of a presentiment entertained by the animal of his approaching dissolution, was recorded. After gratifying a numerous and fashionable company with his performances, in which no falling-off whatever, was visible, he fixed his eyes on the biographer, and, turning to the watch which lay on the floor, and on which he was accustomed to point out the hour, deliberately passed his snout twice round the dial. In precisely four-and-twenty hours from that time he had ceased to exist!

"PROFESSOR WHEEZY inquired whether, previous to his demise, the animal had expressed, by signs or otherwise, any wishes regarding the disposal of his little property.

"MR. BLUNDERUM replied, that, when the biographer took up the pack of cards at the conclusion of the performance, the animal grunted several times in a significant manner, and nodded his head as he was accustomed to do, when gratified. From these gestures it was understood that he wished the attendant to keep the cards, which he had ever since done. He had not expressed any wish relative to his watch, which had accordingly been pawned by the same individual.

"The PRESIDENT wished to know whether any member of the section had ever seen or conversed with the pig-faced lady, who was reported to have worn a black velvet mask, and to have taken her meals from a golden trough.

"After some hesitation a member replied that the pig-faced lady was his mother-in-law, and that he trusted the president would not violate the sanctity of private life.

"The PRESIDENT begged pardon. He had considered the pig-faced lady a public character. Would the honorable member object to state, with a view to the advancement of science, whether she was in any way connected with the learned pig?

"The member replied in the same low tone, that, as the question appeared to involve a suspicion that the learned pig might be his half-brother, he must decline answering it.

"SECTION B.—ANATOMY AND MEDICINE.

"COACH-HOUSE, PIG AND TINDER-BOX.

"PRESIDENT—DR. TOORELL. VICE-PRESIDENTS—PROFESSORS MUFF AND NOGO.

"DR. KUTANKUMAGEN (of Moscow) read to the section a report of a case which had occurred within his own practice, strikingly illustrative of the power of medicine, as exemplified in his successful treatment of a virulent disorder. He had been called in to visit the patient on the 1st of April, 1837. He was then laboring under symptoms peculiarly alarming to any medical man. His frame was stout and muscular, his step firm and elastic, his cheeks plump and red, his voice loud, his appetite good, his pulse full and round. He was in the constant habit of eating three meals *per diem*, and of drinking at least one bottle of wine, and one glass of spirituous liquors diluted with water, in the course of the four-and-twenty hours. He laughed constantly, and in so hearty a manner that it was terrible to hear him. By dint of powerful medicine, low diet and bleeding, the symptoms in the course of three days perceptibly decreased. A rigid perseverance in the same course of treatment for only one week, accompanied with small doses of water-gruel, weak broth, and barley water, led to their entire disappearance. In the course of a month he was sufficiently recovered to be carried down stairs by two nurses, and to enjoy an airing in a close carriage, supported by soft pillows. At the present moment he was restored so far as to walk about, with the slight assistance of a crutch and a boy. It would perhaps be gratifying to the section to learn that he ate little, drank little, slept little, and was never heard to laugh by any accident whatever.

"DR. W. R. FEE, in complimenting the honorable member upon the triumphant cure he had effected, begged to ask whether the patient still bled freely?

"DR. KUTANKUMAGEN replied in the affirmative.

"DR. W. R. FEE.—And you found that he bled freely during the whole course of the disorder?

"DR. KUTANKUMAGEN.—Oh dear, yes; most freely.

"DR. NEESHAWTS supposed, that if the patient had not submitted to be bled with great readiness and perseverance, so extraordinary a cure could never, in fact, have been accomplished. Dr. Kutankumagen rejoined, certainly not.

"MR KNIGHT BELL (M. R. C. S.) exhibited a wax preparation of the interior of a gentleman who in early life had inadvertently swallowed a door-key. It was a curious fact that a medical student of dissipated habits, being present at the *post mortem* examination, found means to escape unobserved from the room, with that portion of the coats of the stomach upon which an exact model of the instrument was distinctly impressed, with which he hastened to a locksmith of doubtful character, who made a new key from the pattern so shown to him. With this key the medical student entered the house of the deceased gentleman, and committed a burglary to a large amount, for which he was subsequently tried and executed.

"The PRESIDENT wished to know what became of the original key after the lapse of years. Mr. Knight Bell replied that the gentleman was always much accustomed to punch, and it was supposed the acid had gradually devoured it.

"DR. NEESHAWTS and several of the members were of opinion that the key must have lain very cold and heavy upon the gentleman's stomach.

"MR. KNIGHT BELL believed it did at first. It was worthy of remark, perhaps, that for some years the gentleman was troubled with night-mare, under the influence of which, he always imagined himself a wine-cellar door.

"PROFESSOR MUFF related a very extraordinary and convincing proof of the wonderful efficacy of the system of infinitesimal doses, which the section were doubtless aware was based upon the theory that the very minutest amount of any given drug, properly dispersed through the human frame, would be productive of precisely the same result as a very large dose administered in the usual manner. Thus, the fortieth part of a grain of calomel was supposed to be equal to a five-grain calomel pill, and so on in proportion throughout the whole range of medicine. He had tried the experiment in a curious manner upon a publican who had been brought into the hospital with a broken head, and was cured upon the infinitesimal system in the incredibly short space of three months. This man was a hard drinker. He (Professor Muff) had dispersed three drops of rum through a bucket of water, and requested the man to drink the whole. What was the result? Before he had drunk a quart, he was in a state of beastly intoxication; and five other men were made dead-drunk with the remainder.

"The PRESIDENT wished to know whether an infinitesimal dose of soda water would have recovered them? Professor Muff replied that the twenty-fifth part of a tea-spoonful, properly administered to each patient would have sobered him immediately. The President remarked that this was a most important discovery, and he hoped the Lord Mayor and Court of Aldermen would patronize it immediately.

"A Member begged to be informed whether it would be possible to administer—say, the twentieth part of a grain of bread and cheese to all grown-up paupers, and the fortieth part to children, with the same satisfying effect as their present allowance.

"PROFESSOR MUFF was willing to stake his professional reputation on the perfect adequacy of such a quantity of food to the support of human life—in workhouses; the addition of the fifteenth part of a grain of pudding twice a week, would render it a high diet.

"PROFESSOR NOGO called the attention of the section to a very extraordinary case of animal magnetism. A private watchman, being merely looked at by the operator from the opposite side of a wide street, was at once observed to be in a very drowsy and languid state. He was followed to his box, and being once slightly rubbed on the palms of the hands, fell into a sound sleep, in which he continued without intermission for ten hours.

"SECTION C.—STATISTICS.

"HAY-LOFT, ORIGINAL PIG.

"PRESIDENT—MR. WOODENSCONSE. VICE-PRESIDENTS—MR. LEDBRAIN AND MR. TIMBERED.

"MR. SLUG stated to the section the result of some calculations he had made with great difficulty and labor, regarding the state of infant education among the middle classes of London. He found that, within a circle of three miles from the Elephant and Castle, the following were the names and numbers of children's books principally in circulation:—

"Jack the Giant-killer	7,943
Ditto and Bean-stalk	8,621
Ditto and Eleven Brothers	2,845
Ditto and Jill	1,998
Total	21,407

"He found that the proportion of Robinson Crusoes to Philip Quarls was as four and a half to one; and that the preponderance of Valentine and Orsons over Goody Two Shoeses was as three and an eighth of the former to half a one of the latter: a comparison of Seven Champions with Simple Simons gave the same result. The ignorance that prevailed, was lamentable. One child, on being asked whether he would rather be Saint George of England or a respectable tallow-chandler, instantly replied, 'Taint George of Ingling.' Another, a little boy of eight years old, was found to be firmly impressed with a belief in the existence of dragons, and openly stated that it was his intention when he grew up, to rush forth sword in hand for the deliverance of captive princesses, and the promiscuous slaughter of giants. Not one child among the number interrogated had ever heard of Mungo Park,—some inquiring whether he was at all connected with the black man that swept the crossing; and others whether he was in any way related to the Regent's Park. They had not the slightest conception of the commonest principles of mathematics, and considered Sinbad the Sailor the most enterprising voyager that the world had ever produced.

"A Member strongly deprecating the use of all the other books mentioned, suggested that Jack and Jill might perhaps be exempted from the general censure, inasmuch as the hero and heroine, in the very outset of the tale, were depicted as going *up* a hill to fetch a pail of water, which was a laborious and useful occupation,—supposing the family linen was being washed, for instance.

" MR. SLUG feared that the moral effect of this passage was more than counterbalanced by another in a subsequent part of the poem, in which very gross allusion was made to the mode in which the heroine was personally chastised by her mother

" 'For laughing at Jack's disaster;'

besides, the whole work had this one great fault, *it was not true*.

" The PRESIDENT complimented the honorable member on the excellent distinction he had drawn. Several other members, too, dwelt upon the immense and urgent necessity of storing the minds of children with nothing but facts and figures; which process the President very forcibly remarked, had made them (the section) the men they were.

"MR. SLUG then stated some curious calculations respecting the dogs'-meat barrows of London. He found that the total number of small carts and barrows engaged in dispensing provisions to the cats and dogs of the metropolis, was one thousand seven hundred and forty-three. The average number of skewers delivered daily with the provender, by each dogs'-meat cart or barrow was thirty-six. Now, multiplying the number of skewers so delivered, by the number of barrows, a total of sixty-two thousand seven hundred and forty-eight skewers daily would be obtained. Allowing that, of these sixty-two thousand seven hundred and forty-eight skewers, the odd two thousand seven hundred and forty-eight were accidentally devoured with the meat, by the most voracious of the animals supplied, it followed that sixty thousand skewers per day, or the enormous number of twenty-one millions nine hundred thousand skewers annually, were wasted in the kennels and dust-holes of London; which, if collected and warehoused, would in ten years' time afford a mass of timber more than sufficient for the construction of a first-rate vessel of war for the use of her majesty's navy, to be called 'The Royal Skewer,' and to become under that name the terror of all the enemies of this island.

"MR. X. LEDBRAIN read a very ingenious communication, from which it appeared that the total number of legs belonging to the manufacturing population of one great town in Yorkshire was, in round numbers, forty thousand, while the total number of chair and stool legs in their houses was only thirty thousand, which, upon the very favorable average of three legs to a seat, yielded only ten thousand seats in all. From this calculation it would appear,—not taking wooden or cork legs into the account, but allowing two legs to every person,—that ten thousand individuals (one-half of the whole population) were either destitute of any rest for their legs at all, or passed the whole of their leisure time in sitting upon boxes.

"SECTION D.—MECHANICAL SCIENCE.

"COACH HOUSE, ORIGINAL PIG.

"PRESIDENT—MR. CARTER. VICE-PRESIDENTS MR. TRUCK AND MR. WAGHORN.

"PROFESSOR QUEERSPECK exhibited an elegant model of a portable railway, neatly mounted in a green case, for the waistcoat pocket. By attaching this beautiful instrument to his boots, any Bank or public-office clerk could transport himself from his place of residence to his place of business, at the easy rate of sixty-five miles an hour, which, to gentlemen of sedentary pursuits, would be an incalculable advantage.

"THE PRESIDENT was desirous of knowing whether it was necessary to have a level surface on which the gentleman was to run.

"PROFESSOR QUEERSPECK explained that City gentlemen would run in trains, being handcuffed together to prevent confusion or unpleasantness. For instance, trains would start every morning at eight, nine, and ten o'clock, from Camden Town, Islington, Camberwell, Hackney, and various other places in which City gentlemen are accustomed to reside. It would be necessary to have a level, but he had provided for this difficulty by proposing that the best line that the circumstances would admit of, should be taken through the sewers which undermine the streets of the metropolis, and which, well lighted by jets from the gas-pipes which run immediately above them, would form a pleasant and commodious arcade, especially in winter-time, when the inconvenient custom of carrying umbrellas, now general, could be wholly dispensed with. In reply to another question, Professor Queerspeck stated that no substitute for the purposes to which these arcades were at present devoted had yet occurred to him, but that he hoped no fanciful objection on this head would be allowed to interfere with so great an undertaking.

"MR. JOBBA produced a forcing-machine on a novel plan, for bringing joint-stock railway shares prematurely to a premium. The instrument was in the form of an elegant gilt weather glass of most dazzling appearance, and was worked behind, by strings, after the manner of a pantomime trick, the strings being always pulled by the directors of of the company to which the machine belonged. The quicksilver was so ingeniously placed, that when the acting directors held shares in their pockets, figures denoting very small expenses and very large returns appeared upon the glass; but the moment the directors parted with these pieces of paper, the estimate of needful expenditure suddenly increased itself to an immense extent, while the statements of certain profits became reduced in the same proportion. Mr. Jobba stated that the machine had been in constant requisition for some months past, and he had never once known it to fail.

"A Member expressed his opinion that it was extremely neat and pretty. He wished to know whether it was not liable to accidental derangement? Mr. Jobba said that the whole machine was undoubtedly liable to be blown up, but that was the only objection to it.

"PROFESSOR NOGO arrived from the anatomical section to exhibit a model of a safety fire-escape, which could be fixed at any time, in less than half an hour, and by means of which, the youngest or most infirm persons (successfully resisting the progress of the flames until it was quite ready) could be preserved if they merely balanced themselves for a few minutes on the sill of their bed-room window, and got into the escape without falling into the street. The Professor stated that the number of boys who had been rescued in the day-time by this machine from houses which were not on fire, was almost incredible. Not a conflagration had occurred in the whole of London for many months past to which the escape had not been carried on the very next day, and put in action before a concourse of persons.

"THE PRESIDENT inquired whether there was not some difficulty in ascertaining which was the top of the machine, and which the bottom, in cases of pressing emergency?

"PROFESSOR NOGO explained that of course it could not be expected to act quite as well when there was a fire, as when there was not a fire; but in the former case he thought it would be of equal service whether the top were up or down."

With the last section, our correspondent concludes his most able and faithful report, which will never cease to reflect credit upon him for his scientific attainments, and upon us for our enterprising spirit. It is needless to take a review of the subjects which have been discussed; of the mode in which they have been examined; of the great truths which they have elicited. They are now before the world, and we leave them to read, to consider, and to profit.

The place of meeting for next year has undergone discussion, and has at length been decided; regard being had to, and evidence being taken upon, the goodness of its wines, the supply of its markets, the hospitality of its inhabitants, and the quality of its hotels. We hope at this next meeting our correspondent may again be present, and that we may be once more the means of placing his communications before the world. Until that period we have been prevailed upon to allow this number of our Miscellany to be retailed to the public, or wholesaled to the trade, without any advance upon our usual price.

We have only to add, that the committees are now broken up, and that Mudfog is once again restored to its accustomed tranquillity,—that Professors and Members have had balls, and *soirées*, and suppers, and great mutual complimentations, and have at length dispersed to their several homes,—whither all good wishes and joys attend them, until next year!

FULL REPORT

OF THE SECOND MEETING OF THE MUDFOG ASSOCIATION FOR THE ADVANCEMENT OF EVERYTHING.

BY CHARLES DICKENS.

In October last, we did ourselves the immortal credit of recording, at an enormous expense, and by dint of exertions unparalleled in the history of periodical publications, the proceedings of the Mudfog Association for the advancement of Everything, which in that month held its first great half-yearly meeting, to the wonder and delight of the whole empire. We announced at the conclusion of that extraordinary and most remarkable Report, that when the Second Meeting of the Society should take place we should be found again at our post renewing our gigantic and spirited endeavors, and once more making the world ring with the accuracy, authenticity, immeasurable superiority, and intense remarkability of our account of its proceedings. In redemption of this pledge, we caused to be despatched per steam to Oldcastle, at which place this second meeting of the Society was held on the 20th instant, the same superhumanly-endowed gentleman who furnished the former report, and who,—gifted by nature with transcendent abilities, and furnished by us with a body of assistants scarcely inferior to himself,—has forwarded a series of letters, which for faithfulness of description, power of language, fervor of thought, happiness of expression, and importance of subject-matter, have no equal in the epistolary literature of any age or country. We give this gentleman's correspondence entire, and in the order in which it reached our office.

"*Saloon of Steamer, Thursday night, half-past eight.*

"When I left New Burlington street this evening in the hackney cabriolet, number four thousand two hundred and eighty-five, I experienced sensations as novel as they were oppressive. A sense of importance of the task I had undertaken, a consciousness that I was leaving London, and stranger still, going somewhere else, a feeling of loneliness and a sensation of jolting quite bewildered my thoughts and for a time rendered me even insensible to the presence of my carpet-bag and hat-box. I shall ever feel grateful to the driver of a Blackwall omnibus, who, by thrusting the pole of his vehicle through the small door of the cabriolet, awakened me from a tumult of imaginings that are wholly indescribable. But of such materials is our imperfect nature composed !

"I am happy to say that I am the first passenger on board and shall thus be enabled to give you an account of all that happens in the order of its occurrence. The chimney is smoking a good deal and so are the crew; and the captain, I am informed, is very drunk in a little house upon the deck, something like a black turnpike. I should infer from all I hear that he has got the steam up.

"You will readily guess with what feelings I have just made the discovery that my berth is in the same closet with those engaged by Professor Woodensconce, Mr. Slug, and Professor Grime. Professor Woodensconce has taken the shelf above me, and Mr. Slug and Professor Grime the two shelves opposite. Their luggage has already arrived. On Mr. Slug's bed is a long tin tube of about three inches in diameter, carefully closed at both ends. What can this contain? Some powerful instrument of a new construction doubtless."

"*Ten minutes past nine.*

"NOBODY has yet arrived, nor has anything fresh come in my way except several joints of beef and mutton, from which I conclude that a good plain dinner has been provided for tomorrow. There is a singular smell below, which gave me some uneasiness at first; but as the steward says it is always there, and never goes away, I am quite comfortable again. I learn from this man that the different sections will be distributed at the Black Boy and Stomach-ache, and the Boot-jack and Countenance. If this intelligence be true, and I have no reason to doubt it, your readers will draw such conclusions as their different opinions may suggest.

"I write down these remarks as they occur to me, or as the facts come to my knowledge, in order that my first impressions may lose nothing of their original vividness. I shall despatch them in small packets as opportunities arise."

"*Half-past nine.*

"SOME dark object has just appeared upon the wharf. I think it is a travelling carriage."

"*A quarter to ten.*

"No, it isn't."

"*Half-past ten.*

"THE passengers are pouring in every instant. Four omnibusesful have just arrived upon the wharf, and all is bustle and activity. The noise and confusion are very great. Cloths are laid in the cabins, and the steward is placing blue platesfull of knobs of cheese at equal distances down the centre of the tables. He drops a great many knobs; but being used to it, picks them up again with great dexterity, and after wiping them on his sleeve, throws them back into the plates. He is a young man of exceedingly prepossessing appearance,—either dirty or a mulatto, but I think the former.

"An interesting old gentleman who came to the wharf in an omnibus has just quarrelled violently with the porters, and is staggering towards the vessel with a large trunk in his arms. I trust and hope that he may reach it in safety; but the board he has to cross is narrow and slippery. Was that a splash? Gracious powers!

"I have just returned from the deck. The trunk is standing upon the extreme brink of the wharf, but the old gentleman is nowhere to be seen. The watchman is not sure whether he went down or not, but promises to drag for him the first thing to-morrow morning. May his humane efforts prove successful!

"Professor Nogo has this moment arrived with his nightcap on under his hat. He has ordered a glass of cold brandy and water, with a hard biscuit and a basin, and has gone straight to bed. What can this mean?

"The three other scientific gentlemen to whom I have already alluded have come on board, and have all tried their beds, with the exception of Professor Woodensconce, who sleeps in one of the top ones, and can't get into it. Mr. Slug, who sleeps in the other top one, is unable to get out of his, and is to have his supper handed up by a boy. I have had the honor to introduce myself to these gentlemen, and we have amicably arranged the order in which we shall retire to rest; which it is necessary to agree upon, because although the cabin is very comfortable, there is not room for more than one gentleman to be out of bed at a time, and even he must take his boots off in the passage.

"As I anticipated, the knobs of cheese were provided for the passengers' supper, and are now in course of consumption. Your readers will be surprised to hear that Professor Woodensconce has abstained from cheese for eight years, although he takes butter in considerable quantities. Professor Grime having lost several teeth, is unable I observe to eat his crusts without previously soaking them in his bottled porter. How interesting are these peculiarities!"

"*Half-past eleven.*

"PROFESSORS WOODENSCONCE and Grime, with a degree of good humor that delights us all, have just arranged to toss for a bottle of mulled port. There has been some discussion whether the payment should be decided by the first toss or the best out of three. Eventually the latter course has been determined on. Deeply do I wish that both gentlemen could win; but that being impossible, I own that my personal aspirations, I speak as an individual, and do not compromise either you or your readers by this expression of feeling, are with Professor Woodensconce. I have backed that gentleman to the amount of eighteenpence."

"*Twenty minutes to twelve.*

"PROFESSOR GRIME has inadvertently tossed his half-crown out of one of the cabin-windows, and it has been arranged the steward shall toss for him. Bets are offered on any side to any amount, but there are no takers.

"Professor Woodensconce has just called 'woman;' but the coin having lodged in a beam is a long time coming down again. The interest and suspense of this one moment are beyond anything that can be imagined."

"*Twelve o'clock.*

"THE mulled port is smoking on the table before me, and Professor Grime has won. Tossing is a game of chance; but on every ground, whether of public or private character, intellectual endowments, or scientific attainments, I cannot help expressing my opinion that Professor Woodensconce *ought* to have come off victorious. There is an exultation about Professor Grime incompatible I fear with greatness."

"*A quarter past twelve.*

"PROFESSOR GRIME continues to exult, and to boast of his victory in no very measured terms, observing that he always does win, and that he knew it would be a 'head' before hand, with many other remarks of a similar nature. Surely this gentleman is not so lost to every feeling of decency and propriety as not to feel and know the superiority of Professor Woodensconce. Is Professor Grime insane? or does he wish to be reminded in plain language of his true position in society, and the precise level of his acquirements and abilities? Professor Grime will do well to look to this."

"*One o'clock.*

"I AM writing in bed. The small cabin is illuminated by the feeble light of a flickering lamp suspended from the ceiling; Professor Grime is lying on the opposite shelf on the broad of his back, with his mouth wide open The scene is indescribably solemn. The ripple of the tide, the noise of the sailors' feet over-head, the gruff voices on the river, the dogs on the shore, the snoring of the passengers, and a constant creaking of every plank in the vessel, are the only sounds that meet the ear. With these exceptions, all is profound silence.

"My curiosity has been within the last moment very much excited. Mr. Slug, who lies above Professor Grime, has cautiously withdrawn the curtains of his berth, and after looking anxiously out, as if to satisfy himself that his companions are asleep, has taken up the tin tube of which I have before spoken, and is regarding it with great interest. What rare mechanical combinations can be obtained in that mysterious case? It is evidently a profound secret to all."

"*A quarter past one.*

"THE behavior of Mr. Slug grows more and more mysterious. He has unscrewed the top of the tube, and now renews his observation upon his companions; evidently to make sure that he is wholly unobserved. He is clearly on the eve of some great experiment. Pray heaven that it be not a dangerous one; but the interests of science must be promoted, and I am prepared for the worst."

"*Five minutes later.*

"HE has produced a large pair of scissors, and drawn a roll of some substance, not unlike parchment in appearance, from the tin case. The experiment is about to begin. I must strain my eyes to the utmost, in the attempt to follow its minutest operation."

"*Twenty minutes before two.*

"I HAVE at length been enabled to ascertain that the tin tube contains a few yards of some celebrated plaster recommended—as I discover on regarding the label attentively through my eye-glass—as a preservative against sea-sickness. Mr. Slug has cut it up into small portions, and is now sticking it over himself in every direction."

"*Three o'clock.*

"PRECISELY a quarter of an hour ago we weighed anchor, and the machinery was suddenly put in motion with a noise so appalling, that Professor Woodensconce, who had ascended to his berth by means of a platform of carpet bags arranged by himself on geometrical principles, darted from his shelf head foremost, and gaining his feet with all the rapidity of extreme terror, ran wildly into the ladies' cabin, under the impression, that we were sinking, and uttering loud cries for aid. I am assured that the scene which ensued baffles all description. There were one hundred and forty-seven ladies in their respective berths at the time.

"Mr. Slug has remarked, as an additional instance of the extreme ingenuity of the steam-engine as applied to purposes of navigation, that in whatever part of the vessel a passenger's berth may be situated, the machinery always appears to be exactly under his pillow. He intends stating this very beautiful, though simple discovery, to the association."

"*Half-past three.*

"WE are still in smooth water; that is to say in as smooth water as a steam-vessel ever can be, for as Professor Woodensconce, who has just woke up, learnedly remarks, another great point of ingenuity about a steamer is, that it always carries a little storm with it. You can scarcely conceive how exciting the jerking pulsation of the ship becomes. It is a matter of positive difficulty to get to sleep."

"*Friday afternoon, six o'clock.*

"I REGRET to inform you that Mr. Slug's plaster has proved of no avail. He is in great agony, but has applied several large additional pieces notwithstanding. How affecting is this extreme devotion to science and pursuit of knowledge under the most trying circumstances!

"We were extremely happy this morning, and the breakfast was one of the most animated description. Nothing unpleasant occurred until noon, with the exception of Dr. Foxey's brown silk umbrella and white hat becoming entangled in the machinery while he was explaining to a knot of ladies the construction of the steam-engine. I fear the gravy soup for lunch was injudicious. We lost a great many passengers almost immediately afterwards."

"*Half-past six.*

"I AM again in bed. Anything so heart-rending as Mr. Slug's sufferings it has never yet been my lot to witness."

"*Seven o'clock.*

"A MESSENGER has just come down for a clean pocket handkerchief from Professor Woodensconce's bag, that unfortunate gentleman being quite unable to leave the deck, and imploring constantly to be thrown overboard. From this man I understand that Professor Nogo, though in a state of utter exhaustion, clings feebly to the hard biscuit and cold brandy and water, under the impression that they will yet restore him. Such is the triumph of mind over matter.

"Professor Grime is in bed, to all appearance quite well; but he *will* eat, and it is disagreeable to see him. Has this gentleman no sympathy with the sufferings of his fellow-creatures? If he has, on what principle can he call for mutton-chops—and smile?"

"*Black Boy and Stomach-ache, Oldcastle, Saturday noon.*

"You will be happy to learn that I have at length arrived here in safety. The town is excessively crowded, and all the private lodgings and hotels are filled with *savans* of both sexes. The tremendous aasemblages of intellect that one encounters in every street is in the last degree overwhelming.

"Notwithstanding the throng of people here, I have been fortunate enough to meet with very comfortable accommodation on very reasonable terms, having secured a sofa in the first floor passage at one guinea per night, which includes permission to take my meals in the bar, on condition that I walk about the streets at all other times, to make room for other gentlemen similarly situated. I have been over the outhouses intended to be devoted to the reception of the various sections, both here and at the Boot-jack and Countenance, and am much delighted with the arrangements. Nothing can exceed the fresh appearance of the sawdust with which the floors are sprinkled. The forms are of unplaned deal, and the general effect, as you can well imagine, is extremely beautiful."

"*Half-past nine.*

"THE number and rapidity of the arrivals are quite bewildering. Within the last ten minutes a stage coach has driven up to the door, filled inside and out with distinguished characters, comprising Mr. Muddlebrains, Mr. Drawley, Professor Muff, Mr. X. Misty, Mr. X. X. Misty, Mr. Purblind, Professor Rummun, The Honorable and Reverend Mr. Long Ears, Professor John Ketch, Sir William Joltered, Doctor Buffer, Mr. Smith of London, Mr. Brown of Edenburg, Sir Hookham Snivey, and Professor Pumpkinskull. The last ten named gentlemen were wet through, and looked extremely intelligent."

"*Sunday, two o'clock*, P. M.

"The Honorable and Reverend Mr. Long Ears, accompanied by Sir William Joltered, walked and drove this morning. They accomplished the former feat in boots, and the latter in a hired fly. This has naturally given rise to much discussion.

"I have just learned that an interview has taken place at the Boot-Jack and Countenance between Sowster, the active and intelligent beadle of this place, and Professor Pumpkinskull, who, as your readers are doubtless aware, is an influential member of the council. I forbear to communicate any of the rumors to which this very extraordinary proceeding has given rise until I have seen Sowster, and endeavor to ascertain the truth from him."

"*Half-past six.*

"I ENGAGED a donkey-chaise shortly after writing the above, and proceeded at a brisk trot in the direction of Sowster's residence, passing through a beautiful expanse of country with red brick buildings on either side, and stopping in the market-place to observe the spot where Mr. Kwakley's hat was blown off yesterday. It is an uneven piece of paving, but has certainly no appearance which would lead one to suppose that any such event had recently occurred there. From this point I proceeded—passing the gas-works and tallow-melter's—to a lane which had been pointed out to me as the beadle's place of residence; and before I had driven a dozen yards further, I had the good fortune to meet Sowster himself advancing towards me.

"Sowster is a fat man, with a more enlarged development of that peculiar conformation of countenance which is vulgarly termed a double chin that I remember to have ever seen before. He has also a very red nose, which he attributes to a habit of early rising—so red, indeed, that but for this explanation I should have supposed it to proceed from occasional inebriety. He informed me that he did not feel himself at liberty to relate what had passed between himself and Professor Pumpkinskull, but had no objection to state that it was connected with a matter of police regulation, and added with peculiar significance, 'Never wos sitch times!'

"You will easily believe that this intelligence gave me considerable surprise, not wholly unmixed with anxiety, and that I lost no time in waiting on Professor Pumpkinskull, and stating the object of my visit. After a few moments' reflection, the Professor, who I am bound to say, behaved with the utmost politeness, openly avowed, I marked the passage in italics, *that he had requested Sowster to attend on the Monday morning at the Boot-Jack and Countenance to keep off the boys; and that he had further desired that the under-beadle might be stationed, with the same object, at the Black Boy and Stomach-ache!*

"Now, I leave this unconstitutional proceeding to your comments and the consideration of your readers. I have yet to learn that a beadle, without the precincts of a church,

church-yard or workhouse, and acting otherwise than under the express orders of churchwardens and overseers in council assembled, to enforce the law against people who come upon the parish, and other offenders, has any lawful authority whatever over the rising youth of this country. I have yet to learn that a beadle can be called out by any civilian to exercise a domination and despotism over the boys of Britain. I have yet to learn that a beadle will be permitted by the commissioners of poor law regulation to wear out the soles and heels of his boots in illegal interference with the liberties of people not proved poor or otherwise criminal. I have yet to learn that a beadle has power to stop up the Queen's highway at his will and pleasure, or that the whole width of the street is not free and open to any man, boy, or woman in existence, up to the very walls of the houses—ay, be they Black Boys and Stomach-aches, or Boot-jacks and Countenances, I care not."

"*Nine o'clock.*

"I HAVE procured a local artist to make a faithful sketch of the tyrant Sowster, which, as he has acquired this infamous celebrity, you will no doubt wish to have engraved for the purpose of presenting a copy with every copy of your next number. The under-beadle has consented to write his life, but it is to be strictly anonymous.

"The likeness is of course from the life, and complete in every respect. Even if I had been totally ignorant of the man's real character, and it had been placed before me without remark, I should have shuddered involuntarily. There is an intense malignity of expression in the features, and a baleful ferocity of purpose in the ruffian's eye, which appals and sickens. His whole air is rampant with cruelty, nor is the stomach less characteristic of his demoniac propensities.

"*Monday.*

"THE great day has at length arrived. I have neither eyes, nor ears, nor pens, nor ink, nor paper, for anything but the wonderful proceedings that have astounded my senses. Let me collect my energies and proceed to the account."

SECTION A.—ZOOLOGY AND BOTANY.

FRONT PARLOR, BLACK BOY AND STOMACH-ACHE.

PRESIDENT—SIR WILLIAM JOLTERED. VICE-PRESIDENTS—MR. MUDDLEBRAINS AND MR. DRAWLEY.

"MR. X. X. MISTY communicated some remarks on the disappearance of dancing bears from the streets of London, with observations on the exhibition of monkeys as connected with barrel-organs. The writer had observed with feelings of the utmost pain and regret, that some years ago a sudden and unaccountable change in the public taste took place with reference to itinerant bears, who being discountenanced by the populace, gradually fell off one by one from the streets of the metropolis, until not one remained to create a taste for natural history in the breasts of the poor and uninstructed. One bear indeed—a brown and ragged animal—had lingered about the haunts of his former triumphs, with a worn and dejected visage and feeble limbs, had had essayed to wield his quarter-staff for the amusement of the multitude; but hunger and an utter want of any due recompense for his abilities, had at length driven him from the field, and it was only too probable that he had fallen a sacrifice to the rising taste for grease. He regretted to add that a similar and no less lamentable change, had taken place with reference to monkeys. Those delightful animals had formerly been almost as plentiful as the organs on the tops of which they were accustomed to sit; the proportion in the year 1829 it appeared by the parliamentary return, being as one monkey to three organs. Owing however to an altered taste in musical instruments and the substitution in a great measure of narrow boxes of music for organs, which left the monkeys nothing to sit upon, this source of public amusement was wholly dried up. Considering it a matter of the deepest importance in connection with national education, that the people should not lose such opportunities of making themselves acquainted with the manners and customs of two most interesting species of animals, the author submitted that some measures should be immediately taken for the restoration of those pleasing and truly intellectual amusements.

"The PRESIDENT inquired by what means the honorable member proposed to attain this most desirable end?

"The AUTHOR submitted that it could be most fully and satifactorily accomplished, if Her Majesty's government would cause to be brought over to England, and maintained at the public expense, and for the public amusement, such a number of bears as would enable every quarter of the town to be visited—say at least by three bears a week. No difficulty whatever need be experienced in providing a fitting place for the reception of those animals, as a commodious bear-garden could be erected in the immediate neighborhood of both houses of Parliament; obviously the most proper and eligible spot for such an establishment.

"PROFESSOR MULL doubted very much whether any correct ideas of natural history were propagated by the means to which the honorable member had so ably adverted. On the contrary, he believed that they had been the means of diffusing very incorrect and imperfect notions on the subject. He spoke from personal observation and personal experience, when he said that many children of great abilities had been induced to believe, from what they had observed in the streets, at and before the period to which the honorable gentleman had referred, that all monkeys were born in red coats and spangles and that their hats and features also came by nature. He wished to know distinctly whether the honorable gentleman attributed the want of encouragement the bears had met with to the decline of public taste in that respect, or to a want of ability on the part of the bears themselves?

"Mr. X. X. MISTY replied, that he could not bring himself to believe but that there must be a great deal of floating talent among the bears and monkeys generally; which in the absence of any proper encouragement, was dispersed in other directions.

"PROFESSOR PUMPKINSKULL wished to take that opportunity of calling the attention of the section to a most important and serious point. The author of the treatise just read had alluded to the prevalent taste for bears' grease as a means of promoting the growth of hair, which undoubtedly was diffused to a very great and, as it appeared to him, very alarming extent. No gentleman attending that section could fail to be aware of the fact that the youth of the present age evinced, by their behavior in the streets, and all places of public resort, a considerable lack of that gallantry and gentlemanly feeling which, in more ignorant times, had been thought becoming. He wished to know whether it were possible that a constant outward application of bears' grease by the young gentlemen about town, had imperceptibly infused into those unhappy persons something of the nature and quality of the bear? He shuddered as he threw out the remark; but if this theory, on inquiry, should prove to be well-founded, it would at once explain a great deal of unpleasant eccentricity of behavior, which, without some such discovery, was wholly unaccountable.

"The PRESIDENT highly complimented the learned gentleman on his most valuable suggestion, which produced the greatest effect upon the assembly; and remarked that only a week previous he had seen some young gentlemen at a theatre eyeing a box of ladies with a fierce intensity, which nothing but the influence of some brutish appetite could possibly explain. It was dreadful to reflect that our youth were so rapidly verging into a generation of bears.

"After a scene of scientific enthusiasm it was resolved that this important question should be immediately submitted to the consideration of the council.

"The PRESIDENT wished to know whether any gentleman could inform the section what had become of the dancing-dogs?

"A MEMBER replied, after some hesitation, that on the day after three glee-singers had been committed to prison as criminals by a late most zealous police magistrate of the metropolis, the dogs had abandoned their professional duties, and dispersed themselves in different quarters of the town to gain a livelihood by less dangerous means. He was given to understand that since that period they had supported themselves by lying in wait for and robbing blind men's poodles.

"MR. FLUMMERY exhibited a twig, claiming to be a veritable branch of that noble tree known to naturalists as the SHAKSPEARE, which has taken root in every land and climate, and gathered under the shade of its broad green boughs the great family of mankind. The learned gentleman remarked, that the twig had been undoubtedly called by other names in its time; but that it had been pointed out to him by an old lady in Warwickshire, where the great tree had grown, as a shoot of the genuine SHAKSPEARE, by which name he begged to introduce it to his countrymen.

"The PRESIDENT wished to know what botanical definition the honorable gentleman could afford of the curiosity?

"MR. FLUMMERY expressed his opinion that it was a DECIDED PLANT."

SECTION B.—DISPLAY OF MODELS AND MECHANICAL SCIENCE.

LARGE ROOM, BOOT-JACK AND COUNTENANCE.

PRESIDENT—MR. MALLET. VICE-PRESIDENTS—MESSRS. LEAVER AND SCROO.

"MR. CRINKLES exhibited a most beautiful and delicate machine, of a little larger size than an ordinary snuff-box, manufactured entirely by himself, and composed exclusively of steel; by the aid of which more pockets were picked in one hour than by the present slow and tedious process in four-and-twenty. The inventor remarked that it had been put into active operation in Fleet Street, the Strand, and other thoroughfares, and had never been once known to fail.

"After some slight delay, occasioned by the various members of the section buttoning their pockets.

"The PRESIDENT narrowly inspected the invention, and declared that he had never seen a machine of more beautiful or exquisite construction. Would the inventor be good enough to inform the section whether he had taken any and what means for bringing it into general operation?

"Mr. Crinkles stated, that after encountering some preliminary difficulties, he had succeeded in putting himself in communication with Mr. Fogle Hunter, and other gentlemen connected with the swell mob, who had awarded the invention the very highest and most unqualified approbation. He regretted to say, however, that those distinguished practitioners, in common with a gentleman of the name of Gimlet-eyed-Tommy, and other members of a secondary grade of the profession whom he was understood to represent, entertained an insuperable objection to its being brought into general use, on the ground that it would have the inevitable effect of almost entirely superseding manual labor, and throwing a great number of highly-deserving persons out of employment.

"The President hoped that no such fanciful objections would be allowed to stand in the way of such a great public improvement.

"Mr. Crinkles hoped so too; but he feared that if the gentlemen of the swell mob persevered in their objection, nothing could be done.

"Professor Grime suggested, that surely in that case, Her Majesty's government might be prevailed upon to take it up.

"Mr. Crinkles said, that if the objection were found to be insuperable, he should apply to Parliament, who he thought could not fail to recognize the utility of the invention.

"The President observed, that up to his time Parliament had certainly got on very well without it; but as they did their business on a very large scale, he had no doubt they would gladly adopt the improvement. His only fear was that the machine might be worn out by constant working.

"Mr. Coppernose called the attention of the section to a proposition of great magnitude and interest, illustrated by a vast number of models, and stated with much clearness and perspicuity in a treatise entitled 'Practical Suggestions on the necessity of providing some harmless and wholesome relaxation for the young noblemen of England.' His proposition was that a space of ground of not less than ten miles in length and four in breadth should be purchased by a new company, to be incorporated by act of Parliament, and inclosed by a brick wall of not less than twelve feet in height. He proposed that it should be laid out with highway roads, turnpikes, bridges, miniature villages, and every object that could conduce to the comfort and glory of Four-in-hand Clubs, so that they might be fairly presumed to require no drive beyond it. This delightful retreat would be fitted up with most commodious and extensive stables for the convenience of such of the nobility and gentry as had a taste for ostlering, and with houses of entertainment furnished in the most expensive and handsome style. It would be further provided with whole streets of door-knockers and bell-handles of extra size, so constructed that they could be easily wrenched off at night, and regularly screwed on again by attendants provided for the purpose, every day. There would also be gas-lamps of real glass, which could be broken at a comparatively small expense per dozen, and a broad and handsome foot-pavement for gentlemen to drive their cabriolets upon when they were humorously disposed—for the full enjoyment of which feat live pedestrians would be procured from the workhouse at a very small charge per head. The place being inclosed and carefully screened from the intrusion of the public, there would be no objections to gentlemen laying aside any article of their costume that was considered to interfere with a pleasant frolic, or indeed to their walking about without any costume at all, if they liked that better. In short, every facility of enjoyment would be afforded that the most gentlemanly person could possibly desire. But as even these advantages would be incomplete, unless there were some means provided of enabling the nobility and gentry to display their prowess when they sallied forth after dinner, and as some inconvenience might be experienced in the event of their being reduced to the necessity of pummelling each other, the inventor had turned his attention to the construction of an entirely new police force, composed exclusively of automaton figures, which, with the assistance of the ingenious Signor Gagliardi, of Windmill-street in the Haymarket, he had succeeded in making with such nicety, that a policeman, cab-driver, or old woman, made upon the principle of the models exhibited, would walk about until knocked down like any real man; nay more, if set upon and beaten by six or eight noblemen or gentlemen, after it was down, the figure would utter divers groans mingled with entreaties for mercy; thus rendering the illusion complete, and the enjoyment perfect. But the invention did not stop even here, for station-houses would be built, containing good beds for noblemen and gentlemen during the night, and in the morning they would repair to a commodious police office where a pantomimic investigation would take place before automaton magistrates,—quite equal to life,—who would fine them so many counters, with which they would be previously provided for the purpose. This office would be furnished with an inclined plane for the convenience of any nobleman or gentleman who might wish to bring in his horse as a witness, and the prisoners would be at perfect liberty, as they were now, to interrupt the complainants as much as they pleased, and to make any remarks that they thought proper. The charge for those amusements would amount to very little more than they already cost, and the inventor submitted that the public would be much benefited and comforted by the proposed arrangement.

"Professor Nogo wished to be informed what amount of automaton police force it was proposed to raise in the first instance.

"Mr. Coppernose replied that it was proposed to begin with seven divisions of police of a score each, lettered from A to G inclusive. It was proposed that not more than half the number should be placed on active duty, and that the remainder should be kept on shelves in the police office, ready to be called out at a moment's notice.

"The PRESIDENT, awarding the utmost merit to the ingenious gentleman who had originated the idea, doubted whether the automaton police would quite answer the purpose. He feared that noblemen and gentlemen would perhaps require the excitement of threshing living subjects.

"MR. COPPERNOSE submitted, that as the usual odds in such cases were ten noblemen or gentleman to one policeman or cab-driver, it could make very little difference in point of excitement whether the policeman or cab-driver were a man or a block. The great advantage would be, that a policeman's limb might be knocked off, and yet he would be in a condition to do duty next day. He might even give his evidence next morning with his head in his hand, and give it equally well.

"PROFESSOR MUFF.—Will you allow me to ask you, sir, of what materials it is intended that the magistrates' heads shall be composed?

"MR. COPPERNOSE.—The magistrates will have wooden heads of course, and they will be made of the toughest and thickest materials that can possibly be obtained.

"PROFESSOR MUFF.—I am quite satisfied. This is a great invention.

"PROFESSOR NOGO.—I see but one objection to it. It appears to me that the magistrates ought to talk.

"MR. COPPERNOSE no sooner heard this suggestion than he touched a small spring in each of the two models of magistrates which were placed upon the table; one of the figures immediately began to exclaim with great volubility that he was sorry to see gentlemen in such a situation, and the other to express a fear that the policeman was intoxicated.

"The section as with one accord declared with a shout of applause that the invention was complete; and the President, much excited, retired with Mr. Coppernose to lay it before the council. On his return,

"MR. TICKLE displayed his newly-invented spectacles,

which enabled the wearer to discern in very bright colors objects at a great distance, and rendered him wholly blind to those immediately before him. It was he said a most valuable and useful invention, based strictly upon the principle of the human eye.

"The President required some information upon this point. He had yet to learn that the human eye was remarkable for the peculiarities of which the honorable gentleman had spoken.

"Mr. Tickle was rather astonished to hear this, when the President could not fail to be aware that a large number of most excellent persons and great statesmen could see with the naked eye, most marvellous horrors on West India plantations, while they could discern nothing whatever in the interior of Manchester cotton-mills. He must know too with what quickness of perception most people could discover their neighbor's faults, and how very blind they were to their own. If the President differed from the great majority of men in this respect, his eye was a defective one, and it was to assist his vision that these glasses were made.

"Mr. Blank exhibited a model of a fashionable annual, composed of copper-plates, gold leaf, and silk boards, and worked entirely by milk and water.

"Mr. Prosee, after examining the machine, declared it to be so ingeniously composed, that he was wholly unable to discover how it went on at all.

"Mr. Blank.—Nobody can, and that is the beauty of it."

SECTION C.—ANATOMY AND MEDICINE.

BAR-ROOM, BLACK BOY AND STOMACH-ACHE.

PRESIDENT—DR. SOEMUP. VICE-PRESIDENTS—MESSRS. PESSELL AND MORTAIR.

"Dr. Grummidge stated to the section a most interesting case of monomania, and described the course of treatment he had pursued with perfect success. The patient was a married lady in the middle rank of life, who having seen another lady at an evening party in a full suit of pearls, was suddenly seized with a desire to possess a similar equipment, although her husband's finances were by no means equal to the necessary outlay. Finding her wish ungratified, she fell sick, and the symptoms soon became so alarming, that he, Dr. Grummidge, was called in. At this period the prominent tokens of the disorder were sullenness, a total indisposition to perform domestic duties, great peevishness and extreme languor, except when pearls were mentioned, at which times the pulse quickened, the eyes grew brighter, the pupils dilated, and the patient, after various incoherent exclamations, burst into a passion of tears and exclaimed that nobody cared for her, and that she wished herself dead. Finding that the patient's appetite was affected in the presence of company, he began by ordering a total abstinence from all stimulants, and forbidding any sustenance but weak gruel; he then took twenty ounces of blood, applied a blister under each ear, one upon the chest and another on the back; having done which, and administered five grains of calomel, he left the patient to her repose. The next day she was somewhat low, but decidedly better; and all appearances of irritation were removed. The next day she improved still further, and on the next again. On the fourth there was some appearance of a return of the old symptoms, which no sooner developed themselves than he administered another dose of calomel, and left strict orders, that unless a decidedly favorable change occurred within two hours, the patient's head should be immediately shaved to the very last curl. From that moment she began to mend, and in less than four-and-twenty hours was perfectly restored; she did not now betray the least emotion at the sight or mention of pearls or any other ornaments. She was cheerful and good-humored, and a most beneficial change had been effected in her whole temperament and condition.

"Mr. Pipkin, M. R. C. S., read a short but most interesting communication in which he sought to prove the complete belief of Sir William Courtenay, otherwise Thom, recently shot at

Canterbury, in the Homœopathic system. The section would bear in mind that one of the Homœopathic doctrines was, that infinitesimal doses of any medicine which would occasion the disease under which the patient labored, supposing him to be in a healthy state, would cure it. Now it was a remarkable circumstance—proved in the evidence—that the diseased Thom employed a woman to follow him about all day with a pail of water, assuring her that one drop, a purely homœopathic remedy, the section would observe, placed upon his tongue after death, would restore him. What was the obvious inference? That Thom, who was marching and countermarching in osier beds, and other swampy places, was impressed with a presentiment that he should be drowned; in which case had his instructions been complied with, he could not fail to have been brought to life again instantly by his own prescriptions. As it was, if this woman, or any other person, had administered an infinitesimal dose of lead and gunpowder immediately after he fell, he would have recovered forthwith. But unhappily the woman concerned did not possess the power of reasoning by analogy, or carrying out a principle, and thus the unfortunate gentleman had been sacrificed to the ignorance of the peasantry."

SECTION D.—STATISTICS.

OUT-HOUSE, BLACK BOY AND STOMACH-ACHE.

PRESIDENT—MR. SLUG. VICE-PRESIDENTS—MESSRS. NOAKES AND STYLES.

"MR. KWAKLEY stated the result of some most ingenious statistical inquiries relative to the difference between the value of the qualification of several members of Parliament as published to the world, and its real nature and amount. After reminding the section that every member of Parliament for a town or borough was supposed to possess a clear freehold estate of three hundred pounds per annum, the honorable gentleman excited great amusement and laughter by stating the exact amount of freehold property possessed by a column of legislators, in which he had included himself. It appeared from this table that the amount of such income possessed by each was 0 pounds, 0 shillings, and 0 pence, yielding an average of the same.—Great laughter.—It was pretty well known that there were accommodating gentlemen in the habit of furnishing new members with temporary qualifications, to the ownership of which they swore solemnly—of course as a mere matter of form. He argued from these *data* that it was wholly unnecessary for members of Parliament to possess any property at all, especially as when they had none, the public could get them so much cheaper."

SUPPLEMENTARY SECTION E.—UMBUGOLOGY AND DITCH-WATERISTICS.

PRESIDENT—MR. GRUB. VICE-PRESIDENTS—MESSRS. DULL AND DUMMY.

"A paper was read by the secretary descriptive of a bay pony with one eye, which had been seen by the author standing in a butcher's cart at the corner of Newgate Market. The communication described the author of the paper as having in the prosecution of a mercantile pursuit, betaken himself one Saturday morning last summer from Somers Town to Cheapside; in the course of which expedition he had beheld the extraordinary appearance above described. The pony had one distinct eye, and it had been pointed out to him by his friend Captain Blunderbore of the Horse Marines, who assisted the author in his search, that whenever he winked this eye he whisked his tail, possibly to drive the flies off, but that he always winked and whisked at the same time. The animal was lean, spavined, and tottering; and the author proposed to constitute it of the family of *Fitfordogsmeataurious*. It certainly did occur to him that there was no case on record of a pony with one clearly-defined and distinct organ of vision, winking and whisking at the same moment.

"MR. Q. J. SNUFFLETOFFLE had heard of a pony winking his eye, and likewise of a pony whisking his tail, but whether they were two ponies or the same pony he could not undertake positively to say. At all events he was acquainted with no authenticated instance of a simultaneous winking and whisking, and he really could not but doubt the existence of such a marvellous pony in opposition to all those natural laws by which ponies were governed. Referring however to the mere question of his one organ of vision, might he suggest the possibility of this pony having been literally half asleep at the time he was seen, and having closed only one eye?

"The PRESIDENT observed, that whether the pony was half asleep or fast asleep, there could be no doubt that the association was awake, and therefore that they had better get the business over and go to dinner. He had certainly never seen anything analogous to this pony; but he was not prepared to doubt its existence, for he had seen many queerer ponies in his time, though he did not pretend to have seen any more remarkable donkeys than the other gentlemen around him.

"PROFESSOR JOHN KETCH was then called upon to exhibit the skull of the late Mr. Greenacre, which he produced from a blue bag, remarking, on being invited to make any observations that occurred to him, 'that he'd pound it as that 'ere 'spectable section had never seed a more gamerer cove nor he vos.'

"A most animated discussion upon this interesting relic ensued; and some difference of opinion arising respecting the real character of the deceased gentleman, Mr. Blubb delivered a lecture upon the cranium before him, clearly showing that Mr. Greenacre possessed the organ of destructiveness to a most unusual extent, with a most remarkable development of the organ of carveativeness. Sir Hookham Snivey was proceeding to combat this opinion, when Professor Ketch suddenly interrupted the proceedings by exclaiming, with great excitement of manner, 'Walker!'

"The PRESIDENT begged to call the learned gentleman to order.

"PROFESSOR KETCH.—'Order be blowed! you've got the wrong 'un, I tell you. It ain't no 'ed at all; it's a coker-nut as my brother-in-law has been acarvin' to hornament his new baked 'tatur-stall vots a-coming down here vile the 'sociation's in the town. Hand over, vill you?'

"With these words Professor Ketch hastily repossessed himself of the cocoa-nut, and drew forth the skull, in mistake for which he had exhibited it. A most interesting conversation ensued; but as there appeared some doubt ultimately whether the skull was Mr. Greenacre's or a hospital patient's, or a pauper's, or a man's, or a woman's, or a monkey's, no particular result was attained."

"I cannot," says our talented correspondent in conclusion, "I cannot close my account of these gigantic researches and sublime and noble triumphs, without repeating a *bon mot* of Professor Woodensconce's, which shows how the greatest minds may occasionally unbend, when truth can be presented to listening ears, clothed in an attractive and playful form. I was standing by, when after a week of feasting and feeding, that learned gentleman accompanied by the whole body of wonderful men entered the hall yesterday, where a sumptuous dinner was prepared; where the richest wines sparkled on the board, and fat bucks—propitiatory sacrifices to learning—sent forth their savory odors. 'Ah!' said Professor Woodensconce, rubbing his hands, 'this is what we meet for; this is what inspires us; this is what keeps us together, and beckons us onward; this is the *spread* of science, and a glorious spread it is!'"

THACKERAY.—IN MEMORIAM.

BY CHARLES DICKENS.

It has been desired by some of the personal friends of the great English writer who established this magazine, [*The Cornhill*,] that its brief record of his having been stricken from among men should be written by the old comrade and brother in arms who pens these lines, and of whom he often wrote himself, and always with the warmest generosity.

I saw him first, nearly twenty-eight years ago, when he proposed to become the illustrator of my earliest book. I saw him last, shortly before Christmas, at the Athenæum Club, when he told me that he had been in bed three days—that, after these attacks, he was troubled with cold shiverings, "which quite took the power of work out of him"—and that he had it in his mind to try a new remedy which he laughingly described. He was very cheerful and looked very bright. In the night of that day week, he died.

The long interval between those two periods is marked in my remembrance of him by many occasions when he was supremely humorous, when he was irresistibly extravagant, when he was softened and serious, when he was charming with children. But, by none do I recall him more tenderly than by two or three that start out of the crowd, when he unexpectedly presented himself in my room, announcing how that some passage in a certain book had made him cry yesterday, and how that he had come to dinner, "because he couldn't help it," and must talk such passage over. No one can ever have seen him more genial, natural, cordial, fresh, and honestly impulsive, than I have seen him at these times. No one can be surer than I, of the greatness and the goodness of the heart that then disclosed itself.

We had our differences of opinion. I thought that he too much feigned a want of earnestness, and that he made a pretence of undervaluing his art, which was not good for the art that he held in trust. But, when we fell upon these topics, it was never very gravely, and I have a lively image of him in my mind, twisting both his hands in his hair, and stamping about, laughing, to make an end of the discussion.

When we were associated in remembrance of the late Mr. Douglas Jerrold, he delivered a public lecture in London, in the course of which, he read his very best contribution to PUNCH, describing the grown-up cares of a poor family of young children. No one hearing him could have doubted his natural gentleness, or his thoroughly unaffected manly sympathy with the weak and lowly. He read the paper most pathetically, and with a simplicity of tenderness that certainly moved one of his audience to tears. This was presently after his standing for Oxford, from which place he had dispatched his agent to me, with a droll note (to which he afterwards added a verbal postscript), urging me to "come down and make a speech, and tell them who he was, for he doubted whether more than two of the electors had ever heard of him, and he thought there might be as many as six or eight who had heard of me." He introduced the lecture just mentioned, with a reference to his late electioneering failure, which was full of good sense, good spirits, and good humor.

He had a particular delight in boys, and an excellent way with them. I remember his once asking me with fantastic gravity, when he had been to Eton where my eldest son then was, whether I felt as he did in regard of never seeing a boy without wanting instantly to give him a sovereign? I thought of this when I looked down into his grave, after he was laid there, for I looked down into it over the shoulder of a boy to whom he had been kind.

These are slight remembrances; but it is to little familiar things suggestive of the voice, look, manner, never, never more to be encountered on this earth, that the mind first turns in a bereavement. And greater things that are known of him, in the way of his warm affections, his quiet endurance, his unselfish thoughtfulness for others, and his munificent hand, may not be told.

If, in the reckless vivacity of his youth, his satirical pen had ever gone astray or done amiss, he had caused it to prefer its own petition for forgiveness, long before:

> I've writ the foolish fancy of his brain;
> The aimless jest that, striking, hath caused pain;
> The idle word that he'd wish back again.

In no pages should I take it upon myself at this time to discourse of his books, of his refined knowledge of character, of his subtle acquaintance with the weaknesses of human nature, of his delightful playfulness as an essayist, of his quaint and touching ballads, of his mastery over the English language. Least of all, in these pages, enriched by his brilliant qualities from the first of the series, and beforehand accepted by the Public through the strength of his great name.

But, on the table before me, there lies all that he had written of his latest and last story. That it would be very sad to any one—that it is inexpressibly so to a writer—in its evidences of matured designs never to be accomplished, of intentions begun to be executed and destined never to be completed, of careful preparation for long roads of thought that he was never to traverse, and for shining goals that he was never to reach, will be readily believed. The pain, however, that I have felt in perusing it, has not been deeper than the conviction that he was in the healthiest vigor of his powers when he wrought on this last labor. In respect of earnest feeling, far-seeing purpose, character, incident, and a certain loving picturesqueness blending the whole, I believe it to be much the best of all his works. That he fully meant it to be so, that he had become strongly attached to it, and that he bestowed great pains upon it, I trace in almost every page. It contains one picture which must have caused him extreme distress, and which is a masterpiece. There are two children in it, touched with a hand as loving and tender as ever a father caressed his little child with. There is some young love, as pure and innocent and pretty as the truth. And it is very remarkable that, by reason of the singular construction of the story, more than one main incident usually belonging to the end of such a fiction is anticipated in the beginning, and thus there is an approach to completeness in the fragment, as to the satisfaction of the reader's mind concerning the most interesting persons, which could hardly have been better attained if the writer's breaking-off had been foreseen.

The last line he wrote, and the last proof he corrected, are among these papers through which I have so sorrowfully made my way. The condition of the little pages of manuscript where Death stopped his hand, shows that he had carried them about, and often taken them out of his pocket here and there, for patient revision and interlineation. The last words he corrected in print, were, "And my heart throbbed with exquisite bliss." God grant that on that Christmas Eve when he laid his head back on his pillow and threw up his arms as he had been wont to do when very weary, some consciousness of duty done and Christian hope throughout life humbly cherished, may have caused his own heart so to throb, when he passed away to his Redeemer's rest!

He was found peacefully lying as above described, composed, undisturbed, and to all appearance asleep, on the twenty-fourth of December, 1863. He was only in his fifty-third year; so young a man, that the mother who blessed him in his first sleep, blessed him in his last. Twenty years before, he had written, after being in a white squall:

And when, its force expended,
The harmless storm was ended,
And, as the sunrise splendid
  Came blushing o'er the sea;
I thought, as day was breaking,
My little girls were waking,
And smiling, and making
  A prayer at home for me.

Those little girls had grown to be women when the mournful day broke that saw their father lying dead. In those twenty years of companionship with him, they had learned much from him; and one of them has a literary course before her, worthy of her famous name.

On the bright wintry day, the last but one of the old year, he was laid in his grave at Kensal Green, there to mingle the dust to which the mortal part of him had returned, with that of a third child, lost in her infancy, years ago. The heads of a great concourse of his fellow-workers in the Arts, were bowed around his tomb.

THE WILL OF CHARLES DICKENS.

The following is a copy in full of the last Will and Testament of Charles Dickens.

"I, Charles Dickens, of Gad's Hill Place, Higham, in the County of Kent, hereby revoke all my former wills and codicils, and declare this to be my last will and testament. I give the sum of £1,000, free of legacy duty, to Miss Ellen Lawless Ternan, late of Houghton Place, Ampthill Square, in the County of Middlesex. I give the sum of 19 guineas to my faithful old servant, Mrs. Anne Cornelius. I give the sum of 19 guineas to the daughter and only child of the said Mrs. Anne Cornelius. I give the sum of 19 guineas to each and every domestic servant, male and female, who shall be in my employment at the time of my decease, and shall have been in my employment for a not less period of time than one year. I give the sum of £1,000, free of legacy duty, to my daughter, Mary Dickens. I also give to my said daughter, Mary, an annuity of £300 a year during her life, if she shall so long continue unmarried, such annuity to be considered as accruing from day to day, but to be payable half-yearly, the first of such half-yearly payments to be made at the expiration of six months next after my decease. If my said daughter Mary shall marry, such annuity shall cease, and in that case, but in that case only, my said daughter shall share with my other children in the provision hereinafter made for them. I give to my dear sister-in-law, Georgina Hogarth, the sum of £8,000, free of legacy duty. I also give to the said Georgina Hogarth all my personal jewelry not hereinafter mentioned, and all the little familiar objects from my writing-table and my room, and she will know what to do with those things. I also give to the said Georgina Hogarth all my private papers whatsoever and wheresoever, and I leave her my grateful blessing, as the best and truest friend man ever had. I give to my eldest son, Charles, my library of printed books, and my engravings and prints. I also give to my said son, Charles, the silver salver presented to me at Birmingham, and the silver cup presented to me at Edingburgh, and my shirt-studs, shirt-pins, and sleeve-buttons; and I bequeath unto my said son Charles and my son Henry Fielding Dickens, the sum of £8,000 upon trust to invest the same, and from time to time to vary the investments thereof, and to pay the annual income thereof to my wife during her life, and after her decease the said sum of £8,000 and the investments thereof shall be in trust for my children (but subject as to my daughter Mary to the proviso hereinbefore contained), who, being a son or sons, shall have attained or shall attain the age of twenty-one years, or, being a daughter or daughters, shall have attained or shall attain that age, or be previously married, in equal shares if more than one. I give my watch (the gold repeater presented to me at Coventry), and I give the chains and seals, and all appendages I have worn with it, to my dear and trusty friend John Forster of Palace

Gatehouse, Kensington, in the County of Middlesex aforesaid. And I also give to the said John Forster such manuscripts of my published works as may be in my possession at the time of my decease. And I devise and bequeath all my real and personal estate (except such as is vested in me as a trustee or mortgagee) unto the said Georgina Hogarth and the said John Forster, their heirs, executors, administrators and assigns respectively, upon trust, that they, the said Georgina Hogarth and John Forster, or the survivor of them, or the executors or administrators of such survivor, do and shall at their, his or her uncontrolled and irresponsible direction, either proceed to an immediate sale or conversion into money of the said real and personal estate (including my copyrights), or defer and postpone any sale or conversion into money till such time or times as they, he, or she shall think fit, and in the mean time may manage and let the said real and personal estate (including my copyrights) in such manner in all respects as I myself could do if I were living and acting therein, it being my intention that the trustees or trustee for the time being of this my will shall have the fullest power over the said real and personal estate which I can give to them, him, or her. And I declare that until the said real and personal estate shall be sold and converted into money, the rents and annual income thereof respectively shall he paid and applied to the person or persons in the manner and for the purposes to whom and for which the anuual income of the moneys to arise from the sale or conversion thereof into money would be payable or applicable under this my will, in case the same were sold or converted into money; and I declare that my real estate shall, for the purpose of this my will be considered as converted into personalty upon my decease; and I declare that the said trustees or trustee for the time being do and shall, with and out of the moneys which shall come to their, his, or her hands, under or by virtue of this my will and the trusts thereof, pay my just debts, funeral and testamentary expenses, and legacies. And I declare that the said trust funds, or so much thereof as shall remain after answering the purposes aforesaid, and the annual income thereof, shall be in trust for all my children (but subject, as to my daughter Mary, to the proviso hereinbefore contained) who, being a son or sons, shall have attained or shall attain the age of twenty-one years, and, being a daughter or daughters, shall have attained or shall attain that age, or be previously married, in equal shares if more than one—provided always that, as regards my copyrights and the produce and profits thereof, my said daughter Mary, notwithstanding the proviso hereinbefore contained with reference to her, shall share with my other children therein, whether she be married or not; and I devise the estates vested in me at my decease, as a trustee or mortgagee, unto the use of the said Georgina Hogarth and John Forster, their heirs and assigns, upon the trusts and subject to the equities affecting the same respectively; and I appoint the said Georgina Hogarth and John Forster, executrix and executor of this my will, and guardians of the persons of my children during their respective minorities; and lastly, as I have now set down the form of words which my legal advisers assure me are necessary to the plain objects of this my will, I solemnly enjoin my dear children always to remember how much they owe to the said Georgina Hogarth, and never to be wanting in a grateful and affectionate attachment to her, for they know well that she has been through all the stages of their growth and progress their ever-useful, self-denying and devoted friend. And I desire here simply to record the fact that my wife, since our separation by consent, has been in the receipt from me of an annual income of £600; while all the great charges of a numerous and expensive family have devolved wholly upon myself. I emphatically direct that I be buried in an inexpensive, unostentatious, and strictly private manner, that no public announcement be made of the time or place of my burial, that at the utmost not more than three plain mourning-coaches be employed, and that those who attend my funeral wear no scarf, cloak, black bow, long hat-band, or other such revolting absurdity. I direct that my name be inscribed in plain English letters on my tomb without the addition of 'Mr.' or 'Esquire.' I conjure my friends on no account to make me the subject of any monument, memorial, or testimonial whatever. I rest my claims to the remembrance of my country upon my published works, and to the remembrance of my friends upon their experience of me; in addition thereto I commit my soul to the mercy of God through our Lord and Saviour Jesus Christ, and I exhort my dear children humbly to try to guide themselves by the teachings of the New Testament in its broad spirit, and to put no faith in any man's narrow construction of its letter here or there. In witness whereof I, the said Charles Dickens, the testator, have to this my last will and testament set my hand this twelfth day of May, in the year of our Lord one thousand eight hundred and sixty-nine. CHARLES DICKENS."

"Signed, published, and declared by the above-named Charles Dickens, the testator, as and for his last will and testament, in the presence of us (present together at the same time), who in his presence, at his request, and in the presence of each other have hereunto subscribed our names as witnesses.

"G. HOLDSWORTH, No. 26 Wellington-st., Strand.

"HENRY WALKER, No. 26 Wellington-st., Strand.

"I, Charles Dickens, of Gad's Hill Place, near Rochester, in the county of Kent, Esquire, declare this to be a codicil to my last will and testament, which will bear date the 12th day of May, 1869. I give to my son Charles Dickens the younger all my share and interest in the weekly journal called *All the Year Round*, which is now conducted under articles of partnership made between me and William Henry Wills and the said Charles Dickens the younger, and all my share and interest in the stereotypes, stock, and other effects belonging to the said partnership, he defraying my share of all debts and liabilities of the said partnership which may be outstanding at the time of my decease, and in all other respects I confirm my said will. In witness whereof I have hereunto set my hand the 2d day of June, in the year of our Lord one thousand eight hundred and seventy. CHARLES DICKENS."

"Signed and declared by the said Charles Dickens, the testator, as and for a codicil to his will, in the presence of us (present at the same time) who, at his request, in his presence, and in the presence of each other, hereunto subscribe our names as witnesses,

"G. HOLDSWORTH, No. 26 Wellington-st., Strand.

"H. WALKER, No. 26 Wellington-st., Strand."

Proved at London, with a codicil, 19th July, 1870, by the oath of Georgina Hogarth, spinster, and John Forster Esq., the executors, to whom administration was granted.

THE END.

THE DICKENS CONTROVERSY.

FROM THE PUBLISHERS' CIRCULAR OF JUNE 1ST, 1867.

T. B. PETERSON & BROTHERS, 306 Chestnut Street, Philadelphia, the only publishers of Dickens's Works in America from 1851 to 1867, over fifteen years, beg leave to call the attention of the American Public to the following article, including a card from them, taken from the editorial columns of the "American Literary Gazette and Publishers' Circular" of June 1st, 1867, as follows:

THE DICKENS CONTROVERSY.—Several matters are presented by the letters, advertisements, and facts recently made public respecting the republication of Mr. Dickens's works in this country, which present suggestive topics of reflection. We desire, however, to advert now simply to the fact that Mr. Dickens, in his published letter to Ticknor & Fields, not only speaks in a most disparaging and flippant manner of substantial payment received by him from this country, but, in our judgment, deals with the facts in a style that is almost next of kin to dishonesty. We regret to say this, but justice to members of the trade requires it, and the circumstances of the case justify it. The letter of Mr. Dickens is as follows:

"GAD'S HILL PLACE, HIGHAM-BY-ROCHESTER, KENT,
"*Tuesday, 16th April*, 1867.

"MESSRS. TICKNOR & FIELDS:

"MY DEAR SIRS:—I have read the newspaper cutting you have sent me, in which it is stated that I have an interest in—have derived, do derive, or am to derive pecuniary advantage from—certain republications of my collected works in the United States not issued by you. Once for all, receive my personal authority to contradict any such monstrous misrepresentations. If they originate in any distorted shadow of truth, they have been twisted into being from the two irrelevant facts: Firstly, That Messrs. Harper of New York, through their agents, Messrs. Sampson, Low & Co., of London, purchased advanced sheets of my three latest novels—'A Tale of Two Cities,' 'Great Expectations,' and 'Our Mutual Friend'—as each appeared serially, for simultaneous republication in America. Secondly, that Messrs. Hurd & Houghton not long since bought of my publishers a hundred impressions of the illustrations to the Pickwick Papers, and have never had any other transaction whatever with them or with me.

"In America the occupation of my life for thirty years is, unless it bears your imprint, utterly worthless and profitless to me.

"Faithfully yours,
"CHARLES DICKENS."

After the appearance of this letter, Mr. Sampson Low published the following note:

"To the Editor of the Pall Mall Gazette:

"Sir:—Most unwilling as I am to intrude upon your space, or to intrude myself before your readers, I cannot refrain from remarking upon the paragraph in this day's journal, based upon the absence of an international copyright law between this country and the United States, and referring to a letter published in the American papers, as from Mr. Dickens to an American publishing house, abounding in expressions of peculiar gratification at the display of their honor ble dealing as publishers in remitting to him the sum of two hundred pounds as part profits of their edition of his works, at the same time implying that such payment is so extraordinary as to be looked upon as an isolated act of honesty on the part of the American publishers. Now, having myself, as the agent of Messrs. Harper & Brothers, paid to Mr. Charles Dickens many thousands of pounds for and on account of his works, when no other publishing house had paid anything, I do not think such payments should be wholly overlooked in the exuberance which he feels at being put into the possession of this additional honorarium from American publishers. Messrs. Harper & Brothers do not seek from Mr. Dickens any such acknowledgment to be used by them as a public advertisement, but they have a right to claim from Mr. Dickens exemption from the only inference to be drawn from the communication, that his claims upon them have hitherto been disregarded.

"Yours obediently,

"Sampson Low.

"59 *Ludgate Hill, May* 7, 1867."

Now, we regard this letter of Mr. Dickens as ungenerous, if not dishonest. Would anybody suppose, upon reading it, that the writer had actually received £3,900 sterling, nearly $20,000 in gold, from a single American firm—that of Harper & Brothers? Why does Mr. Dickens ignore that fact? Why does he say that "in America the occupation of my life for thirty years is, unless it bears your imprint, *utterly worthless and profitless to me?* Are £3,900 received within the last "thirty years," such trash as to be "worthless?" or has that large sum melted away so as to be "profitless?"—not taking into account various respectable sums received from Lea & Blanchard, and other publishers. Even if we suppose that Mr. Dickens measured his words with a micrometer, and is speaking strictly and solely of "collected editions," we cannot help thinking that a frank and gentlemanly nature would not have failed to recognize voluntary liberality as respects *particular* works, even if it did not, in form, extend to *collected* works. It would have been in much better taste if Mr. Dickens had not sought to cover up and suppress the fact that he had received very large remittances from a single publishing house in this country. Yet this very fact he coolly pronounces "*irrelevant.*" Were £3,900 ever before "irrelevant" to an author, unless in view of a prospective speculation? We do not care to dwell on this matter. We respect the talent of Mr. Dickens as a writer of fiction, but we can assure him that his letter is generally regarded by our publishers here as ungenerous, illiberal, and ungentlemanlike; and its results, unless corrected in some way, are likely to prejudice the general pecuniary interests of English authors among us. Still, Mr. Dickens may have one standard, and we another, for measuring what is gentlemanlike. That may be said to be a matter of opinion. Whether his letter, however, is or is not, as we have said above, dishonest, may be regarded as a matter not of opinion, but of fact. He states that Messrs. Harper purchased advance sheets of my three latest novels,—'A Tale of Two Cities,' 'Great Expectations,' and 'Our Mutual Friend.'" That is true as far as it goes. The payments for those three stories amounted to £3,250. But it is not the whole truth, the same firm also paid £400 additional for "Bleak House," and £250 for "Little Dorritt." Is this forgotten by Mr. Dickens? These £650 are doubtless "worthless and profitless" and "irrelevant facts," but they show that Mr. Dickens is only within about seventeen per cent. of the truth, which is pretty fair for a novelist.

We do not suppose that either the trade or the public will, under the circumstance of the case, pay the slightest regard to the wishes that have been expressed by Mr. Dickens on this subject. There is no courtesy on his part which calls very urgently for courtesy from us, and we are aware of no usage of the trade which justifies an author in an endeavor to injure or drive out of the market long-established editions of his works which have been for years before the public, and which represent a heavy amount of capital. Mr. Dickens is himself, in this very case, a flagrant violator of usage, for he or his publisher, having sold advance-sheets of his latest novels to one firm, and received good pay thereor, he now seeks to transfer to another house an exclusive interest in those very works.

We subjoin a communication received by us from Messrs. T. B. Peterson & Brothers, of this city, who have been the only publishers of the works of Charles Dickens in America for the past fifteen years, which speaks for itself:

GEORGE W. CHILDS, ESQ.,

Publisher of the American Literary Gazette and Publishers' Circular.

DEAR SIR :—For the last fifteen years we have been considered in the trade the only authorized publishers in America of the works of Charles Dickens. In the absence of an international copyright, it has always been held that the house which purchased the advance-sheets from an English author had the equitable right to the exclusive use of his works in the United States. As far back as 1851, we bought the stereotype plates, steel illustrations, and wood-cuts of all of Dickens's Works that had ever been printed in this country, among them those made by Carey, Lea & Blanchard, Stringer & Townsend, Jesper Harding, G. P. Putnam, and Harper & Brothers. In a letter just published by you, Mr. Henry C. Lea has stated that his firm had been in the habit of paying Mr. Dickens for the novels they reprinted ; and Harper & Brothers followed the same custom. We supposed, when we purchased these plates, that we were buying the equitable right (as against any other American publishers) to reprint these works ; and it was always regarded in the trade that we had acquired such a right. At that time the sale of Mr. Dickens's works was small in the United States, and there had been no uniform editions issued of them. Many of the plates we bought to get them out of the market, and these we melted down and sold for old metal. We then began stereotyping and publishing uniform editions of Charles Dickens's works, advertising them very extensively, and so creating a demand for them—a demand of which other publishers now seek to avail themselves. We have continued to issue various editions since, twenty-three in all, at prices ranging from twenty-five cents to five dollars a volume, according to the size, quality of paper, number of illustrations, and binding of the edition. When Harper & Brothers arranged with Charles Dickens for the early sheets of his later works, we were considered by them as the only house, according to the usages of the trade, entitled to publish them in book form in America, and offered us copies of the advance-sheets on condition that we paid part of the purchase-money, and bought the stereotype plates and illustrations made by them of each novel. In this way we became possessed of the rights which Harper & Brothers had purchased from Mr. Dickens. To show that the sums thus received by Mr. Dickens for his last *five* works were not illiberal, we give below* a letter from Harper & Brothers, dated May 21st, 1867, in which they state that they paid in all £3,900

---

* FRANKLIN SQUARE, NEW YORK, *May* 11, 1867.

MESSRS. T. B. PETERSON & BROTHERS :

DEAR SIRS :—In reply to yours of yesterday, we append herewith a statement of the payments we have made for Mr. Dickens's works, as far as we can at present ascertain :

A Tale of Two Cities. - - - - -	£1,000
Great Expectations. - - - - -	1,250
Our Mutual Friend. - - - - - -	1,000
Bleak House. - - - - - - -	400
Little Dorritt. - - - - - - -	250

Respectfully,

HARPER & BROTHERS.

(three thousand nine hundred pounds sterling), in round numbers about twenty thousand dollars in gold.* Some of these payments were made when gold was at a very large premium, so that the amount, in United States currency, was considerably greater.

We contend that, under the circumstances, we are the owners of all the rights ever possessed by Carey, Lea & Blanchard, and Harper & Brothers. It appears also, that in place of Charles Dickens never having received any thing from this country, he has been paid liberally, considering the absence of any international copyright. Further, we suggest that it is a very doubtful proceeding on his part, in the face of these facts, to offer to sell to any other house in America, privileges which, it appears, he had sold before.

Respectfully yours,

T. B. PETERSON & BROTHERS.

PHILADELPHIA, *May* 25, 1867.

The following is the letter written by Henry C. Lea, Esq., (of the old firm of Carey, Lea & Blanchard,) to George W. Childs, Esq., which was printed in the Publishers' Circular of May 15th, 1867. It gives facts and speaks to the point.

MY DEAR MR. CHILDS:

In November, 1836, Carey, Lea & Blanchard ventured to reprint the first four numbers of the immortal "Pickwick." The author was unknown, and the enterprise a doubtful one; so the edition, printed from type, was only 1,500 copies, and the numbers were issued at the price of 45 cents, in one volume, in the thin duodecimo shape, bound in boards, with which all readers of old novels are doubtless familiar. The venture was successful, and by December, 1837, when the fifth and concluding volume was published, the edition had been materially increased, while small quantities of the earlier volumes had been reprinted, and two rival and cheaper editions had been started in New York. The only advantage which the author derived from this publication, beyond the reputation which the name of "Boz" acquired in this country, was a remittance of £50, made to him in 1838, by the house, in acknowledgment of the success of his work. That success had led, in 1837, to the republication of the collected "Sketches by Boz," of which but 1,250 copies were printed. This does not seem to have been a fortunate undertaking, for I find no trace of another edition being called for until many years afterwards, when we included it in a collective edition of the works, and though it contains many of the happiest touches of Dickens's early manner, its sale always was very limited.

"Oliver Twist" appeared in 1838, in "Bentley's Miscellany," a periodical which was regularly reprinted in this country. Our house

* In July, 1842, after his American tour, Mr. Dickens sent a circular letter to the leading English authors, stating that he would never, from that time, "enter into any negotiation with any person for the transmission across the Atlantic of early proofs of anything I may write," and volunteering to "forego all profit derivable from such a source." Yet, after this, he *did* receive £3,900 in gold, from Messrs. Harper, for early proofs of five of his works!

endeavored to treat with Mr. Dickens for an early copy of the conclusion of the book, but Mr. Bentley claimed the right to control it, and received £60 for the manuscript of the latter portion in advance—an advantage which proved of little practical benefit to us, for a cheaper edition was printed in New York immediately on its appearance.

In the correspondence with Mr. Dickens during 1838, I find a suggestion that he should secure for himself the control of early sheets in his subsequent arrangements with his publishers, and an offer to him of £100 apiece for advance copies of his future novels. This apparently did not reach him in season for "Nicholas Nickleby," and as the publishers of that work refused to treat for early sheets, nothing seems to have been paid for it.

It is illustrative of the difficulties of business in those days, before steamers were fairly established, that a letter from Mr. Dickens, announcing the forthcoming appearance of "Master Humphrey's Clock," though dated November 29th, 1839, was not received until February 5th, 1840, having been sent by a sailing packet to Halifax. The firm at once wrote to their London agent authorizing him to pay £300 for sheets thirty days in advance, but in consequence of the previous delay the letter did not reach him until after he had, on his own responsibility, made a different arrangement, viz.: £2 10*s*. for each number, a little ahead of regular publication. Under this agreement, the payments made for "The Old Curiosity Shop" amounted to £112 10*s*., and for "Barnaby Rudge" to £107 10*s*.

In the present era of enormous sales and plentiful greenbacks, these sums may not appear large, but in the fearful depression of business before and after the fall of the Bank of the United States they were as much as any house could afford to pay. Within twenty-four hours after the appearance of each number it was reprinted bodily in a dozen newspapers, whose readers thus obtained it for nothing, while rival editions were rapidly brought out in the style of the cheap publications which sprang up about that time, when the "New World" and "Brother Jonathan" flourished, and Winchester & Co. would issue a novel in the shape of a quarto newspaper at a retail price of 15 or 25 cents.

For many years after his visit to this country in 1842, Mr. Dickens refused to countenance any American editions of his works. As business commenced to revive, we authorized our London agent to pay for "Martin Chuzzlewit" double the price that had been paid for "Barnaby Rudge" and the "Old Curiosity Shop," but Mr. Dickens refused to supply the advanced sheets, or to permit his publishers to do so. We were therefore obliged to print that work, "David Copperfield," and "Dombey & Son," without an arrangement with him.

During all this period we were the publishers of the only complete editions of these works in this country, the stereotyped plates and illustrations of which we sold in 1851, and they passed into the hands of Messrs. T. B. Peterson & Brothers, forming the basis of the numerous editions since issued by that house.

But I have allowed my pen to run on further and faster than I intended, or than your space can well afford.

Very respectfully,

Philadelphia, May 10, 1867. HENRY C. LEA.

BEST COOK BOOKS PUBLISHED.

The Young Wife's Cook Book,..Cloth, $1 75
Miss Leslie's New Cookery Book,....................................Cloth, 1 75
Mrs. Hale's New Cook Book,...Cloth, 1 75
Mrs. Goodfellow's Cookery as it Should Be,........................Cloth, 1 75
Petersons' New Cook Book,..Cloth, 1 75
Widdifield's New Cook Book,...Cloth, 1 75
The National Cook Book. By a Practical Housewife,.........Cloth, 1 75
Miss Leslie's New Receipts for Cooking,...........................Cloth, 1 75
Mrs. Hale's Receipts for the Million,...............................Cloth, 1 75
The Family Save-All. By author of "National Cook Book,".Cloth, 1 75
Francatelli's Celebrated French, Italian, German, and English Cook Book. The Modern Cook. With Sixty-two illustrations. Complete in six hundred large octavo pages,..................Cloth, 5 00

WORKS BY THE VERY BEST AUTHORS.

The following books are each issued in one large duodecimo volume, in paper cover, at $1.50 each, or each one is bound in cloth, at $1.75 each.

The Initials. A Love Story. By Baroness Tautphœus,..................$1 50
Why Did He Marry Her? By Miss Eliza A. Dupuy,...................... 1 50
The Macdermots of Ballycloran. By Anthony Trollope,.................. 1 50
Lost Sir Massingberd. By the author of "Carlyon's Year,"............ 1 50
The Planter's Daughter. By Miss Eliza A. Dupuy,...................... 1 50
Dream Numbers. By T. Adolphus Trollope, author of "Gemma,"... 1 50
Leonora Casaloni; or, the Marriage Secret. By T. A. Trollope,..... 1 50
The Forsaken Daughter. A Companion to "Linda," 1 50
Love and Liberty. A Revolutionary Story. By Alexander Dumas, 1 50
Family Pride. By author of "Pique," "Family Secrets," etc......... 1 50
Self-Sacrifice. By author of "Margaret Maitland," etc................ 1 50
The Woman in Black. A Companion to the "Woman in White," ... 1 50
A Woman's Thoughts about Women. By Miss Muloch,.................. 1 50
Flirtations in Fashionable Life. By Catharine Sinclair,.................. 1 50
Rose Douglas. A Companion to "Family Pride," and "Self Sacrifice," 1 50
False Pride; or, Two Ways to Matrimony. A Charming Book,...... 1 50
Family Secrets. A Companion to "Family Pride," and "Pique,"... 1 50
The Morrisons. By Mrs. Margaret Hosmer,.................................. 1 50
Beppo; The Conscript. By T. A. Trollope, author of "Gemma,".... 1 50
Gemma. An Italian Story. By T. A. Trollope, author of "Beppo," 1 50
Marietta. By T. A. Trollope, author of "Gemma,"........................ 1 50
My Son's Wife. By author of "Caste," "Mr. Arle," etc................ 1 50
The Rich Husband. By author of "George Geith,"........................ 1 50
Harem Life in Egypt and Constantinople. By Emmeline Lott,...... 1 50
The Rector's Wife; or, the Valley of a Hundred Fires.................. 1 50
Woodburn Grange. A Novel. By William Howitt,......................... 1 50
Country Quarters. By the Countess of Blessington,...................... 1 50
Out of the Depths. The Story of a "Woman's Life,"..................... 1 50
The Coquette; or, the Life and Letters of Eliza Wharton,............... 1 50
The Pride of Life. A Story of the Heart. By Lady Jane Scott,..... 1 50
The Lost Beauty. By a Noted Lady of the Spanish Court,............. 1 50
Saratoga. An Indian Tale of Frontier Life. A true Story of 1787,.. 1 50
Married at Last. A Love Story. By Annie Thomas,...................... 1 50
The Quaker Soldier. A Revolutionary Romance. By Judge Jones,.... 1 50
The Man of the World. An Autobiography. By William North,... 1 50
The Queen's Favorite; or, The Price of a Crown. A Love Story,... 1 50
Self Love; or, The Afternoon of Single and Married Life,............ 1 50

The above books are each in paper cover, or in cloth, price $1.75 each.

☞ Books sent, postage paid, on Receipt of the Retail Price, by T. B. Peterson & Brothers, Philadelphia, Pa.

WORKS BY THE VERY BEST AUTHORS.

The following books are each issued in one large duodecimo volume, in paper cover, at $1.50 each, or each one is bound in cloth, at $1.75 each.

The Dead Secret. By Wilkie Collins, author "The Crossed Path,"...$1 50
Memoirs of Vidocq, the French Detective. His Life and Adventures, 1 50
The Crossed Path; or Basil. By Wilkie Collins,........................ 1 50
Indiana. A Love Story. By George Sand, author of "Consuelo," 1 50
The Belle of Washington. With her Portrait. By Mrs. N. P. Lasselle, 1 50
Cora Belmont; or, The Sincere Lover. A True Story of the Heart,. 1 50
The Lover's Trials; or Days before 1776. By Mrs. Mary A. Denison, 1 50
High Life in Washington. A Life Picture. By Mrs. N. P. Lasselle, 1 50
The Beautiful Widow; or, Lodore. By Mrs. Percy B. Shelley,...... 1 50
Love and Money. By J. B. Jones, author of the "Rival Belles,"... 1 50
The Matchmaker. A Story of High Life. By Beatrice Reynolds,.. 1 50
The Brother's Secret; or, the Count De Mara. By William Godwin, 1 50
The Lost Love. By Mrs. Oliphant, author of "Margaret Maitland," 1 50
The Roman Traitor. By Henry William Herbert. A Roman Story, 1 50
The Bohemians of London. By Edward M. Whitty,.................... 1 50
The Rival Belles; or, Life in Washington. By J. B. Jones,.......... 1 50
The Devoted Bride. A Story of the Heart. By St. George Tucker, 1 50
Love and Duty. By Mrs. Hubback, author of "May and December," 1 50
Wild Sports and Adventures in Africa. By Major W. C. Harris, 1 50
Courtship and Matrimony. By Robert Morris. With a Portrait,... 1 50
The Jealous Husband. By Annette Marie Maillard,..................... 1 50
The Refugee. By Herman Melville, author of "Omoo," "Typee," 1 50
The Life, Writings, Lectures, and Marriages of Fanny Fern,......... 1 50
The Life and Lectures of Lola Montez, with her portrait, on steel,... 1 50
Wild Southern Scenes. By author of "Wild Western Scenes,"...... 1 50
Currer Lyle; or, the Autobiography of an Actress. By Louise Reeder. 1 50
Coal, Coal Oil, and all other Minerals in the Earth. By Eli Bowen, 1 50
The Cabin and Parlor. By J. Thornton Randolph. Illustrated,..... 1 50
Jealousy. By George Sand, author of "Consuelo," "Indiana," etc. 1 50
The Little Beauty. A Love Story. By Mrs. Grey,....................... 1 50
Secession, Coercion, and Civil War. By J. B. Jones,.................... 1 50
The Count of Monte Cristo. By Alexander Dumas. Illustrated,... 1 50
Camille; or, the Fate of a Coquette. By Alexander Dumas,......... 1 50
Six Nights with the Washingtonians. By T. S. Arthur,................ 1 50
Lizzie Glenn; or, the Trials of a Seamstress. By T. S. Arthur,..... 1 50
Lady Maud; or, the Wonder of Kingswood Chase. By Pierce Egan, 1 50
Wilfred Montressor; or, High Life in New York. Illustrated,....... 1 50
The Old Stone Mansion. By C. J. Peterson, author "Kate Aylesford," 1 50
Kate Aylesford. By Chas. J. Peterson, author "Old Stone Mansion,". 1 50
Lorrimer Littlegood, by author "Hary Coverdale's Courtship,"...... 1 50
The Red Court Farm. By Mrs. Henry Wood, author of "East Lynne," 1 50
Mildred Arkell. By Mrs. Henry Wood, author of "Red Court Farm," 1 50
The Earl's Secret. A Love Story. By Miss Pardoe,...................... 1 50
The Adopted Heir. By Miss Pardoe, author of "The Earl's Secret," 1 50
Cousin Harry. By Mrs. Grey, author of "The Gambler's Wife," etc. 1 50
The Conscript. A Tale of War. By Alexander Dumas, ... 1 50
The Tower of London. By W. Harrison Ainsworth. Illustrated,... 1 50
French, German, Latin, Spanish, and Italian without a Master,...... 1 50
Shoulder Straps. By Henry Morford, author of "Days of Shoddy," 1 50
Days of Shoddy, and The Coward. By Henry Morford, each......... 1 50
The Cavalier, and Lord Montague's Page. By G. P. R. James, each 1 50
Rose Foster. By George W. M. Reynolds, Esq.,............................ 1 50

The above books are each in paper cover, or in cloth, price $1.75 each.

Hans Breitmann's Ballads, complete and entire, with a full glossary, $3 00

☞ **Books sent, postage paid, on receipt of the Retail Price, by**
T. B. Peterson & Brothers, Philadelphia, Pa.

WORKS BY THE VERY BEST AUTHORS.

The following books are each issued in one large octavo volume, in paper cover, at $1.50 each, or each one is bound in cloth, at $2.00 each.

The Wandering Jew. By Eugene Sue. Full of Illustrations,........$1 50
Mysteries of Paris; and its Sequel, Gerolstein. By Eugene Sue,.... 1 50
Martin, the Foundling. By Eugene Sue. Full of Illustrations,..... 1 50
Ten Thousand a Year. By Samuel C. Warren. With Illustrations, 1 50
Washington and His Generals. By George Lippard...................... 1 50
The Quaker City; or, the Monks of Monk Hall. By George Lippard, 1 50
Blanche of Brandywine. By George Lippard,............................ 1 50
Paul Ardenheim; the Monk of Wissahickon. By George Lippard,. 1 50
The above books are each in paper cover, or in cloth, price $2.00 each.

The following are each issued in one volume, bound in cloth, gilt back.

Charles O'Malley, the Irish Dragoon. By Charles Lever,...............$2 00
Harry Lorrequer. With his Confessions. By Charles Lever,.......... 2 00
Jack Hinton, the Guardsman. By Charles Lever,......................... 2 00
Davenport Dunn. A Man of Our Day. By Charles Lever,............ 2 00
Valentine Vox, the Ventriloquist. By Harry Cockton,............ ..... 2 00

NEW AND GOOD BOOKS BY BEST AUTHORS.

The Last Athenian. From the Swedish of Victor Rydberg. Highly recommended by Fredrika Bremer. Paper $1.50, or in cloth,......$2 00
Comstock's Elocution and Reader. Enlarged. By Andrew Comstock and Philip Lawrence. With 236 Illustrations. Half morocco,......2 00
Comstock's Colored Chart. Every School should have a copy of it....5 00
Across the Atlantic. Letters from France, Switzerland, Germany, Italy, and England. By C. H. Haeseler, M.D. Bound in cloth,... 2 00
Colonel John W. Forney's Letters from Europe. Bound in cloth,... 1 75
The Ladies' Guide to True Politeness and Perfect Manners. By Miss Leslie. Every lady should have it. Cloth, full gilt back.... 1 75
The Ladies' Complete Guide to Needlework and Embroidery. With 113 illustrations. By Miss Lambert. Cloth, full gilt back,......... 1 75
The Ladies' Work Table Book. With 27 illustrations. Cloth, gilt,. 1 50
The Story of Elizabeth. By Miss Thackeray, paper $1.00, or cloth,... 1 50
Life and Adventures of Don Quixote and his Squire Sancho Panza, complete in one large volume, paper cover, for $1.00, or in cloth,.. 1 50
The Laws and Practice of Game of Euchre. By a Professor. Cloth, 1 00
Whitefriars; or, The Days of Charles the Second. Illustrated,........1 00

HUMOROUS ILLUSTRATED WORKS.

Each one full of Illustrations, by Felix O. C. Darley, and bound in Cloth.

Major Jones' Courtship and Travels. With 21 Illustrations,.........$1 75
Major Jones' Scenes in Georgia. With 16 Illustrations,................. 1 75
Simon Suggs' Adventures and Travels. With 17 Illustrations,...... 1 75
Swamp Doctor's Adventures in the South-West. 14 Illustrations,... 1 75
Col. Thorpe's Scenes in Arkansaw. With 16 Illustrations,............ 1 75
The Big Bear's Adventures and Travels. With 18 Illustrations,...... 1 75
High Life in New York, by Jonathan Slick. With Illustrations,.... 1 75
Judge Haliburton's Yankee Stories. Illustrated,........................ 1 75
Harry Coverdale's Courtship and Marriage. Illustrated,............... 1 75
Piney Wood's Tavern; or, Sam Slick in Texas. Illustrated,.......... 1 75
Sam Slick, the Clockmaker. By Judge Haliburton. Illustrated,... 1 75
Humors of Falconbridge. By J. F. Kelley. With Illustrations, ... 1 75
Modern Chivalry. By Judge Breckenridge. Two vols., each........ 1 75
Neal's Charcoal Sketches. By Joseph C. Neal. 21 Illustrations,... 2 50

☞ Books sent, postage paid, on Receipt of the Retail Price, by T. B. Peterson & Brothers, Philadelphia, Pa.

CHARLES DICKENS' WORKS.

☞ GREAT REDUCTION IN THEIR PRICES. ☜

PEOPLE'S DUODECIMO EDITION. ILLUSTRATED.

Reduced in price from $2.50 to $1.50 a volume.

This edition is printed on fine paper, from large, clear type, leaded, that all can read, containing One Hundred and Eighty Illustrations on tinted paper, and each book is complete in one large duodecimo volume.

Our Mutual Friend,	Cloth,	$1.50	Little Dorrit,	Cloth,	$1.50
Pickwick Papers,	Cloth,	1.50	Dombey and Son,	Cloth,	1.50
Nicholas Nickleby,	Cloth,	1.50	Christmas Stories,	Cloth,	1.50
Great Expectations,	Cloth,	1.50	Sketches by "Boz,"	Cloth,	1.50
David Copperfield,	Cloth,	1.50	Barnaby Rudge,	Cloth,	1.50
Oliver Twist,	Cloth,	1.50	Martin Chuzzlewit,	Cloth,	1.50
Bleak House,	Cloth,	1.50	Old Curiosity Shop,	Cloth,	1.50
A Tale of Two Cities,	Cloth,	1.50	Dickens' New Stories,	Cloth,	1.50

American Notes; and The Uncommercial Traveler,..............Cloth, 1.50
Hunted Down; and other Reprinted Pieces,..............Cloth, 1.50
The Holly-Tree Inn; and other Stories,..............Cloth, 1.50

Price of a set, in Black cloth, in nineteen volumes,.............. $28.00
" " Full sheep, Library style,.............. 38.00
" " Half calf, sprinkled edges,.............. 47.00
" " Half calf, marbled edges,.............. 53.00
" " Half calf, antique,.............. 57.00
" " Half calf, full gilt backs, etc.,.............. 57.00

ILLUSTRATED DUODECIMO EDITION.

Reduced in price from $2.00 to $1.50 a volume.

This edition is printed on the finest paper, from large, clear type, leaded, Long Primer in size, that all can read, the whole containing near Six Hundred full page Illustrations, printed on tinted paper, from designs by Cruikshank, Phiz, Browne, Maclise, McLenan, and other artists. The following books are each contained in two volumes.

Our Mutual Friend,	Cloth,	$3.00	Bleak House,	Cloth,	$3.00
Pickwick Papers	Cloth,	3.00	Sketches by "Boz,"	Cloth,	3.00
Tale of Two Cities,	Cloth,	3.00	Barnaby Rudge,	Cloth,	3.00
Nicholas Nickleby,	Cloth,	3.00	Martin Chuzzlewit,	Cloth,	3.00
David Copperfield,	Cloth,	3.00	Old Curiosity Shop,	Cloth,	3.00
Oliver Twist,	Cloth,	3.00	Little Dorrit,	Cloth,	3.00
Christmas Stories,	Cloth,	3.00	Dombey and Son,	Cloth,	3.00

The following are each complete in one volume, and are reduced in price from $2.50 to $1.50 a volume.

Great Expectations,......Cloth, $1.50 | Dickens' New Stories,...Cloth, $1.50
American Notes; and The Uncommercial Traveler,..............Cloth, 1.50
Hunted Down; and other Reprinted Pieces,..............Cloth, 1.50
The Holly-Tree Inn; and other Stories,..............Cloth, 1.50

Price of a set, in thirty-three volumes, bound in cloth,.............. $49.00
" " Full sheep, Library style,.............. 66.00
" " Half calf, antique,.............. 99.00
" " Half calf, full gilt backs, etc.,.............. 99.00

☞ Books sent, postage paid, on receipt of the Retail Price, by T. B. Peterson & Brothers, Philadelphia, Pa.

CHARLES DICKENS' WORKS.

ILLUSTRATED OCTAVO EDITION.

Reduced in price from $2.50 to $1.75 a volume.

This edition is printed from large type, double column, octavo page, each book being complete in one volume, the whole containing near Six Hundred Illustrations, by Cruikshank, Phiz, Browne, Maclise, and other artists.

Our Mutual Friend,.....Cloth,	$1.75	David Copperfield,.......Cloth,	$1.75
Pickwick Papers,.........Cloth,	1.75	Barnaby Rudge,..........Cloth,	1.75
Nicholas Nickleby,......Cloth,	1.75	Martin Chuzzlewit,......Cloth,	1.75
Great Expectations,......Cloth,	1.75	Old Curiosity Shop,......Cloth,	1.75
Lamplighter's Story,....Cloth,	1.75	Christmas Stories,.......Cloth,	1.75
Oliver Twist,..............Cloth,	1.75	Dickens' New Stories,...Cloth,	1.75
Bleak House,..............Cloth,	1.75	A Tale of Two Cities,...Cloth,	1.75
Little Dorrit,..............Cloth,	1.75	American Notes and Pic-Nic Papers,........Cloth,	1.75
Dombey and Son,........Cloth,	1.75		
Sketches by "Boz,".....Cloth,	1.75		

Price of a set, in Black cloth, in eighteen volumes,......................$31.50
" " Full sheep, Library style,................................ 40.00
" " Half calf, sprinkled edges,.............................. 48.00
" " Half calf, marbled edges,................................ 54.00
" " Half calf, antique,.. 60.00
" " Half calf, full gilt backs, etc.,.......................... 60.00

"NEW NATIONAL EDITION" OF DICKENS' WORKS.

This is the cheapest complete edition of the works of Charles Dickens, "Boz," published in the world, being contained in *seven large octavo volumes*, with a portrait of Charles Dickens, and other illustrations, the whole making nearly *six thousand very large double columned pages*, in large, clear type, handsomely printed on fine white paper, and bound in the strongest and most substantial manner.

Price of a set, in Black cloth, in seven volumes,......................$20.00
" " Full sheep, Library style,.............................. 25.00
" " Half calf, antique,.. 30.00
" " Half calf, full gilt back, etc.,.......................... 30.00

CHEAP SALMON PAPER COVER EDITION.

Each book being complete in one large octavo volume.

Pickwick Papers,....................	35	Christmas Stories,..................	25
Nicholas Nickleby,..................	35	The Haunted House,...............	25
Dombey and Son,.....................	35	Uncommercial Traveler,..........	25
David Copperfield,...................	25	A House to Let,.....................	25
Martin Chuzzlewit,...................	35	Perils of English Prisoners,.....	25
Old Curiosity Shop,..................	25	Wreck of the Golden Mary,......	25
Oliver Twist,..........................	25	Tom Tiddler's Ground,............	25
American Notes,......................	25	Our Mutual Friend,................	35
Great Expectations,..................	25	Bleak House,.........................	35
Hard Times,............................	25	Little Dorrit,.........................	35
A Tale of Two Cities,................	25	Joseph Grimaldi,....................	50
Somebody's Luggage,...............	25	The Pic-Nic Papers,................	50
Message from the Sea,.............	25	No Thoroughfare.....................	10
Barnaby Rudge,......................	25	Hunted Down,........................	25
Sketches by "Boz,".................	25	The Holly-Tree Inn,................	25

Mrs. Lirriper's Lodgings and Mrs. Lirriper's Legacy,...................... 25
Mugby Junction and Dr. Marigold's Prescriptions,......................... 25

☞ Books sent, postage paid, on receipt of the Retail Price, by T. B. Peterson & Brothers, Philadelphia, Pa.

CHARLES LEVER'S BEST WORKS.

Charles O'Malley,.................. 75
Harry Lorrequer,.................... 75
Jack Hinton, the Guardsman,... 75
Tom Burke of Ours,................ 75
Knight of Gwynne,.............. 75
Arthur O'Leary,.................... 75
Con Cregan,.......................... 75
Davenport Dunn,................... 75

Above are each in paper, or a finer edition in cloth, price $2.00 each.

Horace Templeton,................ 75
Kate O'Donoghue,................ 75

EMERSON BENNETT'S WORKS.

The Border Rover,.............. 1 50
Clara Moreland,.................... 1 50
Viola; or Adventures in the Far South-West,................ 1 50
Bride of the Wilderness,........ 1 50
Ellen Norbury,..................... 1 50
The Forged Will,.................. 1 50
Kate Clarendon,..................... 1 50

The above are each in paper cover, or in cloth, price $1.75 each.

The Heiress of Bellefonte, and Walde-Warren,.................. 75
Pioneer's Daughter and the Unknown Countess,........... 75

WILKIE COLLINS' BEST WORKS.

The Crossed Path, or Basil,.... 1 50
The Dead Secret. 12mo........ 1 50

The above are each in paper cover, or in cloth, price $1.75 each.

Hide and Seek,..................... 75
After Dark,.......................... 75
The Queen's Revenge,........... 75
Mad Monkton,...................... 50
Sights a-Foot,...................... 50
The Stolen Mask,................. 25
The Yellow Mask,................ 25
Sister Rose,......................... 25

MISS PARDOE'S WORKS.

Confessions of a Pretty Woman, 75
The Wife's Trials,................. 75
The Jealous Wife,................. 50
The Rival Beauties,.............. 75
Romance of the Harem,......... 75

The five above books are also bound in one volume, cloth, for $4.00.

The Adopted Heir. One volume, paper, $1.50; or in cloth,..........$1 75
The Earl's Secret. One volume, paper, $1.50; or in cloth, ... 1 75

MRS. HENRY WOOD'S BOOKS.

George Canterbury's Will,...... 1 50
Roland Yorke, ... 1 50
The Channings,..................... 1 50
Red Court Farm,.................... 1 50
Elster's Folly,........................ 1 50
St. Martin's Eve,.................... 1 50
Mildred Arkell,...................... 1 50
Shadow of Ashlydyat,........... 1 50
Oswald Cray,........................ 1 50
Verner's Pride,...................... 1 50
Lord Oakburn's Daughters; or, the Earl's Heirs,............... 1 50
Squire Trevlyn's Heir; or, Trevlyn Hold,.................. 1 50
The Castle's Heir; or, Lady Adelaide's Oath,................ 1 50

Above are each in paper cover, or each one in cloth, for $1.75 each.

The Mystery,....................... 75
A Life's Secret,.................... 50

Above are each in paper cover, or each one in cloth, for $1.00 each.

Orville College,.................... 50
The Runaway Match,............ 50
The Lost Will,...................... 50
The Haunted Tower,.............. 50
The Lost Bank Note,............. 75
Foggy Night at Offord,.......... 25
William Allair,...................... 25
A Light and a Dark Christmas, 25

MISS BRADDON'S WORKS.

Aurora Floyd,....................... 75
For Better, For Worse,.......... 75
The Lawyer's Secret,............. 25

☞ **Books sent, postage paid, on receipt of the Retail Price, by T. B. Peterson & Brothers, Philadelphia, Pa.**

ALEXANDER DUMAS' WORKS.

Title	Price	Title	Price
Count of Monte Cristo,.........	1 50	Memoirs of a Physician,.........	1 00
The Iron Mask,.....................	1 00	Queen's Necklace,.................	1 00
Louise La Valliere,................	1 00	Six Years Later,.....................	1 00
Adventures of a Marquis,.......	1 00	Countess of Charney,.............	1 00
Diana of Meridor,.................	1 00	Andree de Taverney,..............	1 00
The Three Guardsmen,..........	75	The Chevalier,........................	1 00
Twenty Years After,..............	75	Forty-five Guardsmen,...........	75
Bragelonne; the Son of Athos,	75	The Iron Hand,.....................	75
The Conscript. A Tale of War,	1 50	Camille, "The Camelia Lady,"	1 50

Love and Liberty. A Tale of the French Revolution of 1792,.......... 1 50

The above are each in paper cover, or in cloth, price $1.75 each.

Title	Price	Title	Price
Edmond Dantes,..................	75	Man with Five Wives,...........	75
Felina de Chambure,............	75	Twin Lieutenants,.................	75
The Horrors of Paris,...........	75	Annette, Lady of the Pearls,....	50
The Fallen Angel,................	75	Mohicans of Paris,................	50
Sketches in France,..............	75	The Marriage Verdict,...........	50
Isabel of Bavaria,.................	75	The Corsican Brothers,.........	50

Count of Moret,......... 50 | George,....... 50 | Buried Alive,.......... 25

GEORGE W. M. REYNOLDS' WORKS.

Title	Price	Title	Price
Mysteries of Court of London,..	1 00	Mary Price,...........................	1 00
Rose Foster. Sequel to it,.....	1 50	Eustace Quentin,..................	1 00
Caroline of Brunswick,..........	1 00	Joseph Wilmot,.....................	1 00
Venetia Trelawney,...............	1 00	Banker's Daughter,...............	1 00
Lord Saxondale,....................	1 00	Kenneth,................................	1 00
Count Christoval,..................	1 00	The Rye-House Plot,............	1 00
Rosa Lambert,......................	1 00	The Necromancer,................	1 00

The above are each in paper cover, or in cloth, price $1.75 each.

Title	Price	Title	Price
The Opera Dancer,................	75	The Soldier's Wife,...............	75
Child of Waterloo,................	75	May Middleton,.....................	75
Robert Bruce,.......................	75	Duke of Marchmont,.............	75
Discarded Queen,..................	75	Massacre of Glencoe,............	75
The Gipsy Chief,..................	75	Queen Joanna; Court Naples,	75
Mary Stuart, Queen of Scots,...	75	Pickwick Abroad,.................	75
Wallace, the Hero of Scotland,	1 00	Parricide,..............................	75
Isabella Vincent,...................	75	The Ruined Gamester,...........	50
Vivian Bertram,.....................	75	Ciprina; or, the Secrets of a Picture Gallery,...................	50
Countess of Lascelles,............	75	Life in Paris,.........................	50
Loves of the Harem,..............	75	Countess and the Page,.........	50
Ellen Percy,..........................	75	Edgar Montrose,...................	50
Agnes Evelyn,.......................	75		

EUGENE SUE'S GREAT WORKS.

Title	Price	Title	Price
Wandering Jew,..................	1 50	First Love,............................	50
Mysteries of Paris,...............	1 50	Woman's Love,.....................	50
Martin, the Foundling,.........	1 50	Female Bluebeard,................	50
Above in cloth at $2.00 each.		Man-of-War's-Man,...............	50

Life and Adventures of Raoul De Surville,.................................. 25

MADAME GEORGE SAND'S WORKS.

Title	Price	Title	Price
Consuelo,............................	75	Fanchon, the Cricket, paper,...	1 00
Countess of Rudolstadt,.........	75	Do. do. cloth,...	1 50
First and True Love,............	75	Indiana, a Love Story, paper,.	1 50
The Corsair,........................	50	Do. do. cloth,...	1 75
Jealousy, paper,..........	1 50	Consuelo and Rudolstadt, both in one volume, cloth,..........	2 00
Do. cloth,..........	1 75		

☞ **Books sent, postage paid, on receipt of the Retail Price, by T. B. Peterson & Brothers, Philadelphia, Pa.**

HUMOROUS AMERICAN WORKS.

Beautifully Illustrated by Felix O. C. Darley.

Major Jones' Courtship,......... 75
Major Jones' Travels,............ 75
Simon Suggs' Adventures and Travels,.......................... 75
Major Jones' Chronicles of Pineville,.......................... 75
Polly Peablossom's Wedding,.. 75
Mysteries of the Backwoods,... 75
Widow Rugby's Husband,....... 75
Big Bear of Arkansas............ 75
Western Scenes; or, Life on the Prairie,...................... 75
Streaks of Squatter Life,....... 75
Pickings from the Picayune,... 75
Stray Subjects, Arrested and Bound Over,................... 75
Louisiana Swamp Doctor,...... 75
Charcoal Sketches,............... 75
Misfortunes of Peter Faber,.... 75
Yankee among the Mermaids,.. 75
New Orleans Sketch Book,..... 75
Drama in Pokerville,............. 75
The Quorndon Hounds,......... 75
My Shooting Box,................ 75
Warwick Woodlands,............ 75
The Deer Stalkers,................ 75
Peter Ploddy,....................... 75
Adventures of Captain Farrago, 75
Major O'Regan's Adventures,.. 75
Sol. Smith's Theatrical Apprenticeship,......................... 75
Sol. Smith's Theatrical Journey-Work,....................... 75
The Quarter Race in Kentucky, 75
Aunt Patty's Scrap Bag,........ 75
Percival Mayberry's Adventures and Travels,............. 75
Sam Slick's Yankee Yarns and Yankee Letters,................ 75
Adventures of Fudge Fumble,. 75
American Joe Miller,............ 50
Following the Drum,............ 50

D'ISRAELI'S WORKS.

Henrietta Temple,................ 50
Vivian Grey,....................... 75
Venetia,............................. 50
Young Duke,........................ 50
Miriam Alroy,...................... 50
Contarina Fleming,............... 50

FRANK FAIRLEGH'S WORKS.

Frank Fairlegh,.................. 75
Lewis Arundel,................... 75
Harry Racket Scapegrace,..... 75
Tom Racquet,...................... 75

Finer editions of above are also issued in cloth, at $1.75 each.

Harry Coverdale's Courtship, 1 50
Lorrimer Littlegood,............ 1 50

The above are each in paper cover, or in cloth, price $1.75 each.

C. J. PETERSON'S WORKS.

The Old Stone Mansion,......... 1 50
Kate Aylesford,................... 1 50

The above are each in paper cover, or in cloth, price $1.75 each.

Cruising in the Last War,...... 75
Valley Farm,....................... 25
Grace Dudley; or, Arnold at Saratoga,......................... 50

JAMES A. MAITLAND'S WORKS.

The Old Patroon,................. 1 50
The Watchman,.................... 1 50
The Wanderer,..................... 1 50
The Lawyer's Story,............. 1 50
Diary of an Old Doctor,........ 1 50
Sartaroe,............................ 1 50
The Three Cousins,.............. 1 50

The above are each in paper cover, or in cloth, price $1.75 each.

WILLIAM H. MAXWELL'S WORKS.

Wild Sports of the West,........ 75
Stories of Waterloo,............. 75
Brian O'Lynn,..................... 75

WILLIAM HARRISON AINSWORTH'S WORKS.

Life of Jack Sheppard,.......... 50
Life of Guy Fawkes,.............. 75
Above in 1 vol., cloth, $1.75.
Court of the Stuarts,............ 75
Windsor Castle,.................... 75
The Star Chamber,............... 75
Old St. Paul's,...................... 75
Court of Queen Anne,............ 50
Life of Dick Turpin,.............. 50
Life of Davy Crockett,........... 50
Tower of London,.................. 1 50
Miser's Daughter,................. 1 00
Above in cloth $1.75 each.
Life of Grace O'Malley,......... 50
Life of Henry Thomas,.......... 25
Desperadoes of the New World, 50
Life of Ninon De L'Enclos,.... 25
Life of Arthur Spring,........... 25
Life of Mrs. Whipple and Jessee Strang,........................ 25

G. P. R. JAMES'S BEST BOOKS.

Lord Montague's Page,......... 1 50
The Cavalier,....................... 1 50

The above are each in paper cover, or in cloth, price $1.75 each.

The Man in Black,............... 75
Mary of Burgundy,............... 75
Arrah Neil,.......................... 75
Eva St. Clair,....................... 50

DOW'S PATENT SERMONS.

Dow's Patent Sermons, 1st Series, $1.00; cloth,.......... 1 50
Dow's Patent Sermons, 2d Series, $1.00; cloth,.......... 1 50
Dow's Patent Sermons, 3d Series, $1.00; cloth,.......... 1 50
Dow's Patent Sermons, 4th Series, $1.00; cloth,.......... 1 50

SAMUEL C. WARREN'S BEST BOOKS.

Ten Thousand a Year,...paper, 1 50
Do. do. cloth, 2 00
Diary of a Medical Student,... 75

Q. K. PHILANDER DOESTICKS' WORKS.

Doesticks' Letters,................ 1 50
Plu-Ri-Bus-Tah,.................. 1 50
The Elephant Club,............... 1 50
Witches of New York,........... 1 50

The above are each in paper cover, or in cloth, price $1.75 each.

GREEN'S WORKS ON GAMBLING.

Gambling Exposed,.............. 1 50
The Gambler's Life,.............. 1 50
The Reformed Gambler,........ 1 50
Secret Band of Brothers,........ 1 50

Above are each in paper cover, or each one in cloth, for $1.75 each.

MISS ELLEN PICKERING'S WORKS.

The Grumbler,...................... 75
Marrying for Money,............ 75
Poor Cousin,........................ 50
Kate Walsingham, ... 50
Orphan Niece,..................... 50
Who Shall be Heir?............. 38
The Squire,.......................... 38
Ellen Wareham,................... 38
Nan Darrel,.......................... 38

CAPTAIN MARRYATT'S WORKS.

Jacob Faithful,...................... 50
Japhet in Search of a Father,.. 50
Phantom Ship,...................... 50
Midshipman Easy,................ 50
Pacha of Many Tales,............ 50
Frank Mildmay, Naval Officer, 50
Snarleyow,........................... 50
Newton Forster, ... 50
King's Own,......................... 50
Pirate and Three Cutters,...... 50
Peter Simple,........................ 50
Percival Keene,................... 50
Poor Jack,........................... 50
Sea King,............................ 50

☞ **Books sent, postage paid, on receipt of the Retail Price, by T. B. Peterson & Brothers, Philadelphia, Pa.**

MRS. GREY'S CELEBRATED NOVELS.

Cousin Harry,......................	1 50	The Little Beauty,...............	1 50

The above are each in paper cover, or in cloth, price $1.75 each.

A Marriage in High Life,.......	50	The Baronet's Daughters,.......	50
Gipsy's Daughter,.................	50	Young Prima Donna,............	50
Old Dower House,................	50	Hyacinthe,..........................	25
Belle of the Family,..............	50	Alice Seymour,.....................	25
Duke and Cousin,.................	50	Mary Seaham,......................	75
The Little Wife,...................	50	Passion and Principle,..........	75
Lena Cameron,.....................	50	The Flirt,............................	75
Sybil Lennard,......................	50	Good Society,......................	75
Manœuvring Mother	50	Lion-Hearted,......................	75

J. F. SMITH'S WORKS.

The Usurer's Victim; or, Thomas Balscombe,............	75	Adelaide Waldegrave; or, the Trials of a Governess,........	75

REVOLUTIONARY TALES.

The Brigand,.......................	50	Old Put; or, Days of 1776,.....	50
Ralph Runnion,....................	50	Legends of Mexico,..............	50
Seven Brothers of Wyoming,..	50	Grace Dudley,......................	50
The Rebel Bride,..................	50	The Guerilla Chief,..............	75
The Flying Artillerist,...........	50	The Quaker Soldier, paper,.....	1 50
Wau-nan-gee,......................	50	do. do. cloth,.....	1 75

T. S. ARTHUR'S HOUSEHOLD NOVELS.

The Lost Bride,....................	50	The Divorced Wife,..............	50
The Two Brides,...................	50	Pride and Prudence,............	50
Love in a Cottage,................	50	Agnes; or, the Possessed,......	50
Love in High Life,...............	50	Lucy Sandford,....................	50
Year after Marriage,.............	50	The Banker's Wife,..............	50
The Lady at Home,..............	50	The Two Merchants,............	50
Cecelia Howard,...................	50	Trial and Triumph,..............	50
Orphan Children,.................	50	The Iron Rule,.....................	50
Debtor's Daughter,...............	50	Insubordination; or, the Shoemaker's Daughters,............	50
Mary Moreton,......................	50		

Six Nights with the Washingtonians. With nine original Illustrations. By Cruikshank. One volume, cloth $1.75; or in paper,...$1.50

Lizzy Glenn; or, the Trials of a Seamstress. Cloth $1.75; or paper, 1.50

LIEBIG'S WORKS ON CHEMISTRY.

Agricultural Chemistry,.........	25	Liebig's celebrated Letters on the Potato Disease,............	25
Animal Chemistry,...............	25		

Liebig's Complete Works on Chemistry, is also issued in one large octavo volume, bound in cloth. Price Two Dollars.

RIDDELL'S MODEL ARCHITECT.

Architectural Designs of Model Country Residences. By John Riddell, Practical Architect. Illustrated with twenty-two full page Front Elevations, colored, with forty-four Plates of Ground Plans, including the First and Second Stories, with plans of the stories, full specifications of all the articles used, and estimate of price. Price Fifteen Dollars a copy.

FRANK FORRESTER'S GREAT BOOK.

Frank Forrester's Sporting Scenes and Characters. By Henry William Herbert. With Illustrations by Darley. Two vols., cloth,.. $4 00

☞ **Books sent, postage paid, on receipt of the Retail Price, by T. B. Peterson & Brothers, Philadelphia, Pa.**

EXCITING SEA TALES.

Title	Price
Adventures of Ben Brace,......	75
Jack Adams, the Mutineer,....	75
Jack Ariel's Adventures,........	75
Petrel; or, Life on the Ocean,.	75
Life of Paul Periwinkle,........	75
Life of Tom Bowling,............	75
Percy Effingham,.................	75
Cruising in the Last War,......	75
Red King,..........................	50
The Corsair,........................	50
The Doomed Ship,................	50
The Three Pirates,...............	50
The Flying Dutchman,..........	50
The Flying Yankee,..............	50
The Yankee Middy,..............	50
The Gold Seekers,................	50
The King's Cruisers,.............	50
Life of Alexander Tardy,.......	50
Red Wing,...........................	50
Yankee Jack,.......................	50
Yankees in Japan,................	50
Morgan, the Buccaneer,.........	50
Jack Junk,..........................	50
Davis, the Pirate,................	50
Valdez, the Pirate,..............	50
Gallant Tom,.......................	50
Harry Helm,........................	50
Harry Tempest,...................	50
Rebel and Rover,.................	50
Man-of-War's-Man,.............	50
Dark Shades of City Life,......	25
The Rats of the Seine,.........	25
Charles Ransford,................	25
The Iron Cross,....................	25
The River Pirates,...............	25
The Pirate's Son,.................	25
Jacob Faithful,.....................	50
Phantom Ship,.....................	50
Midshipman Easy,................	50
Pacha of Many Tales,............	50
Naval Officer,......................	50
Snarleyow,..........................	50
Newton Forster,...................	50
King's Own,........................	50
Japhet,..............................	50
Pirate and Three Cutters,......	50
Peter Simple,......................	50
Percival Keene,...................	50
Poor Jack,..........................	50
Sea King,...........................	50

GEORGE LIPPARD'S GREAT BOOKS.

Title	Price
The Quaker City,.................	1 50
Paul Ardenheim,..................	1 50
Blanche of Brandywine,.........	1 50
Washington and his Generals; or, Legends of the American Revolution,......................	1 50
Mysteries of Florence,............	1 00
Above in cloth at $2.00 each.	
The Empire City,..................	75
Memoirs of a Preacher,..........	75
The Nazarene,......................	75
Washington and his Men,......	75
Legends of Mexico,...............	50
The Entranced,....................	25
The Robbers,......................	25
The Bank Director's Son,......	25

MILITARY NOVELS. BY BEST AUTHORS.

With Illuminated Military Covers, in five Colors.

Title	Price
Charles O'Malley,................	75
Jack Hinton, the Guardsman,	75
The Knight of Gwynne,.........	75
Harry Lorrequer,.................	75
Tom Burke of Ours,..............	75
Arthur O'Leary,...................	75
Con Cregan,........................	75
Kate O'Donoghue,...............	75
Horace Templeton,..............	75
Davenport Dunn,..................	75
Jack Adams' Adventures,......	75
Valentine Vox,.....................	75
Twin Lieutenants,................	75
Stories of Waterloo,.............	75
The Soldier's Wife,..............	75
Guerilla Chief,....................	75
The Three Guardsmen, ...	75
Twenty Years After,............	75
Bragelonne, Son of Athos,......	75
Forty-five Guardsmen,..........	75
Tom Bowling's Adventures,...	75
Life of Robert Bruce,............	75
The Gipsy Chief,..................	75
Massacre of Glencoe,............	75
Life of Guy Fawkes,.............	75
Child of Waterloo,...............	75
Adventures of Ben Brace,......	75
Life of Jack Ariel,...............	75
Wallace, the Hero of Scotland,	1 00
Following the Drum,...........	50
The Conscript, a Tale of War. By Alexander Dumas, ...	1 50

☞ **Books sent, postage paid, on receipt of the Retail Price, by T. B. Peterson & Brothers, Philadelphia, Pa.**

GUSTAVE AIMARD'S WORKS.

The White Scalper,...............	50	Trapper's Daughter,............	75
The Freebooters,..................	50	The Tiger Slayer,..............	75
The Prairie Flower,..............	75	The Gold Seekers,...............	75
The Indian Scout,................	75	The Rebel Chief,................	75
The Trail Hunter,................	75	The Smuggler Chief,............	75
The Indian Chief,................	75	The Border Rifles,...............	75
The Red Track,....................	75	Pirates of the Prairies,.........	75

LANGUAGES WITHOUT A MASTER.

French without a Master,.......	40	German without a Master,......	40
Spanish without a Master,......	40	Italian without a Master,.........	40
Latin without a Master,.........	40		

The above five works on the French, German, Spanish, Latin, and Italian Languages, whereby any one or all of these Languages can be learned by any one without a Teacher, with the aid of this book, by A. H. Monteith, Esq., is also published in finer style, in one volume, bound, price, $1.75.

HARRY COCKTON'S WORKS.

Sylvester Sound,..................	75	The Sisters,........................	75
Valentine Vox, in paper,........	75	The Steward,.......................	75
do. finer edition, cloth,	2 00	Percy Effingham,...................	75

WAR NOVELS. BY HENRY MORFORD.

Shoulder-Straps,..................	1 50	The Days of Shoddy. A History of the late War,...........	1 50
The Coward,........................	1 50		

Above are each in paper cover, or each one in cloth, for $1.75 each.

LIVES OF HIGHWAYMEN.

Life of John A. Murrel,.........	50	Life of Davy Crockett,...........	50
Life of Joseph T. Hare,.........	50	Life of Sybil Grey,...............	50
Life of Col. Monroe Edwards,.	50	Life of Jonathan Wild,..........	25
Life of Jack Sheppard,..........	50	Life of Henry Thomas,..........	25
Life of Jack Rann,...............	50	Life of Arthur Spring,...........	25
Life of Dick Turpin,.............	50	Life of Jack Ketch,...............	25
Life of Helen Jewett,............	50	Life of Ninon De L'Enclos,.....	25
Desperadoes of the New World,	50	Lives of the Felons,..............	25
Mysteries of New Orleans,......	50	Life of Mrs. Whipple,.	25
The Robber's Wife,...............	50	Life of Biddy Woodhull,.........	25
Obi; or, Three Fingered Jack,	50	Life of Mother Brownrigg,......	25
Kit Clayton,........................	50	Dick Parker, the Pirate,........	25
Life of Tom Waters,.............	50	Life of Mary Bateman,..........	25
Nat Blake,...........................	50	Life of Captain Blood,...........	25
Bill Horton,.........................	50	Capt. Blood and the Beagles,..	25
Galloping Gus,......................	50	Sixteen-Stringed Jack's Fight for Life,..............................	25
Life & Trial of Antoine Probst,	50	Highwayman's Avenger,........	25
Ned Hastings,......................	50	Life of Raoul De Surville,.......	25
Eveleen Wilson,...................	50	Life of Rody the Rover,.........	25
Diary of a Pawnbroker,.........	50	Life of Galloping Dick,.........	25
Silver and Pewter,................	50	Life of Guy Fawkes,..............	75
Sweeney Todd,.....................	50	Life and Adventures of Vidocq,	1 50
Life of Grace O'Malley,.........	50		

MILITARY AND ARMY BOOKS.

Ellsworth's Zouave Drill,.......	25	U. S. Light Infantry Drill,.....	25
U. S. Government Infantry & Rifle Tactics,....................	25	The Soldier's Companion,......	25
		The Soldier's Guide,............	25

☞ **Books sent, postage paid, on Receipt of the Retail Price, by T. B. Peterson & Brothers, Philadelphia, Pa.**

WORKS AT 75 CENTS. BY BEST AUTHORS.

Hans Breitman's Party. With other Ballads. By Charles G. Leland, 75
Hans Breitmann In Church, with other Ballads. By C. G. Leland, 75
Hans Breitmann about Town, with other Ballads. By C. G. Leland, 75
Webster and Hayne's Speeches in Reply to Colonel Foote,............ 75
The Brigand; or, the Demon of the North. By Victor Hugo,......... 75
Roanoke; or, Where is Utopia? By C. H. Wiley. Illustrated,...... 75

The Banditti of the Prairie,...	75	Flirtations in America...........	75
Tom Racquet,.....................	75	The Coquette,......................	75
Red Indians of Newfoundland,	75	Thackeray's Irish Sketch Book,	75
Salathiel, by Croly,..............	75	Whitehall,............................	75
Corinne; or, Italy,...............	75	The Beautiful Nun,...............	75
Ned Musgrave......................	75	Mysteries of Three Cities,......	75
Aristocracy, ...	75	Genevra. By Miss Fairfield,..	75
The Inquisition in Spain,.......	75	New Hope; or, the Rescue,.....	75
Elsie's Married Life,.............	75	Crock of Gold. By Tupper,...	75
Leyton Hall. By Mark Lemon,	75	Twins and Heart. By Tupper,	75

WORKS AT 50 CENTS. BY BEST AUTHORS.

The Woman in Red. A Companion to the "Woman in Black,"...... 50
Twelve Months of Matrimony. By Emelie F. Carlen,................... 50

Leah; or the Forsaken,.........	50	The Admiral's Daughter,.......	50
The Greatest Plague of Life,..	50	The American Joe Miller,......	50
Clifford and the Actress,........	50	Ella Stratford,.....................	50
The Two Lovers,.................	50	Josephine, by Grace Aguilar,..	50
Ryan's Mysteries of Marriage,	50	The Fortune Hunter,............	50
The Orphans and Caleb Field,.	50	The Orphan Sisters,.............	50
Moreton Hall,......................	50	Robert Oaklands; or, the Outcast Orphan,....................	50
Bell Brandon,......................	50		
Sybil Grey,..........................	50	Abednego, the Money Lender,.	50
Female Life in New York,......	50	Jenny Ambrose,..................	50
Agnes Grey,........................	50	Father Tom and the Pope, in cloth gilt, 75 cents, or paper,	50
Diary of a Physician,............	50		
The Emigrant Squire,...........	50	The Romish Confessional.......	50
The Monk, by Lewis,............	50	Victims of Amusements,........	50
The Beautiful French Girl,...	50	Violet,................................	50
Father Clement, paper,..........	50	Alieford, a Family History,...	50
do. do. cloth,...........	75	General Scott's $5 Portrait,...	1 00
Miser's Heir, paper,..............	50	Henry Clay's $5 Portrait,......	1 00
do. do. cloth,..............	75	Tangarua, a Poem,...............	1 00

WORKS AT 25 CENTS. BY BEST AUTHORS.

Aunt Margaret's Trouble, ...	25	The Mysteries of Bedlam,.....	25
The Woman in Grey,............	25	The Nobleman's Daughter,...	25
The Deformed,....................	25	Madison's Exposition of Odd Fellowship, ...	25
Two Prima Donnas,.............	25		
The Mysterious Marriage,......	25	Ghost Stories. Illustrated,....	25
Jack Downing's Letters,.........	25	Ladies' Science of Etiquette,...	25
The Mysteries of a Convent,...	25	The Abbey of Innismoyle,......	25
Rose Warrington,................	25	Gliddon's Ancient Egypt.......	25
The Iron Cross,...................	25	Philip in Search of a Wife,.....	25
Charles Ransford,................	25	Rifle Shots,.........................	25

THE SHAKSPEARE NOVELS.

Shakspeare and his Friends,...	1 00	The Secret Passion,..............	1 00
The Youth of Shakspeare,......	1 00		

Above three Books are also in one volume, cloth. Price Four Dollars.

☞ **Books sent, postage paid, on receipt of the Retail Price, by T. B. Peterson & Brothers, Philadelphia, Pa.**

www.ingramcontent.com/pod-product-compliance
Lightning Source LLC
LaVergne TN
LVHW020913110826
845150LV00004B/659

* 9 7 8 1 4 2 5 5 5 6 8 0 8 *